Cool Careers For D

Sheet

30 great careers most people wouldn't have thought of

Acoustics specialist

Attorney specializing in outer space issues

Audiologist (a master's-level job with doctor's prestige)

Biological weapons deterrence specialist

Celebrity personal assistant (assistant to the stars)

Child-life specialist (helps chronically ill kids adapt to life in the hospital)

Counselor to college-bound athletes

Dating coach

Graphologist (handwriting analyst, usually hired by police, FBI, etc.)

Holographer (makes holograms for festivals, trade shows, etc.)

Hydrologist (collects and tests water samples from mountain streams, glaciers, etc.)

Laser engineer

Locksmith

Mediator

Muralist (for freeway underpasses, eyesore buildings, etc.)

Neon sign maker (a dying art, yet high-demand)

Newborn photographer (takes pictures of newborns, moms, and dads in the hospital)

Nurse anesthetist

Prosthetist (makes artificial limbs)

Restaurant menu designer

Rock band photographer

Special occasions cake baker

Sports information director (provides info to the media on a college's sports teams)

Tile setter

TV show casting director

Venture capitalist

Virtual reality computer programmer

Volcanologist (studies volcanoes)

Winemaker

Work-family manager (helps companies create more family-friendly workplaces)

Chapter 2 has scoops on these 30 plus 482 more great careers.

How to convince someone to hire you instead of someone with more degrees

Write a letter that . . .

- Says something like, "I deliberately chose to upgrade my skills without going back for another degree because I knew I would learn more of value."
- Describes what you did and what you learned.
- Says something like, "I believe I chose substance over form, but now I come to the moment of truth. Will you interview me?"

For a model letter, see Chapter 8.

BUSINESS AND GENERAL REFERENCE BOOK SERIES FROM IDG

Cool Careers For Dummies®

Shortcuts to a cool career

These careers offer many of the benefits of a prestigious career in a fraction of the time and cost. Here are a few examples:

The Long Route	***The Short Route***
Doctor	Physician's assistant
Lawyer	Mediator
Psychologist	Personal coach

For more, see Chapter 2.

Four not-pushy ways to land a job

- Join online discussion groups.
- Sign up at "push" Web sites, which deliver on-target job openings right to your e-mail box.
- Write a letter or e-mail to a senior person at your dream employers.
- Attend job fairs.

For details, see Part III.

Three musts for successful self-employment

- **Do a mini-business plan.** It will help you decide whether this business is for you, and provide a blueprint for your success.
- **Realize that you may need less capital than you think.** Choose a service rather than a product, start your business at home or at a government-subsidized small business incubator, avoid hiring help, and resist the temptation to buy expensive furniture and equipment.
- **Use the marketing methods you're most comfortable with.** The best method in the world is useless if you won't use it.

See Chapter 19 for much more advice on going solo.

Six cool career Web sites

CareerPath (`www.careerpath.com`): Search instantly through the want ads currently running in 60 major newspapers, a total of 260,000 fresh job openings.

CoolWorks (`www.coolworks.com`): Links to 35,000 jobs and volunteer opportunities at vacation spots: ski resorts, national parks, cruise ships, resorts, and so on.

Career Resource Center (`www.careers.org`): This site has a master list of career-related online discussion groups, plus much more.

Entrepreneurial Edge (`www.edgeonline.com`): A jam-packed site for the self-employed. Just one feature: a searchable database of 5,000 documents and book chapters on small business.

JobSmart (`www.jobsmart.org`): Some of the best career advice on the Net.

The Riley Guide (`www.dbm.com/jobguide`): Your wish list of links to other great career sites.

Six ways to make any job better

- Propose to lead a project you'd find fun.
- Recruit an all-star team of supporters (for example, a knowledge guru, a wise old soul, and a fun person).
- With coworkers, trade tasks that use your weaknesses for tasks that use your strengths.
- To get what you want from your boss, figure out whether he or she is persuaded by facts or feelings.
- Even if you're a clerk, think like a CEO: Come up with new ways to improve things — and make sure you get the credit!
- When your job has become dead-end, get out before you get stale.

Chapter 18 has much more on making any job better.

Cheat Sheet $2.95 value. Item 5095-0.

For more information about IDG Books, call 1-800-762-2974.

...For Dummies: Bestselling Book Series for Beginners

Praise for Cool Careers For Dummies

"A career guide that REALLY works — thorough, reliable, and amazingly helpful."

— James C. Gonyea, nationally recognized career guidance expert; Host: Gonyea Online Career Center on AOL

"Whenever you have the opportunity to get career advice from Marty Nemko, you've got to listen. He's terrific!

— John Lucht, author of *Rites of Passage at $100,000+, the Insider's Guide to Executive Job-Changing and Faster Career Progress*

"If you don't have a career coach, you must invest in *Cool Careers For Dummies*. It both brims over with information and offers solid, nurturing advice. Whether you're going to get that first job, considering a career change, or learning, not leaping, into self-employment, *Cool Careers For Dummies* has something to offer. Technology and demographics will shape the 21st century labor market, and *Cool Careers For Dummies* is one of the key resources that will make this market easier to navigate.

— Julianne Malveaux, Economist and Syndicated Columnist, Washington, D.C.

"If you think you're doomed to boring jobs, you haven't read *Cool Careers For Dummies*. This essential, ingenious book provides hundreds of thought-provoking ideas for jobs you would actually love. The authors also provide clear, step-by-step directions for making your dream job a reality."

— Bob Goldman, Syndicated Columnist, "Work Daze"

"Finally, a book where career idealism, realism, and practical career management advice come together. Loaded with great ideas to help you select, plan, or change your career. Whether you're starting your career, are in a corporation, profession, or your own business, this is a read to succeed."

— Kent Black, formerly Group Vice-President, Drake Beam Morin, Inc., the world's largest career transitions consulting firm

"Highly recommended for anyone confused about choosing a career or wondering "what's next?", *Cool Careers For Dummies* takes the mystery, fear, and drudgery out of getting ahead!"

— Mary-Ellen Mort, Project Director, Job Smart, top-rated careers Web site

"If you're looking for work that gives you more than just a steady paycheck, *Cool Careers For Dummies* is a great place to begin your search. The straight-talking authors first provide an unusual array of 500 career possibilities and then offer useful advice on how to land a job in the area you choose. It's a fun read that may be of invaluable help in making one of life's big decisions."

— Jack Kahn, Director of Program Development, PBS-TV *Nightly Business Report*

"*Cool Careers For Dummies* provides a fast-moving, humor-filled tour through questions about careers, including self-employment, job interviews, determining one's interests, creating opportunities, and making decisions."

— Dr. Robert A. Scott, President, Ramapo College of New Jersey

"Whether you're looking for a job or want to switch careers, Marty Nemko will show you the tricks you need. His thorough knowledge and direct style have helped thousands of my listeners."

— Ronn Owens, Talk Show Host, KGO, San Francisco/KABC, Los Angeles

"*Cool Careers For Dummies* is a breath of fresh air! It guides readers through the career planning process in a new way and provides lots of interesting, practical suggestions that really make a difference."

— Marilyn E. Maze, Career Software Designer, ACT, Inc.

"Anyone who dreads the 9-to-5 rut will embrace *Cool Careers For Dummies*. It offers readers the options they need to find the right career, the guidance to get there, and the inspiration to do it."

— Dave Murphy, Career Search Editor, *San Francisco Examiner*

"A lively, irreverent, funny, and really helpful book for all those millions of people who are trying to figure out a new cool career. It's jammed with good advice, lots of new possibilities, and it sure takes the sting out of a difficult process."

— Ann Sparks, Program Director, Alumnae Resources, San Francisco's largest career development organization

"Extra-strength resources to continually re-launch your career search . . . cool!"

— Jeffrey Taylor, Founder, The Monster Board, a leading employment Web site

"Remarkably effective. Takes you from clueless to a career."

— Bob Rosner, Author of *Working Wounded: Advice That Adds Insight to Injury*

COOL CAREERS FOR DUMMIES®

by Marty Nemko and
Paul & Sarah Edwards

IDG Books Worldwide, Inc.
An International Data Group Company

Foster City, CA ♦ Chicago, IL ♦ Indianapolis, IN ♦ New York, NY

Cool Careers For Dummies®

Published by
IDG Books Worldwide, Inc.
An International Data Group Company
919 E. Hillsdale Blvd.
Suite 400
Foster City, CA 94404
www.idgbooks.com (IDG Books Worldwide Web site)
www.dummies.com (Dummies Press Web site)

Library of Congress Catalog Card No.: 98-86167

ISBN: 0-7645-5095-0

Printed in the United States of America

10 9 8 7 6 5 4 3 2 1

1B/ST/QX/ZY/IN

Distributed in the United States by IDG Books Worldwide, Inc.

Distributed by Macmillan Canada for Canada; by Transworld Publishers Limited in the United Kingdom; by IDG Norge Books for Norway; by IDG Sweden Books for Sweden; by Woodslane Pty. Ltd. for Australia; by Woodslane (NZ) Ltd. for New Zealand; by Addison Wesley Longman Singapore Pte Ltd. for Singapore, Malaysia, Thailand, Indonesia and Korea; by Norma Comunicaciones S.A. for Colombia; by Intersoft for South Africa; by International Thomson Publishing for Germany, Austria and Switzerland; by Toppan Company Ltd. for Japan; by Distribuidora Cuspide for Argentina; by Livraria Cultura for Brazil; by Ediciencia S.A. for Ecuador; by Ediciones ZETA S.C.R. Ltda. for Peru; by WS Computer Publishing Corporation, Inc., for the Philippines; by Unalis Corporation for Taiwan; by Contemporanea de Ediciones for Venezuela; by Computer Book & Magazine Store for Puerto Rico; by Express Computer Distributors for the Caribbean and West Indies. Authorized Sales Agent: Anthony Rudkin Associates for the Middle East and North Africa.

For general information on IDG Books Worldwide's books in the U.S., please call our Consumer Customer Service department at 800-762-2974. For reseller information, including discounts and premium sales, please call our Reseller Customer Service department at 800-434-3422.

For information on where to purchase IDG Books Worldwide's books outside the U.S., please contact our International Sales department at 650-655-3200 or fax 650-655-3297.

For information on foreign language translations, please contact our Foreign & Subsidiary Rights department at 650-655-3021 or fax 650-655-3281.

For sales inquiries and special prices for bulk quantities, please contact our Sales department at 650-655-3200 or write to the address above.

For information on using IDG Books Worldwide's books in the classroom or for ordering examination copies, please contact our Educational Sales department at 800-434-2086 or fax 317-596-5499.

For press review copies, author interviews, or other publicity information, please contact our Public Relations department at 650-655-3000 or fax 650-655-3299.

About the Authors

Marty Nemko has several cool careers. He has a successful career counseling practice. His column appears every Sunday in the *Los Angeles Times* employment section and in the *San Francisco Examiner/Chronicle,* right above *Dilbert.* He's entering his tenth year as producer and host of the hour-long *Work with Marty Nemko,* heard weekly on a National Public Radio affiliate in San Francisco. He is a frequent guest on TV and radio shows, and has appeared nationally on CBS, CNN, and PBS. He has been the primary interview source for dozens of articles, including *The Washington Post, The Wall Street Journal,* and *Money*. He holds a Ph.D. from the University of California, Berkeley and subsequently taught there. He does find a few moments for hobbies: he loves to breed new varieties of roses and to play romantic songs on the piano.

Paul & Sarah Edwards' career and self-employment books have sold over a million copies. Their weekly column is syndicated by the *Los Angeles Times* News Syndicate, and they write monthly columns for *Entrepreneur's Home Office* and Price Costco's *Connection.* They have been regular commentators, guests, and hosts on CNBC, HGTV, and Lifetime and appear frequently on radio and TV shows across the country. Since 1988, they have produced and co-hosted their hour-long show, *Working From Home,* on the Business News Network. Occasionally their show, broadcast from their Southern California home, is enriched by the barks of Billy, their toy Manchester Terrier, and Blue, an Italian greyhound.

Ask the Authors

Phone or in-person career counseling: One of this book's authors, Marty Nemko, directs a career counseling practice. For information, phone 510-653–0100.

Presentations: The authors offer practical yet fun presentations and seminars for organizations and campuses. For information, call 510-653–0100.

Self-employment support: The Edwards provide a wealth of ongoing information, resources, and support, including updates, marketing tips, excerpts from their nine books on self-employment, and daily messages at `www.paulandsarah.com`. And for updates on this book and other cool stuff, visit the authors' Web site at `www.coolcareers.com`.

ABOUT IDG BOOKS WORLDWIDE

Welcome to the world of IDG Books Worldwide.

IDG Books Worldwide, Inc., is a subsidiary of International Data Group, the world's largest publisher of computer-related information and the leading global provider of information services on information technology. IDG was founded more than 25 years ago and now employs more than 8,500 people worldwide. IDG publishes more than 275 computer publications in over 75 countries (see listing below). More than 90 million people read one or more IDG publications each month.

Launched in 1990, IDG Books Worldwide is today the #1 publisher of best-selling computer books in the United States. We are proud to have received eight awards from the Computer Press Association in recognition of editorial excellence and three from *Computer Currents*' First Annual Readers' Choice Awards. Our best-selling *...For Dummies®* series has more than 50 million copies in print with translations in 38 languages. IDG Books Worldwide, through a joint venture with IDG's Hi-Tech Beijing, became the first U.S. publisher to publish a computer book in the People's Republic of China. In record time, IDG Books Worldwide has become the first choice for millions of readers around the world who want to learn how to better manage their businesses.

Our mission is simple: Every one of our books is designed to bring extra value and skill-building instructions to the reader. Our books are written by experts who understand and care about our readers. The knowledge base of our editorial staff comes from years of experience in publishing, education, and journalism — experience we use to produce books for the '90s. In short, we care about books, so we attract the best people. We devote special attention to details such as audience, interior design, use of icons, and illustrations. And because we use an efficient process of authoring, editing, and desktop publishing our books electronically, we can spend more time ensuring superior content and spend less time on the technicalities of making books.

You can count on our commitment to deliver high-quality books at competitive prices on topics you want to read about. At IDG Books Worldwide, we continue in the IDG tradition of delivering quality for more than 25 years. You'll find no better book on a subject than one from IDG Books Worldwide.

John Kilcullen
CEO
IDG Books Worldwide, Inc.

Steven Berkowitz
President and Publisher
IDG Books Worldwide, Inc.

Eighth Annual Computer Press Awards ≥1992

Ninth Annual Computer Press Awards ≥1993

Tenth Annual Computer Press Awards ≥1994

Eleventh Annual Computer Press Awards ≥1995

Dedications

Marty: To my parents. As teenagers, they were wrested from their home in Poland and into concentration camps. After the war, they were placed on a cargo ship and dropped in New York City with no money, no family, no education, no English, but plenty of Holocaust scars. Despite it all, they succeeded. They are my inspiration.

Paul and Sarah: To our son, Jon, who followed his own career path. I, Paul, was told from Day 1 that I should be a lawyer. I followed the script and did graduate from law school but took the first chance I got to go in a different direction. I, Sarah, was told that my best bet was to be a teacher. I got the education I needed to teach but never spent a day as a classroom teacher. So we were careful not to push Jon into a career. The result is that Jon is doing something he likes: He designs computer games. We salute Jon for choosing his own career and for all the hard work it took to succeed.

Authors' Acknowledgments

To the thousands of career searchers who taught us so much of what is in this book: the callers to our radio shows, the career searchers at Alumnae Resources, and most of all, Marty's clients.

To our wise reviewers: Jim Gonyea, career forums host on America Online; Marilyn Maze, director of career products for American College Testing; Howard Figler, dean of career counselors; and the queens of online career searching: *JobSmarts'* Mary Ellen Mort and *The Riley Guide's* Margaret Riley Dikel. Special thanks to Dave Murphy, Marty's editor at the *San Francisco Examiner.* No matter how hard Marty tries to excise every unneeded word, Dave cuts 10 percent more — and it reads better.

To the other talented people whose ideas enrich these pages: Christina Fox, Dodge Johnson, Jennifer Murphy, Julie Petrie, Michael Scriven, and Marty's dear friends, David Wilens and Allan Gold.

To Kelly Manzer, Marty's sounding board. Thank you for patiently listening to my rants and raves before offering your common-sense, occasionally brilliant responses—an awesome gift.

To Joyce Acosta. Paul and Sarah deeply appreciate Joyce's good spirit and ability to get things done as their administrative assistant. She makes their lives run. They thank their lucky stars for Joyce.

To our consiglieri: agent Jan Miller and august Doubleday editor emeritus, Luther Nichols.

To the good people at IDG: Mark Butler and Kathy Welton for believing we were the right authors for this book, Tim Gallan for his zen-like project editing, Kathleen Dobie for her copy editing with a human touch, and Allison Solomon for handling administrative tasks with unusual intelligence and diligence. A special thanks to Clark Scheffy, who had to leave the project when U.C. Berkeley called, but first educated us on what works in a *...For Dummies* book.

And finally, Marty wants to thank his wife, Barbara Nemko, who despite being in the middle of an exhausting election campaign, patiently reviewed much of this book and, throughout, remained wise and kind.

Publisher's Acknowledgments

We're proud of this book; please register your comments through our IDG Books Worldwide Online Registration Form located at `http://my2cents.dummies.com`.

Some of the people who helped bring this book to market include the following:

Acquisitions, Editorial, and Media Development

Project Editors: Clark Scheffy, Tim Gallan

Acquisitions Editor: Mark Butler

Copy Editor: Kathleen Dobie

General Reviewer: Marilyn Maze

Research Coordinator: Heather Prince

Editoral Coordinator: Maureen Kelly

Editorial Manager: Leah P. Cameron

Media Development Manager: Heather Heath Dismore

Editorial Assistant: Donna Love

Production

Project Coordinator: Regina Snyder

Associate Project Coordinator: Tom Missler

Layout and Graphics: Lou Boudreau, Angela F. Hunckler, Brent Savage, J. Tyler Connor, Maridee V. Ennis, Todd Klemme, Jane E. Martin, Drew R. Moore, Heather N. Pearson, Janet Seib, Deirdre Smith, Kate Snell

Proofreaders: Kelli Botta, Henry Lazarek, Nancy Price, Janet M. Withers

Indexer: Sherry Massey

General and Administrative

IDG Books Worldwide, Inc.: John Kilcullen, CEO; Steven Berkowitz, President and Publisher

IDG Books Technology Publishing: Brenda McLaughlin, Senior Vice President and Group Publisher

Dummies Technology Press and Dummies Editorial: Diane Graves Steele, Vice President and Associate Publisher; Mary Bednarek, Director of Acquisitions and Product Development; Kristin A. Cocks, Editorial Director

Dummies Trade Press: Kathleen A. Welton, Vice President and Publisher; Kevin Thornton, Acquisitions Manager

IDG Books Production for Dummies Press: Michael R. Britton, Vice President of Production and Creative Services; Beth Jenkins Roberts, Production Director; Cindy L. Phipps, Manager of Project Coordination, Production Proofreading, and Indexing; Kathie S. Schutte, Supervisor of Page Layout; Shelley Lea, Supervisor of Graphics and Design; Debbie J. Gates, Production Systems Specialist; Robert Springer, Supervisor of Proofreading; Debbie Stailey, Special Projects Coordinator; Tony Augsburger, Supervisor of Reprints and Bluelines

Dummies Packaging and Book Design: Robin Seaman, Creative Director; Jocelyn Kelaita, Product Packaging Coordinator; Kavish + Kavish, Cover Design

♦

The publisher would like to give special thanks to Patrick J. McGovern, without whom this book would not have been possible.

♦

Contents at a Glance

Cartoons at a Glance

By Rich Tennant

"So what if you have a Ph.D. in physics? I used to have my own circus act."

page 165

"I'm sure there will be a good job market when I graduate. I created a virus that will go off that year."

page 335

"When choosing a career I ignored my heart and did what my brain wanted. Now all my brain wants is Prozac."

page 5

"We don't care where you see yourself in five years, as long as you can see where our clients will be."

page 309

"My sense is you're personalizing your resume too much."

page 191

Fax: 978-546-7747 • E-mail: the5wave@tiac.net

Table of Contents

Introduction

Twelve years ago, I heard about a little-known career called child-life specialist. When children must go to the hospital for an extended stay, they're assigned a child-life specialist to help them adapt to living without their parents.

When I told my clients about this career, they were glad to hear about it, even if they themselves didn't want to pursue it. It gave them hope that maybe a cool career existed for them that they hadn't heard of.

That started me on my collection. Every time I heard of an interesting career, I added it to my list. I included not only unusual careers but also neat niches within the popular careers: lawyers who arrange adoptions or specialize in outer space issues, for example. Now the list has 512 careers. I got many of the self-employment ideas from my co-authors, Paul and Sarah Edwards, who have written eight books on the subject.

This book contains a brief profile on each of the 512 careers plus the strategies that my clients have found most helpful in choosing a career or in landing a job. I developed many of these strategies because the standard career advice wasn't working for lots of people. These strategies do work. The Edwardses contribute a fine blueprint for how to become successfully self-employed. That's the book in a nutshell. Its ideas have helped a lot of people find a cool career, including many people who were quite stuck.

How This Book Is Organized

The chapters in this book are organized into five parts. Here's what they present:

Part I: Find the Right Career for You, Right Here

Whether you've never had a career before or want to dump your old one and get a new one, this part is for you.

First, follow your heart

Browse the "Cool Careers Catalog" in Chapter 2 — those yellow pages with the quick profiles of the 512 careers — and simply pick out one or more that make your heart beat a little faster. If you don't feel like browsing the entire Catalog, there's a quicker approach. We divide the careers into categories to make it easier to home in on the right ones for you.

Next, use your head

We ask you to list what's really important to you in a career. Don't know? The "20 Most Revealing Questions" in Chapter 3 will help.

Finally, blend head and heart

This part's *virtual career coach* simulates what I do with my private clients so that your final career choice both makes sense and feels good. Last, there's a final check: Does your chosen career have all five signs of being right for you? If the answer is yes, congratulations, you've found your cool career.

Part II: Getting Smart

Choosing a career is one thing; succeeding at it is something else. Often, a key is to get trained well. In this part, we show you how to find the right career preparation for you and how to make the most of it. If a university seems right, we show you how to maximize your chances of admission and how to reap the maximum benefit from your back-to-school stint. But sometimes, you can learn more at what we call *You University,* a custom mix of mentoring, articles, tapes, and seminars. We even show how a You U. "graduate" can get hired over someone with more degrees.

Part III: A Better Way to Land the Job

The standard advice — network, network, network — simply doesn't work for lots of people. They either don't have many contacts to network with or are uncomfortable asking people for help with their career. This part shows you an effective way to land the job even if you're shy and don't have a 500-person rolodex. For my clients with a tendency to procrastinate, this approach has been a godsend.

Part IV: Customizing Your Career

When you buy a suit, it will probably look just okay off-the-rack. To really look good, it needs to be tailored and accessorized. Same with your career. This part shows you how to make any job better by tailoring it to your strengths and by using savvy approaches with your boss and co-workers. Another approach to customizing your career is to become self-employed. Chapter 19 takes the exciting but scary thought of being your own boss and shows you how to maximize your chances of success.

Part V: The Part of Tens

Many good ideas don't require a long explanation. So we plunk every good idea that's self-explanatory into this part. Are 512 careers not enough? Here, we show you ten ways to find many more. Suffering from the heartbreak of procrastinitis? Stall no more. We give you ten (actually 29) extra-strength cures. Interviews make you sweat? No sweat. We offer ten questions that make job interviewees squirm — and honest ways to survive them. Finally, we offer ten keys to success for the self-employed. Don't miss the Part of Tens!

Plus we offer an afterword with our best thoughts on how to be happy with your worklife (our very favorite pages in this book).

Finally, right before the index, we give you the Cool Career Finder — a way for you to find careers in such categories as "Too much fun to be work" and "Make a big difference in the world."

Icons Used in This Book

Of course, we think that every word in this book is golden, but there are some ideas we really don't want you to miss, so we mark them with one of these icons:

Your basic good idea.

Good ideas that few people use.

Avoid these common pitfalls and you're unlikely to bomb out.

This icon lets us brag. These are the ideas we're most proud of.

Many people will procrastinate on their career search if it's drudgery. So, over the past twelve years, I've worked hard to find approaches that are fun yet effective, and put them all in this book. This icon makes sure that you don't miss them.

A key strategy that you won't want to forget.

Where to Go from Here

If you think you might procrastinate in the beginning of your career search, why not start by checking out the fun stuff? For example, sneak a peek at the "Cool Careers Catalog" in Chapter 2. Flip through the book and stop to gawk at the Unconventional Wisdom and Fun Yet Effective icons.

And when you're finally in the mood to get at least slightly serious, just turn the page. You are going to benefit. Can you picture it: finally satisfied with your career, eager to get out of bed on workday mornings, not watching the clock at work. And just think of what you'd do with the money. Okay, stop daydreaming and turn the page. Let's get started!

Part I

Find the Right Career for You, Right Here

"When choosing a career I ignored my heart and did what my brain wanted. Now all my brain wants is Prozac."

In this part . . .

We get right to it. This part walks you, step by step, through our proven effective (and rather fun) process of finding a career that's right for you: from how to make the most of the Cool Careers Catalog to finding the courage to say, "Yes! This is the right career. I'm going to go for it!"

Chapter 1
Sandy's Tale

In This Chapter

- A little morality tale on career planning

Sure, some people come out of the womb knowing what they want to be when they grow up — the five-year-old violin prodigy comes to mind. But most of us aren't so lucky — and we don't get much help.

Some parents tell you, "It's your life. You decide." Other parents go to the other extreme, expecting you to follow in their footsteps: "Hazardous waste disposal is a great career." Before you even learn how to tie your shoes, they're pushing: "Come on, let's visit Daddy's toxic waste dump."

In high school, you take a career test that asks what you're interested in. How the heck are you supposed to know? If you're like most teens, you spend most of your school life studying such career irrelevancies as the symbolism in *Romeo & Juliet,* quadratic equations, and the slave ships of 1628. After school, you play soccer and are forced to take piano lessons (a skill for which only your mother thinks you have talent). You spend summers with friends at Camp Kowabonga, during which your career exploration consists of observing your counselor go postal. How in the world are you supposed to validly answer test questions about your career interests? It's little surprise that many high school students laugh at their career test results: funeral director, clergy, or the utterly useless, "Your interests suggest that you could pursue a wide range of careers."

Many students remain undaunted. They figure that career clarity will come in college. Trouble is, most colleges proudly proclaim that their courses are *not* for career preparation but for general education. Worse, college courses are taught by professors — people who have deliberately opted out of the real world. So many college students' career sights are limited.

As college graduation approaches, panic often sets in and the same students who procrastinated endlessly trying to ensure that they made the perfect career decision, suddenly force themselves into a choice, often based on very little. Their entire reasoning often fits on a bumper sticker:

- "I want to help people, so I'll be a doctor."
- "I'm lousy in science and I like to argue, so I'll go to law school."
- "I want to make a lot of money, so I'll go into business."
- "I don't know what I want to do, so I'll get a master's in something."

None of the above would work for Sandy. He was sick of school. So he headed to the college's career center where he was pointed to a career library and encouraged to "explore." That's inadequate guidance for most of us. He did, however, fall into a job. His cousin was the custodian at Western Widget Waxing, Inc., and put in a good word for Sandy: "He has always been interested in widgets." Sandy wrote a letter to Western Widget Waxing, Inc., that began, "I believe I'm well-suited for a career in the widget waxing industry." He got an interview. He wore that conservative suit he swore he'd never wear and told old WWW, Inc., that ever since his childhood, he spent much of his spare time waxing widgets. He got the job.

Within days of starting at WWW, Inc., Sandy realized that widget waxing wasn't all it was cracked up to be. Now what? WWW's human resources manager told Sandy only about options in widget waxing. "Well, Sandy, you *are* on track to becoming a widget waxing supervisor, and down the road, I think you have the potential to become a waxing director." On seeing Sandy's face go flat, she tried, "Well, you could join our sales department. Would you like to sell widget waxing? How about the accounting department? Shipping? Well, what *do* you want, Sandy?" That was the problem. Sandy didn't know.

In desperation, Sandy decided to seek help from a professional — even though it used up the money he'd been saving for that vacation. "What's a thousand bucks if it can land me a cool career? I'll make ten times that much at a job I'm happy in."

Alas, when Sandy showed up at his appointment with the career counselor, there were those tests again.

Counselor: Well, Sandy, on the Myers-Briggs Type Indicator, you're an INFP. That means you're an introverted, intuitive, feeling perceiver.

Sandy: So what should I do for a career?

Counselor: Sandy, you can't rush this. That would be premature foreclosure. We need to review the results of the Campbell Interest and Skills Survey. You're an RIC. That stands for realistic-investigative-conventional. Let's interpret that.

Sandy: So what should I do for a career?

Counselor: Well, Sandy, use what information you've learned about yourself from the Myers-Briggs Type Indicator and from the Campbell Interest and Skills Survey, by exploring in the career library.

Sandy: Nooooooh, not again!

Instead, Sandy returned to Western Widget Waxing, Inc.

Too often, career counseling is like psychoanalysis: You gain insight into yourself, but your life is no better.

One day, Sandy heard about a book called, *Find Your Career Joy While Doing What You Love and the Money Will Come While Your Flower Opens*. So off Sandy trotted to the bookstore, and although daunted by the book's thickness and its 66 worksheets, he figured it was only $15.99 — the cost of two movie tickets. Such a deal. Sandy bit.

Five years later, our hero, now 30, was still on worksheet #6. His mother, his friends, even his haircutter, were asking him, "Well, Sandy, what *are* you going to be when you grow up?" Sandy decided to get serious. He pulled out his aging copy of *Find Your Career Joy While Doing What You Love and the Money Will Come While Your Flower Opens,* and actually managed to complete all 66 worksheets. This gave him a complete inventory of his skills, interests, values, job requirements, personality attributes, and inter-ocular focal length.

But wait a minute! Doing all that still didn't tell Sandy how to figure out which career fits best.

I swear we are not exaggerating. Even the best-selling career guides do not take you through that crucial next step: Which careers fit? They state or imply that if you do all their worksheets, you will somehow divine your dream career.

Sandy cried, and Sandy stayed on at Western Widget Waxing, Inc. "Maybe I'm meant to be in widget waxing," he told himself. He worked hard, and indeed the human resources manager's prediction came to pass. At age 40, Sandy became director of Widget Waxing. But he still wasn't happy.

Then Sandy was sure he found a solution: the computer. WWW, Inc., progressive firm that it is, bought a career-finding computer, and made it available to its employees. Sandy was first in line. A couple of hours and voilà, 15 best-fit careers popped out. Some of the careers made sense but didn't excite him enough to make him quit his now-comfortable job at WWW to go back and get retrained for a profession he wasn't even sure he'd end up liking better. After all, Sandy had become a director and was fully vested in WWW's retirement plan. A few of the generated careers did excite Sandy, but they were careers that excite too many people —TV broadcasting, for example. So what if Sandy would love to anchor the nightly news? So would half the people on the continent.

Although Sandy didn't know it, many computer programs often fail because they eliminate careers if the career seeker lacks even one ostensibly necessary skill or personality trait. In the real world, many careers don't have rigid skill and personality requirements. Take book editors. Some succeed primarily because of their aesthetic sense, others because of their feel for the bottom line. And aren't some editors introverts, others extroverts? Even if Sandy was lacking a key skill, if he found a career that excited him, he may well have been willing and able to put the energy into compensating for his weakness. But the computer program never gave him the chance.

Krishna Rama (nee Sandy) now resides at the Harmonic Transcendent monastery in Berkeley, California, hoping to find career nirvana through meditation.

All jokes aside (at least for the moment), despite taking career tests, plowing through fat career guides, and/or meditation, many people end up falling into their careers more by chance than by choice. Not a good way to ensure career happiness. There has to be a better way.

There is. Read on.

Chapter 2

The Cool Careers Catalog

In This Chapter

- How to use the Cool Careers Catalog
- All kinds of good careers
- A few not-so-cool careers

The first step in finding the right career may be the most fun: browsing the Cool Careers Catalog.

We're especially excited about the Catalog because it gives you a fast yet substantive introduction to over 500 good careers, including many unlikely suspects. Think of the Catalog as you would a favorite mail-order catalog. Scan the names of the careers, and when one intrigues you, read its short *scoop:* a quick introduction to that occupation. For now, just jot down the names of any careers that, based on gut feeling, seem like possibilities.

What Makes a Cool Career Cool?

Competition for a spot in the Cool Careers Catalog was fierce. First, a career had to be either

- A popular mainstream career
- A little-known niche within a mainstream career
- A little-known career
- A self-employment opportunity that we believe offers relatively low-risk and high payoff

We narrowed the careers down further by choosing only those that scored highest overall on these criteria:

- Potential to make a difference in society
- Potential for at least a middle-class income
- A good job market

Using the Cool Careers Catalog

To make it easy to home in on the right career for you, we divide the careers into categories, but the scoops are short and fun-to-read enough that you may want to read them all just for the heck of it. Who knows? Your dream career may be in a category you wouldn't have picked.

The categories

A career can require skill with *people,* with *data,* with *words,* and/or with *things*. In the Catalog, we categorize the careers accordingly. (See the Table of Contents for the complete list of categories.) For example, the attorney scoop is in the "Words/People" category. Most attorneys must excel at using words and must also have good people skills.

Puhleeze, don't treat a career's category as gospel. The individual job you land may be different. For example, one lawyer may mainly write contracts, in which case, he doesn't need exceptional people skills. Another reason not to take the categories too seriously is that quite a few careers fall on the border between two categories. They can easily fit in another category.

So if you have the patience, ignore the categories and just skim the Catalog from beginning to end. That way you won't miss anything. Don't worry; it won't take long. If, however, you want a shortcut, pick a category as a better-than-random starting place.

And speaking of shortcuts, the Appendix of this book has 16 special lists of careers: for example, the careers most likely to impress your family, those that are too much fun to be work, those offering the surest routes to big bucks, and those likely to make the biggest difference to society. You can start by browsing the careers on one of those lists.

The catalog's icons

Sometimes, a picture is worth 1,000 words. Not so with these pictures; they're worth maybe three or four. Here's what they mean:

Careers marked with this icon have significant self-employment potential.

Each scoop has an education icon to let you know the minimum amount of schooling you need to start out in that career. Many people in the field may have more than the minimum, but if you have at least the amount listed, you have a shot at the job.

No degree required. Training may involve an on-the-job program, an apprenticeship, or a college-based certificate program that takes a year or less.

Some college required.

Bachelor's degree required.

Master's or other post-bachelor's education required.

Doctoral degree required.

Careers marked with this icon are profiled in-depth in the *Occupational Outlook Handbook,* an authoritative government source available in most libraries, and online at www.bls.gov/ocohome.htm.

Careers marked with this icon are profiled in-depth in *Best Home Businesses for the 90s,* by Paul Edwards and Sarah Edwards.

To make it easy to find out more about a career, most of the scoops include the address and Web site of the field's professional association, which is often a source of valuable information. If you don't have Web access, most associations prefer that you write rather than phone. Request information useful for people considering the career in that field and information on becoming a member. Associations will at least provide the latter, often useful in itself. Member benefits usually include a magazine covering what's new and important in the field, a member directory, and placement on a mailing list for the field's upcoming events.

What price prestige?

We hold some unusual views about choosing a career. To ensure that our biases aren't foisted upon you unwillingly, we place them in an Afterword. That way, to read them, you have to take an affirmative step. There is, however, one bit of iconoclasm that we think we should share with you right here:

The Cool Careers Catalog covers the popular professions such as doctor, lawyer, and psychologist, but as you know, those careers require years of graduate school. Many people in these fields believe that their education did not really prepare them for their careers despite the years of effort and enough money to buy a house. Before committing to all that schooling, know that many people find great career satisfaction and good income in similar careers that require far less time behind a student desk. Examples:

- Aspire to be a doctor? Physician's assistants realize most of a doctor's benefits: They command a good salary, get to treat patients, and because they don't treat serious illnesses, most of their patients get well.
- Leaning toward the law? Consider becoming a mediator: less confrontational work, fewer ethical temptations, and shorter training.
- Motivated to become a psychologist? Personal coaches not only train for a shorter time, but because they deal with healthier people, they see more progress.

So in addition to the popular high-status professions, consider checking out the Catalog's many other options.

One more thing. Career passion usually comes *after* you've been in the job for a while. So don't browse the Catalog expecting to find a career that makes you yell, "Eureka! I have found it!" The wisest approach is not to hold out for immediate ecstasy, but to just pick out the career(s) that, for you, feels better than the others.

Okay, enough preliminaries. We tried to make each career scoop fun to read even if you're not interested in the career. So enjoy.

Work with People

Caretaking and Coaching

Mediator. Traditionally, the way that divorcing husbands and wives avoid killing each is by hiring two attorneys and letting the lawyers slug it out. That's expensive, adversarial, and often, just plain yucky. An increasingly popular alternative is to hire a mediator. In addition to divorce mediation, these peacemakers can make a living in community mediation. Example: You're furious at your neighbor for playing loud music every night. Your neighbor is equally furious at your constant complaints: "Loud music is my way of having fun at the end of the work day, and you are not going to deny me my rights." A really good mediator needs the listening skills of a suicide counselor, the patience of Job, and the wisdom of Solomon. But, not to worry, mediation can be a rewarding career even for mere mortals. *American Arbitration Association Center for Mediation: www.adr.org; 140 W. 51st St., New York, NY 10020; 212-484-4000.*

(Neat Niche) **Ombudsperson.** As conflict in the workplace grows, many organizations hire ombudspersons to resolve disputes. For example, every federal agency is required to have at least one. Universities also hire them. *The Ombudsman Association: c/o Carole Trocchio, 5521 Greenville Ave. #104-265, Dallas, TX 75206; 214-553-0043.*

(Neat Niche) **Intercultural Mediator.** As schools, workplaces, and neighborhoods integrate, intercultural conflicts are increasing. So is the need for mediators who can understand and inspire trust among people from diverse backgrounds.

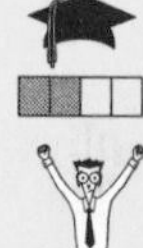

Geriatric Care Manager. Imagine that you had aging parents living in another city. They need help dealing with a health care provider or insurance company, finding someone to look in on them, or dealing with minor legal matters. You want to keep them out of a nursing home. You'd help out if you were local, but you're not. The answer? Hire a geriatric care manager. *National Association of Professional Geriatric Care Managers: 1604 North Country Club Rd., Tucson, AZ 85716; 520-881-8008. See also: the United States government's Web site on aging: www.aoa.dhhs.gov.*

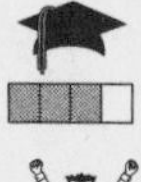

Clinical Psychologist. This field has a hidden benefit. We all know that it's compassionate, has status, and can pay well, but although few practitioners will admit it, psychology's unspoken appeal is that it's voyeuristic: You get to hear people's deepest intimacies. A downside of psychology is that many clients don't get better. Too often, clients gain insight into their problems, but their lives don't improve much. Nevertheless, demand for psychologists is growing because more health plans are covering psychologists' visits, because it's tough to cope with life's ever-greater demands, and because new therapies *are* more effective. For example, brief solution-oriented therapy, sometimes combined with new drugs, is rapidly replacing prolonged analysis of childhood angst. A master's degree is usually sufficient, although a Psy.D. (a practically-oriented doctorate) is the big kahuna degree. Ph.D. programs are generally better for aspiring researchers and professors, not practicing psychologists. *American Psychological Association: www.apa.org; 750 First St., N.E., Washington, DC 20002; 202-336-5500. American Counseling Association: www.counseling.org; 5999 Stevenson Ave., Alexandria, VA 22034; 703-823-9800. See also: www.wesleyan.edu/spn/psych.htm.*

(Neat Niche) **Relationship Acceptance Therapist.** New evidence suggests that couples counseling is most effective when it helps partners learn to accept each other as they are rather than trying to change each other. (This makes sense. How easy is it to make *you* change?) A study reported in *U.S. News and World Report* found that after just six months of acceptance therapy, 90 percent of couples considering divorce reported "dramatic" increases in satisfaction and none split up.

(Neat Niche) **Sports Psychologist.** A golfer has trouble concentrating. A pitcher freaks out under pressure. Teammates hate each other's guts. Enter the sports psychologist, who frequently uses guided visualization and hypnosis. *The Academy for Psychology of Sports International: 6161 Busch Blvd., Columbus, OH 43229.*

(Neat Niche) **Men's Therapist.** The 1990s saw a great increase in therapists for women and for people of color. Men are now starting to seek counselors specializing in men's issues. *American Men's Studies Association: www.cybersales.net/amsa; 329 Afton Ave., Youngstown, OH 44512-2311; 330-782-2736.*

(Neat Niche) **Infant Mental Health Counselor.** This career emerged because more and more children are born with severe mental or physical problems, or into homes with parents ill-equipped to be parents. The counselor advises parents on how to bring up a challenging baby while retaining their sanity. *World Association for Infant Mental Health: www.msu.edu/user/waimh; Kellogg Center, Ste. 27, Michigan State University, East Lansing, MI 48824; 517-432-3793.*

(Neat Niche) **Money Therapist.** Money makes some people miserable: Some hoard it, others spend it too fast, baby boomers can't talk with their aging parents about it. Enter the money shrink.

(Neat Niche) **School Psychologist.** This can be a great job: nine-month year, high status, low stress. Typical project: Johnny is doing lousy in school. What should school and parents do? In comes the school psychologist: Observe the kid; test him; pow-wow with parent, teacher, kid, and special education teacher; and write jargon-filled report. School psychologists may also do parenting workshops and screen students for gifted students programs. *National Association of School Psychologists: www.naspweb.org; 4340 East West Highway, Bethesda, MD 20814; 301-657-0270.*

Alas, programs for gifted students are getting eliminated. Why do slow learners have the right to special, high-cost instruction, psychological and other services, but gifted students, with so much potential to contribute to society, increasingly get zilch? But I digress.

Personal Coach. Do you like to help others but would rather deal with problems easier to address than reconstructing a personality? Personal coaching is some combination of goal-setting advisor, time-management consultant, motivator, sounding board, confidant, dream-builder, and etiquette instructor. A big plus for becoming a coach rather than a shrink is the much shorter training time. Certification offered through *Coaches Training Institute: 415-451-6100,* and *Coach U. in Dallas, TX: www.coachu.com; 800-48COACH. See also: International Coaches Federation: www.coachfederation.org; 888-ICF-3131* and *www.islandnet.com/~rcarr/referral.html.*

(Neat Niche) **Career Coach.** Not everyone owns this book, and even if they did, some of them still enjoy having a human coach. Career coaches help people change jobs or make the most of the jobs they have. The need for career coaches is skyrocketing because people change jobs more than ever and the jobs they move to are ever more challenging. Both *U.S. News and World Report* and *Entrepreneur* magazines rate career coaching one of the hottest consulting activities. You'll be more effective and find it easier to get clients if you specialize: for example, in executives, lawyers, physicians, engineers, educators, or psychologists.

(Neat Niche) **Life Purpose Coach.** More than 46 percent of men and 40 percent of women say they are still trying to figure out the meaning and purpose of their life. So it's not surprising that some people are earning their livelihoods as life purpose consultants. There are over 300 practicing Life Purpose Consultants and their number has been growing 25 percent a year. Life Purpose Consultants may help people during times of transition: recovering from illness, searching for more fulfilling work, retiring, living after a divorce, and coping when children leave the nest. Some Life Purpose Consultants work to help organizations or companies clarify their corporate vision or mission. This new field is especially appealing to helping professionals who want to open a private practice without having to rely on third-party insurance payments.

(Neat Niche) **Time Management Coach.** When someone asks, "How are you?" The answer is as likely to be "Busy" as "Fine." Enter the time-management coach — the person who tries to help wring 25 hours from a 24-hour day. Many people are willing to pay for that advice, and so are many employers. Doing time-management seminars in workplaces not only gets you a fee, it gives you a way to recruit individual clients. Prepare by doing the equivalent of writing a term paper. Read a few books and articles on time-management, do a Web search, and write down every potentially useful strategy so that you have plenty of different strokes for different folks.

Time management is all about making choices; we can't do it all. The question is what to do full-bore, what to do half way, what to delegate, and what to say no to.

(Neat Niche) **Fitness Coach.** We all want to be fit but we don't all have the discipline to do it ourselves. A fitness trainer hovering over us can help. As a result, membership in the International Association of Fitness Professionals has gone from 742 in 1991 to over 7,000 in 1998. Fitness coaching sounds fun and easy, but there are downsides: You have to be a good marketer, and you usually have to work when your client isn't working — sayonara evenings and weekends. There's controversy about the importance of certification, but there's no question that you need sound knowledge of fitness principles, how to prevent and deal with injuries, and, of course, how to make a weak-willed client do those last ten sit-ups. Certification is offered by the *Aerobics and Fitness Association of America: www.afaa.com; 800-225-2322; 15250 Ventura Blvd. Suite 200, Sherman Oaks, CA 91403* and by the *American Council on Exercise: www.acefitness.org; 619-535-8227; P.O. Box 910449, San Diego, CA 92121.*

(Neat Niche) **Parenting Coach.** Whether it's a newborn or an adult child who just moved back home, many parents worry that they're not good-enough parents. They don't want a therapist, they just want help in getting their pride and joy to not drive them crazy. You can market to individual parents, for example, by offering free seminars at Lamaze classes. School districts and social service organizations may also hire parenting coaches.

(Neat Niche) **Shyness Coach.** Ninety percent of people say they're shy. This is an almost completely untapped market. You role-play stressful situations with clients, and help clients realize that the worst-case scenario isn't so bad or so likely.

(Neat Niche) **Dating Coach.** L.A. dating coach, Bart Ellis, doesn't just talk with his clients, he sends them out with a staffer on a mock date. The staffer writes a report analyzing the client's strengths and weaknesses as a date, and then Ellis reviews the results with the client.

(Neat Niche) **Etiquette Coach.** You're one of those 20-somethings whose idea of a fancy meal is a pizza with two toppings. All of a sudden, you're hired by the firm of Dewey, Cheatham & Howe, Inc., and you need to make well-heeled customers think you're worth your firm's well-heeled fees. Yeah, competence counts, but you'd better know how to make small talk without sounding trite, and how to spear a cherry tomato without the seeds spraying onto your shirt. The etiquette coach can help. Our marketing suggestions include getting corporations to hire you to run seminars for its employees, visiting the Web sites of local companies and e-mailing your pitch to top executives, and contacting private schools. (*Public* schools rarely cooperate with anything that is profit-making.) A variation on this theme is becoming a cross-cultural etiquette coach. Examples: Don't belch, slurp, or smack your lips. That's good advice in the United States, but in Asia, the lack of satisfied sounds may offend your host.

(Neat Niche) **Executive Coach.** Many executives are just a beat off. They're a bit too intense, too detail oriented, too something. Companies or the executives themselves hire coaches to help get them back in the rhythm.

(Neat Niche) **Personal Organizer.** With the paperless office the most incorrect prediction in history, our desks are piled high and our mailboxes are stuffed full. In addition, we're saddled with more trappings than ever. So it's no surprise that the demand for personal organizers is soaring. A neat subniche is that of a children's personal organizer. Parents go nuts trying to get their kids to do their homework, organize their notebooks, and get themselves off to school in the morning. Want to help? Since 1993, membership has doubled in the *National Association of Professional Organizers: www.napo.net.*

(Neat Niche) **Witness Coach.** Style counts, and attorneys know it. So, especially in big cases, attorneys often hire a coach to help witnesses improve speaking style, wardrobe, even such subtleties as posture, gait, and how to look at the jury.

Health Educator. HMOs know that an ounce of prevention is not only better than a pound of cure, it costs less. HMOs' ounce of prevention is to hire health educators to teach people such things as how to lose weight, fit exercise into a busy day, or lower their cholesterol (as though people don't know that broccoli is good and cheeseburgers are bad). Nonetheless, a job conducting health seminars is, as jobs go, pretty salubrious.

Retirement Consultant. A company with older workers sometimes feels a triple whammy: Older employees are more expensive, lower-energy, and lower-tech than many younger employees. The company would like some of its grayer employees to leave but can't risk downsizing them for fear of age-discrimination lawsuits. One solution is to hire a retirement consultant. The consultant meets with older workers to help them figure out how to make retirement work financially and what they'll do with their time. In addition to corporate work, retirement consultants can attract individual clients by offering free retirement-planning seminars. An ad in a local publication that appeals to people over 50 may say, "Nervous about retirement? Free seminar offers solutions to such problems as 'How will I afford it?' and 'What will I do with my time?'" At the end of the seminar, announce that you work with individuals to help them develop and implement a personalized plan. Your career should grow as boomers age.

Athletic Coach. I coached an Oakland Boys Club basketball team. I went in with visions of using hoop to help kids triumph over their life circumstances, but that proved overly ambitious. Just getting them to pay attention took everything I had. It was fun though, unearthing the neighborhood ringers and convincing them to play on my team. And the games were a rush: constantly figuring out what to do to give your team an edge, and trying to be the role model of calm intensity to tame the kids' scatteredness so that they could stay in control yet still give 100 percent.

The usual starting job is a high school coaching position, but you only start to earn a decent income at the college level. There, you have additional responsibilities such as meeting with the media and big-time donors. And you must make recruiting trips to convince some high school athletes that even though their SAT score is 750 (the verbal *plus* the math) and they have a C average at a weak high school, they can succeed in college classes. Because of Title IX regulations, the number of female sports teams is increasing, so job opportunities are good for women and not so good for men. *National High School Athletic Coaches Association: P.O. Box 2569, Gig Harbor, WA 98335; 253-853-6777. Job openings: Online Sports Career Center: www.onlinesports.com. Job openings for high school and college football coaches: www.coachhelp/jobs/htm.*

A&R Representative. A&R stands for "Artists and Repertoire," but that still doesn't explain what an A&R rep does. An A&R rep works for a record label to find people with talent and sign them with her company. Finding talented people can be a fun process: going to clubs, concerts, and talent shows. An A&R rep may also try to lure performers from other labels, and reviews tapes from performers who'd kill for a contract. After signing the talented few, the rep works with the artist to find the best stuff to record and then lobbies the label's PR department to generate the maximum buzz. *National Academy of Recording Arts and Sciences: www.grammy.org; 3402 Pico Blvd., Santa Monica, CA 90405; 310-392-3777.*

Literary, Artist's, or Performer's Agent. Most artistic types aren't entrepreneurial. Left to their own devices, they'd hang out, practice their craft, and the checks would somehow arrive in the mail. The agent's job is to make that happen. Agents help polish the sample product, pitch it to prospective buyers, and negotiate the deal for 10–15 percent of the take. Why is being an agent a cool career? You get to pick out and then champion the talented people you want to represent, work closely with them to ensure that their product is well packaged, and help your star reach as large an audience as possible. Plus, being an agent requires no formal credentials. Most agents learn the business as an agent's assistant or as a talent buyer — acquisitions editor for a publishing company, for example. *Association of Author's Representatives: 10 Astor Pl., New York, NY 10003; 212-353-3709. See also: www.producerlink.com.*

(Neat Niche) **Agent for Multimedia Game Developers.** Some of the hottest talent never gets on stage. This talent stays up 'til four in the morning cranking out code for a cool computer game. An agent is usually better able than a geeky programmer to get a software publisher to "Show me the money!"

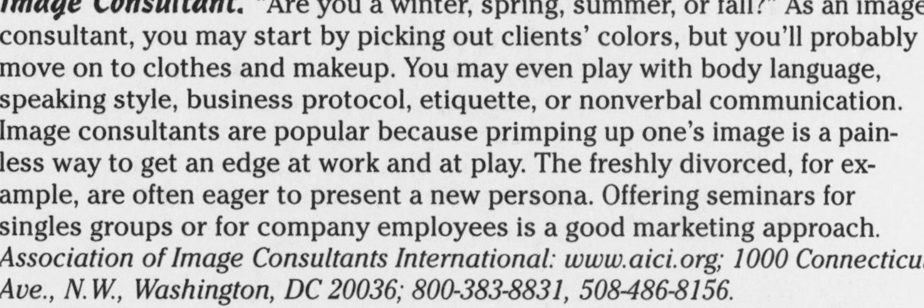

Image Consultant. "Are you a winter, spring, summer, or fall?" As an image consultant, you may start by picking out clients' colors, but you'll probably move on to clothes and makeup. You may even play with body language, speaking style, business protocol, etiquette, or nonverbal communication. Image consultants are popular because primping up one's image is a painless way to get an edge at work and at play. The freshly divorced, for example, are often eager to present a new persona. Offering seminars for singles groups or for company employees is a good marketing approach. *Association of Image Consultants International: www.aici.org; 1000 Connecticut Ave., N.W., Washington, DC 20036; 800-383-8831, 508-486-8156.*

Golf Seminar Instructor. Suzanne Woo, a former lawyer, now makes her living teaching individuals and groups the rules and etiquette of golf — equipment purchase, golf teacher selection, and the real draw: how to use golf for networking and to learn about co-players. Behavior on the course usually mirrors behavior in business.

Social Worker. Many people and families just can't make it without help. A child is abused; an older adult has Alzheimer's disease; a single parent with eight children, on top of it all, gets AIDS. Few jobs are more intimate and human than the social worker's. Despite the frustrations and low pay, most social workers who make it past the first two years love their jobs. Even if they can't solve the entire problem, the small steps feel rewarding enough. A bachelor's degree often gets you hired, a master's gets you promoted. To open a private practice, many states require a master's degree. *National Association of Social Workers: www.socialworkers.org; 750 First St., N.E., Washington, DC 20002-4241; 202-408-8600.*

Child Life Specialist. Imagine that your child is told she has a serious illness and must suddenly move from home into a hospital for a long stay filled with painful treatments. The child life specialist's job is to help her adapt to living without their parents and to psychologically prepare them for scary medical encounters. Child life specialists also help ensure that these kids get an education and a bit of fun in their lives. Because child life services are often mandated by hospital accreditation agencies, jobs are available, especially for graduates of top training programs such as those at Boston's Wheelock College or Mills College in Oakland, California. *Child Life Council: 11820 Parklawn Dr., Suite 202, Rockville, MD 20852; 301-881-7090.*

School Guidance Counselor. The modern version of this job is much more complicated than dealing with kids kicked out of class for chewing gum. School counselors may coordinate sex education, health awareness, career counseling, even on-site social work services. And yes, counselors still spend a lot of time telling Johnny that he better shape up or else. *American School Counselor Association: www.schoolcounselor.org; 801 N. Fairfax, Suite 310, Alexandria, VA 22304; 800-306-4722.*

Baby-Sitting Trainer. The only training most baby-sitters get is, "Call 911 in case of emergency." But what's the best way to respond if the baby cries? If the toddler won't go to sleep? Or if Munchkin misses mommy? You may be able to convince local recreation departments, adult schools, or human services agencies to hire you to teach baby-sitting training seminars. Baby-sitters may be glad to sign up so that they feel more confident and can let prospective customers know that they're certified. Quite reassuring to parents.

Nanny. The training is short; the task is doable, often pleasurable; and you may get to work in an environment most people only dream about: a wealthy person's home. That's not a bad combination, even if the pay is low. If you're good with kids, you won't have trouble finding a job. With the increase in single parents, and with two-parent families working very full-time, even many middle-class people find that a nanny is a must. The key to enjoying nannyhood is to get hooked up with a great family. Attending nanny school maximizes your chances. Why? Because many desirable families search for their nannies by contacting nanny schools. *American Council of Nanny Schools Delta College: University Center, MI 48710; 517-686-9417. National Academy of Nannies: 1681 S. Dayton St., Denver, CO 80231; 303-333-NANI.*

Doula. The most exhausting period in many women's lives is childbirth and the month after. Unlike a nanny, who cares for the child, the doula focuses on the mom; giving her instructions on breast-feeding, running errands, cooking, and cleaning — all to ease the transition to motherhood. Doula services are mushrooming. Doulas of North America, which refers clients to pre- and post-partum doulas, has seen membership skyrocket from 85 in 1992 to 2,000 now. *Doulas of North America: www.dona.com; 1100 23rd Ave. E, Seattle, WA 98112; 206-325-0472.*

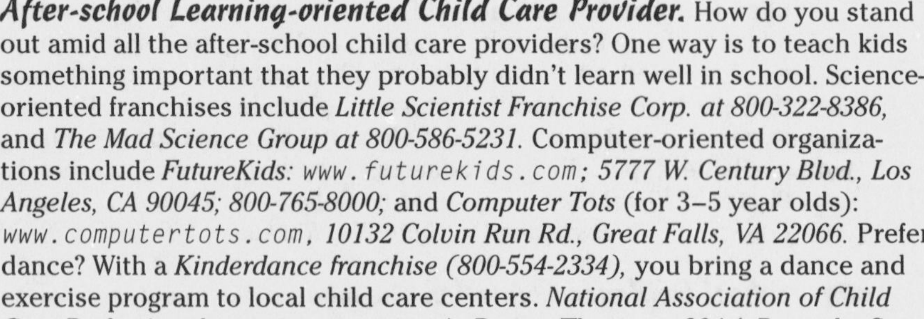

After-school Learning-oriented Child Care Provider. How do you stand out amid all the after-school child care providers? One way is to teach kids something important that they probably didn't learn well in school. Science-oriented franchises include *Little Scientist Franchise Corp. at 800-322-8386,* and *The Mad Science Group at 800-586-5231.* Computer-oriented organizations include *FutureKids:* `www.futurekids.com`*; 5777 W. Century Blvd., Los Angeles, CA 90045; 800-765-8000;* and *Computer Tots* (for 3–5 year olds): `www.computertots.com`*, 10132 Colvin Run Rd., Great Falls, VA 22066.* Prefer dance? With a *Kinderdance franchise (800-554-2334),* you bring a dance and exercise program to local child care centers. *National Association of Child Care Professionals: www.naccp.org; c/o Donna Thornton, 304-A Roanoke St., Christianburg, VA 24073; 800-537-1118.*

Dial a Wife. Beth Berg will plan the meal, wait for the plumber, even do the initial househunting. Sounds like a traditional wife, but she gets paid $25 an hour. In today's world of the vanishing housewife, everyone from newly divorced men to overworked women are eager to pay for the privilege of having their very own June Cleaver. Beth Berg's first ad simply said, "Buy time."

Celebrity/Executive Personal Assistant. According to the *New York Post,* a typical day in the life of Olympia Dukakis's personal assistant consists of rendering a second opinion on a movie contract, picking up her dog's gourmet dog food, suggesting ideas for marketing Dukakis's new salad dressing, and picking up her dry cleaning. Salaries range from $30,000-$100,000, plus perks. What sort of perks? Well, this isn't typical, but Carol Burnett gave her assistant a Land Rover for her birthday. *Association of Celebrity Personal Assistants: 132 W. 22nd St., New York, NY 10001.*

Corporate Concierge. Marcia's concierge service, operating in the lobbies of residential and office buildings, helps tenants with the mundane tasks of life such as picking up dry cleaning, returning videos, and taking cars in for oil changes. Marcia can often get an employer to pay for her services, because the boss knows that many employees sneak time off work to take care of life's necessities. By paying Marcia to take care of these chores for her employees, the boss gets full use of the employees, and gets grateful workers as a bonus.

Media Escort. (The kind that keeps clothes on. This is a family-oriented book.) The proud author is on tour to hawk a magnum opus. He's just arrived in Kansas City; he's never been to Kansas City before now. Instead of struggling with the car-rental map, getting lost three times on the way from the airport to the hotel, wandering in circles trying to find KZUX radio — hopefully before the show begins — and then rushing to get to Barnes & Noble for the book signing, the author lets an escort take charge of it all. As an escort, you get to chat with all sorts of mucky mucks. Don't count on making big bucks, but it's fun work, and you can learn a lot from the celebs. You can often get clients by contacting the publicity director at major book publishers.

Bringing People Together

Personnel Recruiter. Get past the image of the recruiter coming onto campus to recruit top graduates. Today's recruiter starts before jobs are even advertised. She develops ongoing relationships with the sorts of people the employer is likely to want to hire. For example, a company that uses Java programmers may routinely post tips and tricks on Java discussion groups on the Net to elicit positive feelings toward the recruiter. When a job opens, the recruiter posts it on the Web and sets up software to electronically screen applicants. Increasingly, she conducts the first interview online and by phone. Even final interviews are beginning to be conducted electronically, via videoconference. The applicant in Dubuque heads to the nearest Kinko's where he interviews with hirers anywhere in the world. *National Association of Personnel Services: www.napsweb.org; 3133 Mount Vernon Ave., Alexandria, VA 22305; 703-684-0180.*

(Neat Niche) **Employment Interviewer.** You've been on the other side of the table: "Mr. Job Applicant, why do you want to work for this company?" (You think, "Because I'm desperate. I'll work anywhere." You answer, "Because I'm impressed with your fine line of products.") How'd you like a career where in which *you're* the interviewer? Private employment agencies hire interviewers, sometimes without a college degree, to screen applicants, prep them for interviews, and then sell them to prospective employers. Don't like the selling part? Try working for the government. Your job is simply to match applicants with the available openings.

(Neat Niche) **Executive Recruiter (Headhunter).** As a headhunter, you work for a private agency engaged by corporations to lure top execs from other companies. What makes this a neat niche is that you get to work with highly accomplished people, and that you can earn big money if you're savvy enough to sniff out the real winners and convince them to interview with your client. Gotta tell you, though; headhunters' job prospects aren't great. Employers increasingly prefer to use the Internet to ferret out hot execs. Indeed, many independent headhunters now operate online.

Matchmaker. Today, few of us have the time, let alone the inclination, to hang out at meet markets on the off-chance of finding Mr. or Ms. Right. Matchmakers who set up online or classified ad voice-mail dating services should prosper in the small, growing cities whose markets are less likely to be saturated. These dating services not only save time, they offer an easy way to safely screen hundreds of prospects. For ideas, check out these Web sites: *match.com; as.org; couple-link.com; cupidnet.com; datecentral.com; mm.org; meetmeonline.com; one-and-only.com; personalsnetwork.com; vous.com; singlesonline.com; webmatch.com; and 1st-site.com. A franchise is available. International Society of Introduction Services: 818-222-1367.*

(Neat Niche) **Friend Finder.** If you're too busy to find a romantic partner, you're even less likely to take the time to find a friend, although most people want someone to pal around with. Many homebound seniors especially crave someone to keep them company. The biweekly nurse just doesn't do it. They want someone who has similar interests, time for schmoozing, and who won't stick them with needles. Enter the friend finder, the platonic version of the matchmaker. This is a virtually untapped market, and you can probably find success just by replicating the successful formula used by the romantic online, newspaper ad/phone dating services.

(Neat Niche) **Homework-Helper Finder.** In several cities, children home alone can call a number for "Grandma, Please!" and reach an adult who has the time to talk with them, sing to them, or help them with homework.

Tutor Broker. Millions of parents are concerned that their children aren't learning. So parents frequently seek one-on-one tutors but have a hard time finding one. As a tutor broker, you accumulate a stable of teachers, college students, and high-school students, willing and able to tutor, and match them to parent needs. To find tutors, place ads in local college newspapers. To find students needing tutoring, place ads in the local PTA newsletters. National chains such as Sylvan Learning, Score!, and Kumon Math offer tutoring, so your hook may be to provide tutors who make house calls.

TV/Radio Community Affairs Director. Every TV and radio station is required to do public service. Your job is to coordinate it. You might produce a show on teen pregnancy, public service announcements for older adults, or a community job fair. A common approach to landing the job is taking an internship in a station's community affairs department. For job listings, *www.tvjobs.com.*

School-to-Work Coordinator. Schools are finally realizing that they graduate too many students ill-equipped for real-world jobs. So high schools are hiring school-to-work coordinators. A coordinator may arrange for teachers to visit local workplaces. Many teachers, on seeing what it takes to succeed in today's workplace, change what they do in the classroom. School-to-work coordinators may also help students in career planning by bringing community members to schools to talk about their jobs, and arranging student job shadowing and internships. *National Alliance of Business: www.nab.com; 1201 New York Ave., N.W., Suite 700, Washington, DC 20005; 800-787-2848.*

Casting Director. Would you find it fun to cast a sitcom? An epic motion picture? A feminine hygiene commercial? Casting director is one of those little-known but fun Hollywood careers. Here's how casting works: You write a breakdown (a list of all the needed characters) and e-mail them to agents and wait for submissions (photos and resumes). Then you pick people to audition. The bad news: You usually have to start as a volunteer. Check the *Casting Director's Directory* for firms that might need a slave like you. *Casting Society of America: 213-463-1925. See also: www.hollywoodreporter.com2/ index* and *www.showbizjobs.com.*

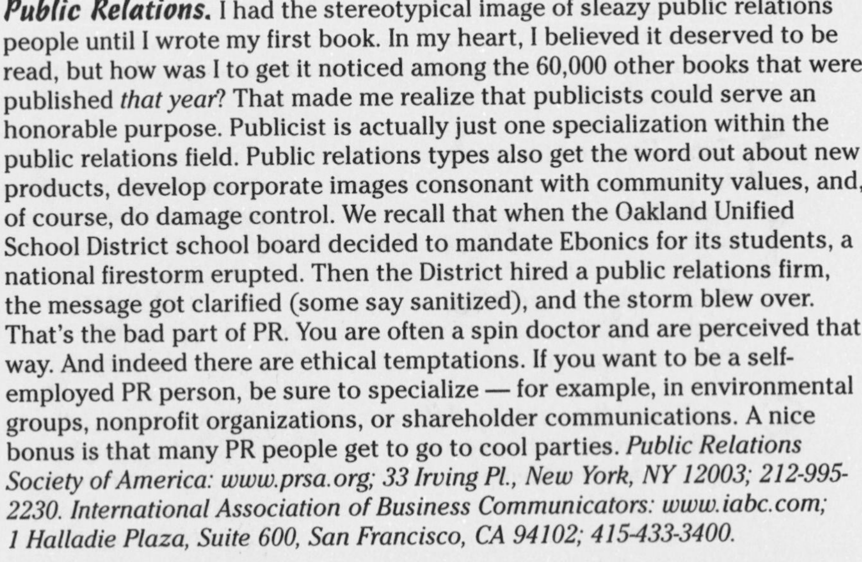

Public Relations. I had the stereotypical image of sleazy public relations people until I wrote my first book. In my heart, I believed it deserved to be read, but how was I to get it noticed among the 60,000 other books that were published *that year*? That made me realize that publicists could serve an honorable purpose. Publicist is actually just one specialization within the public relations field. Public relations types also get the word out about new products, develop corporate images consonant with community values, and, of course, do damage control. We recall that when the Oakland Unified School District school board decided to mandate Ebonics for its students, a national firestorm erupted. Then the District hired a public relations firm, the message got clarified (some say sanitized), and the storm blew over. That's the bad part of PR. You are often a spin doctor and are perceived that way. And indeed there are ethical temptations. If you want to be a self-employed PR person, be sure to specialize — for example, in environmental groups, nonprofit organizations, or shareholder communications. A nice bonus is that many PR people get to go to cool parties. *Public Relations Society of America: www.prsa.org; 33 Irving Pl., New York, NY 12003; 212-995-2230. International Association of Business Communicators: www.iabc.com; 1 Halladie Plaza, Suite 600, San Francisco, CA 94102; 415-433-3400.*

(Neat Niche) **Public Relations for the Travel Industry.** Paul Plawin, in *Careers for Travel Buffs,* writes, "In order to write about the delights of the Doral Beach Spa in Miami Beach, a Royal Caribbean Cruise, the beaches of the Bahamas, the fun and frivolity of Southern California, or the fjords of Alaska, public relation people must visit those destinations." Definitely a neat niche.

Celebrity Locator. A big-name speaker can help a nonprofit organization to raise big bucks. The problem is that most nonprofits don't know a celebrity. We can hear you saying, "But neither do I!" The secret is that most bigwigs are happy to do fund-raisers, either because they are charitable sorts, because they want to enhance their visibility, or simply because it feeds their egos. There are lots of ways to find brand-name speakers. For example, contact local TV personalities at the station and national celebs via special directories (ask at your library). An Internet search often yields clues on how to find your target star. Finding your hero may take you only a few hours, but many nonprofits will gladly pay you hundreds of dollars to recruit someone who will net them thousands.

Expert Witness Service Broker. Attorneys constantly need experts willing to testify that their client is an innocent babe. Your job is to identify a stable of experts and provide the right one to attorneys, retaining a percentage of the expert's fee.

Jury Selection Consultant. Attorneys are ever more aware that a jury's composition can make the difference between winning and losing. So law firms are spending big bucks to hire consultants to predict how potential jury members might vote. It's a cool career for lawyers who don't want to argue, psychologists who don't want to listen to patients' problems all day, and market researchers who'd rather deal with people than survey data. Demand is strong and growing. If the trend continues, each side will hire a jury selection consultant for important jury trials.

Sales-oriented work

Salesperson. When we say "salesperson," what's the first word that comes to mind? Sleazy? Pushy? While those types are around, many successful salespeople don't fit the stereotype. They are, however, self-starters, pleasantly persistent, good at listening to the customer, explaining how a product can solve the customer's problems, and aren't reluctant to ask for the sale. A career in sales is one of the few routes to high income without college. Sales offers flexible hours and, if you're an outside sales rep, a chance to travel. Plus, it's nice to know that your income is directly related to your performance: The more you sell, the more you make. Problem is, it's tough to know how much you'll sell. Even good salespeople will fail if the product, territory, or commission rate stinks. Many salespeople are surprised to find that they actually spend less than half of their time selling. They answer technical questions, write proposals, take care of problems with product or delivery, and write reports to management. *National Association of Sales Professionals: www.nasp.com; 8300 N. Hayden Rd., Suite 207, Scottsdale, AZ 85258; 602-951-4311.*

Many companies cut commission rates if salespeople do too well. So before taking a sales job, speak with other salespeople to find out about the commission schedule, your proposed territory, and, of course, whether the product is easy to sell.

(Neat Niche) **Ethnic Market Sales.** The Asian, African American, Native American, and Hispanic ethnic markets haven't been fully tapped. Like many people, members of these groups tend to like to buy from salespersons of their own ethnic group, so if you are a person of color, this is a niche to consider.

(Neat Niche) **Commercial Security Sales.** Employees and customers increasingly view employers as fat cats and are ever more willing to — let's be blunt — rob them. Of course, your basic off-the-shelf theft is popular, but creativity seems to know no bounds. Current ruses include selling the company's internal data to competitors and starting a company to sell a former employer's product that's been tweaked just enough to avoid getting caught. Corporations are eager to hear from salespeople with products and services that can stem the losses.

(Neat Niche) **Database Information Sales.** If you're selling hats through the mail, you'd love to get your hands on a list of people who have bought hats before, or who have the demographic and psychographic characteristics of people who buy hats. Well, now you can get those lists. Companies are compiling enormous amounts of information on all of us. (Yes, it's a bit scary.) Other firms are willing to pay big bucks for a list of on-target prospects.

(Neat Niche) **Electrical Components Sales.** Electrical parts aren't sexy — unless you're an equipment manufacturer. But demand for these components is high, and few salespeople have the technical expertise to sell them effectively. An engineering background is a plus.

(Neat Niche) **Sales of Instruments and Consumables to Biotech Companies.** The biotech industry is booming and its companies use a lot of expensive consumables.

(Neat Niche) **Pharmaceutical Products Sales to HMOs.** Your goal is to get your drug onto the HMO's formulary — the list of drugs approved for doctors to prescribe. A bachelor's in science or nursing is generally required.

(Neat Niche) **Software Sales to Specialized Markets.** The software that banks use to back up all their data costs each bank, on average, $500,000.

(Neat Niche) **Internet Ad Sales.** Seemingly unlimited opportunity.

(Neat Niche) **Radio and Cable TV Advertising Sales.** Ditto.

(Neat Niche) **Big-Ticket Item Sales.** Like golf courses and airplanes.

College Admissions Recruiter. The United States has almost 5,000 colleges and vocational-technical schools, 98 percent of which must recruit to fill their classrooms. Your title may be College Admissions Counselor or Admissions Officer, but a more accurate description is salesperson. You need to be able to soft-sell — sell without appearing to be selling. *National Association for College Admission Counseling: www.nacac.com; 1631 Prince St., Alexandria, VA 22314; 703-836-2222.*

Don't confuse College Admissions Recruiter with a College Admissions Counselor. The recruiter is hired by a college to recruit students to that particular college, whereas the college counselor's job is to help students find a college matching their needs from among the 5,000 in the United States.

(Neat Niche) **International Student Recruiter.** International students usually pay full tuition, which is music to colleges' ears. It's easiest to get hired if you're fluent in an Asian or Middle Eastern language.

(Neat Niche) **Grades K through 12 School Recruiter.** Private, and even some public, K–12 schools are now hiring people to convince parents to enroll their kids.

Fundraiser/Development Specialist. This field has come a long way from scattershot mass mailings. You may wonder, "Why the term 'development'?" Because a nonprofit organization *develops* prospective donors into actual donors — ideally, big donors. Colleges are among development's more aggressive practitioners. Your alma mater attempts to develop you in the beginning by sending you mailers and by staging events designed to make you feel closer to the college — to remind you of the good old days, even if, in fact, they weren't so good. Low-cost tickets to the football game, newsletters with stories designed to make you feel close to the college, and dinners with speeches by the best professors they can find are all part of the cultivation process. Then, once you're feeling warm and fuzzy, the college starts with the solicitations — usually with direct mail campaigns and telemarketing banks. Plus, if according to the alumni questionnaire you filled out, you're a potential big donor, the college assigns an already-donating alumnus with similar interests (for instance, they pair jocks with jocks, corporate titans with other corporate titans) to individually solicit you. A development office keeps precise records of how much you donate. The more you donate, the more they ask for the next time. A development officer's crowning achievement is convincing you to put the organization in your will. Development jobs include event coordinators, database managers, writers for cultivation publications and pitch letters, grant proposal writers, and direct solicitors, who usually have expertise in wills and trusts. *American Association of Fundraising Council: 25 W. 43rd St., New York, NY 10036; 212-354-5799. See also: www.clark.net/pub/pwalker/Fundraising_and_Giving* and *www.philanthropy-journal.org.*

(Neat Niche) **Fundraiser for Arts Organizations.** Fundraising for the theater or the symphony, and so on, lets you spend time around artistic types without having to fight the long odds against making a living on stage.

Auctioneer. "$100 bid, now two, now two, will ya give me $200? $200 bid, now three, now three, will ya give me $300?" When we think of auctioneers, we think of one thing: fast talkers. But there's more. Auctioneers must enjoy selling and be masters at creating a sense of urgency while conveying a sense of humor. Acting skills can help. Side note: The auctioneer chants not just because it keeps the audience interested but because it makes things go quickly. At an average household estate auction, the auctioneer's chant helps sell an average of 60 items per hour. Automobile auctioneers frequently sell 125 to 175 cars per hour, and tobacco auctioneers may sell 500 to 600 lots per hour! Auctions used to focus on antiques and estates. Today, half of the auction events are real estate and business liquidations. Real estate developers now realize that holding an auction is a much faster way to sell a house than waiting for buyers. Auctions are used to sell everything from skyscrapers to amusement parks. With more and more businesses going under, people going bankrupt, and homes, boats, RVs, and private planes going into foreclosure, good auctioneers are selling for high bids. And you don't need a lot of school to start chanting. Only 25 percent of auctioneers have a college degree. Many auctioneers learn on the job, and others attend short training programs. *National Auctioneers Association: www.auctioneers.org; 8880 Ballentine, Overland Park, KS 66214; 913-541-8084.*

(Neat Niche) **Fundraising Auctioneer.** Many nonprofit groups, from elementary school PTAs to the United Way, have fundraisers. Auctions are among the most lucrative ways to raise money, but most are conducted by amateur auctioneers. That results in far lower bids than with a professional.

Other people-oriented careers

Producer. Whether it's a TV news segment on legalizing prostitution, a local production of *Deathtrap,* or a multimedia virtual trip to France, few things are more fun than coming up with an idea and putting the pieces together so that it gets done — which is what a producer does. With cable stations growing and more local network affiliates adding news programs, producer opportunities are increasing. Start as an intern or production assistant, be a go-getter, and make lots of friends. The *Association of Independent Video and Film Makers* posts internships at *www.aivf.org.* Everyone wants to work for feature motion pictures, so at least for starters, go where they ain't: Find a corporate filmmaker or do commercials. Get some experience and you'll probably make it into entertainment films faster than if you try to start in entertainment. Remember also, the fun part is more the moment-to-moment work than the final product. If you want to work on entertainment films, rather than make the pilgrimage to Hollywood, contact your nearest large city's or state film commission. They'll tell you who's slated to shoot what. Because getting ahead in this biz is all about relationships, you'd better make friends easily. Bradley Richardson, author of *JobSmarts,* recommends that to find out what's happening now, search the Web for "film industry," "music industry," or "television industry." *Producers Guild of America: www.producersguild.com; 400 S. Beverly Dr., Beverly Hills, CA 90212; 310-557-0807. See also: www.producerlink.com. National Association of Performing Arts Managers: www.napama.org; 137 E. 30th St., New York, NY 10016; 212-683-0801.* How to Make it in Hollywood *by Linda Buzzell.*

(Neat Niche) **Expo/Show Producer.** As an expo producer, you may put on a bridal show, a plastic manufacturer's convention, or a conference on nanotechnology. Identify a need, get a lot of attendees and exhibitors, and you may be able to make a good year's salary in two or three months. *International Association for Exposition Management: www.iaem.org; P.O. Box 802425, Dallas, TX 75380; 972-458-8002.*

(Neat Niche) **Multicultural Festival Producer.** The demand for these festivals continues to grow as government and special interest groups encourage celebrations of diversity. Multicultural festivals are potentially lucrative, but are large, challenging projects. You must stay very organized amid complexity and be able to negotiate calmly with everyone from skittish government officials to temperamental artists.

Event Planner. This is similar to being a producer without the financial risk. Someone else is the producer, and she pays you a salary. This career is the compulsive's dream — with an infinite number of details to get right, all by an unmovable deadline, plus a frantic client usually adding to the stress. To boot, you frequently have to give up your nights and weekends. To tell you the truth, we can't imagine why anyone likes this career, but many people do. Indeed, it's one of the most popular career choices among my female clients, which is the only reason we've included it. In addition to being detail-oriented, you need a ready stable of reliable suppliers, from caterers to entertainers. The good news is that this is a huge field. The meeting industry, predominantly conventions and expos, has a national market of over $70 billion! *Meeting Planners International: 4455 LBJ Freeway, Dallas, TX 75244.*

(Neat Niche) **Convention, Trade Show, or Expo Planner.** Planning these events offers big bucks in exchange for big headaches.

(Neat Niche) **On-Site Staffing Provider.** Coordinating a meeting long-distance can be especially difficult. An on-site staffing service provides temporary personnel for meetings, conventions, and other special events.

(Neat Niche) **Reunion Planner.** "I can't believe it. Back when we were in school, he had a full head of hair!" Family and class reunions are intriguing events, but who has time to do all the work: mail invitations, take reservations, hire bands, find food, arrange hotels, line up child care, and plan activities to make the reunion memorable? The reunion planner. It's a neat niche because reunions are especially exciting events, yet reunion planning is less crowded than other event planning specialties. Another plus: Tracking down missing class members adds a detective component to an already fun job. *National Association of Reunion Managers: www.reunions.com; P.O. Box 23211, Tampa, FL 33623; 800-586-2586. See also: Class Reunion, Inc. for a self-study program on becoming a reunion planner: 847-677-4949.*

(Neat Niche) **Wedding Planner.** Twenty years ago, there were no wedding planners, but as couples marry later in life, many lives are too full to handle all the details of a wedding (like how to make the Elks Club look like the Ritz). *Association of Bridal Consultants: www.trainingforum.com/ASN/ABC/index.html; 200 Chestnutland Rd., New Milford, CT 06776; 860-355-0464.*

(Neat Niche) **Singles Events Planner.** Fern bars, the meet markets of the '80s and '90s, are growing passe. Most singles would rather meet in a less alcohol-centered environment. Bringing singles together offers an entrepreneurial opportunity for you. One of the simplest approaches is to place an ad in the relationship section that advertises dinners for eight single people. You host the event and provide dinner. Franchises are available. *See www.franchise.org* or *www.entrepreneurmag.com.*

Business Network Organizer. A business network organizer addresses most small businesses' number one priority: getting new customers. A network organizer sets up weekly meetings for small businesspeople to trade referrals and strategies for acquiring customers.

Specialty Temp Agency Owner. This is one of *Entrepreneur* magazine's "Hot Picks." Many full-time jobs with benefits are gradually being replaced by temp positions. How can you capitalize? Start a temp agency. You can't compete with megacompanies, such as Manpower or Olsten, so pick a field where it's tough to find good employees — especially one you know a lot about. Examples include: association executives, court reporters, disabled employees, short-order cooks, medical secretaries, pharmacists, escrow personnel, and optical engineers. If you're successful, you can consider franchising your operation. *National Association of Temporary and Staffing Services: www.natss.com; 119 South St., Alexandria, VA 22312; 703-549-6287.*

Relocation Consultant. You're moving. You have to figure out where to live, the best places to shop, and where the good schools are. A relocation specialist can help you. Based on answers to a detailed questionnaire about your wants and needs, the relocation consultant points you in the right direction. It's like having a wise, local relative. How do you get a job as a relocation consultant? Approach the local offices of national real estate chains. They're the most likely to be involved in long-distance relocations, and may offer relocation consultants free to their customers. Coldwell Banker offers a training program, graduates of which receive a Certified Residential Relocation Certificate. *Employee Relocation Council: www.erc.org; 1720 N St., N.W., Washington, DC 20036; 202-857-0857.*

Personal Care Facility Owner. Many aging boomers can't stand their varicose veins, wrinkles, cellulite, and receding hairlines. And because the surgeries have become easier, more people are lining up to restore that fresh-faced look. Cosmetic surgery clinics are popping up, but we believe the need, especially in small cities, is far from saturated. Don't worry, you don't need to be a doctor. You can be the entrepreneur who opens the clinic, does the marketing, and hires the doctors to staff it.

Worksite Day Care Operator. Corporations are starting to open on-site childcare for their employees, but this trend is just beginning. It's a great time to jump on the bandwagon. Review what other on-site child care operators are doing, adopt your favorite ideas, meet with corporations to outline choices, and set up programs. You'll relieve hundreds of parents' child care worries. *National Association of Child Care Professionals: ww.naccp.org; c/o Donna Thornton; 304-A Roanoke St., Christianburg, VA 24073; 800-537-1118.*

BHB

Home Health Care Business Owner. This field is exploding because the population is aging, patients are discharged from the hospital earlier, and it's easier to provide skilled care at home thanks to new medicines and technologies. Providing home health nurses and companions is an opportunity for the small businessperson. Family Friend Management Systems offers franchises at $15,000, which gets you software and training to go with it, and the documents needed to start such a business. *National Association for Home Care at the Institute of Consulting Careers: www.nahc.org.*

BHB

Clown. Are you a complete clown? If not, you can be in just eight weeks, and tuition's free! If a career as Bozo fills you with mirth, check out *Barnum & Bailey Clown College, P.O. Box 9, Vienna, VA 22183; 800-755-9637.* The curriculum is "rich in juggling, pie-throwing, and stilt-walking, but your clownology courses will also teach pantomime, wire walking, magic, makeup, unicycling, prop building, costume construction, acrobatics, and, of course, pratfalls." If you survive, you get to audition for a low-paying spot in the circus. (Don't tell your family just yet.) No experience necessary for Clown College, but to assess your potential, they do want to see a videotape. A bit of advice: Don't try to impress them by getting shot out of a cannon. *Clowns of America International: www.clowns.org.*

> (Neat Niche) **Clown at Corporate Events and Children's Birthday Parties.** Nice second j ob for evenings and weekends. Franchise: *Party Animals, Inc., 7716 Praver Drive West, Jacksonville, FL 32217; 904-731-0701.*

Children's Birthday Party Entertainer. Even if you're no clown, this can be a fun second career. Tom Stewart never thought he'd end up as a Teenage Mutant Ninja Turtle, Superman, or Elvis Presley. Yet he makes a good living pulling costumes out of his car trunk to perform for kids. His wife is also a party performer, blowing up and tying her balloon art into a zoo of party favors. Other birthday party entertainers paint kids' faces and mesmerize kids with magic tricks or with a collection of creepy crawlies such as leapin' lizards, hissing snakes, and spiders big enough to pet. Some parents may pay a lot for a photo of a boa constrictor wrapped around their six year-old!

Work with Data

Scientific data

Biologist. No field has done more to improve life. In the last decade alone, people working in biology/biotechnology have developed:

- Food crops that can grow in a previously infertile section of Latin America that covers 800,000 square miles — an area larger than the size of Mexico. Thousands of formerly starving people now can eat.
- Breakthrough drugs — like new proteins that lessen the effect of heart attacks, and protease inhibitors that greatly extend the life span of people with HIV.
- Corn that produces its own natural pesticides.
- A method to identify a criminal (DNA analysis) that is thousands of times more accurate than older, conventional methods.
- Genetically altered bacteria that can clean up oil spills and chemical leaks by rendering the toxic materials harmless.
- Genetically engineered growth hormones to reduce organ transplant rejection.

I recently had the good fortune to attend a presentation by five Nobel Prize winners. One of the few things they agreed on was that the field that will make the greatest impact on humankind in the coming decades is molecular biology/biotechnology. Many of us, when we think of biology, think of *macrobiology:* studying different animals and plants, their roles in the ecosystem, and their structures. I recall, in high school, trying to remember the difference between a stamen and a pistil. I also remember seeing lots of cute pictures of endangered furry creatures. Indeed, many people choose to major in biology with those visions in mind. But fact is, if you're considering a career in biology, know that most careers in biology focus on molecules. It is now widely agreed that most of science's answers will be found on the molecular and genetic levels. From here forward, biology is mainly math.

Actually, the name "biologist" is now misleading. Today's biologist is part biologist, part chemist, part mathematician, with at least a dollop of computer programmer and/or robotics engineer. Those with a whole-animal biology background — for example, "environmental biology" — will usually be limited to positions as low-level lab assistants or high school biology teachers. *American Institute of Biological Sciences: www.aibs.org; 1444 Eye St., N.W.,*

Washington, DC 20005; 202-628-1500. Industrial Biotechnology Organization: 1625 K Street, N.W., Washington, DC 20006; 202-857-0244. See also: www.gene.com; www.bio.com; and *www.biospace.com/sd/career.*

(Neat Niche) **Biotech careers at the bachelor or master level.** A long-standing oversupply of biology Ph.D.'s, makes competition for Ph.D.-level jobs in biotech fierce. The good news is that there are ample bachelors and masters level jobs at biotech and pharmaceutical firms. True, you aren't top banana, but you do have plenty of interesting opportunities. You get to produce the actual genetically engineered plants, animals, and drugs; you get to run experiments, perhaps assisting in designing them; write up studies; and even co-present at conferences. In short, you get many of the benefits of a Ph.D. with less school and less difficulty landing a job. Choose your job carefully, though. In some labs, a bachelor's degree entitles you to clean the rat cages.

There are conflicting predictions about the job market for Ph.D. bioscientists. We believe that you'll be fine as long as you're multidisciplinary: some background in computer science, engineering, or communications to go along with a solid molecular biology or genetics background. Focus your job search on small biotech companies. They're doing most of the hiring.

(Neat Niche) **Rational Drug Development.** Until recently, drugs were developed in a fairly unsystematic way. Researchers tried this and they tried that until they found something that worked. Often, nothing did. Now, it's all changing. We are starting to understand the molecular changes that occur when a disease strikes. We are, at the same time, developing the capability to create drugs, molecule by molecule, to counteract those molecular changes. These drugs constitute true cures. It is only a matter of time until we develop a drug consisting of molecules that interrupt the HIV virus's ability to multiply, and create a molecule to stop the myelin disintegration that causes multiple sclerosis.

(Neat Niche) **Genomics.** Many diseases and behavior states — such as personality and intelligence — are significantly affected by our genes. In the next few years, genomic biologists will finish mapping the human genome. Then genomics can focus on using that knowledge to prevent and cure diseases, and to enhance human potential. This is a computer-intensive career. Most genomists spend more than three-quarters of their time in front of a computer. This is a career for people who really want to make a difference: Many experts believe that genomists will make the largest contribution to improved human health in the coming generation. *American Society of Human Genetics: www.faseb.org/genetics; 9650 Rockville Pike, Bethesda, MD 20814; 301-571-1825. See also: www.academicinfo.net/biotech.html#centers.*

(Neat Niche) **Bioinformatics.** A mind-boggling 3.5 *billion* genes and DNA structures must be archived to map the human genome and in the just-described rational drug development. There is large unmet demand for bioinformaticians, the people who develop and use the software to manage this mountain of crucial information. The University of Pennsylvania and George Mason University have top programs, but employers will gladly settle for any institution's B.S. in computer science with a masters in biochemistry, or vice versa.

Toxicologist. The Texas A&M Toxicology home page begins, "Hardly a week goes by without hearing about a chemical that may threaten our health: pesticides in the food we eat, pollutants in the air we breathe, chemicals in the water we drink, toxic dump sites near our homes. Are these chemicals really dangerous? How much does it take to cause harm? What are the effects of the chemicals? Cancer? Nervous System Damage? Birth Defects?" Toxicologists answer these questions. *Society of Toxicology: www.toxicology.org; 1767 Business Center Dr., Reston, VA 20190; 703-438-3115.*

Biological Weapons Deterrence Specialist. Saddam Hussein makes us ever more aware that biological weapons can be as threatening as nuclear weapons, and much more portable. At a news conference, Vice President Gore held up a five-pound sack of sugar and warned that the same amount of anthrax released from a plane over the District of Columbia could kill 300,000 people. And creating that much anthrax is easy: For $10,000, and materials easily obtainable from scientific supply houses, a smart biochemistry major could produce five pounds of anthrax in a week. At the National Press Club, Ross Perot said, "If we can't keep drugs out of our prisons which we highly control, how can we keep biological weapons out of our country?" The need for deterrence experts is obvious and the field far from saturated. Hey, if you're intelligent, please get into this career. You could save our lives! *Institute for Defense and Disarmament Studies; 675 Massachusetts Ave., Cambridge, MA 02139; 617-354-4337. Center for Nonproliferation Studies at the Monterey Institute of International Studies in Monterey, CA: www.cns.miis.edu; 425 Van Buren Street, Monterey, CA 93940; 408-647-4154. Federation of American Scientists: www.fas.org; 307 Massachusetts Avenue, N.E., Washington, DC 20002.*

Environmental Analyst. An environmental analyst figures out what's wrong or could go wrong with our air, earth, and water, and how to fix it. In an area with higher-than-normal cancer rates, environmental analysts look for aberrations in the composition of the air, soil, and water, and then play detective and try to figure out what's causing the problem. Often in such a situation, the analysts find unexpected chemicals in the air, and then they check to see if local factories are culprits. When the polluter is found, environmental analysts use subtle, and not-so-subtle ways to get the polluter to clean up its act. Environmental analysts are hired by federal, state, and local environmental protection agencies such as EPA or OSHA or through consulting firms hired by governments, corporations, or citizen groups. *National Registry of Environmental Professionals: www.nrep.org; P.O. Box 2099, Glenview, IL 60025; 847-724-6631. See also: www.eco.org.*

Hydrologist. This field isn't all wet. Tom Stienstra, author of *Sunshine Careers,* reminds us that without water we have nothing. Hydrologists ensure that our water is as safe as possible. They gather data and then make water-saving proposals to corporations or government agencies. While some hydrologists work in labs, many have offices in the great outdoors. Hydrology is one of the few outdoors professions that pays a middle-class living and requires only a bachelor's degree. Can you picture yourself hiking into wilderness areas to take and analyze water samples, sneaking in reveries by a flowing stream? Just remember, many hydrologists spend a lot of time at the water's source: snowy mountains and glaciers. *American Institute of Hydrology: www.aihydro.com; 2499 Rice St., St. Paul, MN 55113; 612-484-8169.*

(Neat Niche) **Stream Restorationist.** Soil erosion, dams, and pollutants are causing streams to dry up or become inhospitable to fish. Stream restorationists try to fix all that, whether it be an isolated mountain stream or one of the urban brooks that soothe our stressed lives.

Meteorologist. Believe it or not, they're getting much better at predicting the weather — not only tomorrow's weather, but next year's. This has profound implications. For example, imagine you are a farmer and know how wet and warm the next season will be. You can pick the perfect crop for that weather, which greatly reduces your chance of crop failure. Don't worry, you can be a meteorologist even if you're too shy to be on the nightly news. Weather affects everything, so in addition to radio and TV, government service, or chasing hurricanes and tornadoes, meteorologists also work in agriculture, for cruise lines, ski resorts, the Department of Defense, and airlines. A *Philadelphia Inquirer* piece by Dodge Johnson began, "In the next several hours, Federal Express meteorologists will make forecasts for the 160 cities where FedEx flies." Meteorology is for the math and computer person who doesn't want to be a programmer. Of course, it helps if you're fascinated with the weather. Meteorology made it onto our list of cool careers because it's rewarding, but the job market is tight. Half of meteorologists are hired by the National Weather Service, and the N.W.S. increasingly requires a master's degree for the cool jobs. Because predicting the weather requires integrating information from around the globe, a foreign language is a plus. *American Meteorological Society: www.ametsoc.org/ams; 45 Beacon Street, Boston, MA 02108; 617-648-1000.*

Volcanologist. When will a volcano erupt? Volcanologists better not guess wrong. If they predict an imminent gusher and nothing happens, many people have been needlessly terrified and evacuated. If the volcanologist says, "No problem," and it blows, you have a fried community. The United States has fewer than 200 volcanologists, and most have a Ph.D. We include very few careers with such poor prospects of landing a job and that require so much training, but volkies really love their career, so we couldn't resist. Volcanologists spend a lot of time in exotic places studying a fascinating phenomenon. Their work can save lives and property, and because children are so fascinated with volcanoes, they visit many schools, usually leaving an auditorium full of wide-eyed kids. And, for Ph.D.s, volkies are a fun-loving lot.

OOH

Agricultural Scientist. A career for the scientist who doesn't want to be in a lab all day. Your job is to find better ways to grow crops. You may work on a better way to control spider mites on rose bushes, or powdery mildew on grapes, or to keep oxalis weeds from taking over broccoli fields — all with minimal impact to the environment. Rather than work on control, you may work on prevention: developing plant varieties genetically engineered to be resistant to pests and disease. The largest employers are the government and university extension services. A master's degree is often required. *American Society of Agronomy: www.agronomy.org; 677 S. Segoe Rd., Madison, WI 53711; 608-273-8080.*

(Neat Niche) **Soil Scientist.** You advise farmers on what to add to the soil to grow bigger crops. You tell housing developers which soil is good for the recreation area and which should be stuck under a house. The more environmentally oriented answer questions such as: How do we stop the erosion of this land? How is the pesticide moving through the soil? Will it reach the groundwater? *Job openings: www.nrcan.gc.ca/~bcampbel.*

(Neat Niche) **Entomologist.** Here or in remote jungles, you may gather and study data on the thousands of new insect species discovered each year. Which are threats? Allies? How to deal with them? Or you may visit a farm infested with some little terror and figure out how to nuke it without nuking the rest of us. *Entomology Society of America: 9301 Annapolis Rd., Lanham, MD 20706: Attn: Public Relations Coordinator.*

(Neat Niche) **Plant Pathologist.** You specialize in plant health, much as a physician specializes in human health. Just as with humans, your job is to diagnose and treat the wide range of diseases affecting the patient. One difference: You're more likely to eat your patient. *American Phytopathological Society: www.scisoc.org; 3340 Pilot Knob Rd., St. Paul, MN 55121; 612-454-7250.*

OOH

Food Scientist. How can we make a better tasting frozen pizza? Can we make a hot dog that tastes good without cancer-causing nitrites? How can chicken processors reduce the amount of pyelobacteria — which sickens thousands of people each year? Food scientists work for food processing companies to make better foods, and increasingly, for government agencies to ensure that the foods you eat don't make you puke. *Institute of Food Technologists: www.ift.org; 221 N. LaSalle St., Chicago, IL 60601; 312-782-8424.*

(Neat Niche) **Flavorist.** The company says, "We need to make a packaged chicken soup mix that tastes like Grandma's. The flavorist's job is to create natural and chemical concoctions that simulate the real thing. The flavorist usually starts by combining items from existing products and/or a library of flavors.

OOH

Statistician. Statisticians ensure that appearances aren't misleading. In the final poll on the morning of the election, when 51 percent of those surveyed favor Candidate A and 49 percent prefer Candidate B, how confident can Candidate A be? It depends on how many people were polled and how similar that group is to the people who will actually vote. The statistician tells us how likely it is that the two percent difference occurred by chance. They also present numerical data in a way that mortals can understand, such as pie charts. One-fourth of all statisticians work for the federal government — most commonly, on the census. Yeah, you can lie with statistics, and everything can't be reduced to probabilities, but statistics do often lead to good decision-making. Not a bad payoff for one's career efforts. Florence Nightingale said that statistics is the most important science in the whole world: for upon it depends the practical application of every other science. *The American Statistical Association: www.amstat.org; 1429 Duke St., Alexandria, VA 22314-3402.*

(Neat Niche) **Biostatisticians.** You answer questions such as "How effective is this new drug? How sure are we that a gene truly is located where the marker suggests it is? What is the probability of a side effect among pregnant women?" In the hundreds of job openings for statisticians that we've looked at, by far the largest number is for biostatisticians.

Cancer Registrar. Because most cancers don't have a single foolproof cure, many treatment protocols are tried for each type of cancer. One way to figure out which methods work best for whom (for example, males in their sixties with leiomyosarcoma and diabetes) is to accumulate treatment records of every cancer case. Most hospitals and consortia do that, and the person in charge is the cancer registrar. This person doesn't just enter submitted information into the database; he often speaks with the physician, and even the patient for clarification. May you never get a call from a cancer registrar. *National Cancer Registrar's Association: www.ncra-usa.org/main.html; 8310 Nieman Rd., Lenexa, KS 66214; 913-438-6272.*

Computer data

Computer Programmer. No surprise, this will continue to be one of the professions in greatest demand, especially in languages such as C++, Visual C++, Delphi for both UNIX and Windows, and Java. Employers will especially go wild for you if you have expertise in a content area such as chemistry, engineering, or economics as well as in programming

Today's programming language of choice is tomorrow's dinosaur, so to be a happy, successful programmer, you need to like the idea of continually reeducating yourself. Jobs abound in mundane areas such as intranet development (company computers communicating with vendors and customers), upgrading computers that run on old languages and operating systems, and the year-2000 problem, but check out the neat niches:

(Neat Niche) **Virtual Reality Programmer.** You write software that is the ultimate training method: putting students in a virtual duplicate of the actual situation — military officers in war zones, doctors in surgery, and astronauts in spaceships.

(Neat Niche) **Education Software Programmer.** Do you like the idea of creating software so that kids actually learn something? Although teacher unions are unlikely to trumpet this, evidence is growing that students learn more from a good computer program than from a live teacher. Industry and parents are currently the biggest consumers of education software, but schools are increasingly being dragged along. *International Society for Technology in Education: www.iste.org; 480 Charnelton, Eugene, OR 97401; 800-336-5191. For an MA in instructional design/computer science at San Diego State University: allisonrossette@mail.sdsu.edu; 619-594-6088.*

(Neat Niche) **Web Programmer.** The explosion in Web sites means a great need for HTML, Java, and CGI specialists. Also, large companies are moving their databases to the Web. These databases were written in ancient languages such as Cobol and Fortran. So programmers in these vintage languages should not consider them useless.

(Neat Niche) **Entertainment Software Programmer.** Okay, so this niche is very well-known, but it's too cool. Had to include it.

The preceding niches increasingly use multimedia approaches. These groups keep you up to speed. *Association for Interactive Media: www.interactivehq.org; 1301 Connecticut Ave., N.W., Washington, DC 20036; 202-408-0008. See also: the New York New Media Group: www.nynma.org, newsgroup: comp.multimedia.*

(Neat Niche) **Computer Security Programmer.** From both inside and outside the organization, hackers steal information from company computers. This produces a strong demand for programmers, often called firewall developers, to foil the thieves. Also, corporations, the FBI, and the Department of Justice hire cybersleuths to surf the Internet to nab software pirates. The Business Software Alliance estimates that nearly one in two software applications is pirated. *Computer Security Resource Clearinghouse: csrc.nist.gov.*

(Neat Niche) **Consulting Programmer.** According to an Arthur Anderson study, 70 percent of small- to mid-sized firms upgraded their computer systems in 1997 and 10 percent plan to add a Web site in 1998. Opportunities abound in Web site and database development, preparing computers for the year 2000, and general PC doctoring. *Independent Computer Consultants Association: www.icca.org; 800-774-4222.*

Webmaster (some prefer "Webmaster or Webmistress"). A Webmaster is the person who puts the Internet or intranet (within a company) site together. In the late '90s, she may simply have been a manager, directing the techies. But increasingly, she also does some programming, sets up the hardware so that it runs, and fixes bugs as they come up. According to a survey by the Texas State Occupational Information Coordinating Commission, the best way to learn is to "just get in there and create a Web page. Then keep up with technology." Solid HMTL plus some C++ and Javascript are basic requirements. *Webmaster's Guild: www.webmaster.org. National Association of Webmasters: www.naw.org; 888-564-6629. See also: www.cio.com; www.webpro.org; alt.webgod;* and *alt.webmaster.*

(Neat Niche) **Web Site Maintainer.** This is an easier job than being a Webmaster and less obvious. It's been said that maintenance is the monster behind the monitor. A typical business often makes a huge effort to develop its site, and then, once it's up and running, leaves it alone. Fact is, most sites need ongoing care and feeding: tweaking weaknesses, fixing bugs, and, most importantly, updating content so that people want to keep coming back.

Database Administrator. The U.S. Department of Labor projects this to be the single fastest-growing occupation through 2006. The information explosion has to be categorized some way and that way is often a database. Database administrators supervise and often implement design, programming, and protocol updating.

Soundtrack Sound Designer. Increasingly, soundtracks, especially for computer games, are created as much by computer cut-and-pasters as by musical wizards. Instead of standing in the orchestra pit, this conductor sits in front of a computer with a library of sounds, special effects, voice and music clips, and cuts and pastes together the mood of a computer game, commercial, or film trailer. *Audio Engineering Society: www.aes.org; 60 E. 42nd St., New York, NY 10165; 212-661-8528. Pro Sound: www.prosound.com; 2 Park Ave., New York, NY 10016; 212-213-3444. Job openings: www.hollywoodreporter.com2/index* and *www.showbizjobs.com.*

Business data

Actuary. How much should an insurance company charge each employee of the Western Widget Company for health insurance? That's a typical question an actuary answers. Becoming an actuary is a good option for someone who wants a prestigious career that applies math to practical decisions, and that offers salaries that, if you're a good communicator and not just a mathhead, can reach six figures. More good news: You can achieve the highest level of actuary (Fellow) without a graduate degree. You do have to pass ten arduous exams for which you can study at home or take classes at local actuary clubs or at universities. *Society of Actuaries: www.soa.org; 475 N. Martingale Rd., Schaumburg, IL 60173; 847-706-3500. Insurance jobs: www.insjobs.com.*

Economist. This is another career for the math-centric person who wants to do something that is at least somewhat practical. Economists answer such questions as, "How will our company be affected if the minimum wage goes up?" "What are the economic costs and benefits of legalizing gambling in this county?" "What has happened to solar cell production and why?" In other words, economists predict and analyze production and consumption trends to help governments and companies make policy. Problem is, people's actual behavior often doesn't follow the predicted model. We're always amused when we read a panel of blue-ribbon economists' predictions. They rarely agree. Nevertheless, a master's or doctoral degree is often required. *American Economics Association: www.vanderbilt.edu/AEA; 2014 Broadway, Nashville, TN 37203; 615-322-2595.*

(Neat Niche) **Environmental Economist.** You figure out the economic impacts of activities such as building a theme park, restricting auto traffic in national parks, and creating a federally subsidized oil deal with Venezuela. *Job openings: www.eco.org and www.environmental-jobs.com. See also www.princeton.edu/~oa/careeroe.html.*

Mortgage Rate Auditor. Suspicious people say it's deliberate, more trusting types call it inadvertent, but it's clear that too many of the 12 million people holding adjustable mortgages have their rates adjusted too high. Mortgage holders are starting to turn to mortgage rate auditors to figure out if they're being shortchanged. Momentum Technology Group (800-942-1522) offers a $1,500 mortgage rate auditor training program that includes software and a year of technical support. You then send a mailing that says, "If I get you a refund, I get a third of it; if I don't, you owe me nothing," to residents in zip codes with a high percentage of homeowners.

Expense Reduction Consultant. A perfect career for a cheapskate. Your job is to review all a business's buying decisions: long-distance service, office supplies, printing, insurance — everything — to make sure they're buying as wisely as possible.

Property Tax Reduction Specialist. According to the National Taxpayers Union, 60 percent of property in the United States is over-assessed. How do you turn this into a business? You learn the rules for property assessment in your county, and then obtain, from the county, a mailing list of all property owners. You send each property owner a letter explaining that with their permission, you will attempt to lower their property tax. If you can't, they owe nothing. If you can, you keep half of their first year savings and the property owner keeps all the savings from then on. A *New York Times* article wrote about one such firm, Tax Reductions Plus. It said that the firm claims to have represented over 1,500 property owners and only 12 failed to get a tax reduction.

Government Procurement Consultant. The nation's largest customer is the government — and it may be willing to pay $85 for a screw. That's the sort of customer that all businesses love, but most companies don't know how to get the government to buy from them. Your job is to teach them. You can get an introduction by visiting the following sites. *Huge U.S. government Web site: www.business.gov. See also: Matthew Lesko's Info Power III: www.lesko.com; 800-955-7693.*

Credit Risk Manager. This isn't a sexy job but it's high-paying and in-demand. Credit risk managers work for organizations that extend credit: credit card companies and other corporations, universities, even government agencies. Your job is to figure out who should get credit and how much. You must be computer-savvy and have at least a bachelor's degree in statistics, economics, computer science, math, or operations research. Salaries of $80,000–$150,000 are common after just three to ten years of experience. *National Association of Credit Management: www.nacm.org; 8815 Centre Park Dr., Columbia, MD 21045; 410-740-5560.*

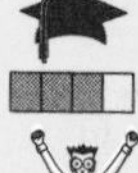

Pre-Employment Screening Consultant. To avoid making costly hiring mistakes and to avoid charges of discrimination in hiring, employers are increasingly supplementing interviews with formal testing. Consultants select off-the-shelf instruments or develop customized tests that sample the actual job, and test candidates to predict the candidate likely to do the job best. *Society for Industrial & Organizational Psychology: www.siop.org; P.O. Box 87, Bowling Green, OH 43402.*

Securities Analyst. Would you find it fun to figure out if a company's stock or bond is a bargain? That's what securities analysts do. They're mathematical detectives who interview company employees and crunch a lot of numbers. One fringe benefit is that securities analysts are in a good place to get fresh-off-the-press tips on stocks likely to go up. *Association for Investment Management and Research: P.O. Box 3668, Charlottesville, VA 22903; 800-247-8132.*

SEC rules prohibit trading based on inside information before it's released to the public, but one wonders how government regulators can keep insiders from buying the stock early — if not in their own name, in Aunt Sally's, but I digress.

(Neat Niche) **Portfolio Manager.** Pension funds and mutual funds hire portfolio managers to buy the stocks and bonds most likely to increase in value and to decide when the previously bought securities should be dumped. With the proliferation of new mutual funds (1,500 in the past three years alone) portfolio managers are sought-after as never before. *Institute of Chartered Financial Analysts: www.aimr.org; P.O. Box 3668, University of Virginia, Charlottesville, VA 22901; 804-977-6600.*

Stock Trading Specialist. This is the true inside trader. He stands at a trading post (that's actually what it's called) on the floor of a stock exchange and functions as a combination auctioneer/matchmaker — the keeper of order amid the apparent mayhem. He matches the waving hand of a buyer's representative (a floor broker) willing to pay the highest price, with the waving hand of a seller willing to sell at the lowest price. When there's an excess of either buyers or sellers, the specialist must buy or sell the stock from his own account to correct the imbalance. That keeps price swings moderate. You'd think that specialists would lose money, but because they, more than anyone, know the pent-up demand or lack thereof, they do just fine. Marty Schwartz, one of the world's most successful stock traders said, "I'll give you my view on specialists: Never in my life have I met a less talented group of people who make a disproportionately large amount of money relative to their skills." *New York Stock Exchange: www.nyse.com.*

Floor Broker. When you place an order to buy or sell a stock, bond, or commodity, that order is transmitted to the floor of a stock exchange. There, a floor broker tries to execute it for you by flailing her arms at the stock trading specialist, or increasingly, by entering your order on a handheld computer. One would think that computers would put floor brokers out of a job, but for reasons we don't understand, demand for floor brokers is actually increasing. *New York Stock Exchange: www.nyse.com.*

Insurance Underwriter. Is an insurance company wise to insure a particular applicant? Using computer programs, underwriters decide which risks are worth taking. It's a balancing act: If the underwriter is too conservative, the company loses business to competitors; if he is too liberal, the company loses money in claims payouts. The number of underwriting jobs will stay flat because software now does some of the work more precisely than a human can. *American Institute for Chartered Property and Casualty Underwriters: www.insweb.com; 720 Providence Rd., Malvern, PA 19355-0716; 610-644-2100. See also: www.connectyou.com/talent for links to insurance sites; for insurance jobs: www.insjobs.com.*

Estate Appraiser. A great career for people curious about how much things are worth. Demand is strong because bankruptcies are at an all-time high. (Most bankruptcies require an appraisal of a person's estate.) Also, as the population ages, more deaths occur, which often triggers estate appraisals. *American Society of Appraisers: www.appraisers.org.*

Work with Words

Writer. Self-expression — it's a powerful driver for many people, including your authors. Our lives gain meaning when we know that many others will hear what we have to say. And written self-expression has particular power because there's time to be more reflective. In addition, the result of your labor is more permanent than when speaking. (My parents love it when I send them clips.) Although your odds of making a living as a novelist or poet are about as good as O.J. Simpson being named Husband of the Millennium, there are neat writing niches that allow you to write without having to donate plasma to make the rent. Whatever the niche, though, most writers must free-lance. To survive as a free-lancer, it's not enough to send clips. You must pitch story ideas that are in sync with the publication, propose a compelling approach to the piece, and importantly, explain why you're the ideal person to do it. *National Writers Association: www.nationalwriters.com; 1450 S. Havana, Aurora, CO 80012; 303-751-7844. See also: www.inkspot.com* and *www.writers.com.*

(Neat Niche) **Medical Writer.** Writing *Seven Steps to Preparing for Your Hysterectomy* is a typical assignment for medical writers. They explain prevention practices and treatments in plain English. Sources of work include HMOs and other health insurers, hospitals, clinics, and magazines that appeal to older readers. *American Medical Writers Association: www.amwa.org; 9650 Rockville Pike, Bethesda, MD 20814; 301-493-0003.*

(Neat Niche) **Politician's Writer.** Every politician needs one, from a school board member to the president. Political writers craft fundraising letters, speeches, and see-how-much-I'm-doing-for-you newsletters. One approach to landing a job is to write a fundraising letter for your favorite politician for free. Send it as a sample of what you can do.

(Neat Niche) **Industry Publications Writer.** Ever thought of writing for *Pizza Today?* It's the glossy magazine written for people in the pizza business. There are thousands of such publications, and they tend to pay writers well.

(Neat Niche) **Ghostwriter.** Here's a back-door route into ghostwriting, which is a very cool gig. Instead of pitching publishing companies, contact celebrities. Ask if they'd like you to write a book about them. If they agree, develop a proposal together and send it, probably through an agent, to publishing houses. When the book comes out, the star is listed as the author in huge type and your name is microscopic, if it appears at all. The name of Hilary Clinton's ghostwriter of *It Takes a Village* never appeared on the book. Nevertheless, celeb ghostwriting may be the fastest route to a decent-paying, if secret, book deal.

(Neat Niche) **Copywriter.** This offers one of the surer routes to a non-starving writing career. Many copywriters think first about working for ad agencies, but also consider lesser-known niches: company annual reports, mail-order or Web catalog copy, telemarketing scripts, consumer information booklets, and restaurant menus. The number of small businesses is increasing, as is the number of media outlets. That, of course, increases the need for copywriters. As with most fields, specialization helps. Employers prefer to hire an expert at the type of writing they need. So become the whiz on one thing: roses, carpentry tools, mutual fund brochures, whatever.

(Neat Niche) **Technical Writer.** In this in-demand niche, you develop user manuals, articles about new products, instruction booklets, press releases, and online help files. *Society for Technical Communication: www.stc.org; 901 N. Stuart St., Arlington, VA 22203; 703-522-4114. See also: user.itl.net/~gazza/techwr.htm. Newsgroups: alt.books.technical; misc.books.technical; biz.books.technical; bit.listserv.techwr-1. For job listings: www.mindspring.com/~panin/writers.htm.*

Social Science Analyst. Like to read? The federal government employs 15,000 people under this job title, and their main job is to read and research material on such issues as drug abuse, urban planning, and adult literacy. Employment prospects are better with a graduate degree. State agencies also offer such jobs under varying job titles. Similar jobs may also be available at universities, think tanks, and in corporations.

Information Abstractor. Love to read nonfiction? Would you enjoy synthesizing articles into a paragraph or two? The job market is good because of the need to distill that relentless information explosion. You'll be particularly in demand if you have content expertise, perhaps in law, medicine, engineering, or real estate. *National Federation of Abstracting & Information Services: www.well.com/user/asi; 1429 Walnut St., Philadelphia, PA 10102; 215-563-2406. See also: Newsgroup: sci.finance.abstracting.*

BHB

Indexer. An index can make the difference between a book and a good book. Peter Farrell, author of *Make Money from Home,* calls a good index, "a minor work of art but also the product of clean thought and meticulous care." That work of art must usually be done quickly — a publisher usually gives the indexer a manuscript just a few weeks before publication. Indexing is a self-employed occupation that requires a person with the odd combination of enjoying the solitary work of creating an index and the ability to go out there, ask for business, and insist on reasonable compensation: $2-3 per manuscript page or $20-30 an hour. Degrees are unnecessary. For a good, inexpensive indexing home study course, contact the *United States Dept. of Agriculture at 202-720-7123. American Society of Indexers: www.asiindexing.org; P.O. Box 48267, Seattle, WA 98148-0267.*

(Neat Niche) **Internet Indexer.** The major search engines such as Yahoo! and AltaVista are ever looking to develop sophisticated ways to search the Internet and other databases.

Court Reporter. You record courtroom drama (or courtroom tedium), as the perfectionist who must get it right at 300 words per minute. Don't worry, there's special shorthand. Training for this difficult-sounding profession typically takes less than a year. And salaries are good: $40,000–$80,000, which makes court reporting one of the best-paying, non-dangerous careers that don't require a four-year degree. In urban areas, knowledge of a foreign language is a big plus. *National Court Reporters Association: www.ncraonline.org; 8224 Old Courthouse Rd., Vienna, VA 22182; 703-556-6272 or 800-272-6272. See also: www.verbatimreporters.com.*

OOH

(Neat Niche) **Stenocaptioner.** Using a court-reporter-like technique, you caption live TV programming for the hearing-impaired.

Scopist. When a court reporter records the proceedings at 300 words a minute, the transcript is understandably rough. The scopist edits it so that it's ready for the judge's and lawyers' persnickety eyes. Training is short and convenient; you can get a 16-week, at-home course by calling At-Home Professions: 800-359-3455. To land a job, try calling court reporting agencies listed in your Yellow Pages. *National Court Reporters Association: www.ncraonline.org; 8224 Old Courthouse Rd., Vienna, VA 22182; 703-556-6272.*

BHB

Legal Transcript Digester. Here's an interesting legal career in which you don't have to be a lawyer or even a paralegal. Preparation for complex trials can require hundreds of hours of depositions (interviews) and hundreds more hours of trial. The verbatim court reporter transcript is too cumbersome, so attorneys hire transcript digesters to condense the material. *A full training course is available from Hillside Digesting Services' Transcript Digesting Manual: P.O. Box 2888, Fallbrook, CA 92088; 800-660-3376. See also: www.drblank.com/hbotrans.htm for a minicourse.*

BHB

Radio Guide Publisher. TV listings are ubiquitous, yet in most locales, it's difficult to find radio listings: who will be on the talk shows, what music will be played when, etc. We believe this is a terrific publishing opportunity. One approach is to collect the program listings, sell the collection to local newspapers, and also print it as an advertisement-funded freebie to be distributed at supermarkets.

Graphologist. Handwriting analysts are not only found in carnivals. Police departments, attorneys, and employers use graphologists to catch forgers or to verify that you wrote the ransom note. Also, there's evidence that personality characteristics can be discerned from handwriting. In a job interview, you may say, "I'm hard-working," but your handwriting — something you can't control as well as your tongue — may say something different. Besides, if you're a graphologist, you can be the instant center of attention at a party. *National Society for Graphology: 250 W. 57 St., New York, NY 10107; 212-265-1148.*

Work with Things

Artistically done

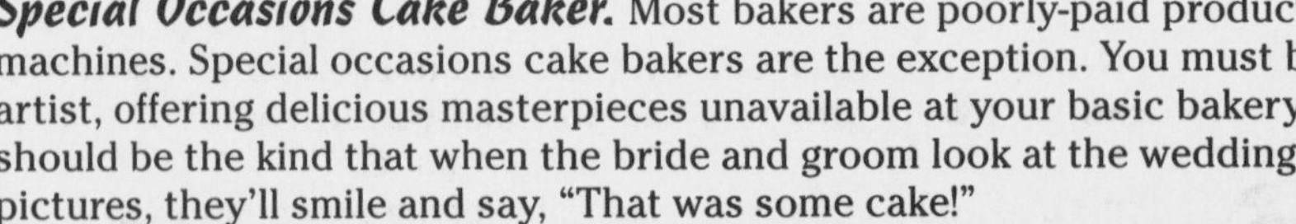

Special Occasions Cake Baker. Most bakers are poorly-paid production machines. Special occasions cake bakers are the exception. You must be an artist, offering delicious masterpieces unavailable at your basic bakery. It should be the kind that when the bride and groom look at the wedding pictures, they'll smile and say, "That was some cake!"

Artist/Graphic Designer. Get real. If you have visions of hanging out in your loft, splattering paint on some enormous abstract canvas, congratulations — you have a cool hobby. Your chances of turning that into a career that nets you more than 50 cents an hour is about as good as being bitten by a rattlesnake in your bed. The *Princeton Review* profile on artists claims that "as a purely self-expressing career, 90 percent of artists make under $1,000 per year on their art." If you expect to make a living as an artist, burnish this into your brain: 75 percent of the art available for view in the

OOH

United States is produced by the advertising industry. And almost all of that is computer-generated art. The most common term for that career, of course, is "graphic designer." The good news is that demand is growing. As more and more publications and products vie for people's attention, companies are turning to graphic designers to ensure that their steak sizzles. More good news: In graphic design, degrees don't count; your portfolio does. Send samples of your portfolio to lots of art directors at ad agencies or to the new design/marketing agencies — and don't forget the small houses. Beware, in some workplaces, graphic designers are expected to be production machines. "I went into graphic design because I wanted to be creative. Instead I'm a robot, cranking out page after page of look-alike junk-mail catalog pages." And you better like computers. In almost all graphics design jobs, you're chained to a computer all day. Oh, and one more sad truth: Only a third of people who start a career in graphic design last five years. *Graphic Artists Guild: www.gag.org; 90 John St., New York, NY 10038; 212-791-3400. See also: www.wwac.org.*

(Neat Niche) **Demonstrative Evidence Specialist.** Demonstrative evidence specialists create those large computer-generated drawings, slides, and videos that attorneys use to present their cases to judges and juries. Because each situation is different, you're not a robot, and because the stakes are high, you make more than slave wages.

(Neat Niche) **Technical Illustrator.** Three of my most dreaded words: some assembly required. I am slow when it comes to putting something together, and the "easy-to-follow" drawings created by technical illustrators don't usually help. Maybe you'll do a better job. Technical illustrators tackle projects more important than my patio furniture. They may, for example, create drawings of coronary by-pass surgery or the inner workings of a rocket engine. *American Institute of Technical Illustrators: 2424 Sylvan Avenue, Suite 908, Alton, IL 62002-5502; 618-462-3720. Society of Illustrators: www.societyillustrators.org; 128 E. 63rd St., New York, NY 10021-7303; 212-838-2560.*

(Neat Niche) **Muralist.** If you can't get a National Endowment for the Arts grant, convince the city or local merchants to hire you to paint inspiring murals on graffitied buildings, in restaurants, apartment house or office building lobbies, on freeway underpass walls, even on billboard-size signs. *National Society of Mural Painters, American Fine Arts Society: www.anny.org/orgs/0041/001p0041.htm; 215 W. 57th St., New York, NY 10019.*

(Neat Niche) **Commission Artist.** If you can create paintings that would look good on the walls of rich people's living rooms, place an ad in a magazine read by the local wealthy that explains that you can "create a gallery-quality painting to their specifications for a fraction of the cost."

(Neat Niche) **Animator.** An architect develops a blueprint for a house, but the customer is nervous. Will it really be livable? So an animator develops a walk-through animation of the house. Now the customer can do as many virtual walk-throughs as she likes before the first nail is hammered. This is just one of the suddenly endless opportunities for animators. Why suddenly? For the first time, computers can, at moderate cost, do animations previously impossible at any price, animations sophisticated enough to appeal to adults. Science and industry, cable TV, films, Internet sites, computer games, and commercials are all jumping on the animation bandwagon. Downsides are low pay and highly structured work. This is not the career for free-wheeling artists. The top animation schools are the California Institute of the Arts and Sheridan College in Toronto. *The International Animation Association: www.swcp.com/~asifa/; c/o Deanna Morse, School of Communications, Lake Superior Hall, Grand Valley State University, Allendale, MI 49401; 616-895-3101. National Cartoonists Society: P.O. Box 20267, New York, NY 10023; 212-627-1550. Best Web site is www.bergen.org/AAST/computeranimation.*

Conservator. A conservator's idea of bliss is restoring something old (like paintings, furniture, autographs, books, and musical instruments) to its former glory. A combination painter, refinisher, and chemist (watch those fumes), most conservators are hired by major museums. Government agencies sometimes hire them to restore historic properties. Alas, few jobs are available. *American Institute for Conservation of Historic and Artistic Works: www.palimpsest.stanford.edu/aic; 1717 K St., N.W., Washington, DC 20006; 202-452-9545. National Trust for Historic Preservation: www.nationaltrust.org; 1785 Massachusetts Ave., N.W., Washington, DC 20036; 800-944-6847.*

Holographer. Looking for a career that melds art and science? Wanna make something cool? Try holography. Holographs are no longer just '60s-cool psychedelia — the field is growing. Holographs are used to promote new products, on ID and credit cards, in movie special effects, even in medical diagnosis. Though some holographers learn on the job, others attend a special school, notably the one at *The Museum of Holography in Chicago: 1134 W. Washington Blvd., Chicago, IL 60607; 312-226-1007. Optical Society of America: www.osa.org; 2010 Massachusetts Ave., N.W., Washington, DC 20036; 202-223-8130.*

Biomedical Visualization Specialist. This field used to be called medical illustration, but it's come a long way. Thanks to software and imaging equipment, medical and scientific illustrators are no longer limited to what they can hand-draw. For example, they can use computer-generated brain maps to demonstrate differences between a Nobel prize winner and a retarded person, or between the parts of the brain that are activated when thinking about math or thinking about sex. *The Association of Medical Illustrators: www.medical-illustrators.org; 1819 Peachtree Street, NE, Atlanta, Georgia 30309; 404-350-7900.*

Diemaker. This is one metal artist who can expect to earn a living. Working from a blueprint or instructions, you develop the forms (dies) for metal or plastic products — from coins to auto parts. Though you still need artistic skills, you now have lots of help. Die design is computer-assisted, as is the cutting. There is a shortage of diemakers, so job and salary prospects are good, and no college is required. Most diemakers learn as apprentices. *The Precision Machined Products Association: www.pmpa.org; 6700 W. Snowville Rd., Brecksville, OH 44141; 440-526-0300. Precision Metal Forming Association: 27027 Chardon Rd., Richmond Heights, OH 44143.*

Cinematographer. It seems that everyone wants to be a film director, but what are the odds of making a living at it? Think lottery. How can you derive many of directing's benefits with fewer people competing for your jobs? Try cinematography. Cinematographers also are directors on film sets. The major difference is that instead of directing people, they're directing what the camera is doing: figuring out the right lighting and photographic techniques and, after the shoot, reviewing and critiquing what they designed. *American Society of Cinematographers: www.cinematography.com; 1782 N. Orange Dr., Hollywood, CA 90028; 800-448-0145. Job openings: www.hollywoodreporter.com2/index* and *www.showbizjobs.com.*

Lighting Designer. In the end, what's most fun about a career in theater or the movies is the creativity and the people. Trying to land a movie/theater career through the front door by being an actor or director is a long shot, but there are back doors, one of which is lighting director. You train for this career in college-based stagecraft programs (like the ones at UC Irvine and Cal Poly, Pomona). Lighting directors are hired not only in film and theater, but for trade shows, and for lighting major buildings — hotels, corporate lobbies, museums, concerts, and theme parks. *International Association of Lighting Designers: Suite 487, Merchandise Mart, Chicago, IL 60654; 312-527-3677. Links: www.nsicorp.com/proorg.htm.*

Neon Sign Maker. How'd you like a career of twisting colored glass into special shapes? This is a dying art, yet demand is high — a nice combination for you. There are only three regulated training programs in the United States, including the highly-regarded National Neon Institute in Benicia, California (800-626-4217). Just 14 weeks to certification, and director Lee Champaign says that you can get a job almost anywhere in the United States. Don't worry, you needn't be a Rembrandt. An artist creates the design. Your job is to bend the glass to match the design.

Foley Artist. Remember the sounds of that steamy sex scene between Leonardo DiCaprio and Kate Winslett in *Titanic?* Probably created by a foley artist making dispassionate love to his own wrist. That crunching snow as the avalanche rescuers try to save the day? Walking on cornstarch in a burlap bag. When someone lands a punch? Socking a hunk of steak. Rib cuts are perfect because they have bones to giving a crunching effect. Foley artists create sounds that are easier to record than those made during the actual shoot. The good foley artist must be an "audile": able to look at an object and imagine what type of sound it can produce. Take, for example, that vampire flick in which a character's guts get pulled out: raw chicken. Foley artists must also have a good sense of timing, which may be why many Foley artists are also musicians. So next time you see a movie car crash, think pie plate. *Job openings: www.hollywoodreporter.com2/index* and *www.showbizjobs.com.*

Exhibit Designer/Builder. Many artistic types who like to sling a hammer dream of becoming theater set designers, but that market is extraordinarily tight. But exhibit designing/building, a similar field, is less known and therefore easier to break into. You build the equivalent of theater sets for trade shows, expos, and museums. *Exhibit Designers and Producers Association: www.edpa.com; 5775 Peachtree Dunwoody Rd., Atlanta, GA 30342; 404-303-7310. See also: www.exponet.com.*

Structured procedures

Heart-Lung Perfusionist. In open-heart surgery, the surgeon can't work on the heart if blood is squirting all over the place. So a machine is hooked up to an artery to receive the blood. The machine then, like a heart and lungs, pumps blood and air out to an artery on the other side of the heart and lungs, and circulation continues. Meanwhile, the heart is relatively bloodless so that the surgeon can work. The surgeon does the hooking up and the perfusionist runs the machine. Sounds straightforward, but talk to any perfusionist and he'll mention one word: stress. One mistake can be one too many for the bypass patient. There are upsides: You are intimately involved in saving people's lives, and salaries are excellent — except in rural areas; *starting* salaries exceed $60,000. Only a bachelor's degree is required. Perfusion is the smallest health care profession with only 3,500 practitioners in the United States. *American Society for Extracorporeal Technology: www.amsect.com; 11480 Sunset Hills Rd., Reston, VA 20190; 703-435-8556.*

Dental Technologist. You're the person who makes false teeth and braces. It's a good career for people who want to be self-employed, working with your hands on small, precise work. To make a good living, you need to specialize in an area that's in demand, like geriatric bridges and other appliances. Most dental technologists get their training on the job, but there are 46 American Dental Association-accredited training programs. *National Association of Dental Laboratories: www.nadl.org; 8201 Greensboro Drive, McLean, VA 22105; 703-610-9035.*

Musical Instrument Repairperson. There are thousands of junior high school orchestras and bands. Junior high school students are not known for their tender treatment of anything, so there are plenty of broken violins, trumpets, and flutes that need repair. And, of course, even some older folks' instruments need work. This is a great career for fix-it types who'd prefer to avoid things electrical. You should know how to play the instrument. Otherwise, how would you know if you fixed it? Noted training institutions include Badger State Repair in Wisconsin, Renton Technical College in Washington (WA), and Red Wing Technical Institute in Minnesota. *National Association of Professional Band Instrument Repair Technicians: www.napbirt.org; P.O. Box 51, Normal, IL 61761; 309-452-4257.*

(Neat Niche) **Piano Technician/Tuner.** This is a low-stress job. Working conditions are ideal, usually in quiet, pleasant surroundings, and you're nearly always assured of pleasing your customer. Also, time is rarely of the essence. Though some of the work is routine, pianos require a range of repairs, so the work offers adequate novelty. Despite the presence of electronic aids, piano tuners need a good ear. *Piano Technicians Guild: www.ptg.org; 3930 Washington St., Kansas City, MO 64111; 816-753-7747.*

Avionics Technician. In a $20 million airplane, $16 million is avionics (electronic equipment). It's been said that today's airplanes are flying computers. That means plenty of avionics to fix and plenty to upgrade. Electronics are always getting better, so many people are retrofitting — much cheaper than buying a new plane. Avionics technology is a career for tinkerers who read magazines like *Popular Mechanics,* and, of course, who like airplanes. *Professional Aviation Maintenance Association: 1200 18 St., N.W., Washington, DC 20036; 202-216-9220.*

Network Technologist. "The system is down. What the heck happened?" "Oh my God! I lost my data!" Computer network technologists install and repair those oh-so-complicated contraptions. You're a combination mega-tinkertoys assembler, computer programmer, and fix-it person. You get to see how all the pieces fit together, and there's variety: some diagnostic brainwork, some hands-on; plus you're crucial to everyone who uses the network. This is no 9-to-5 job. You work until it's fixed. You are well paid, though. The Department of Labor projects great demand through 2006. *International Society of Certified Electronics Technicians: www.iscet.org; 2708 West Berry Street, Fort Worth, TX 76109; 817-921-9101. Electronics Technicians Association: www.eta-sda.com; 602 N. Jackson, Greencastle, IN 46135; 765-653-4301. For job openings: www.computerworld.com.*

Conference Taping Specialist. Tens of thousands of professional meetings are held each year in the United States alone. Only a fraction offer tape-recorded sessions for sale to those who missed sessions. This is a simple business. Equipment needs are modest: tape recorders, microphones, and a tape duplicating machine. Marketing is straightforward — almost all the world's associations are listed, along with their size in the *Encyclopedia of Associations,* which is available at most libraries. Just call the largest associations in your local area, and make your pitch to the conference coordinator. You may be able to get a yes simply by touting the convenience to the organization's members, but your chances multiply if you offer the association a piece of the action.

High-Tech Repairperson. As products become ever more electronic, ever more people are needed to repair them. It's a nice job with a pleasant work environment, the opportunity to use your brains to diagnose the problem, and high demand. *International Society of Certified Electronics Technicians: www.iscet.org; 2708 West Berry St., Ft. Worth, TX 76109; 817-921-9101.*

BHB

(Neat Niche) **Notebook Computer Repairperson.** Talk about a field with huge demand. More and more people use notebook computers, and because the notebooks are delicate and moved around so much, they break. More good news for you: Training doesn't require a Ph.D. Three to six months should do.

(Neat Niche) **Music Synthesizer Repairperson.** Most bands have a synthesizer player. Moving these delicate electronic orchestras from gig to gig means plenty of breakdowns, and plenty of employment for you.

(Neat Niche) **Hard Disk Repairperson.** People will pay through the nose to retrieve the data they should have been backing up.

(Neat Niche) **Robotics Technologist.** Does building and fixing robots sound like fun? Today, robots mainly weld cars and elevated highway beams, but soon they'll assist with hip replacement surgery, climbing and painting rusty utility towers, and installing space stations. Oh, one, perhaps surprising, job requirement: You have to be able to lift 50 pounds. Robots haven't yet been to WeightWatchers. *Optical Society of America: www.osa.org; 2010 Massachusetts Ave., N.W., Washington, DC 20036; 202-223-8130.*

(Neat Niche) **Personal Digital Assistant Repairperson.** These pocket-sized combination rolodex, calendar, and mini-computer have become ubiquitous and are expensive enough to justify repairing. Their portability increases their dropability and, in turn, your employability.

(Neat Niche) **Biomedical Equipment Repairperson.** This high-tech repair gig pays well because the machine must often be fixed now. A patient on a heart-lung machine can't wait long.

Telecommunications Technologist/Installer. Computers are booming, telecommunications are booming, so no surprise, the intersection is, well, booming. Telecommunications specialists connect computers with communication equipment. A typical project involves installing a voice-mail, e-mail, and videoconferencing system so that all branches of a multinational company can communicate with each other. Some programming usually is required. *International Communications Industries Association: www.icia.org; 11242 Waples Mill Rd., Fairfax, VA 22030; 800-659-7469.*

Solar Energy Technologist/Installer. There are many technologist careers, but few that nurture the soul of the environmentally conscious like this one. Not only are you keeping the air clean, you're probably working for clients who are similarly minded because, fact is, solar energy is generally not as cost-effective as petroleum-based energy. Of course, demand is increasing as solar energy gets ever more cost-effective. Solar energy is now being used to power entire housing subdivisions. The Sacramento Municipal Utilities District has a photovoltaic plant that powers 660 homes. Most solar installers learn on the job, although some community colleges offer programs. *American Solar Energy Society: www.ases.org/solar; 2400 Central Ave., Boulder, CO 80301; 303-443-3130. Solar Energy Industries Association: www.seia.org; 122 C St., N.W., Washington, DC 20001; 202-383-2600.*

Millwright. Millwrights install and repair heavy industrial equipment. Few high school graduates picture themselves as crucial to the operation of a mega-corporation, yet millwrights are. And it can be a rewarding job. It can feel great to be called on to figure out what's wrong, and under the gun of time pressure, solve a problem that affects an entire plant's operation. You're also called on when a new piece of million-dollar heavy machinery is delivered. You're there to unload, inspect, and move it into position. That can mean deciding which ropes, cables, and hoists to use. It can even mean building a special foundation using the manufacturer's blueprints. Fast-growing specialties include robotics, telecommunications, medical diagnostic, and truck manufacturing equipment. Most millwrights learn as apprentices or in community college programs. *The Millwright Group: 2750 Prosperity Ave., Fairfax, VA 22031; 703-698-0291.*

Noise Control Serviceperson. Many owners of residences and workplaces near airports, freeways, schools, and factories are willing to pay for some peace and quiet. This is a high-value specialty, yet the skills required are often modest. Often, all you're doing is insulating roofs and double-glazing and weatherstripping windows and doors.

I do not understand why leaf blowers are legal. They are the noisiest things this side of an atom bomb, and the noise lasts longer. Plus their engines spew out carcinogens. And for what? To blow leaves around? What's wrong with a rake?

Electrician. We're shocked that more people aren't becoming electricians. If you'd get a charge out of a career that requires working with both your hand and your brain, and are unlikely to blow a fuse when having to fix a problem right now, this career could light up your life. And job prospects are spiking — the Department of Labor projects strong demand for electricians through 2006. While many electricians plug in via a four- or five-year apprenticeship, others get wired on the job, supplemented with classroom or correspondence courses. *International Brotherhood of Electrical Workers: www.ibew.org; 1125 15th St., N.W., Washington, DC 20005.*

(Neat Niche) **Phone Cable Installer.** Demand is exploding as people install more phone lines for computers and telecommunications.

Automotive Technician (Car Mechanic). Get that image out of your mind: a grease-covered dude, hands covered with nicks from trying to turn a wrench in a too-tight space. Today's automotive technician may spend almost as much time with a computer as with a wrench. Cars are now heavily computer controlled, as is the equipment used to diagnose problems. If you have the ability to understand a complicated repair manual and a nose for diagnosing what's wrong, this is a much better career than it used to be. More good news: Most automotive techs get their first professional job with no training other than having played around with their own car. There are excellent opportunities for women, as the work is more automated, and physical strength is less important. *National Institute for Automotive Service Excellence: www.asecert.org; 13505 Dulles Technology Dr., Herndon, VA 20171; 703-713-3800.*

(Neat Niche) **Diesel Engine Technicians.** Large need, higher salary, fewer applicants. Why? "Diesel engine" doesn't sound as sexy as "Corvette," but with regard to the actual work, a piston is a piston.

(Neat Niche) **Mobile Auto Repairperson.** Every car needs tune-ups, oil changes, and brake jobs, and nearly every car owner finds getting those things done inconvenient: Drop off the car and somehow get to work in the morning, and then somehow get back to the shop after work. Enter the mobile auto repairperson. She does the work right where you park your car for work. What a business: huge demand, little competition, and ample markup.

Used Car Inspector. You finally find a used car you're excited about, but, of course, you want it inspected first. AAA often has a long waiting list, and you'd rather go to an inspection specialist than a general car repair shop, but few exist. This appears to be a large unmet need. If you'd like a blueprint for a used car inspection service, consider a franchise — for example, *Automotive Appraisal Services Group: 91398 World Way Center, Los Angeles, CA 90009; 800-495-2525.*

Mobile Car Detailer. Many of us would like our car polished and cleaned inside and out but don't have the time to do it ourselves or to take it to a shop where we have to sit around waiting for it to be done. Enter the mobile car detailer. While the customer's car is parked at work or at home, the mobile car detailer does the job. This is another of those low-investment, no-brains, high-markup, easy-to-satisfy-the-customer businesses. One marketing approach is to get local new car dealers, especially luxury brands, to give a coupon for a half-price detailing to each new car purchaser. Luxury car buyers have just bought a new car and want it kept looking good, and you know they have disposable income. One no-profit detailing may yield a customer who'll keep buying your service for years.

Surveyor. Where does United States airspace end? What are a park's legal boundaries? Where does your neighbor's land end? Surveyors figure these things out. They still use the old-fashioned theodolites on tripods, but increasingly use Global Positioning Systems (GPS) satellite systems to do the measurement. Surveying is a fine career for someone who does not have a college degree, is comfortable around algebra and geometry, likes to learn as an apprentice, and wants an outdoor career with some status. We spoke with the director of California's state apprenticeship programs, who said that if he had a child, of the hundreds of apprenticeable careers, he'd say that surveying was, overall, the best. The job market is tight. The key to upping your chances is to know the new surveying technologies such as GPS and remote sensing. *American Congress on Surveying and Mapping: www.landsurveyor.com/acsm; 5410 Grosvenor Ln., Bethesda, MD 20814; 301-493-0200.*

Drafter. Can you picture it? Sitting at a drafting table with triangles and a T-square drawing blueprints. Forget it. Although you still need free-hand drawing skills, most drafting today is done at a computer with a Computer-Assisted-Drafting (CAD) program. The market is hottest for electronic drafters: those who draw circuit boards and schematic diagrams. *American Design Drafting Association: www.adda.org; P.O. Box 799, Rockville, MD 20848-0799; 301-460-6875.*

Tile Setter. This strikes us as the perfect construction career. The work is physically easy, progress is steady and readily apparent, and the results look pretty. Training is short, usually on-the-job, although apprenticeships are available. And here's the kicker — for a reason we can't understand, pay is higher than for most construction trades. Perhaps it's because half of tile setters are self-employed, which is double the rate in other construction trades. That may be a sign that tile setters find it relatively easy to get work. *International Masonry Institute: www.imiweb.org; 823 15th St., N.W., Washington, DC 20005.*

Locksmith. This is the only career in which you don't get arrested for picking locks. This is one of the better hands-on occupations: great need, short training, physically undemanding, and many grateful customers: all those people locked out of their homes or cars, and companies and home owners who need to keep the bad guys out. The latter is where the money is. Training can often be done by correspondence. *Associated Locksmiths of America: www.aloa.org; 3003 Live Oak St., Dallas, TX 75204; 214-827-1701.*

Gemologist. A gem of a career: looking at beautiful jewelry all day and deciding how much each piece is worth. Even better, only a few months and you can become one of only 1,000 people to be certified by the Gemological

Institute of America. Never again will anyone be able to pawn off a cubic zirconium as a diamond on you. If you can live with rhinestone pay, you may find this a sparkling career. *Gemological Institute of America: www.gia.org.*

Hydroponics Farmer. In winter in most states, food markets must get their vegetables from California or Mexico. Not exactly fresh from the field. With hydroponics (soilless greenhouse growing), you can provide farm-fresh veggies even in February in Minnesota. To be cost-effective, focus on high-priced produce. For example, you might grow gourmet lettuces such as arugula, baby romaine, and radicchio, cut 'em up, mix 'em up, and you've got $3.00 a pound gourmet salad that cost you well under a buck. You'd be surprised how many markets will say yes as long as you can be counted on to deliver, day in and day out. Don't forget about non-obvious outlets such as convenience stores and high-class restaurants. Hydroponics farmers can also grow exotic plants. Fancy restaurants, hotels, and flower shops will often pay big money for tropical crotons and lush ferns in winter. Beyond profit, hydroponics offers an easier way to be a farmer: no tractors, no plowing, no weeding, no heavy pesticide use, no weather problems. And the feeding and watering is all automatic. *Hydroponics Society of America: P.O. Box 3075, San Ramon, CA 94583; 510-743-9605.*

Arborist. A career in which you start at the top — top of the tree, that is: pruning it, topping it, bracing it, spraying it. When you climb down, you also advise on which tree to put where, how to plant and care for it so that — unlike the feeble ash in front of my house — it thrives. Do a good job and you'll have bolstered Joyce Kilmer's case: "I think that I shall never see a poem lovely as a tree." *International Society of Arboriculture: www.ag.uiuc.edu/~isa; P.O. Box 3129, Champaign, IL 61826; 217-355-9411.*

Dog Trainer. Do you have the patience to teach Rover not to chew up the furniture or pee on the floor when Rover's owner can't? Do you like the challenge of convincing a dog to let you walk it rather than have it walk you? Consider dog training. Best way for *you* to get trained is to visit a few local training centers, watch a few trainers work, and ask your favorite for an apprenticeship. There are no professional standards for dog trainers, so choose carefully. *National Association of Dog Obedience Instructors: www.kimberly.uidaho.edu/nadoi; 729 Grapevine Hwy., Hurst, TX 76054.*

(Neat Niche) **Service Dog Trainer.** We all know about guide dogs for the blind, but there's increasing demand for dogs for the deaf. Your job is to train the dog to alert the master to specific sounds like a smoke alarm, a ringing phone, and a knock at the door. Because these dogs are generally large, and much of the training requires moving the dog, service dog trainers must be physically strong. *National Service Dog Center: www.petforum.com/deltasociety/dsb000.htm; 289 Perimeter Rd. E., Renton, WA 98055; 800-869-6898.*

(Neat Niche) **Working Dog Trainer.** What sort of work do working dogs do? Typical jobs are sniffing out drugs for the United States Customs Service and finding injured people in wreckage for local police departments.

Pet Sitter. Americans are nuts about their pets. Forty-three percent of United States households have pets, more than the percentage of households with kids! Because pet owners travel just like other people, pet-sitting services are gaining customers. There are three ways to pet-sit. You can open your home to Muffin, live in Muffin's home while its owners are gone, or make daily stops at Muffin's home. In all three scenarios, you feed, walk, and play with the Muffmeister, and perhaps a menagerie of rabbits, hamsters, and tarantulas. Don't think that pet sitting is the same as pet playing. There are crises, for example, when Muffin is sick upon arrival or develops a case of separation anxiety when you show up. In such cases, you must instantly become PetShrink or you may find yourself with a pooch who refuses to go for a walk, or with a bite out of your leg. More often, it's a matter of accommodating to idiosyncrasies, like the cat who likes to roll around in the tub each morning after its owner showers. To keep the cat happy, the pet-sitter moistened the tub and put the cat in. The only way to make a middle-class income from pet sitting is to have a staff of sitters, but then again, that means you don't get to play with Muffin. *National Association of Professional Pet Sitters: www.petsitters.org; 1200 G St., N.W., Washington, DC 20005; 202-393-3317.*

BHB

Fireworks Display Specialist. Staging pyrospectaculars sounds like a blast, but it's not easy to skyrocket into this field. The problem is that it's dominated by a small number of private, mainly family-run businesses, that like to keep their sky shows to themselves. But if this career sounds more exciting than a pyrofinale, here are some good ways to start. Contact *American Fireworks News: www.barrettwebs.com/afn; P.O. Box 30, Dragomons Ferry, PA 18328; 717-828-8417;* and *Bob Weaver's Web site at www.znet.com~rjweaver.* Your next step is to attend a shooter's training: either one offered during the spring by a local fireworks company or the two-day shooter's certification course offered each year by *Pyrotechnics Guild International (www.pacificnet/~pgi),* or maybe the more academic, week-long seminar offered at *Washington College in Maryland.* It's also worth working as an assistant at a July 4th show or two. It's seasonal work for most people in the field, but a small percentage keep busy year-round shooting fireworks for movies, TV, theater, concerts, and sporting events. *International Pyrotechnics Society: c/o IIT Research Institute, Attn: James Austing, 10 W. 35th St., Chicago, IL 60616. Pyrotechnical Guild International: 18021 Baseline Ave., Jordan, MN 55352; 612-492-2061.*

Product Tester. How'd you like to play with toys for a living? Be a toy tester for Mattel or Hasbro. Michael Ferraro tastes Godiva Chocolate for a living. Jack Brashears' job is tasting Jack Daniels whiskey. There are product testers for everything from software to cars. There are limits, though. A rather lazy person contacted the Simmons Mattress Company to ask if it uses mattress testers. They said no.

Work with People and Data

Optometrist. "Better with lens A or lens B?" After a while, I can never tell, and feel like a dunce. But I digress. Optometrists examine, diagnose, and treat eye conditions, most often by prescribing glasses or contact lenses. In some states, they're even allowed to do some minor surgery. Optometry is among the most rewarding health careers because it identifies serious problems that usually have a ready cure. And because the population is aging, and because optometrists are a lower-cost alternative to ophthalmologists (medical eye doctors), the job market for optometrists is good. *American Optometric Association: www.aoa.net; 243 N. Lindbergh Blvd., St. Louis, MO 63141; 314-991-4100.*

(Neat Niche) **Sports Optometrist.** New research has found that it's possible to train athletes to see moving objects better.

(Neat Niche) **Optometrist specializing in the hard-to-fit.**

Orthoptist. This is another good career for people who'd like to be a doctor but don't have the grades or desire to spend that much time in school. Just like an eye doctor (ophthalmologist), but under his general supervision, you check vision, perform tests from depth perception to color blindness, and do patient education. Any bachelor's degree plus a two-year program earns you a 35K salary to start and a career that many orthoptists say feels rather like being a physician. Orthoptics is a small profession in great demand. There are more jobs available than orthoptists to fill the vacancies. *American Orthoptic Council: lw.france@hosp.wisc.edu; 3914 Nakoma Rd., Madison, WI 53705; 608-233-5383.*

Pharmacist. Mushing medicines together with mortar and pestle? Forget about it. Today's pharmacist is often a front-line health care provider teaching diabetics how to inject themselves with insulin, assisting with blood pressure monitoring, and ensuring that people know how to take their medications. The latter isn't as easy as it sounds. Many older people must take many medications, each of which must be taken at a different time, some of which must be taken on an empty stomach, others when not drowsy. Perhaps the most important thing a pharmacist does is ensure that drugs can be taken together. The TV show *Dateline* did a test in which an obviously pregnant woman walked into ten pharmacies asking whether two drugs could be taken together. Six of the ten pharmacists said yes. In fact, when a pregnant woman takes those two drugs together, it's lethal. Each year, thousands of people are hospitalized because they take prescription medications improperly. MIT researchers are working on a *precision pill* — a single pill that would deliver a variety of medicines, each released at the right time. Until that pill becomes available, though, pharmacists can be lifesavers.

Some insiders say that the coolest pharmacy jobs are in drug companies' research departments. *Academy of Pharmacy Practice and Management: www.aphanet.org; c/o Susan Winckler, 2215 Constitution Ave., N.W., Washington, DC 20037; 800-237-APHA or 202-628-4410.*

Genetic Counselor. We are becoming ever more aware that our children are greatly affected by their genes. The upshot of recent *Time* and *Newsweek* cover stories is that our personalities and intelligence are significantly mediated by our biology. What do genetic counselors do? Typical example: a married couple both suffer from severe depression. They're thinking about having a child. A genetic counselor helps them understand the risk that their child will suffer from depression, facilitates their deciding whether to get pregnant, and helps them make peace with their decision. People enter this field from a wide range of disciplines including biology, genetics, psychology, nursing, public health, and social work. *National Society of Genetic Counselors: members.aol.com/nsgcweb/nsgchome.htm; 233 Canterbury Dr. Wallingford, PA 19086; 610-872-7608.*

Dietitian. They're not just in the hospital basement any more. As we get more health conscious, corporations hire dietitians to plan healthy meals for their employee cafeterias and to promote sensible eating habits. (Frankly, I'd rather have a sausage pizza with extra cheese.) Food manufacturers and supermarket chains use dietitians to evaluate prepared foods and put interesting low-calorie recipes such as endive salad with radicchio and sun-dried tomatoes into their ads.

Those three items — endive, radicchio, and sun-dried tomatoes — are undeniably trendy, but why? They are three of the world's worst-tasting edibles. How do such things become in? But I digress.

Health spas, weight-loss clinics and prisons use dietitians to make sure that visitors lose weight while having that oh-so-important balanced diet. Now we don't want to miss our share of the four basic food groups, now do we? My daughter says that our refrigerator seems to have a different four basic food groups: snack foods, jams, condiments, and science experiments.

By the way, why do prisoners get dietitians to ensure that their diet carefully reflects the four basic food groups when your average teenager's diet is more out of balance than a unicyclist? But I digress again.

The previously mentioned dietitian careers are growing, but most dietitians are still kept busy with hypertension, diabetes, and obesity in hospitals, clinics, and in their own private practices. I'm still hungering for that sausage pizza, but I'll settle for some chow fun (fat, greasy, delicious Chinese noodles). *American Society for Clinical Nutrition: www.faseb.org/ascn; 9650 Rockville Pike, Bethesda, MD 20814; 301-530-7110. American Dietetic Association: www.eatright.org; 216 W. Jackson Blvd., Chicago, IL 60606; 312-899-0040.*

(Neat Niche) **Geriatric Nutrition.** This may be *the* boom niche within dietetics. As our population ages and moves into assisted-care facilities, there's more demand for dietitians to plan meals to meet elders' special needs.

Manager. Many people like to manage projects and other people. It's a good thing. Despite all the downsizing, the United States still has 36 million managers. And recently, hiring started again. What makes a management position good? The particular industry or government agency isn't so crucial. These things are

- An organization with enough money to do things right and pay you reasonably
- An organizational culture that values excellence *and* its people
- A pleasant work environment
- Compatible co-workers, supervisees, and supervisors

Ask about those things before accepting a position.

That's what *you're* looking for, but what are employers craving? Kathryn and George Petras, in *Jobs,* describe the employable manager at the millennium: "Multilingual, a generalist with technical skills, computer literate, a doer, not a follower, a team player or team leader, a change agent." For all that, companies should pay 100 grand, don't you think? *American Management Association: www.amanet.org; P.O. Box 169, Saranac Lake, NY 12983; 800-262-9699. Links: www.sceneserver.com.*

(Neat Niche) **Government Manager.** Aspiring managers should not overlook government positions. Eighty percent of government jobs are managerial and professional compared with 25 percent in the private sector. In addition to quantity, government jobs offer quality: good benefits, stability, and colleagues dedicated to the public interest. Plus, government agencies are encouraging a more customer-service orientation among their employees, so the stereotype of the semi-comatose government worker is becoming less accurate. *www.usajobs.opm.gov lists all federal openings, as does a menu-driven telephone system: 202-606-2700. America's Job Bank at www.ajb.dni.us lists many thousands of state government jobs. For your state employment service, check the front of your White Pages. American Society for Public Administration: www.aspanet.org; 1120 G Street, N.W., Suite 700, Washington, DC 20005; 202-393-7878.*

(Neat Niche) **Work-Family Manager.** According to *Self* magazine, this job title didn't even exist a decade ago. Yet today, hundreds of companies have hired managers to develop and implement family-friendly work policies such as flexible work scheduling, dependent care, and family leave. Most such managers have a human resource background. Average salary: $66,000. Work-family managers are overwhelmingly female. *Society for Human Resource Management: www.shrm.org; 1800 Duke St., Alexandria VA 22314; 703-548-3440. For job openings, see: www.hrworld.com; www.hrcomm.com;* and *www.hrimmall.com.*

(Neat Niche) **Facilities Manager.** You run a corporation's facilities: from deciding where to lease, to hiring the maintenance crew. *International Facilities Management Association: www.ifma.org; 1 E. Greenway Plaza, Houston, TX 77046; 713-623-IFMA.*

(Neat Niche) **Association Manager.** There are many thousands of professional organizations, each of which uses managers. Associations employ over 1,000,000 people! Particularly ripe for picking are small organizations that have been volunteer-run and are ready for a step up. Or start your own organization. Surprisingly, many fields don't have one. What does an association manager do? Typically she ensures that new members are recruited, the membership list is maintained, dues are collected, the newsletter is sent out, and meetings and conferences are planned and promoted. *American Society of Association Executives: www.asaenet.org; 1575 I St., N.W., Washington, DC 20005; 202-626-2723.*

(Neat Niche) **Brand Manager.** Can you get excited about marketing toilet paper? It's actually more fun than you may think. It's like running your own business. You have a budget and have to figure out the smartest way to spend it so that your product sells.

(Neat Niche) **Restaurant Manager.** This career fails to meet one of our criteria for a cool career because many people find it draining — it's not easy getting entry-level folks to crank out hundreds of meals a day and serve them all with a smile. But restaurant manager eked into the august group of cool careers because as Bradley Richardson, author of *JobSmarts* asserts, it's one of the few careers in which you can become the boss within a year and have a realistic shot at a six-figure salary within five years. *Educational Foundation of the National Restaurant Association: www.edfound.org; 250 S. Wacker Dr., Chicago, IL 60606.*

(Neat Niche) **Environmental Manager.** Government agencies and corporations hire environmental managers to develop plans to minimize pollution to water, air, and soil quality, and to develop remediation plans when things go awry. Corporate environmental managers also draft environmental impact reports before expanding operations. *National Registry of Environmental Professionals: www.nrep.org; P.O. Box 2099, Glenview, IL 60025; 847-724-6631. For job openings: www.eco.org; www.environmental-jobs.com;* and *www.princeton.edu/~oa/careeroe.html.*

(Neat Niche) **Nonprofit Manager.** It's true that nonprofit management is especially difficult because staff is often largely volunteer and funds are limited, but The Cause is sometimes enough to make it all worthwhile. *Nonprofit management links: www.nptimes.com.*

Manager positions requiring more-specialized skills (health care manager, for example) are covered in separate listings.

Military Officer. This job title is a catchall for hundreds of occupations, from manager to doctor to engineer. A military career has many pluses: excellent free training, extensive benefits, a noble mission, and esprit de corps unmatched in most civilian jobs. Of course, you do have to accept a life of uniforms, the bureaucracy to end all bureaucracies, and transfers to places you'd otherwise never choose. (Aberdeen, Texas, anyone?) And, oh yes, you can get your head blown off. There are many routes in ROTC, enlistment, Officers Candidate Schools, and the prestigious service academies. The latter arguably offer the finest undergraduate experience anywhere. If you think you might like to "be all you can be," start by checking out the clearinghouse for military-related careers: *www.militarycareers.com/index.html.*

Human Resources Manager. You generally get to be the nice guy. While the other managers' main job is to make the workers do more, better, faster, your job is to keep things human. Yes, you're also trying to indirectly build the bottom line, but your efforts have a more compassionate quality. *Society for Human Resources Management: www.shrm.org; 1800 Duke St., Alexandria, VA 22314; 703-548-3440.*

(Neat Niche) **Employee Benefits Specialist.** The fun part of the job is being a teacher: explaining benefits to employees — from pension plans to mental illness coverage. It's not as fun to have to explain what they don't qualify for. Even less fun is all the paperwork, with rules ever-changing. Subniche: health care benefits management. *American Society for Healthcare, Human Resources Administration: www.ashhra.org; 1 N. Franklin, Chicago, IL 60606; 312-422-3721. For job openings: www.ifebp.org/jobs; www.hrworld.com; www.hrcomm.com;* and *www.hrimmall.com.*

Succession Planning Consultant. One of the most difficult periods in a family business is when one generation realizes that it must let go and allow the next generation to take over. Family members are often too emotionally involved to develop a wise succession plan on their own. Enter the consultant, a combination psychologist and businessperson. *Canadian Association of Family Enterprise: bulwark1.ic.gc.ca/SSG/mi00899e.html; 1163 Sylvester St., P.O. Box 136, Lefroy, ON, Canada L0L IW0. Family Business Advisor: 800-551-0633.*

Advertising Manager. Advertising is divided into the creative side (the writers and the artists) and the business side (the people who coordinate, buy, and sell advertising). We cover the creative side under the "writer" and "artist" listings. Here we talk about the business side, and except for the neat niche described next, this career doesn't meet our requirements as a cool career. The main career on the business side is account manager, the liaison between the creative and the client. This career is tough to break into, requires long hours, and has very high turnover in the first few years. And even if you survive, only a small percentage make real money. Besides, do you really want to devote your work life to convincing people to buy Fab rather than Tide? *American Advertising Federation: www.aaf.org; 1101 Vermont Ave., N.W., Washington, DC 20005; 202-898-0089. The Advertising Council: www.adcouncil.org; 261 Madison Ave., New York, NY 10016; 212-922-1500.*

(Neat Niche) **Advertising Planner.** Advertising firms are turning to creative-thinking, inquisitive outsiders to help design their ad campaigns. The *Wall Street Journal* reported that Citicorp was wondering how to differentiate its MasterCard from the countless others. It hired an account planner who interviewed consumers and discovered that many of them delighted in racking up free miles. "One woman confessed that she was going to return a sweater she had bought with another credit card so she could buy it all over again with her mileage-earning AAdvantage card." A few years ago, the job title "account planner" didn't even exist. Now there's a professional association of account planners, with over 500 people attending each year's convention.

Conference Hall Exhibit Manager. A professional organization can derive significant income from renting exhibit hall space at its conferences. Most organizations, however, are not expert at recruiting exhibitors, negotiating with them, collecting fees from them, or with the logistics of exhibit area setup and tear down. So organizations are often willing to outsource exhibit management to a specialist. This is a cool career because it's little-known, requires almost no investment, and identifying your prospective clients is easy. The *Encyclopedia of Associations* lists the dates of thousands of organizations' future conferences. Your Chamber of Commerce may have a list of upcoming local ones.

Casino Manager. This career abysmally fails our "makes a difference" criterion but offers other advantages. As state governments get ever more strapped, they reluctantly look to legalized gambling. In 1989, casino gambling was legal only in two states. Now it's legal in 48. The broken-nosed pit boss from the Bugsy days need not apply, but according to Vince Eade, director of the University of Nevada, Las Vegas International Gaming Institute, it takes only a few months to learn casino games in a community college training program. Salary for a floor manager or pit boss starts at around $40,000, and with just a few years of successful experience, it's a decent bet that you can land an $80,000 job as a gaming corporation executive. *Casino Institute of Atlantic Community College in Atlantic City: 609-343-4862. Community College of Southern Nevada: 702-383-6641.*

Professional Employer Service. These organizations take care of hiring, benefits, paperwork, and payroll, and lease the employee to another company. Companies are increasingly using a professional employer service because it handles the detail-oriented, administrative tasks, and helps insulate companies against wrongful termination suits. This career is one of *Entrepreneur* magazine's Hot Picks. *National Association of Professional Employer Organizations: www.napeo.org; 901 N. Pitt St., Alexandria, VA 22314; 703-836-0466.*

Labor Relations Specialist. Most of the work is done before you ever sit down at the negotiating table. Through the year, your job is to learn the needs of both labor and management, and to resolve disputes as they arise. If you work for a union, you may be trying to unionize workplaces. Come contract time, the bulk of your work is still away from the negotiating table. Your main job is to do the research needed to bolster your side's position. And then, of course, during negotiations, you get to play hardball, win-win, and poker. Good training opportunity: *AFL-CIO Organizing Institutes, Department for Professional Employees: www.aflcio.org; 815 16th St., N.W., Washington, DC 20006; 202-637-5000.*

Political Campaign Manager. Everyone who runs for office, from school board member in Lost Gulch, Wyoming, to president of the United States, needs a campaign manager. The campaign manager researches the opinions and voting patterns in the district, helps develop the candidate's themes, schedules the fundraisers, coordinates the direct mail, manages the database, hires staff, trains the phone bank workers, coordinates the door-to-door campaign, excites the media with a nonstop barrage of "news," and even helps design the campaign button. It's an exciting job: You're in charge of a winner-take-all contest that can make a difference in society. *www.politicalresources.com. See also: National Political Index: www.politicalindex.com for links.*

In our crazy system, our leaders get elected largely on who presses the most flesh, buys the best database of expected voters, makes the speech with the most soundbites, and, most importantly, extracts the most dollars from special interest groups. If I had my way, elections would be just two weeks long and funded completely with tax dollars. Each registered voter would receive a booklet with a statement and voting record from each candidate. During those two weeks, the candidate could use the tax dollars to campaign as he or she saw fit and would be required to participate in at least one televised debate sponsored by the League of Women Voters. That's it. Substance, not fluff, and much less chance of our politicians landing in the hip pockets of special interests. Perhaps most importantly, because of the brief, honorable campaign, outstanding candidates, daunted by what it currently takes to get elected, would more likely come forward.

Fee-Only Financial Planner. This is an especially good field for the older career-seeker. Most people with money are older and tend to trust people their own age. Especially as baby boomers age and worry about how in the world they're going to save that zillion dollars they say we'll need for retirement, the need for financial planners is accelerating. Social security is unlikely to help. The author of *JobSmarts,* Bradley Richardson, reports that a survey found that more 20-somethings believe in UFOs than believe they'll ever see a penny of social security. And with the ever wider range of investment and insurance options, there are many confused people who want help. The good financial planner is as much a financial therapist as a number cruncher or mutual fund picker. Unfortunately, the traditional financial planner has a conflict of interest: She makes more money if you buy high-commission investments and insurance, and makes even more if you buy and sell often. Enter the fee-only financial planner. These folks get paid a flat fee, so their only motivation is to please the client. Some say that the best financial planner training is the one you get if a brokerage house hires you. Others recommend the two-year, $2,000 self-study course offered by the *College for Financial Planning: www.icfp.org; 800-945-IAFP. Institute of Certified Financial Planners: www.icsp.org; 3801 E. Florida Ave., Denver, CO 80231; 303-759-4900. National Association of Personal Financial Advisors: www.napfa.org; 355 W. Dundee Rd., Buffalo Grove, IL 60089; 888-FEE-ONLY.*

Credit Consultant. Like many addictions, overspending can devastate your life. Credit card debt and bankruptcies are at all-time highs, and couples argue more about money than anything else. As a result, a new profession, credit counselor, is emerging. You help people find ways to be happy without spending, develop a plan for reducing debt, and may even contact creditors to negotiate an easier-to-meet payment schedule. *Institute for Personal Finance: 3900 E. Camelback Rd., Phoenix, AZ 85018.*

(Neat Niche) **Commercial Debt Negotiator.** Many businesses accumulate too much debt. They hire you to negotiate with banks, collection agencies, and other creditors to accept a discount in exchange for immediate payment. You get clients by cold-calling businesses, or from bankers or collection agencies that refer customers having problems. Check to be sure that, in your state, it's legal to represent debtors in this way. *American Collectors' Association: www.collector.com; Box 39106, Minneapolis, MN 55439; 612-926-6547.*

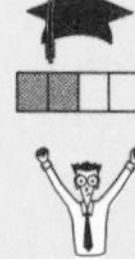

College Financial Aid Counselor. Guess how much it costs to send two kids to a name-brand private college for their bachelor's and master's degrees? $500,000! So, it's no surprise that frantic parents are flocking to financial aid counselors. These counselors function like tax accountants, helping you figure out how to plan and fill out the college and government forms to maximize your financial aid.

Done right, financial aid planning is an honorable profession, but there are many scams. Learn more from the *National Association of Student Financial Aid Administrators: www.nastaa.org; 1920 L St., N.W., Washington, DC 20036; 202-785-0453.*

BHB

Computer Tutor. Many of us would like to improve our computer skills. There's great demand for by-phone and in-person computer tutors. Get referrals from computer retailers. Or emulate the guerrilla marketer who got all the clients he wanted by standing in the parking lot in front of a major computer store, and every time he saw someone walking out with a new computer, gave his pitch, and made an appointment on the spot.

Work with People and Words

Public speaking

Radio/TV News Reporter. This is one of those long-shot glamour professions that may be worth the risk. You get to investigate fast-breaking stories and report your findings on the air. And with the thousands of local news broadcasts, it isn't absurd to think you could land a job, at least if you're willing to start out in a small market. Musts are good writing skills, a good memory, and an authoritative on-air presence. *Radio-Television News Directors Foundation: www.spj.org; 1000 Connecticut Ave., N.W., Washington, DC 20036; 202-659-6510. See also: www.tvjobs.com for a list of nationwide job openings in TV. Investigative Reporters and Editors, School of Journalism: 138 Neff Annex, Columbia, MO 65211; 573-882-2042.*

Professional Speaker. This is another fantasy career with reasonable prospects. Despite the plethora of electronic alternatives, people want to hear live speakers. A few thousand Americans, including some no-names, make a living spreading their gospel at conventions, college campuses, corporate headquarters, and general public forums. Even cruise ships are adding speakers to their menu of entertainment. Find a topic you are or can become expert in that would appeal to many people. Then read books such as *Speak and Grow Rich,* study tapes of great speakers, craft a solid outline, build in some multimedia, and practice, practice, practice until you're able to say something of real substance while making a powerful connection with your audience. Consider joining a local chapter of Toastmasters where you learn public speaking techniques and get to give talks to fellow members, a sympathetic audience. When you have a knock-your-socks-off sample videotape, send it everywhere — including lecture bureaus. They can help market you. *National Speakers Association: nsaspeakers.org; 1500 S. Priest Dr., Tempe, AZ 85281; 602-968-2552.*

(Neat Niche) **Speaking Coach.** Most of us are called on to "say a few words," whether it be at a staff meeting, a professional conference, or a toast at our child's wedding. If you're a good public speaker, why not teach others what you've learned. Market by giving talks on how to give a speech at professional conferences or at local corporations. Don't forget about law firms — they earn their living as smooth talkers.

OOH

BHB

Employee Trainer. The need for training has never been greater. More students graduate from high school and even college unable to read their diplomas at the same time the modern workplace requires them to be communication whizzes and techno-mavens. Even those who graduated college with enough skills soon find that they need to upgrade. A trainer's topic range is wide: from basic reading to advanced UNIX, peak performance to planning for retirement, database management to diversity management. A current challenge for trainers is how to make people in welfare-to-work programs employable in such demanding workplaces. *American Society for Training and Development: www.astd.org; 1640 King St., Alexandria, VA 22313; 800-628-2783 or 703-683-8100.*

(Neat Niche) **Software Trainer.** New software and new versions of old software continue to be released. Heaven forbid you should be saddled with Version 7.0 when Version 8.0 is available. As a trainer, it's a plus if you are certified by the software's manufacturer.

(Neat Niche) **Gender Equity/Sexual Harassment Trainer.** The field is burgeoning. You use techniques such as role-playing and controlled confrontation to help change attitudes and behavior.

(Neat Niche) **Internet Trainer.** The Three R's now have a Fourth: *R*etrieving information from the Net and other sources. *Information Technology Training Association: www.itta.org; 8400 N. MoPac Expressway, Austin, Texas 78759; 512-502-9300.*

(Neat Niche) **Specialty Trainer.** Train clients for those difficult-to-get-into fields to which many people aspire: rock star, talk show host, athlete, comedian, artist, sports, screenplay writer, voiceover artist, film director, Webmaster, for example.

OOH

Teacher. Here's how the Princeton Review Web site describes teaching: "Usually beginning at 8 a.m., teachers must begin the difficult task of generating interest in their often sleepy students. A good sense of humor and the ability to think like their students helps." Don't get seduced by 3 p.m. dismissal bells and summers off. Teaching today is no cushy gig. Schools now put everyone from the mentally challenged to the mentally gifted in the same class. It takes exceptional talent to develop no-snooze lessons for that wide a range of students, often including immigrant kids who may speak

Spanish, Chinese, or Tagalog, but little English. Also, teachers have far less power to remove children who chronically disrupt the class — and it only takes one. Students with severe behavior and emotional problems used to be placed in special classes. Now, except in the most extreme cases, they're mainstreamed. And new teachers, despite having the least experience, are often given the toughest classes. Now add the many hours after school preparing interesting yet valuable lessons, correcting papers, and dealing with parents who complain that Johnny's individual needs aren't being met. Finally, remember that teachers are with kids all day, so they don't get much intellectual stimulation. You need a special mentality to do that for 25 years. We paint this stark picture because we believe that teaching is among the very most important professions. That's the main reason it is on our list of cool careers. Because most public school teachers, after just two years, receive tenure for life, a bad teacher saddled by the golden handcuffs of job security, can be tempted to stay in the profession forever, damaging 30 kids at a time, year in and year out. So we want to encourage teachers to enter the profession with full knowledge of its realities. Too often, people decide to become teachers based on their own years as a student or on a rewarding experience as a one-to-one tutor. The experience of many of today's classroom teachers is quite different. *American Federation of Teachers: www.aft.org; 555 New Jersey Ave, N.W., Washington, DC 20001. See also: www.teacherjobs.com.*

(Neat Niche) **Program Specialist.** Elementary schools increasingly use specialists to visit classrooms to teach art, music, technology, or special education. This tends to be a rewarding job because you're the breath of fresh air in a student's humdrum day, and because you're able to focus on your specialty.

(Neat Niche) **English-as-a-Second-Language Teacher for Adults.** Immigration continues to jump. This increases the need for people to teach English as a second language. ESL teachers are hired by community colleges, adult schools, and by corporations for their immigrant employees. This career is often gratifying because most students are highly motivated. *See: www.ncbe.gwu.edu/links/biesl/index.html for links, and for job openings: www.bilingual-jobs.com.*

(Neat Niche) **Music or Art Teacher**. After years of decline, the schools are finally starting to hire more music and art teachers. A recent *New York Times* piece reported that education budgets throughout the country are showing restorations of money for art and music classes.

There's something wrong when the National Endowment for the Arts gives millions of dollars to a relative handful of artists who produce work that most of the public finds unappealing or even distasteful, and millions of schoolchildren receive little or no art instruction, something that can so enrich the lives even of non-artistic kids.

(Neat Niche) **Non-School-Based Teacher.** Theme parks, zoos, state and national parks hire teachers as guides and seminar leaders.

(Neat Niche) **Vocational/Technical Teacher.** Community colleges and post-secondary career colleges hire specialists to teach in fields such as technology repair, business education, agriculture, plumbing, and protective services.

(Neat Niche) **Distance-Learning Teacher.** People are less willing and able to show up Tuesdays and Thursdays from 7 to 9 p.m. for a college class. At the same time, technology is improving so that it's possible for you to sit in your living room and decide to start and stop a multimedia course whenever you like. *United States Distance Learning Association: www.usdla.org.*

School Administrator. You wouldn't think that turnover would be high among school principals. It's a prestigious job with an important mission. Yet turnover *is* high, and here's why: One of the principal's key roles is to evaluate teachers. Because public school teaching is completely unionized, the rules for evaluation are highly prescribed. Principals report that it typically takes two years of time-consuming, highly stressful, lawyer-filled effort to have even a chance of getting rid of an incompetent teacher, so most principals feel forced to look the other way, and instead, must take the flak from complaining parents and students. Another source of principals' stress is that many of today's principals must take on more tasks than in the past. For example, they're charged with establishing school-based drug/alcohol/crime prevention programs and developing partnerships with local businesses. Yet another demoralizer is salary. The very strong teachers' unions have gotten solid salary increases for teachers, but administrators' salaries have not kept pace, so that teacher salaries are now often nearly equal to principals'. The silver lining in all of this is that the job market for aspiring principals has never been better. And a principalship is a launching pad for often more-rewarding jobs as district or county school administrators. *American Association of School Administrators: www.aasa.org; 1801 N. Moore St., Arlington, VA 22209; 703-528-0700.*

College Student Affairs Administrator. This career has nothing to do with steamy dorm room flings. College student affairs administrators coordinate the non-academic part of student life, from student orientation to graduation. For example, they supervise the fraternities, coordinate intramural sports and residence hall activities, and sponsor anti-drug programs. *National Association of Student Personnel Administrators: www.naspa.org; 1875 Connecticut Ave., N.W., Washington, DC 20009; 202-265-7500.*

Employee Assistance Planner. Workers show up with more problems than they used to: drug abuse, violence-proneness, financial disarray, and need for elder care. Employee assistance planners coordinate programs to deal with these problems. On a more positive note, EAPs may establish physical fitness programs, sponsor workshops on time management or career planning, even arrange carpools. *Employee Assistance Professional Association: www.eap-association.com; 2101 Wilson Blvd., Arlington, VA 22201, 703-522-6272.*

Clergy. A clergyperson told me that the very thing I thought was most important in a cleric turns out not to be a requirement at all: She said that many clergy have serious doubts about the existence of God. They are, however, strongly committed to helping people live richer lives using religion as a foundation. Sometimes this help is direct: sermons, religious classes, and ministering to people at high and low points of their lives, but clergy also spend a surprising amount of time in indirect service: fundraising and administrative work. Except for the long hours and having to be on-call at all hours, the clergy is a wonderful profession: high status, reasonable pay, unmitigated do-gooding, and a good job market except for Protestant ministers (because their churches are merging). The situation is better for rabbis, and excellent for Catholic priests — lifetime celibacy is increasingly unpopular. Indeed, the Catholic Church has run full-page ads attempting to "collar" future priests. The first step toward investigating a career in the clergy: Speak with a clergyperson you respect, then contact the ordination organization for your denomination.

One-on-one

Speech-Language Pathologist. Think of how you feel when you listen to a stutterer. Imagine how he feels. The speech-language therapist treats stuttering and dozens of other voice and speaking problems, from cleft palate to limited vocabulary to stroke victims trying to recover their speech. This is yet another field that has made rapid advances in recent years. For example, not long ago, it was believed that stuttering came from psychological trauma. Now, scientists have found a brain anomaly in stutterers, and as a result, have developed more successful treatments. For a wide range of speech problems, speech therapists can now use computers to create custom exercises that the client can work on at home — the computer says a word, the patient repeats it, and the computer provides feedback. Cool. *American Speech-Language-Hearing Association: www.asha.org; 10801 Rockville Pike, Rockville, MD 20852; 301-897-5700. See also: www.rehaboptions.com.*

(Neat Niche) **Accent Reduction Specialist.** Many immigrants, especially those in professional jobs, are eager to improve their accents. You can help. To find clients, try contacting human resource departments at high-tech corporations. They often recruit from Asia to fill programmer, engineer, and scientist positions.

College Admission Consultant. "Which college should I go to?" "How do I get in?" "How do I find the money?" In high schools, college counselors typically help students answer these questions with individual counseling and group presentations. They may also get writer's cramp from cranking out all those student recommendations. In private practice, the work is one-on-one. As always, it's wise to specialize, for example, in students aiming for designer-label colleges or in students with learning problems. *National Association for College Admission Counseling: www.nacac.com; 1631 Prince St., Alexandria, VA 22314; 703-836-2222.*

(Neat Niche) **College-Bound Athlete Counselor.** Many high school students are pulled kicking and screaming into doing their college applications. Not so with college athletes. They may not care any more than their peers about the joys of learning, but they do care about playing ball. These motivated clients make your job fun. You help Bruiser figure out which colleges will let him play a lot and otherwise make him happy. You answer such questions as, Where are the best summer programs for high school athletes? How to best impress the college coaches? How to deal with recruiters? How to negotiate the best deal? You're like a junior Jerry McGuire: "Show me the scholarship!"

Academic Tutor/Learning Specialist. This is an unusually rewarding career. Many people find one-on-one tutoring rewarding and infer that they'd enjoy classroom teaching, only to find that it's a whole different ball game. The good news is that demand for tutors is virtually unlimited. Parents these days worry more than ever that schools aren't adequately educating their children. Tutoring often can help, and after-school chains such as Sylvan Learning, Score-Kaplan, and Kumon Math are growing faster than a kid packing his books when the bell rings. Because many kids prefer to be tutored in-home, tutors willing to make house calls and/or work by phone, fax, and e-mail should thrive. *The Complete Guide to Starting and Operating a Home Tutoring Business: 801-278-4324.*

Call yourself a learning specialist rather than a tutor. Tutor implies $10 an hour, learning specialist $50.

Home Schooling Consultant. With disenchantment with the public schools rising, over a half-million school children are now home schooled. But home schooling is no easy feat. As a consultant, you can help parents and children design their learning program and iron out problems. *National Homeschool Association: www/n-h-a.org; P. O. Box 290, Hartland, MI 48353.*

Adventure Travel Organizer. With Americans going back to nature in record numbers, this market is expanding. Hiking, bird watching, backpacking, and other forms of recreation have seen double-digit growth since the early '80s according to the United States Forest Service. And in our search for the exotic, markets are building for the likes of dog sledding, hang gliding, sky diving, and trips such as mountain climbing in the Himalayas,

BHB

and exploring Antarctica or the Brazilian jungle. We believe the market for general adventure travel is getting crowded, so nichecraft is particularly important here. *Adventure Travel Society: www.adventuretravel.com; 6551 S. Revere Pkwy., Englewood, CO 80111; 303-649-9016. See also: outside.starwave.com.*

(Neat Niche) **Social Activism Tour Operator.** Medea Benjamin's "Reality Tours" allows vacationers to picket Nike firms in Southeast Asia, witness elections in dicey democracies, and so on.

(Neat Niche) **Adventure-Spiced Meeting Organizer.** Jim Zuberbuhler runs Out There, which adds a short outdoor escapade to groups that want to include an adventure component in their meeting agenda. "We introduce 'perceived risk' into people's lives and put them into situations where tough choices must be made, providing them with very real moments of clarity."

(Neat Niche) **Spiritual Tour Operator.** Our search for meaning is extending beyond our work, relationships, and traditional religion, to such things as women's ritual retreats in the desert.

Police Detective. Jane is suspected of running a cocaine operation. You, ace detective, wearing plainclothes, might follow her around, examine bank accounts for clues, interview her associates, perhaps infiltrate her organization by pretending to be a prospective buyer, and then bust the sucker. This is one of the more rewarding but dangerous police gigs, and a plum reserved for top police officers. That's the problem: You gotta go through some years of some pretty tough duty as a cop before you get a shot at a detective position. Detective jobs are especially subject to affirmative action, so minorities' prospects are particularly enhanced here.

Mystery Shopper. How good is the food and service in each Red Lobster? Are NationsBank employees doing a good job of serving and selling customers? Are employees at Rite-Aid stealing merchandise? (Employees account for two-thirds of shoplifting.) Mystery shopper is one of *Entrepreneur* magazine's Top 10 Home Businesses. You send independent contractors to pose as customers in retail stores, restaurants, and banks. They then report on their experiences. There is a large unmet need for mystery shoppers. It is estimated that mystery shoppers are used by only 10 percent of businesses, government, and nonprofit organizations that would benefit from them.

Political Aide. Most politicians have paid aides. They research problems, draft legislation, and sub for the pol at rubber chicken dinners. This is a satisfying job: You actually have some power, and the work is varied and fast-paced. The usual route in is to start as an intern or campaign volunteer, ask for more responsibility, and prove yourself.

Lobbyist. You're a lobbyist for the National Abortion Rights League. There's a law you'd like passed that would allow young teens to have an abortion without parental permission. You may have actually drafted the legislation, and you certainly dug up research that proves the benefits of the legislation — for example, that the legislation would result in fewer teen moms, avoid unsafe abortions, and that the current prohibition is largely ignored anyway. You host a cocktail party for key legislators and just enough other folks to make your goal less obvious. You write press releases and try to get on TV and radio to expound your position. That's the life of a lobbyist: professional persuader of politicians. It's easier to land a lobbyist position for a corporate group than for a nonprofit one because, for example, more people would rather lobby for the National Abortion Rights League than for the Tobacco Institute. A law degree is a plus, but many lobbyists with just a bachelor's degree have worked their way up by starting as an intern or junior staffer for a lobbying group. These jobs are much like the sought-after jobs working for a senator or congressperson, but are easier to land. *American League of Lobbyists, Washington, DC: P.O. Box 30005, Alexandria, VA 22310; 703-960-3011.*

Work with People and Things

Polygraph Operator. Would you find it fun to make a living figuring out if people are lying? That's what polygraph (lie detector) operators do. Hook up your subject to a machine that monitors heart rate and brain waves. If things start spiking when you ask, "Did you murder your husband?", your subject may be a step closer to Ol' Sparky. Most polygraph operators work for law enforcement agencies, but polygraph tests are also used by attorneys to prove that their client is an upstanding citizen, and in pre-employment testing in sensitive industries such as health care and day care centers. You don't want your darling child to be cared for by a pedophile. *American Polygraph Association: www.polygraph.org; P.O. Box 8037, Chattanooga, TN 37414; 800-272-8037.*

We'd love it if someone developed a pocket-sized lie detector, and every time someone lied to you, it would beep. We'd pay a lot of money for one of those babies.

Occupational Therapist. You help a stroke patient relearn how to drive. You help find an alternative for an arthritis patient who can no longer button a shirt. You devise activities to rebuild dexterity and to remind patients of life's simpler pleasures. Using a combination of psychology, computers, braces, and a healthy dose of common sense, the occupational therapist is the practical soul who tries to put it all together. Bonus: Just a bachelor's degree in OT should do. The Department of Labor projects fast growth through 2006. *American Occupational Therapy Association: www.aota.org. See also: www.rehaboptions.com.*

Horticultural Therapist. These professionals know just how therapeutic plants and gardening can be, and they plan and implement gardening projects to help senior citizens and those with emotional and physical disabilities. This career usually pays less than dirt, is in less demand than an overripe tomato, but can be as rewarding as a garden of earthly delights. *American Horticultural Therapy Association: www.ahta.org; 362-A Christopher Ave., Gaithersburg, MD 20879; 301-948-3010.*

Funeral Director. Many people cringe at this profession, but the people in it are extraordinarily proud of their work. When you look beneath the surface, death care turns out to be a psychologically and financially rewarding career. Most of your work is with the survivor, not the deceased. When there's a death, a funeral director who can help family members make arrangements that feel right can be a real benefit in a time of need. Alas, too many funeral directors take that opportunity to sell $5,000 caskets when a $500 one would do: "You wouldn't want to be cheap with your mother, now would you?" Training is moderate (2–4 year college training program), rewards are great, and demand is growing thanks to aging baby boomers and because of the many funeral directors about to retire. Not a bad combination. Do us a favor, though — be sure to spend some time at a funeral home before deciding on this career.

Despite projected fast growth in this field, it is not easy to land a job. Because the field is financially and psychologically rewarding and training is relatively short, most people keep this business in the family. It may take a while to convince an employer that you're, pardon the expression, dying for the job. *National Funeral Director Association: www.nfda.org; 11121 W. Oklahoma Ave., Milwaukee, WI 53227; 800-228-6332. The American Board of Funeral Service Education: www.abfse.org; 13 Gurnet Rd., Suite 316, Brunswick, ME 04011; 207-798-5801. See also: www.funeralnet.com/classifieds/index.html.*

(Neat Niche) **Low-Cost Funeral Director.** A tasteful funeral service needn't require a second mortgage. Work with local memorial societies (groups that help find low-cost options for people) to create affordable options. To get the scoop on the profession from the consumer advocate's side: *Funeral & Memorial Societies of America: www.funerals.org/famsa; P.O. Box 10, Hinesburg, VT 05461; 802-482-3437.*

Mastectomy Lingerie Consultant. Many home-based businesses offer clients a one-on-one sensitivity that no big outfit can match. There's no better example than Rhonda Webb, who fits women who have had mastectomies with prosthetic breasts and special lingerie. Webb markets through surgeons and oncologists and meets clients in their own homes. She says, "People are very appreciative. It's so much more relaxed than walking into a cold department store with everyone hearing what your problem is."

Electro-Neurodiagnostic (END) Technician (formerly EEG Technician). END techs monitor brain waves. Why would you want to do that? In surgery, brain waves indicate how well the anesthesia is working. In a sleep clinic, they can help figure out what's causing a person's insomnia. Doctors use them to determine how well a medication is helping an epileptic. This is a cool career because, despite its important health care role, it can be learned on the job, and employment prospects are good. *American Society of Electroneurodiagnostic Technologists: www.aset.org; 204 W. 7th St., Carroll, IA 51401; 712-792-2978.*

Diagnostic Medical Sonographer. Commonly known as ultrasound technologists, these technicians perform sonograms to determine how a pregnant mom and baby are doing, as well as use newer techniques to evaluate a heart problem non-invasively, for example. *Society of Diagnostic Medical Sonographers: www.sdms.org; 12770 Coit Rd., Dallas, TX 75251; 972-239-7367.*

Low-Investment Food Operations Owner. Simple, limited- or no-seating food operations can be relatively low-risk routes to high income.

(Neat Niche) **Pizza by the Slice Business Owner.** Pizza never goes out of style, has a large markup, and is a relatively simple business. One secret to success is to open your shop within smelling distance of a busy walk-in entrance to a college campus. To keep rent costs down, we recommend a take-out operation with just a few seats. Also important: The pizza has to be to-die-for. Find an ever-crowded pizzeria that serves yumbo pizza that is located far enough from your proposed location so that the owner won't fear your competition. Ask the head pizza maker to teach you how to make it, and pay for your lessons if necessary.

(Neat Niche) **Drive-Through Coffee/Espresso House Owner.** Espresso-based drinks, such as cappuccino, are among the legal products with the highest markup. A cup of cappuccino costs about a dime to make and sells for two bucks, a 2,000 percent gross profit margin. And coffee and espresso aren't going out of style. Coffee bars have been a staple in Europe for centuries, and after a few years in this country, gourmet coffee drinking has not faded like a fad, but continues to grow. Franchises are available. *One example: Xpresso Drive Through Café: 1304 5th St., Golden, CO 80403; 303-215-0373 for franchise information.*

(Neat Niche) **Juice Bar Owner.** This is the new-millennium version of the malt shop, with yogurt/fruit/juice blended drinks or your basic fresh-squeezed fruit juices. High-markup, an easy-to-produce product, and one of *Entrepreneur's* Hot Picks.

(Neat Niche) **Soup Restaurant Owner.** Cheap, fast, low-calorie, high-profit margin, simple to make, likely to stay popular. And it's comfort food. It's another of *Entrepreneur's* Hot Picks.

(Neat Niche) **Food Cart Owner.** The most important thing about a food outlet is location. Subject to zoning restrictions, carts allow you to vary location so that you can be in front of a busy office building at lunch time, at the main exit of the local high school at 3 p.m., in front of a busy movie theater in the evening, and near the stadium on game days. Good candidates for cart-based businesses: sandwiches, soup, espresso, and pastries.

Parking Lot Oil Change Business Operator. Every car needs oil changes, and nearly every car owner finds getting them inconvenient. At best, you sit around at a while-you-wait oil change service. Otherwise, it's drop off the car, somehow get to work, and somehow get back to the shop. Instead, imagine that when you pull into a parking lot at work, in a shopping center, or at the airport, you can request an oil change done while your car is parked. Isn't that more convenient? What a business: big demand, large income potential, small investment, no extraordinary skills required, and no real competition. Just find a large parking lot owner who'd like a new profit center. Shouldn't be too tough. *The Automotive Oil Change Association: www.aoca.org; 12860 Hillcrest, Dallas, TX 75230; 800-331-0329.*

Curbside Address Number Painter. This requires no brains, minimal effort, and a total investment of $50. In night-time emergencies, it is difficult for police or ambulances to see street addresses. You are the solution. Buy a can of black and a can of white police-approved reflective paint, available at many major paint shops. Also buy six-inch stencils of the numbers 0–9. On a weekend, when people are more likely to be home, go door-to-door in a neighborhood with ample disposable income and offer to paint their address on the curb for $10. It takes you one minute. You can likely get ten customers per hour, a cool hundred bucks an hour. It's not a prestigious business, but it may be the fastest way to $100,000 a year, even if you have no talent or money to invest.

Personal Shopper. A career for those whose motto is "Shop 'til you drop." Formerly an extravagance of the idle rich too busy playing croquet to shop, now personal shoppers often serve the busy professional who has barely enough time for respiration. Get hired by upscale department stores. Recruit your own clients with ads in local publications that cater to busy professionals and by cross-promoting with hairdressers or image consultants.

Balloon Delivery Service. We like this business: minuscule start-up costs, makes everyone happy, and is mainly a night-and-weekend business, so you can keep your day job. Ask bakeries and supermarkets if you can put your brochures on the display case with the birthday/anniversary cakes to market your service. *Fooledya: www.fooledya.com/balloon.*

Work with Words and People

Librarian. If you picture a mousy bookworm, update your stereotype. Today's librarian is a cyberwhiz who's also social. This job increasingly focuses on helping patrons retrieve obscure information from the mountain of electronic and print resources. Librarians who specialize in medicine, other sciences, law, or engineering will make more money, but as the *AboutWork* Web site points out, "You're less likely to take home the books for a little casual relaxation." A bachelor's, and increasingly a master's, degree is required. *American Library Association Library Resources: www.ala.org; 50 E. Huron St., Chicago, IL 60611; 800-545-2433. American Society for Information Science: 8720 Georgia Ave., Silver Spring, MD 20910; 301-495-0900. Special Libraries Association: www.sla.org; 1700 18th St., N.W., Washington, DC 20009; 202-234-4700.*

(Neat Niche) **Cooperative Cataloger.** Today, a modem enables you to access information at any library in the world, so it helps if there's a unified cataloging system. Dozens of librarians are creating one. More are needed. For information: *Library of Congress: e-mail; dellapor@mail.loc.gov.*

(Neat Niche) **Private Librarian:** Hospitals, government agencies, prisons, magazines, TV and radio station news departments, corporations' and nonprofit organizations' research departments all have libraries. Would you have thought about a library at Revlon? The Brookings Institute think tank? The United States Air Force? *Newsweek* magazine? Most large law firms? They all hire librarians.

(Neat Niche) **Information Retriever.** We're already overwhelmed with information, and it's only going to get worse. Our savior is the information retriever (sometimes called information broker) who, for a fee, goes beyond what a librarian has time to do. Retrievers surf the Net and databases such as Dialog and Nexus, search print sources, phone interview the right people, and give you a digest of the best information. The information glut is so overwhelming that information brokers must specialize. Some non-obvious specializations are demographics and psychographics, patents, and competitive intelligence. In the latter, a company wants to develop a next-generation widget, so it hires an information broker to find out what other widget makers are doing. *Association of Independent Information Professionals: www.aiip.org; 234 W. Delaware Ave., Pennington, NJ 08534; 609-730-8759. See also: www.onlineinc.ocm/pempress/super/toc.htm for profiles.*

Foundation Grantmaker. Here, you make a career of giving away other people's money. Most large corporations and ultra-wealthy families set up foundations to give their billions to nonprofit organizations. But which organizations? Answering that question is your job. You develop guidelines and review proposals from hopeful applicants. These jobs are tough to get, requiring relentless networking. An MBA, especially with a specialization in foundation management, will help. This job may be worth the effort. *The Foundation Center: www.fdncenter.org; 79 5th Ave., New York, NY 10003; 800-424-9836. See also: www.foundation.org.*

Attorney. You're lousy at science and like to argue, so you go to law school, right? Catch this: 80 percent of lawyers wish they were doing something else. Seventy-five percent of attorneys recommend that their children not be lawyers. Despite these statistics and a reputation for sleaze matched only by politicians, armies of college graduates run off to law school seeking money, status, and a *Law and Order* wardrobe. It's a myth that law is an easy route to a six-figure income. The attorneys who make big bucks typically work 70-hour weeks — some corporate law firms buy futons for their offices so the lawyers can sleep there. And many attorneys don't make big money. Indeed, more and more lawyers are forced to work as powerless paralegals who often make no more than garbage collectors.

It's a myth that lawyers spend most of their time in a courtroom. Even litigators spend only a fraction of their time before a judge, and transactional attorneys, who draft agreements, spend little or no time in court. *American Bar Association: www.abanet.org; 750 N. Lake Shore Dr., Chicago, IL 60611; 800-621-6159. See also: attorneysatwork.com. For law jobs: www.lawjobs.com* and *www.legalemploy.com.*

There's money to be made in them there hills. Most lawyers choose to live in or near big cities, but there's plenty of need (well, plenty of desire) for lawyers in rural areas, and less competition. A small town is a good place to start and perhaps to stay.

(Neat Niche) **Patent Law.** When we think of patents, contraptions may come to mind, but today, patents often are awarded on such things as genes, computer chips, and genetically engineered mice. (Anti-biotech gadfly, Jeremy Rifkin, is attempting to patent a half human/half animal as a test case.) Companies usually patent a product as they *start* to develop it — otherwise, the risk of piracy is too great. The patent lawyer's job is to get that patent. The lawyer must understand both the science and the law to convince the United States Patent and Trademark Office that the new product will be truly different from existing products. So it's no surprise that most patent lawyers have a science or engineering background in addition to a law degree. Robert Benson, patent attorney at Human Genome Sciences loves his job. "In the lab, you can only do so much research work, but as a patent attorney you get to experience literally hundreds of lifetimes of research work." Note that patent law is a subspecialty of intellectual property law, a burgeoning field.

(Neat Niche) **Sports Agent.** Ever since Cuba Gooding yelled "Show me the money!" sports agents have gained a higher profile, not only among the public, but among pro athletes. Most sports agents now work for full-service sports management companies, such as ProServ, that help with everything from product endorsements to estate planning. *Sports Lawyers Association: 11250-8 Roger Bacon D., Reston, VA 20190; 703-437-4377. See also: www.onlinesports.com/pages/careerCenter.html.*

(Neat Niche) **Adoption Specialist.** How different this is from traditional adversarial lawyering — helping to match a child needing parents with parents wanting to adopt a child. A far cry from the other sort of family law: divorcing couples ready to kill each other over an armoire. *American Academy of Adoption Attorneys: www.adoptionattorneys.org; P.O. Box 33053, Washington, DC 20033; 202-832-2222.*

(Neat Niche) **Bankruptcy Lawyer.** Bankruptcies are at an all-time high and continue to skyrocket. And lawyers tell us that bankruptcy law is among the easier types of law to practice. The procedures are straightforward and minimally adversarial.

(Neat Niche) **Mediator/Arbitrator.** Many people and many contracts require mediation or arbitration of disputes. If you're an attorney who has tired of the adversarial nature of practicing law, this may be for you. Retired judges are often tapped because of their credibility, but background as a decent human being and having a calming personality may be as important. To succeed in this field, you must spend a lot of time marketing yourself to gatekeepers: accountants, therapists, and other attorneys. *American Arbitration Association Center for Mediation: www.adr.org; 213-383-7059. Alternative Dispute Resolution: www.adr.org.*

(Neat Niche) **Education Lawyer.** Johnny has gone through 12 years of schooling and still can't read. Who's responsible? Many parents are claiming that the schools should be and are hiring lawyers to file big-dollar lawsuits against school districts. Education lawyers, of course, also defend school districts against these and other claims. A typical case may involve a teacher who was fired for incompetence and claims that due process was violated, or a child who falls off a schoolyard play structure whose parent claims inadequate supervision. *Education Law Association: www.educationlaw.org; 818 Miriam Hall, 300 College Park, Dayton, OH 45469; 937-229-3589.*

(Neat Niche) **Termination Prevention Program Developer.** Courts increasingly find that the lack of a formal termination prevention program is evidence of a hostile workplace for minorities and women. So, companies are scrambling to develop such plans. Wanna help?

(Neat Niche) **Space Lawyer.** As more and more satellites fill the ionosphere, disputes arise. If a satellite above Azerbaijan transmits information to Kuala Lumpur, what rights to the data does a student in Peoria have? Does a country have the right to launch a Star Wars satellite that circles the globe? And looking further, who owns which rights to the moon? Who's responsible for space pollution? What laws can enforce cleanup? They're already selling tickets for commercial space flights. What sorts of contracts are needed to protect the spacelines and the passengers? Space law is, as they used to say in the '60s, a new frontier. *American Bar Association Forum on Space Law: www.abanet.org/forums/airspace; 750 N. Lake Shore Dr., Chicago, IL 60611; 312-988-5000.*

(Neat Niche) **Elder Lawyer.** Family members or nursing home staff, exhausted from caring for senile, incontinent patients, often commit elder abuse: leaving old people unturned so they develop bedsores, or tied down with restraints for the staff's convenience. Lawyers who specialize in elder law argue over whether there's legal liability. *National Academy of Elder Law: www.naela.org; 1604 N. Country Club Rd., Tucson, AZ 85716; 520-881-4005.*

(Neat Niche) **Franchise Lawyer.** The public is attracted to franchises — paint-by-numbers businesses; they are growing at 10 percent a year. Too often, though, the paint quickly begins to fade. Franchisees complain that the promised extensive training turned out to be a quickie, or that the foolproof method wasn't. Of course, for every plaintiff's attorney, there's a defense counterpart, so there's plenty of work to go around. *Franchise Consultants International Association: 3820 Premier Ave., Memphis, TN 38118; 901-368-3877. See also: www.franchise.org.*

(Neat Niche) **Environmental Lawyer.** No one wants to despoil the earth, but companies and government regulators have different ideas of how much despoiling is avoidable. A company may argue for a pollution control system that can get 90 percent pollution control with a system that costs $50,000. The government may insist on 98 percent control, even if that costs the company $100,000. Environmental lawyers argue both sides. Also, even within the government, there's confusion as federal, state, and local regulations often contradict each other. Plenty of fodder for environmental lawyers. *Environmental Law Institute: www.eli.org; 1616 P St., N.W., Washington, DC 20036; 202-939-3800. See also: www.eco.org; www.environmental-jobs.com;* and *www.princeton.edu/~oa/careeroe.html.*

Administrative Law Judge. This is a relatively easy way to become a judge. The difference from the more familiar judges is that administrative law judges rule on the laws and regulations of a public agency, and the process is more informal. Typical role: A school district offers a child with learning difficulties a special class plus speech therapy, but the parents want the district to pay for a special private school. An adminstrative law judge decides. *Association of Administrative Law Judges: www.aalj.org; c/o Joel Elliott, 522 S.W. 5th Ave., Portland, OR 97204; 503-326-3279. The Administrative Law Judge Handbook: An Insiders Guide to Becoming a Federal Administrative Law Judge: To order call 800-296-9611.*

Hearing Officer. You may not need to be a lawyer. A person denied a welfare claim has due process rights, one of which is the right to plead the case before a hearing officer.

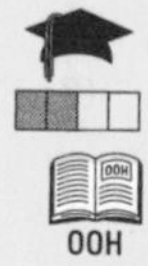

Journalist. Like a career in acting or film directing, journalism is one of those job aspirations likely to result in poverty. I was on a top floor of the Time-Life Building talking with four editors from one of Time-Warner's major magazines, and everyone agreed how obscene it was that colleges continue to welcome more and more journalism majors even though the vast majority will never earn even a subsistence living in the field. So why is journalism on our list of cool careers? Because it's so rewarding and enjoyable that it's worth considering if you love digging up information, interviewing, and cranking out simple, clear prose rapid-fire. To increase your chances of landing a job, specialize — science, technology, and education reporters may have an edge. No matter your specialty, be sure you are a whiz at surfing through many databases to find needed information. *American Society of Journalists and Authors: www.asja.org; 1501 Broadway, New York, NY 10036; 212-997-0947. See also: www.newslink.org/joblink.html.*

(Neat Niche) **Digital Journalist.** Many writers are techno-timid, yet much of the growth in publishing is in online publications. So learn to pepper your writing with sound bites, video clips, and links to Internet sites (we recommend learning HTML). Bradley Richardson, author of *JobSmarts* reports that at a recent journalists' conference, a speaker from Knight-Ridder said that the largest employer of journalists in the next year will not be a newspaper or even a publisher. It will be Microsoft. Microsoft is hiring writers for its many Web offerings. Send clips and story/column ideas to the big cheese listed at a target site.

(Neat Niche) **TV Newswriter.** You write the words that those public-idolized puppets called TV news anchors read, down to the transitions between one story and the next. You have to write very concisely and with edge, and be assiduous about checking your facts.

(Neat Niche) **Computer-Assisted Reporting Specialist.** You use databases plus the Internet to help other reporters get that compelling statistic or statement that contradicts what the politician said.

Book/Magazine/Web Site Editor. Some cool jobs exist here, but get ready for a long, low-paying road, especially in the struggling book industry (except for IDG Books). The fun part is finding great projects, convincing your editorial/publication board to say yes, and then helping the author to mold it into something wonderful and salable. But getting the first job is tough, and it's usually low paying with long hours. If you insist on the book business, consider moving to the Big Apple, which has 90 percent of the business. One possible starting place is as an agent's assistant. You read lots of unsolicited submissions (called the slush pile), and make connections with editors. Scan the acknowledgments in recent books to find beloved agents. In magazines, try to get a first job as a fact-checker or researcher. Whether seeking a book or magazine editorship, it's a plus if you're a subject matter expert. Health care background? Try a health care publisher. Former chef? Pester editors in charge of cookbooks. *American Society of Magazine Editors: 919 3rd Ave., New York, NY 10022; 212-872-3700. For Web site jobs, e-mail Web site editors-in-chief. Their addresses are often listed at the site.*

Family Historian/Biographer. How many parents ask their college student, "What in the world are you going to do with a degree in history?" Well, tell your parents about Martha Webb. Her consulting firm, Making History, produces custom-ordered family histories. It has grown from a one-woman, one-room shop to a staff of five that fills four rooms. We're not surprised that she's successful. Most of us are egocentric. Deep down, we'd love to have a book written about us. How do you turn that into a business? You can contact famous people who are in real or psychological need of a boost. Offer to write their biography. When they agree, write a book proposal and find a literary agent to peddle it for you. Also, just plain folks may want their stories recorded as personal legacies for future generations. Or someone may like a biography of his aging parent or a volume that tells his family history. Simply place ads in upscale community newspapers or market through reunion planners. Videobiography is a variation on this theme. A video can include people, places, photos, films, heirlooms, and other precious moments that capture the story. *Association of Personal Historians: www.PersonalHistorians.com.*

Anthropologist. Many people think of anthropology — the study of man's physical, cultural, and social development — as a fast route to underemployment, but there are neat niches. *American Anthropological Association: www.ameranthassn.org; 4350 N. Fairfax Dr., Arlington, VA 22203; 703-528-1902.*

(Neat Niche) **Medical Anthropologist.** The AIDS epidemic and the low safe-sex rates in some communities has resulted in an increase in demand for anthropologists to try to figure out why. *Society for Medical Anthropology: www.ameranthassn.org/sma.htm.*

(Neat Niche) **Corporate Anthropologist.** You conduct focus groups to discover consumer wants undetectable by statistical or survey methods.

(Neat Niche) **Housing Anthropologist.** Working with urban planners, you help to develop housing projects that are less likely to become infested with crime and drugs.

Foreign Service Officer. Imagine working in the United States embassy or consulate in one of 250 foreign countries. (The government's choice! Bosnia or Indonesia, anyone?) Your job may include keeping abreast of political and economic conditions so that you can brief United States policy makers, or provide advice to United States firms doing business in your resident country. Or you may arrange cocktail parties with business and political leaders and the public of your host country to enhance relations between the two nations. An entry-level job may have you helping some American schnook who lost a passport. A cool career, but here's the rub: It sounds cool to too many people. Every year, there are 200 foreign service openings. Guess how many people apply? 10,000. Better be a good reader and writer. *U.S. Dept. of State, Foreign Service Recruitment Division: www.state.gov; Box 9317, Arlington, VA 22219; 703-875-7490. Executive Council on Foreign Diplomacy: 818 Connecticut Ave., N.W., Washington, DC 20006; 202-466-5199.*

Foreign Language Interpreter or Translator. If you're fully bilingual, this is a pretty easy job: Just repeat what you heard or read. And the field is booming. Membership in the American Translators Association has grown 40 percent in the past five years. Asian companies setting up shop in the U.S.; U.S. firms importing Asian scientists, engineers, and computer programmers; and increased numbers of immigrants in the court and medical systems are factors contributing to the increased need for translators. Most in-demand languages are Spanish, Russian, Japanese, Arabic, Chinese, French, and German. Good money is possible if you specialize. Medical, legal, and engineering interpreting are your best bets. No matter your niche, it helps if you're not just bilingual but bicultural. Understanding both cultures enables you to translate the nuances. The largest employer of interpreters and translators is the federal government. Other large employers are the United Nations and the Organization of American States. *American Translators Association: www.atanet.org; 1800 Diagonal Rd., Alexandria, VA 22314; 703-683-6100.*

(Neat Niche) **Translation.** Instead of the spoken word, you translate written text. Translating written material is less stressful because you have time to think, or heaven forbid, look up a word in the dictionary. Plus, the work hours are more normal. Interpreters have to attend events wherever or whenever they occur.

College Teacher. There are many upsides. There's the joy of creating knowledge and the opportunity to help others acquire it through your classes, advising, writings, and professional presentations. You have intelligent, civilized (usually) colleagues, and after a few years, tenure for life. After tenure, your workload is modest. If you're working hard, it's because you choose to. Plus, you get to work in one of the most beautiful work environments: a college campus. But there are downsides. More and more students are utterly unqualified to do college work and unwilling to work hard, yet routinely complain about too-hard grading if they get a C. (See the eye-opening book, *Generation X Goes to College,* by Pulitzer prize nominee, Peter Sacks.) Despite students' virtual illiteracy, professors usually need a doctorate, except at two-year colleges, which takes an average of 6–12 post-bachelor's years to complete, depending on the field. Does tenure sound good? Be aware that colleges increasingly hire part-timers and temp faculty. Prospects for a full-time job are best in engineering, business, and computer science.

Colleges are among the first to proclaim the importance of treating labor fairly, yet they're a leader in hiring part-timers to avoid paying employee benefits.

There's often pressure to publish journal articles when you'd rather be teaching. Ernest Boyer, former vice president of the Carnegie Foundation for the Advancement of Teaching wrote, "Winning the campus teaching award is often the kiss of death for promotion and tenure." A final minus: On many campuses, there is pressure to be politically correct — to assign certain types of readings, express certain views, and even to pass students of certain races, even if you believe their work does not justify a passing grade. *American Association of University Professors: www.aaup.org; 1012 14th St., N.W., Washington, DC 20005; 202-737-5900. See also: www.chronicle.com* and *www.apnjobs.com.*

Thesis Completion Consultant. Many graduate students get close to finishing their degree but drop out because they have trouble doing their thesis. You can help. You might help develop the questions to be addressed, plan the structure and analysis, or review a draft. *A useful newsletter is Thesis News: www.asgs.org; 702-831-1399.*

Grant Proposal Writer. Every year, state and federal governments issue thousands of requests for proposals for every imaginable product and service. They may request proposals for 50,000 Navy uniforms, a state-of-the-art English-as-a-Second-Language program, or 300 desks for IRS offices. Organizations hire grant proposal writers to maximize their chances of winning the contract. There is strong demand for proposal writers who can specialize in agriculture, communication, energy, business, education, or space exploration, for example. To become a self-employed proposal writer, try reading the *Commerce Business Daily* to find proposals you'd like to write, contact companies or nonprofit organizations that might want to bid on it, and offer to write the proposal. *The Grantsmanship Center: www.tgci.com; P.O. Box 17220, Los Angeles, CA 90017; 213-482-9860.*

Regulation Compliance Consultant. When a law or regulation changes, it usually means an opportunity for entrepreneurs. For example, North Carolina recently decided to require all high school students to take an earth science course. Well, many of the state's teachers had never taught earth science, so an entrepreneurial woman contacted the state's education department and got to provide earth science training workshops for teachers all across North Carolina. Every time you read a newspaper and hear of a new law or regulation, ask yourself if that creates an opportunity for you.

Work with Data and People

Audiologist. A master's-level job with doctor-level prestige. Plus, the field's terrific new tools make you look like a miracle worker. For example, new hearing aids enable the user to amplify only those frequencies with a hearing loss. Even more impressive, a new hearing aid mimics our natural ability to block out background noise and zero-in on specific sounds. For the self-conscious, some new hearing aids are so tiny that everything fits into your ear canal except the gizmo you pull it out with. The nation's most famous user is Bill Clinton. Many audiologists get out of the office, and spend part of each week in hospitals, rehab centers, and special schools. Oh, there's one part of audiology that isn't prestigious: You spend a fair amount of time removing ear wax. *American Academy of Audiology: www.audiology.com; 8201 Greensboro Drive, McLean, VA 22102; 800-AAA-2336.*

College Financial Aid Officer. At most colleges, more than half the students apply for financial aid. With only so much money to distribute, your job is to distribute it equitably and to mollify or negotiate with students who got less than they had hoped for. It's a nice job because it feels good to allocate money, there are enough breather periods between crunch times, you only need a bachelor's degree, and you get to work on a college campus — one of the nicer work environments. *National Association of Student Financial Aid Administrators: www.finanaid.org; 1920 L St., N.W., Washington, DC 20036; 202-785-0453.*

Systems Analyst. What's the best way to enable a traveling salesperson to connect with the company's databases? How can a computer system enable all the employees, suppliers, and vendors to know the status of each order? How can three different computer systems talk with each other? The systems analyst, working with programmers and managers, develops the blueprint for creating computer-based solutions to problems like these. Knowledge of programming, networking hardware, and software is usually required. The Department of Labor projects this to be among the three fastest-growing occupations through 2006. *Association for Systems Management: www.infoanalytic.com/asm/in; P.O. Box 38370, Cleveland, OH 44138.*

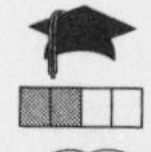

Software Designer/Manager. You lead the team in developing the software design and then coordinate its completion. This rewarding job is perfect for someone who is second-best in everything: programming, managing, art, and marketing. Not surprisingly, managers for Web site development projects are particularly in demand. Contact local Internet service providers (ISPs) and ask them to farm out Web site development work to you. *Internet Professional Publishers Association: www.ippa.org. See also: www.webpro.org; alt.webedit; www.websitebuilder.com; www.wdda.org; and for job openings: www.computerworld.com.*

Operations Research Analyst. One way the United States manages to stay competitive in this global economy is its ability to create efficient production systems. The operations research analyst, a practically-oriented math whiz, is one of the brains behind it all. She may, for example, help the Green Giant figure out how much corn he should plant and when to plant it. A master's is generally required. *Operations Research Society of America: www.informs.org.*

Purchasing Agent. How'd you like to get paid for shopping? Well, it's not quite like at the mall. Purchasing agents do the shopping for companies and government agencies. The jobs that pay well require you to know lots of details about government regulations and product specifications. Of course, it doesn't hurt to have a good instinct for when it is and isn't worth going after a bargain. *National Association of Purchasing Management: www.napm.org; P.O. Box 22160, Tempe, AZ 85285; 800-888-6276. American Purchasing Society: www.american-purchasing.com; 30 W. Downer Pl., Aurora, IL 60506. See also: www.catalog.com/napmsv/jobs.htm.*

Accountant. Not long ago, accountants were just bean counters looking at where money came from and went to. Now, these financial physicians are often asked to look forward. They are involved in decisions about developing new products, raising capital, and even structuring the company. The old stereotype of the accountant as a mumbling recluse no longer holds. If an accountant wants to do more than count beans, he must be a good communicator, often of bad news: "No, you can't deduct that. No, you calculated that incorrectly. No, that is inadequate documentation." That naysayer role is one of the field's biggest downsides. The Big Six firms offer terrific training and challenging if exhausting assignments. These are good jobs, but they're tough to get. Who are the Big Six? KPMG-Peat Marwick, Price Waterhouse, Arthur Anderson, Deloitte & Touche, Ernst & Young, and Coopers & Lybrand. *American Accounting Association: www.rutgers.edu/accounting/raw/aaa; 5717 Bessie Dr., Sarasota, FL 33423; 941-921-7747. American Association of Finance and Accounting: www.aafa.com. American Institute of Certified Public Accountants: www.aicpa.org; 1211 Avenue of the Americas, New York, NY 10036; 212-596-6200. See also: www.accountingnet.com;www.accountingjobs.com;* and *www.financialjobs.com.*

(Neat Niche) **Investigative Accountant.** According to *U.S. News and World Report,* number crunchers are now frequently called in by law firms, government agencies, and corporations to sniff out such indiscretions as phony insurance claims and improper security trading. The Big Six firms alone hire hundreds of forensic accountants each year, and so does the FBI, for example, to investigate the finances of Joey the Blade's cement business. *The Association of Certified Fraud Examiners: www.acfe.org; 716 West Avenue, Austin, TX 78701; 800-245-3321.*

(Neat Niche) **Business Valuator.** Every day, companies merge. You wonder whether eventually there will be a grand total of one company. Every one of those mergers and acquisitions requires someone to figure out the value of the company being merged or acquired. These high stakes mean big bucks for you. Business valuators are also used when wealthy people get divorced or die to determine the real value of wifey's business or hubby's stock options. *Institute of Business Appraisers: www.instbusapp.org; P.O. Box 1447, Boynton Beach, FL 33425; 561-732-3202.*

(Neat Niche) **International Accountant.** The previously closed economies in Eastern Europe and Latin America are open. The North American Free Trade Agreement (NAFTA) and General Agreement on Tariffs and Trade (GATT) have eliminated trade restrictions. As a result, companies are crying, "Find me an international accountant!" Say an American company does business in Beijing. Which accounting and tax laws and principles apply? As the accountant, you would answer these questions. It sure helps if you speak the language.

(Neat Niche) **Health Care Accountant.** When you have an operation, the cost depends on the answers to these questions: Are you on Medicare? Do you have private insurance? Which company? Are you a low-income patient? Not poor and paying your own way? (You pay more.) Not only is there not one price, there isn't one payer — a single surgery often gets paid for by multiple sources: the government, an insurance company, the patient, and sometimes after all that, the hospital has to eat some of it. The health care accountant keeps track of the entire mess.

(Neat Niche) **Environmental Accountant.** As environmentalism has become religion, most government agencies now use environmental accountants to argue that the environmental damages caused by a company outweigh the benefits. And many companies — especially utilities, manufacturers, and chemical companies — hire other environmental accounts to prove that the benefits of production outweigh the liabilities — or simply to comply with the regulations. CPAs who are engineers are in particularly great demand. *See: www.eco.org; www.environmental-jobs.com;* and *www.princeton.edu/~oa/careeroe.html for job openings.*

(Neat Niche) **Management Consulting.** CPAs (accountants who have passed rigorous exams) are frequently called in on a consulting basis, perhaps to computerize a company's accounting function, project a company's growth, facilitate a merger or acquisition, or provide general advice on how to improve operating procedures. The Big Six accounting firms are dominant here.

Investment Banker. Business's growth hormone is money. The investment bankers' job is to get it on the best terms. Are you willing to work into the wee hours and do lots of traveling to get a company the best deal on the money? You don't raise the dough by calling a few banks and saying, "Hi, will you lend us some money?" Here's how investment bankers work: A growing small private company needs more money. Should it go public? Issue bonds? Spin off a division? You do complex calculations (stochastic differential equations and derivations of models like Black-Scholes, words that have absolutely no meaning to us), to help the company come up with the answer. Let's say the company decides to go public and issue stock. You attempt to price it right and then convince banks, mutual fund and pension fund managers to buy millions of dollars of your stock or bond offering. To sell requires much more than a slick tongue, but that helps. You start with a bachelor's as a holding analyst and usually need an MBA before you make the big bucks. *Institute of Financial Education: www.the institute.com; 55 W. Monroe St., Chicago, IL 60603; 800-946-0488. See also www.cob.ohio-state.edu/~fin/jobs/ib2.htm#Link5 for links; www.mbacentral.com; www.mbanetwork.com/meca;* and *www.mbajob for job openings.*

Many people, in part thanks to movies like *Bonfire of the Vanities,* believe that investment bankers do absolutely nothing for the world. The reality is that their job is to help companies raise money so that they can bring a better product to market. Even media-reviled investment banker Michael Milken, by raising money for MCI as investment banker, was key to making the telecommunications industry more competitive, and in turn, lowering all our phone bills. Before deregulation, you were paying 40 cents per long-distance minute. Now, for example, ITD Corp offers long-distance service for just a nickel a minute, an 87 percent savings. Thank an investment banker.

Business Loan Broker. This is a simpler version of an investment banker. Most businesses occasionally must borrow money. Your job is to find it for them. Your sources can include the "capital available" ads in publications ranging from *The Wall Street Journal* to your local newspaper, as well as local banks, finance companies, and the Small Business Administration. Tyler Hicks, author of *199 Great Home Businesses You Can Start (and Succeed in) for Under $1,000,* recommends finding borrowers through classified ads in the "business services" section of your local paper or by directly contacting companies and saying, "I have money available. $10,000 and up." Hicks claims that "Would-be borrowers will break down your door once word spreads."

All businesses, but especially this one, must have business liability insurance. Every so often, a small business in need of money may see you as a source and sue you if things don't go just right.

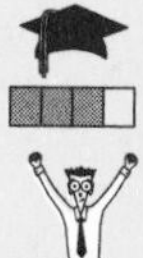

Venture Capitalist. This job involves looking for budding businesses to invest in, usually in computers or biotech. Some of the best investment ideas are discussed at a bar or on the golf course, so it doesn't hurt to be a schmoozer. But if you're not, try contacting CEOs of organizations that have obtained venture capital. They often know of other worthy businesses in need of capital. After you find a prospect, you need the MBA-level quantitative skills to assess the business's future value. But just as important, you need a nose for judging people because a business succeeds or fails as much on its people as on its product. Once you're convinced that a business is worth investing in, you need the ability to convince investors. *National Venture Capital Association: www.nvca.org; 1655 N. Fort Myer Drive, Arlington, VA 22209; 703-524-2549. Institute of Certified Business Counselors: www.nvst.com; 3485 W. 1st Ave., Eugene, OR 97402; 541-345-8064.*

Work with Data, People, and Words

Sports Information Director. The public is mad for information about their team, and you're happy to give it to them. After all, it helps fill the seats. Your job is to create and distribute information to the media and to field their questions. You get great seats to the big game, your working environment is ideal, and you're closer to the team than anyone but the coaches. *College Sports Information Directors of America: Campus Box 114A, Texas A&M University, Kingsville, TX 78363.*

Program Evaluator. "You're judgmental!" That's usually an epithet, but in this profession, you're paid to be judgmental. Typical scenario: You're hired to evaluate an innovation like a new program aimed at improving an inner-city school district's reading performance. You interview students and teachers in the program, look at test scores compared with a control group, and write a report of your findings. It's fun being an evaluator because you get to check out lots of innovative programs, see what works and what doesn't, and make recommendations for improvement. The bad part is that many program sponsors don't really want your input; they've hired you mainly to meet a government requirement. After all, few people like to be told what to change. A master's or doctorate degree filled with statistics courses is usually the admission ticket to the profession, but the fact is, program evaluators rarely use statistics beyond what you'd learn in that intro to stats class that many undergrads take as a less-taxing way to satisfy their college's math requirement. *American Evaluation Association: www.eval.org; 401 E. Jefferson St., Rockville, MD 20850; 301-251-7700.*

(Neat Niche) **Web Site Evaluator**. It seems like there are more Web sites than grains of sand. How do you know which sites are best in class? To help separate the wheat from the chaff, evaluation services such as *www.lycos.com* give awards to top sites.

Sanitarian/Occupational and Environmental Hygienist. "No you can't have a coffee cart at the county fair. The milk wouldn't stay fresh." "No, your factory's wastewater disposal system does not meet state standards." "No, the paint in your tenant's apartment will not work — too much lead." Sanitarians are hired by government agencies to say no, and yes, so that our food, water, air, and housing are as healthy as possible. Any science bachelor's degree will do, but preferred is a master's or certification by the *National Environmental Health Association: 720 S. Colorado Blvd., South Tower, Denver, CO 80246. American Industrial Hygiene Association: www.aiha.org; 2700 Prosperity Ave., Fairfax, VA 22031; 703-849-8888. American Conference of Governmental Industrial Hygienists: 1330 Kemper Meadow Dr., Cincinnati, OH 45240; 513-742-2020.*

City Manager. You're involved in all aspects of running a city, from distributing the budget to overseeing park renovation to hiring key personnel. City managers are among the more powerful government officials who don't have to run for election. A masters in public administration is usually required. *International City/County Management Association: www.icma.org; 777 N. Capitol St., N.E., Washington, DC 20002; 202-289-4262. American Society for Public Administration: www.aspanet.org; 1120 G St., N.W., Washington, DC 20005; 202-393-7878.*

Health Care Administrator. What's a health care system to do? Technology is advancing, health care laws changing, HMOs squeezing, population aging, hospitals closing, stand-alone clinics opening, home health care exploding. Answer: Hire more health care administrators to make sense of the madness. But with increased pressure for cost-control, the number of administrators is not growing. Yes, you can probably land a job with a master's in health administration from one of the 67 accredited programs, but who gets hired first? Doctors with MBAs. It's a good option for the doctor who's had enough patient care and is tired of fighting with HMOs and Medicare to get reimbursed. A recent *Newsweek* article touts the University of California, Irvine, MBA in health care management. An often faster but more expensive approach is the University of Phoenix's online MBA. Job prospects are best in home health agencies and group medical practices. *American College of Health Care Executives: www.ache.org; 1 N. Franklin St., Chicago, IL 60606; 312-424-2800.*

(Neat Niche) **Public Health Administrator.** Working for a government agency, you might coordinate health care programs for the poor, direct a safe-sex campaign, or administer vaccination programs.

(Neat Niche) **Alternative Health Care Administrator.** Health insurers increasingly are covering treatments such as acupuncture and chiropractic but have little experience in evaluating these treatments, identifying qualified providers, or establishing reasonable compensation. That's your job.

Marketer. Your company wants to introduce a product — let's say a piece of edutainment software for teenagers. You review the competition to identify a need. Then, with that general product in mind, you review demographic and psychographic data to find the market segments most likely to buy it. You conduct surveys and focus groups of your target market to see what features they want. You help select packaging and a marketing message that appeals to your target market, and finally, you select the approaches that best get the message out from among radio, TV, direct mail, or the Internet. Demand is great for marketers with technical knowledge — it's easier to develop a marketing campaign for a circuit board if you're an engineer. A bachelor's degree is generally enough, and you needn't major in marketing, but an internship helps land a good job. If you want to be a self-employed marketing consultant, the key, as always, is to carve out a tiny but in-demand niche — for example, showing shopping malls how to set up promotions to bring customers to the mall. *American Marketing Association: www.ama.org; 250 S. Wacker Dr., Chicago, IL 60606; 312-648-0536. See also: www.dmworld.com.*

(Neat Niche) **Online Marketer.** Every Web site wants traffic. Your job is to get it there. Submit the site in the right way to the search engines, conduct e-mail direct marketing campaigns, arrange link exchanges (I'll insert a link to your site if you'll insert a link to mine), make submissions to newsgroups, do cross-advertising on related sites, plus traditional advertising and public relations campaigns. A direct-marketing background is good preparation. Visit these sites and learn a lot and you'll probably find an enormous job market open to you. *The Internet Marketing Association: www.intermarketing.com. Wilson Internet Services (links to resources on Web-based marketing): www.wilsonweb.com. See also: www.ep.com/faq/webannounce.html and the book* NetMarketing, *online: www.ypn.com.*

(Neat Niche) **Focus Group Leader.** A key step in developing a product is to ask a group of people about it. In today's jargon, that's called a focus group. Often, a focus group is simply a structured discussion, but it can be much more sophisticated. For example, before President Clinton gives a speech, he reads a draft to a private audience of citizens carefully selected to be representative of the public audience. Each guinea pig has a dial that he or she can turn from 0 (I hate it) to 10 (I love it). They continually adjust the dial as he speaks. President Clinton can then use only the material that gets a high average rating. The focus group leader runs the proceedings and writes up the results.

(Neat Niche) **Social Marketer.** The same techniques that Madison Avenue uses to convince you to buy a brand of cigarettes, social marketers use to get you to live more wisely. For example, the U.S. government now spends $200 million each year on prime-time commercials, mainly to spread anti-drug or anti-cigarette messages. It's the flip side of product marketing: You're trying to build market share of *non*-use.

How can the same government that sponsors anti-smoking campaigns subsidize tobacco growers?

(Neat Niche) **Film Marketer.** There's plenty to market: getting the domestic movie houses to rent the film and the filmgoers to see it. Then you have overseas, cable and network TV, and, of course videocassette markets. Next, there are the airlines, so we don't get bored on those transcontinental flights. And we're not done yet. We can't forget about the T-shirts and baseball caps, now can we? *American Film Marketing Association: www.afma.org; 10850 Wilshire Blvd., Los Angeles, CA 90024; 310-446-1000. See also: www.hollywoodreporter.com2/index and www.showbizjobs.com for job openings.*

(Neat Niche) **Seminar Promoter.** One of the best ways to market a service is to offer a free or low-cost seminar: Potential customers get to see the service in action, and at the end of the seminar, when they're maximally excited, you can sign them up for the service. Also, even if they don't sign up, you've acquired a valuable mailing list for future solicitations. The key, of course, is getting as many people to your seminar as possible. Often, people with the skills to put on the seminar don't know how to get people to show up. The seminar promoter does, using a combination of well-placed ads, flyers, press releases, and direct mailings. *International Special Events Society: www.ises.com; 9202 N. Meridian St., Indianapolis, IN 46260; 800-688-4737.*

(Neat Niche) **Special Events Marketer.** Every sporting event, multicultural festival, and on-campus lecture series needs to be promoted lest there be an event and no one shows. It's more fun than the usual marketing because you're marketing a special event rather than a widget. *International Special Events Society: www.ises.com; 9202 N. Meridian St., Indianapolis, IN 46260; 800-688-4737 or 317-571-5601.*

(Neat Niche) **Marketing Researcher.** Your job is to design surveys to collect needed information. In addition to in-house marketing departments, you can work for independent polling organizations. Biggies include Yankelovich, Gallup, Field, Harris, and Roper Starch. *Marketing Research Association: www.mra-net.org; 1344 Silas Deane Hwy., Rocky Hill, CT 06067; 860-257-4008.*

BHB

Export Agent. Nearly any manufacturer wants to expand its market, but few know the ins and outs of exporting: how to find the right foreign buyers, how to deal with them and with shippers, customs agents, and with all the regulations. The good news is that you can learn all this easily and inexpensively. Use the U.S. Trade Commission's vast free training and support resources (800-872-8723). Tyler Hicks, author of *199 Great Home Businesses*

You Can Start (and Succeed in) for Under $1,000, suggests an even easier method: "Find foreign companies seeking U.S. products from U.S. Department of Commerce publications such as *Trade Opportunities* and from local and state chambers of commerce and business development groups. If you know a foreign language, concentrate on companies where that language is spoken. Locate U.S. companies selling what foreign buyers want by consulting the *Thomas Register of American Manufacturers (www.thomasregister.com)* or at most large libraries. Tell the U.S. source you have an overseas buyer for a specific number of items at such-and-such a price, and negotiate from there." A *Money* magazine report concluded that, among all home-based businesses, export agents are among the most likely to generate high income. *Manufacturer's Agents National Association: www.manaonline.org; 23016 Mill Creek Rd., Laguna Hills, CA 92654; 949-859-4040.*

OOH

BHB

Management Consultant. Your job is to solve the problems too hard for an organization to solve by itself. Examples: A growing company needs a better system for managing the information flow. A firm wants to start selling in Asia. After acquiring a new division, a company realizes that its structure must be reorganized. It's tough to get hired by the major management consulting firms such as Bain or McKinsey, but there are many small firms, and self-employment is a possibility. One self-marketing strategy is to write a proposal to the ten companies you think you can best help. Or write an article on your specialty and call company executives as part of the research. Your discussion could turn into a consulting assignment. *Institute of Management Consultants: www.imcusa.org; 521 5th Ave., New York, NY 10175; 212-697-8262. See also: www.cob.ohio-state.edu:80/dept.fin.*

Organizational Developer. Today, organizations are as fluid as mercury. They reorganize, downsize, rightsize — anything to avoid capsize. Organizational developers help plan and implement the changes by helping pick the wisest organizational structure, decide who should fill job slots and how those jobs should be configured, and motivate a downsized company's survivors. Organizational developers may also be involved in team building and diversity training. Some insiders, however, report that many ODs approach the latter two activities with trepidation because of past failures. When I recently suggested that a client, an OD with 20 years of experience, might want to do more team building and diversity training, he grimaced, put his hands over his face and moaned, "Nooooh! Anything but that!" *Organizational Development Network: www.odnet.org.*

BHB

Small Business Consultant. Many of the 600,000 people who start a business each year are scared of failing. Many small businesses require expertise in marketing, accounting, finance, and technology, and many owners could use some help. *Institute of Certified Business Counselors: www.nvst.com; 3485 W. 1st Ave., Eugene, OR 97402; 541-345-8064.*

(Neat Niche) **Business Plan Writer.** Many people know that they should have a business plan but don't know how to create one. Inexpensive software packages such as BizPlan Builder can help you make business plans look professional, but the key to being a good business plan writer is understanding what it takes to market, raise money for, and run a business. This sounds like a fun job to us: helping come up with the business idea and implementation plan, but not incurring any financial risk or dealing with the mundane headaches of running the business.

(Neat Niche) **Small Business Financing Consultant.** Two-thirds of new businesses need additional funds. There are many sources of money — family, Small Business Administration, local government, venture capitalists, and conventional banks, creative financing approaches such as leases, bridge loans, and second mortgages. You help your client figure out the smartest approach for the situation, and help land the money.

(Neat Niche) **Client Prospecting Specialist.** Use databases and other tools for helping businesses find customers. You might, for example, develop a targeted mailing list for your client.

(Neat Niche) **Franchising Consultant.** Choosing a franchise is no mean feat. There are thousands to choose from, each with pros and cons, plus the complicated legal documents. Because buying a franchise is a big decision, many people prefer to have a pro walk them through the selection process. Could that pro be you? *Franchise Consultants International Association: 5147 S. Angela Rd., Memphis, TN 38117; 901-682-2951. International Franchise Association: www.franchise.org; 1350 New York Ave., N.W., Washington, DC 20005; 202-628-8000.*

(Neat Niche) **Professional Practice Consultant.** Many doctors are running scared. So are many dentists, chiropractors, osteopaths, podiatrists, psychotherapists, orthodontists, lawyers, and CPAs. They're scared because they increasingly realize that being good practitioners doesn't make them good businesspersons. And as regulations increase and practices merge, it's ever more difficult to be a good businessperson. So professionals in private practice are turning to consultants to help recruit new customers, and to develop better systems for billing and collections, payroll, records management, and personnel. Increasingly, consultants are hired to help a medical professional join an HMO without having to work for peanuts. Especially if you specialize in one profession, this is a desirable consulting job: Demand is great, and you work with educated people who have the money and motivation to pay you well. A franchise opportunity with a fee of $25,000 is available from *Professional Management Group, Box 1130, Battle Creek, Michigan 49016, 800-888-1932.* They'll train you, but they want people with some business background and familiarity with some aspects of the health-care field. *Society of Medical-Dental Management Consultants: www.smdmc.org; 6215 Larson St., Kansas City, MO 64133; 800-826-2264.*

Specialty Consultant. Are you an expert at something? Or could you become one with self-study or formal study? Self-employed consultants can get successful quickly. The keys are to be an expert in something that people want, and to market yourself hard. It helps if many people in your personal network could use your service. Consulting is a great career because you keep all the profits, and your expenses are low because you provide a service rather than a product, and you can work at home, like all three authors of this book. Read *Million Dollar Consulting* by Alan Weiss. Bradley Richardson's *JobSmarts* describes him as "a dynamic one-man show who makes a million dollars a year working for Fortune 500 companies. Alan tells you everything from setting your fees to setting up an office." *Professional and Technical Consultants Association: www.patca.org; 849 Independence Ave., Mountain View, CA 94043; 650-903-8305.*

Work with Data and Things

Archivist. What part of the National Park Service's enormous collection of information should be permanently maintained? Which of those items should be exhibited in national parks? How should the rest of the information be stored so that it can easily be accessed? Archivists answer such questions. The Federal government, for example, can keep only 3 percent of its records. So there's always plenty to do. A major in history and a master's in library science is a good background. *Society of American Archivists: www.archivists.org; 527 S. Wells, Chicago, IL 60607; 312-922-0140.*

Web Site Designer. Most organizations and millions of individuals want a Web site, and if they already have one, two years later it's ready for a facelift. Web site designers who know how to turn a site from functional to fabulous are in big-time demand. The Web site designer uses standard graphic design programs to create the look. The Webmaster (a career described in this catalog) does the programming to put everything together. Web site designers need expertise in interface design plus the three industry standard programs: Photoshop, Director, and Illustrator. Self-employment opportunity: Contact Internet service providers (ISPs) and ask them to farm work out to you. *Internet Professional Publishers Association: www.ippa.org. See also: www.webpro.org; www.Websitebuilder.com; www.webmaster.org; www.cio.com;* and *www.wdda.org. Newsgroups: alt.webmaster* and *alt.webedit.*

(Neat Niche) **Intranet Designer.** More and more companies are building for-employees-only sites. This is a less obvious career path than IntERnet Web site design, so opportunities should be greater and salaries higher.

Desktop Publisher. The Department of Labor predicts this to be one of the fastest growing occupations, expected to jump 74 percent by the year 2006. Not surprising to us. From newsletters on up, typesetting, design, and layout is now rapidly becoming a desktop computer project. *The Desktop publishing forum on Compuserve: "go dtpforum." Newsgroup: comp.text.desktop.*

(Neat Niche) **Newsletter Publisher.** According to the Newsletter Publishing Association, 50 percent of new newsletters succeed, a higher percentage than other small businesses. And if you do things right, your chances are better still.

- Choose a narrow niche. It's easier to sell 1,000 newsletters for home health nurses than 1,000 for nurses.
- Choose a topic that has an endless stream of new information that your target readers lust after.
- Be sure an existing publication doesn't meet the need.
- Consider an online as well as a print version. If you have a large subscriber base, distribution costs will be lower.
- To market a newsletter successfully, you must buy the right mailing lists for solicitations and place ads at highly-targeted Web sites. *Newsletter Publishers Association: www.newsletters.org; 1501 Wilson Blvd., Arlington, VA 22209; 800-356-9302.*

(Neat Niche) **Template Newsletter Publisher.** Professionals such as accountants, lawyers, dentists, and financial planners are always looking for ways to remind clients and potential clients of their existence. A newsletter is more subtle than an advertisement. You, the desktop publisher, create a newsletter for one of these fields, let's say financial planners. With one exception, each financial planner gets the same newsletter to distribute to his or her mailing list. The exception is that each financial planner's stack of newsletters has his or her own front page, with the planner's name in the publication's title, and perhaps a letter to the readers written by that planner. *Newsletter Publisher Association: 1501 Wilson Blvd., Arlington, VA 22209; 800-356-9302. See also: www.newsletter-clearinghse.com* and *www.nlf.com.*

(Neat Niche) **Restaurant Menu Creator.** There are countless restaurants, and each of them needs a menu, many of which need to be changed periodically. Because the menu is what the customer reads at the moment of truth — when deciding how much to spend — an appealing menu design can mean big bucks to the owner. So if you become an expert in menu design, you may be able to charge amply for your services. Start by studying restaurant menus. Compendia are available at hotel concierge desks, in the Entertainment Guide, and online. *National Restaurant Association: www.restaurant.org; 1200 17th St., N.W., Washington, DC 20036; 202-331-5900.*

Acoustics Specialist. We all know that acoustics specialists ensure good sound in a concert hall, but they also keep our offices quiet so that we can concentrate and our homes quiet so that we can sleep. They also help design loudspeakers and microphones, and film and recording studios. Acousticians are the folks who created sonograms — safer alternatives to X rays and invasive diagnostic tests. *Acoustical Society of America: asa.aip.org; 500 Sunnyside Blvd., Woodbury, NY 11797; 516-576-2360.*

Coroner/Medical Examiner. Did Professor Plum do it with the candlestick in the conservatory? Or did he die from natural causes? Medical examiners, who, in many jurisdictions, don't need to be M.D.s, answer such questions. It's not the sort of medical career that makes a great first impression: You cure no one, and you spend your life mucking around with dead people. In fact, however, after a period of desensitization, playing around with corpses begins to feel normal. And it's rewarding work: Coroners determine the cause of death, an interesting investigative process, which one medical examiner described as "The only career in which you enable dead people to save lives." *The National Association of Medical Examiners: www.thename.org; 1402 S. Grand Blvd., St. Louis, MO 63104; 314-577-8298.*

Microscopist. Imagine being able to look at something at 500,000 times magnification, in three dimensions. That's what today's microscopists can do. Why might you want to magnify something so greatly? To examine what happens to diseased cancer cells at the molecular level, to assess the quality of the ceramic coating on a rocket's heat shield, or to determine if the DNA of skin underneath a suspect's fingernails matches that of the strangled person. *Microscopy Society of America: www.microscopy.com; 435 N. Michigan Ave., Chicago, IL 60611; 800-538-3672.*

Cytotechnologist. You're the cancer detector. You examine biopsied cells using microscopes and chemical tests to see what's up. Obviously, this is a career for someone who is very careful. A mistake can be devastating. Only a bachelor's degree is required. *American Society for Cytopathology: www.cytopathology.org; 400 W. 9th St., Wilmington, DE 19801; 302-429-8802.*

Oceanographer. We've all seen them on TV. Diving off a spacious boat on a perfect day, exploring a coral reef in pursuit of new ways to preserve the ecosystem. Those types of oceanographers are still around, but increasingly they're used to restore shorelines and rehabilitate bridges and ports, and in mariculture (sea farming). No matter the specialty, a career in oceanography has downsides that don't make it onto the TV special. Many oceanographers spend months far from home, much of that time freezing in cramped quarters. Something else those TV specials don't highlight is the many hours oceanographers spend far from the sea: in their cubicles, crunching numbers. A master's or Ph.D. in marine science or related field is standard, but people familiar with boats, electronics, or dive apparatus can get onto oceanographic expeditions without a college degree. *The Oceanography Society: www.tos.org; 4052 Timber Ridge Drive, Virginia Beach, VA 23455; 757-464-0131. American Geophysical Union: www.agu.org; 2000 Florida Ave., N.W., Washington, DC 20009; 202-462-6903. International Oceanographic Foundation, Rosenstiel School of Marine and Atmospheric Science: www.rsmas.miami.edu/iof; 4600 Rickenbacker Causeway, Miami, FL 33149; 305-361-4888.*

Geographer. Michael Jordan was a geography major. Can't you just imagine him debating: "Hmm, should I be a geographer or a pro basketball player?" Well, assuming you don't have pro basketball potential, geography offers some pretty cool careers. Don't think that geographers mainly make maps. Only a small percentage do. (They are covered under a separate entry: cartographer.) Geographers do, however, know a lot about how the land is laid out and how humans have used it. Geographers are often experts on such matters as global warming, deforestation, and groundwater pollution. If you decide to become a geographer, you'll be in good company: Mother Teresa started out as a geography teacher. *Association of American Geographers: www.aag.org; 1710 16th St., N.W., Washington, DC 20009; 202-234-1450.*

(Neat Niche) **Location Expert.** It's been said that the three keys to a business's success are location, location, and location. Because geographers know about demographics, transportation, availability of labor, shopping patterns, and how cities expand, geographers are good candidates for helping companies figure out where to open up shop.

(Neat Niche) **Area Specialist.** The government or a corporation wants to understand a country in detail so that its policies and plans are on target. Area specialists brief their bosses based on information from newspapers, radio, TV, magazines, government documents, aerial photos, and intelligence reports.

Geographic Information Specialist. How fast is a forest fire spreading? What's the best location for a highway? Worldwide, which crops will be bumper? (A favorite question of commodities traders.) Geographic information specialists use satellite photos, lasers, and computers to create maps that answer these questions. Sounds like you need a Ph.D., but only a bachelor's or master's is required. *American Congress of Surveying and Mapping: www.landsurveyor.com/acsm; 5410 Grosvenor Ln., Bethesda, MD 20814; 301-493-0200. Job openings: www.ggrweb.com.*

(Neat Niche) **Photogrammetry Technician.** You prepare maps of inaccessible regions using aerial photographs. This career requires just two years of education after high school.

(Neat Niche) **Precision Agriculture.** Instead of blanketing mammoth farms with pesticides and fungicides, precision agriculturists use computers and global positioning systems to enable farmers to apply chemicals on an as-needed basis.

Geologist. The career for people with rocks in their heads and for people who don't. Many geologists — petroleum geologists for example — don't even see the rocks they're studying because they're so far below the earth's surface. The latter usually focus on using computer data to answer one question: Where should we drill for oil? Guess wrong and the company loses millions. Guess right and you're a genius, and you may also have earned yourself a few extra shekels. You, of course, have lots of space-age tools — like gamma ray detectors — to help you guess right. Much of the work is outdoors and can be in a remote location for long periods, so it's a lousy choice if you value family life and a stable work environment. New employers of geologists are seismic data brokering companies, but the largest employers are oil companies and the U.S. Departments of Agriculture, the Interior, and Defense. *American Geological Institute: www.agiweb.org; 4220 King St., Alexandria, VA 22032; 703-379-2480. Geological Society of America: www.geosociety.org; 3300 Penrose Pl., Boulder, CO 80301; 303-447-2020.*

(Neat Niche) **Environmental Geologist.** Analyze rock and soil samples to aid environmental cleanups. For example, a hydrogeologist might trace where contaminants start and stop along waterways. *Job openings: www.eco.org; www.environmental-jobs.com;* and *www.princeton.edu/~oa/careeroe.html.*

(Neat niche) **Interplanetary Geologist.** Is there life on Mars? Could we introduce life onto Venus? The answers may lie on and beneath the planet's surface. Enter the interplanetary geologist.

Silviculturist. Silviculturists are forest builders. You create, restore, or maintain a forest or tree nursery. You're responsible for picking the right tree varieties, supervising the planting, pruning, and harvesting. You may also conduct research on topics such as the best methods for ensuring rapid tree growth, or the effects of animal grazing on growth. Though most silviculturists live in isolated locations, urban forestry is a possibility as cities look to provide islands of respite amid the maelstrom. *American Forestry Association: 710 17th St., N.W., Washington, DC 20006; 800-368-5748.*

Viticulturist. In plain English, this is a grape grower and often, vineyard manager. Typically, you work for a winery and direct its operations: from which grape variety to grow to when to harvest for best flavor. Because you are a manager, it helps if you know accounting. Although you aren't the farmer, you'll find yourself doing a lot of bending unless you're in a research facility or are a consultant, maybe for a University cooperative extension. But don't worry, there's free wine to dull any aches. *American Society for Enology and Viticulture: P.O. Box 1855, Davis, CA 95617; 530-753-3142.*

Mail-Order Business Owner. This is a tough business, but we are bullish on one mail-order product: sell a brief how-to report targeted to a narrow market. Example: *Buying Stamps for Less: Seven Things You Must Know and Probably Don't*. Such how-to reports are inexpensive to develop, reproduce, and ship. They're unbreakable, and they won't rot. To get customers, place small ads in publications (or Web sites) that serve your target audience. For example, if you want stamp collectors to buy your how-to report, advertise in a philatelist magazine. It is important to pick a product that appeals to a very narrow market. Products that are supposed to appeal to everyone seldom appeal to anyone. *Direct Marketing Association: www.the-dma.org.*

Online Store Owner. This may be the best chance for the little guy to successfully sell a product nationally. Some believe that it's too late to jump on the Web, that the big corporations are already set to dominate. We disagree. The cost of developing a cool site is now low enough to allow you to compete. (Hire someone who knows CGI programming.) Also, as long as your product is aimed at a narrow niche, it is not expensive to direct people to your site. For example, Iowa peacock farmer Dennis Fett sells live peacocks and gets 90 percent of his sales from his site *(www.peafowl.com)*. Pluses for Internet stores include no store rent to pay, no theft problems, and far less need for inventory. You may need no inventory at all. Orders simply get forwarded automatically directly to your supplier who fills them. Once you're up and running, the checks could just start coming in. An easy first step to checking your competition is to visit these Internet malls, which contain over 30,000 online businesses: *www.internet-mall.com; www.galaxymall.com;* and *www.21stcenturyplaza.com. See also: www.the-dma.org* and *www.techweb.com/webcommerce.*

(Neat Niche) **Woman-Oriented Sales Site Owner.** Although women make two-thirds of all mail-order purchases, they make only 20 percent of online purchases. Sites that are woman-specific, such as *christinecolumbus.com* — a site that specializes in travel wear for women — should do well.

Work with Things and People

Hands-on health and beauty

Athletic Trainer. Suddenly a player goes down. You race out on the field and must make an instant evaluation: How bad? Do we need the stretcher? A doctor? You don't want to overreact — the player, the team, the fans would all like to see him or her play again, or at least walk off the field. But, of course, better safe than sorry. The athletic trainer's key skill is decision making. She also has important decisions to make before and after the game.

For example, injured athletes are usually champing at the bit to play again. The doctor has given the okay to play, but as you tape the player up, you notice him wincing. What should you do? Another interesting part of the job is developing a conditioning program for the team and a rehab regimen for injured athletes, and motivating them to implement it. Finally, Michael O' Shea, trainer at the University of Louisville, explains, "The trainer is a 24-hour father confessor." Athletic coaching jobs on teams are tough to get, but there's growth at sports medicine clinics and corporate fitness centers. *National Athletic Trainers' Association: www.nata.org; 2952 Stemmons Freeway, Dallas, TX 75247; 214-637-6282.*

Prosthetist/Orthotist. An amputee walks in. You are going to make his or her artificial limb or brace. You must be the sort of person who can work face-to-face with amputees, and work with great care and precision. After all, you are preparing a device on which that person's ability to use hands or feet will depend. *American Academy of Orthotists and Prosthetists: www.oandp.com/organiza/aaop/index.htm; 1650 King St., Alexandria, VA 22314; 703-836-7114.*

Dentist. It's a myth that you have to be good with your hands to be a good dentist. Studies find that your average klutz (with a good brain) can develop the hands-on skills. You do, however, need a good back. Many dentists develop back problems from constantly leaning over patients. Even more problematic — dentistry is stressful. It's no fun to see patients flinch (hopefully, not writhe) in response to your gentle touch. Despite the money and prestige, burnout leads more than a few dentists to stop practicing. The good news is that there are neat niches: *American Dental Association: www.ada.org; 211 E. Chicago Ave., Chicago, IL 60611; 312-440-2500.*

(Neat Niche) **Veterinary Dentist.** You knock Fido out before starting, so there's no flinching (or biting) to stress you out. Also, it's a non-impacted (pun intended) field.

(Neat Niche) **Cosmetic Dentist.** Help turn yellowed and cracked teeth into movie-star whites. Much more pleasant than having to tell unsuspecting patients, "I'm sorry, we'll have to do a root canal." Bonus: Only minimal extra training is required.

Dental Hygienist. More than just cleaning your teeth, a dental hygienist takes and develops X rays, and administers anesthesia. In some states, hygienists even examine patients who are unable to come into the dentist's office. And, of course, part of their job description is to show you ugly pictures of gums to guilt-trip you into flossing more. Dental hygienists must take precautions to avoid carpal tunnel syndrome and back pain. *American Dental Hygienists Association: www.adha.org; 444 N. Michigan Ave., Chicago, IL 60611; 312-440-8900.*

Surgical Technologist. Just a high school diploma plus a one-year program, and you can play a role in the life-and-death drama of the operating room. The surgical technologist preps the patient (I remember having my chest shaved before my appendectomy. Not fun!), provides emotional support (I definitely needed that), and gets the surgical tools and machines ready in the operating room. During the operation, when the surgeon calls, "Sutures! Clamp! Retractor!" or any of those things they yell for on *ER,* the surgical technologist is one being yelled at. According to the Department of Labor, surgical technology is a fast-growing field. *Association of Surgical Technologists: 7108-C S. Alton Way, Englewood, CO 80112; 303-694-9130.*

Cardiovascular Technologist. Heart disease is the leading cause of death in America and the major reason that men die eight years earlier than women. The cardiology technologist plays a key role in diagnosing problems before it's too late. The range of tools for diagnosis has advanced well beyond the traditional electrocardiogram, using non-invasive ultrasound tests to measure blood flow to the extremities, for example. Cardiovascular techs have a stressful job, especially if they're assisting in heart catheterization — an invasive but accurate test for heart blockage. It helps to have a knack for calming people down. Entry-level jobs in this field often just require on-the-job training, but a two-year degree in cardiology technology prepares you for top-level positions. *Alliance of Cardiovascular Professionals: www.atlanticinteractive.com/acp/acp.html; 910 Charles St., Fredericksburg, VA 22401.*

Dispensing Optician. This job is a nice blend: part-technical, part-people. You help people pick out the frames that make them look sexy, intellectual, whatever. You then take some measurements — for example, the distance between the patient's pupils so that the lenses can be made the correct distance from each other. Then you make the actual glasses, grinding oversized lenses until they fit. In states where opticians are licensed, you can make a reasonable living. The growth is in the chains like Pearle and LensCrafters (owned by U.S. Shoe). Most opticians are trained on the job or by apprenticeship. *Opticians Association of America: www.opticians.org; 10341 Democracy Ln., Fairfax, VA 22030; 703-691-8355.*

Massage Therapist. One of the few careers in which nearly every customer is highly satisfied. The best massage therapists are not only wonderful with their hands but somehow demonstrate a sense of caring. Training is short, typically 500 hours, but be sure to enroll in a program accredited by the Commission on Massage Training. A downside is that you're on your feet all day doing physical work. Marketing tip: Develop relationships with concierges. Stressed-out traveling businesspeople often treat themselves to a massage at the end of the day. *American Massage Therapy Association: www.amtamassage.org; 820 Davis St., Evanston, IL 60201; 847-864-0123.*

(Neat Niche) **Corporate Massage.** Trend 1: Massage has gone mainstream. Marketed as a stress buster for the overworked, yup-scale massage storefronts are popping up from Madison Avenue to Rodeo Drive. Trend 2: Employers are forcing employees to do more with less. Enter the corporate massage therapist, a stress buster who gives weekly, short, in-chair (or on a massage table in the conference room) massages to employees. How do you convince tightwad employers to say yes? "No perk costs less and increases morale more. And your company is seen as benevolent, which can boost sales and make it easier to attract quality employees. There's even some evidence that, after a few minutes of post-massage stupor, people are more alert." Lots of corporations are going halfsies: They pay half, the employee pays half. Sounds like a deal to me, but there's at least one employer that isn't quite at ease with on-site massage. The Internal Revenue Service office in San Jose offered on-site massage for its employees, but there was a problem: the sound. Morgan Banks, the agency's health specialist explains, "You can't have taxpayers coming into an audit hearing 'oohs' and 'ahhs.' Now we're looking for a room with thicker walls."

(Neat Niche) **Pet Massage.** It's hard to believe, but sources tell us that pet massage is big in Southern California. We're not sure it will play in Peoria.

Cosmetologist/Makeup Artist. A fun job, making people look attractive while chatting with them. And training is short. Although most cosmetologists don't get rich, some, like my sister, do. Sandy always loved putting makeup on others, so she learned everything she could about it, went to a manufacturer who put Sandy's brand name on ready-made cosmetics, and opened a store called *Let's Make Up* in which Sandy did free makeovers and showed people how to do it themselves. When the women saw how good they looked, they usually ended up buying fistsful of the stuff. Within two years, Sandy was making fistfuls of money. *National Cosmetology Association: www.nca-now.com; 3510 Olive St., St. Louis, MO 63103; 800-527-1683. See also:* Hair, Makeup and Styling Career Guide *(2nd Edition, $40).*

(Neat Niche) **Special Effects Makeup Artist.** How'd you like a career making up puppets and creature masks? According to the *Hollywood Reporter,* "Since 1992, membership in the Los Angeles Makeup Artists and Hairstylists Union has increased by more than 50 percent. There are 720 people working in this field and their handiwork is in demand like never before. . . Michael Westmore, makeup supervisor at Paramount for the *Star Trek* series, says that he's never seen anything like the latest bull market. 'I've hired over 80 people myself.'" But not everyone's a bull. One insider warned that computer technology is replacing a lot of what special effects makeup artists do. *Links for jobs in the entertainment industry: www.hollywoodreporter.com2/index* and *www.showbizjobs.com.*

(Neat Niche) **Wedding Makeup Artist.** Many brides hire a pro to ensure that the bridal party looks luminous, not just for the ceremony, but for the zillion photographs and hours of videotape that immortalize that (hopefully) one-of-a-kind day. The camera often requires that you wear special makeup to avoid looking washed out. *Association of Bridal Consultants: 200 Chestnutland Rd., New Milford, CT 06776; 860-355-0464. See also: www.weddingchannel.com* and *www.weddingcircle.com.*

(Neat Niche) **FBI/CIA Theatrical Effects Specialist.** The CIA Web site says "We are seeking candidates with three years in cosmetology, theatrical makeup, costuming, art/graphics."

(Not-so-Neat Niche) **Funeral Home Restorator.** If the casket's open, its resident has to look good. No need to use hypoallergenic makeup. *National Funeral Director Association: www.nfda.org; 11121 W. Oklahoma Ave., Milwaukee, WI 53227; 800-228-6332. The American Board of Funeral Service Education: www.abfse.org; 13 Gurnet Rd., Brunswick, ME 04011; 207-798-5801. See also www.funeralnet.com/classifieds/index.html.*

Electrologist. Would you like to feel sort of like a doctor, make people look unquestionably better, yet get all your training in just four weeks? Those are the facts about electrology. Many women are self-conscious about having a moustache, beard, or hair outside the bikini line. Electrologists remove it hair by hair by inserting a fine needle into the follicle and then releasing a small amount of electric current using a foot pedal. They say it's painless, but we'll just take their word for it. New laser technology may make electrolysis obsolete, but it's too early to tell. Check it out. *Electrolysis Society of the Northeast: www.esne.org; 815 Stewart Ave., Garden City, NY 11530; 800-656-3769. Society of Clinical and Medical Electrologists: 132 Great Rd., Stow, MA 01775; 978-461-0313.*

Other Things/People Careers

Business Equipment Broker/Lessor. More people are starting businesses, and because most new businesses fail, more people will be ending their businesses. The business equipment broker profits from both by leasing to new business and buying used equipment from companies going bust. And of course, they handle businesses upgrading equipment. As technology advances ever faster, rather than buy, more businesses prefer to take a two-year lease on the latest computer, and in two years, lease the next-generation model. *Equipment Leasing Association: www.elaonline.com; 4301 N. Fairfax Dr., Arlington, VA 22203; 703-527-8655.*

Home Inspector. Buying a home can be love at first sight, but love is often blind. Enter the home inspector. Before consummating the deal, many buyers (or at least their less giddy Realtors) insist that the house be inspected. That can be your job. Construction experience helps, but home inspection franchisors insist that even neophytes can be quickly trained. Pitch your service to local Realtors, real estate attorneys, and mortgage lenders. Give lectures at real estate agencies on "How to Prevent an Inspection from Killing the Deal." Marketing tip: In low-income areas, as few as 3 percent of homes get inspected versus 95 percent in affluent areas. *American Society of Home Inspectors: www.ashi.com; 85 W. Algonquin Rd., Arlington Heights, IL 60005; 800-243-2744. See also: Amerispec: www.servicemaster.com; 1855 W. Katella Ave., Orange, CA 92667; 800-426-2270 and World Inspection Network: 800-967-8127 for franchise opportunities.*

Home Remodeler. Home remodeling sales will go from $115 billion in 1996 to $180 billion by 2005. The National Association of Home Builders estimates that by 2010, spending on remodeling will surpass spending on new homes. *The Remodelers Council: www.nahb.com; 1201 15th St., N.W., Washington, DC 20005; 202-822-0216.*

Golf Course Superintendent. Where should we put that new bunker? How should we schedule the groundskeepers? What's the best way to keep those greens perfect? To answer those questions, every golf course has a superintendent. This is another cool career that doesn't require a bachelor's degree: a two-year degree in turfgrass management will do. Be sure, though, to spend at least one summer as a groundskeeper. *Golf Course Superintendents Association of America: www.gcsaa.org; 1421 Research Park Dr., Lawrence, KS 66049; 800-472-7878.*

Garden Designer. Many of us allow our yards to decline into the too-natural look. Sure, there's the garden-variety gardener, but he doesn't have design skills. Landscape architects have design skills, but you may need a second mortgage to afford one. Enter what we call the Garden Doctor. She makes house calls and performs transplants. Armed with a laptop and software like *3D-Landscape,* the Garden Doctor and client can design the perfect Eden right there on screen without lifting a shovel. When the design is just right, the homeowner can do the job or contract with the Garden Doctor. *Association of Professional Landscape Designers: www.apld.com; 11 S. LaSalle St., Chicago, IL 60603; 312-201-0101.*

(Neat Niche) **Quick-Thumb Gardener.** He creates gardens that require minimal effort to stay looking good.

(Neat Niche) **Interiorscaper.** Hotels, hospitals, restaurants, atriums, malls, universities, and corporate headquarters are potential clients. Our favorite company name: Plant Parenthood.

Fashion Designer. "Next year, I think our line of children's swimsuits should use more tricot in earth tones. Parents are tired of cutesy. For a change, we might also try a loose fit. Here's a sketch of a couple of designs. If you like any of them, I'll cut a few samples. Maybe we could try them out at our sales meeting or at a fashion show." That's the life of the fashion designer. We often think of designers focusing on haute couture, but clothing designers specialize in everything from children's swimsuits to women's lingerie. *International Association of Clothing Designers: www.fashionexch.com; 475 Park Ave. S., New York, NY 10016; 212-685-6602. See also: www.fashionexch.com for job listings.*

OOH

(Neat Niche) **Accessory Design.** Designs for handbags and shoes change almost as often as clothing designs, yet many aspiring clothing designers don't think of this niche, so it isn't quite as crowded.

Moving Specialist. Imagine that when you decide to move to a new place, all your stuff is miraculously packed, whisked to your new place, and set up. That's the job of the moving specialist. Self-employment marketing strategy: Ask moving companies to refer clients to you, perhaps in exchange for a finders fee, if that's legal.

BHB

(Neat Niche) **Elder Mover.** Many older folks want to trade their too-large home for a smaller place, but the project can be intimidating. In addition to the physical tasks, leaving one's home can be emotionally painful. Elder movers take care of everything from hiring the right movers to figuring out what will fit in the new home; from hooking up the VCR to setting their clients' slippers on the right side of the bed so that when they first arrive, it feels like home.

Photographer. Snapping pictures for a living sounds like fun, but can you actually make a living at it? Only if you're an aggressive marketer and you're strategic. For example, many people can take pictures, but far fewer can take pictures with a digital camera and perform postproduction magic to create images that will dazzle and persuade — which is precisely what magazines and ad agencies want. Also consider these neat niches. *Professional Photographers of America: www.ppa-world.org; 57 Forsyth St., N.W., Atlanta, GA 30303; 800-742-7468.*

OOH

(Neat Niche) **Newborn Photographer.** Arrange with local hospitals to take photos of moms, dads, and newborns in the nursery.

(Neat Niche) **Government Photographer.** Government work can be an island of security in the photographer's sea infamous for low pay and irregular employment. The feds might hire you to take aerial photographs. Law enforcement agencies hire forensic photographers: "Did that piece of headlight come from a suspect's car?" Enhanced photographs of evidence can tell the tale. Search the government job listings on the Web. *For federal jobs: www.jobs.opm.gov.*

(Neat Niche) **Industrial Photographer.** This is another photography job that's potentially stable. You may even get a company car. Plus, you get to work with top-of-the-line equipment. The downside is that the work is unlikely to quench your thirst for artistic expression. A typical project may involve taking photos of a prototype product at each stage in its development.

(Neat Niche) **Photojournalist.** As newspapers try to stay competitive in the ever glitzier ways we receive our news, they use more photos. The job market is still tight, but if you have expertise in digital photography and postproduction, this sexy job may be a bit easier to land than in years past. *National Press Photographers Association: www.sunsite.unc.edu/nppa; 3200 Croasdaile Dr., Durham, NC 27705; 919-383-7246.*

(Neat Niche) **Lithograph Cameraperson.** You use computers and camera to lay out magazines and mail-order catalogs.

(Neat Niche) **Rock Band Photographer.** Rock band members have large egos and an insatiable need to market themselves. So this is a fertile, little-known, and fun niche.

(Neat Niche) **School Photographer.** Taking headshots of 100 kids a day isn't the most creative work in the world, but there are plenty of customers out there. At many schools, picture-taking is an annual event. Another plus is that, unlike most photography niches, your evenings and weekends are free. *Professional School Photographers of America, c/o Photo Marketing Association International: www.pmai.org/../sections/pspa.htm; 3000 Picture Pl., Jackson, MI 49201; 517-788-8100.*

Tugboat Operator. This is a sailor's job that pays $50,000–$60,000 and doesn't require long stints away from home. And the job market is good. Fear of oil spills has resulted in regulations requiring most large ships to be towed into dock by a tug. Most tug operators get their experience working on party boats or fishing boats, or by attending a two-year maritime program. *International Organization of Master Mates and Pilots: www.bridgedeck.org; 700 Maritime Blvd., Linthicum Heights, MD 21090; 410-850-8700. See also: jobxchange.com/xisetoc.htm for job listings.*

Sports Umpire/Referee. I loved being an umpire. It was fun making a decision every few seconds that was respected — usually. Somehow, even getting booed wasn't so bad — when I was able to remind myself that in the larger scheme of things, it didn't matter whether it was a ball or a strike. And as a sports fan, umpiring was a way to be a part of the game even if I wasn't a great ballplayer. Don't count on making full-time money as an ump. Sure, top NFL refs make over $250,000, but for most high school and college refs, officiating is a part-time thing, as much for the fun as for the money.

There are perks, though. You get to travel, and it's a fun way to stay in shape, except in baseball, where umps mainly just stand there. The good news is that demand is high. According to a sports officiating Web site, "So great is the need (for officials) that many state athletic associations must constantly recruit new officials . . . just to offset normal attrition." You need the skills of a saint: competent decision-making under pressure and the ability to stay cool when coaches and fans yell in your face (or spit, as did pro baseball player Roberto Alomar). *Harry Wendelstedt School for Umpires: 88 S. St. Andrews Dr., Ormond Beach, FL 32174. A counterpart in basketball is the Nationwide Basketball Referee's Camp: 4525 Jolyn Pl, Atlanta, GA 30342. See also: Officiating Web site: www.gmcgriff.com/refonline. National Association of Sports Officials: www.naso.org; 2017 Lathrop Ave., Racine, WI 53405; 414-632-5448. Sports job listings: Online Sports Career Center: www.onlinesports.com.*

Stunt Person. Ready to dive from a cruise ship into a frigid ocean? How about leaping from a tall building? Getting set on fire? If so, maybe you'd like to be a stunt person. Be sure your health insurance is in place. But the risk doesn't deter aspirants; competition is fierce for stunt jobs. You usually need to be quite an athlete and well-trained. There are only two training schools in the United States: One is Stunts Are Us in, of all places, Kenosha, Wisconsin, 414-859-2379. First step for a career in which you swing from nooses and tumble down stairs is to read Jack Bucklin's *Stuntman: A Freelancer's Guide to the Craft and Landing the Job,* available by calling 800-392-2400. *United Stuntman's Association: www.stunt.simplenet.com. Screen Actor's Guild: www.sag.com; 7065 Hollywood Blvd., Hollywood, CA 90028. Links for jobs in the entertainment Job openings: www.showbizjobs.com;* and *www.hollywoodreporter.com2/index* .

Work with Things and Data

Patent Agent. You get to do everything a patent lawyer does except appear in court. Mary invented a gadget that opens jars more easily and wants to patent it. Your job is first to assess if it's really new enough to justify a patent. If so, you draft an extensive patent application to the U.S. Patent and Trademark Office. It describes, in words and pictures, how the new invention is different from anything that preceded it. A background in science or engineering is almost a requirement. There will always be people wanting to patent their innovations to protect their rights, and the position can't be automated, so there should always be a need for patent agents. *Patent and Trademark Office Society: members.aol.com/societypto; P.O. Box 2089, Arlington, VA 22202.*

Engineer. This is a career for tinkerers who like to use computers to design stuff. For the past ten years, engineering has been among the highest-paid, most in-demand, bachelor's level careers. And future prospects look great: The Department of Labor expects demand to stay hot at least through 2006, especially in electrical and software engineering. The bad news is that the admission ticket for the coolest engineering jobs is increasingly a master's degree. And because this field is so fast-changing, older engineers — often perceived as too many steps behind — face a tough time in the job market. *National Society of Professional Engineering: www.nspe.org; 1420 King St., Alexandria, VA 22314.*

(Neat Niche) **Biomedical Engineer.** Typical projects for these engineers include designing a more functional artificial arm or leg, a computer simulation of brain function, and a monitor for hospital patients, astronauts, or deep sea divers. *Institute of Electrical and Electronics Engineers: www.ieee.org; 1828 L St., N.W., Washington, DC 20036; 202-785-0017.*

(Neat Niche) **Packaging Engineer.** How should a small toy be packaged so that it is theft-resistant yet allows the shopper to play with it just enough to yell, "Mommy, can I have it?" How should a drug be packaged so that it's child-proof yet accessible to an arthritic older person? What's the least expensive packaging that keeps frozen shrimp from smelling fishy after its journey from a Thailand aquafarm to a U.S. supermarket?

(Neat Niche) **Computer Engineer.** The Department of Labor projects this to be the second fastest growing occupation through 2006, expected to jump 118 percent. You design hardware and software. An important subniche is building the architecture for the next-generation replacement for the Internet, which is already cracking under the weight. *Institute of Electrical and Electronics Engineers: www.ieee.org; 1828 L St., N.W., Washington, DC 20036.*

(Neat Niche) **Telecommunications Engineer.** The Olympics are seen instantly with crystal clarity around the world. A paralyzed person talks and a computer types his precise words almost as fast as he can speak. You can check your e-mail with a handheld wireless device. The hero? Telecommunications engineers. What's next? In the next decade, telecommunications engineers will develop an on-your-wrist phone that can search the Internet or phone home.

(Neat Niche) **Optical Engineer.** Typical projects include developing a laser-guided robot that can destroy a minefield before it destroys a soldier, or a telescope lens that can see farther into space than ever before. *Optical Society of America: www.osa.org; 2010 Massachusetts Ave., N.W., Washington, DC 20036; 202-223-8130.*

(Neat Niche) **Sales Engineer.** It often takes an engineer to convince an engineer that her company should buy a high-tech widget. The engineer who can do that sometimes commands a six-figure salary. *American Association of Professional Sales Engineers: 55969 Jayne Dr., Elkhart, IN 46514; 219-522-4837.*

(Neat Niche) **Environmental Engineer.** Companies scared of tougher regulations and public demand for low pollution are spending big to prevent and cure environmental messes. The pollution prevention industry is already $1 billion a year and growing. There are early reports, however, that because engineering graduates have flocked to this field in recent years, environmental engineering is becoming saturated. Best job opportunities may be in Eastern Europe and Asia as they begin environmental cleanup. *American Academy of Environmental Engineers: www.enviro-engrs.org/address.htm; 130 Holiday Ct., Annapolis, MD 20140; See also: www.eco.org; www.environmental-jobs.com;* and *www.princeton.edu/~oa/careeroe.html.*

(Neat Niche) **Spacecraft Engineering.** They're already booking seats on the first commercial space flight. More passenger spacecraft will come, but for the next decade, the real growth will be in designing and building unmanned vehicles. A typical application is monitoring pollution changes on Earth. Another growth area is in low-orbit satellites, which dramatically reduce the cost of satellite communication. Lockheed Martin is already building 60 spacecraft. Other major players are McDonnell Douglas, Boeing, and Rockwell. Many people think that spacecraft engineering mainly involves designing the vehicle itself. Actually, the main work is designing the thousands of computer programs needed to drive the vehicle's many systems. *American Institute of Aeronautics and Astronautics: www.aerospace.net; 1801 Alexander Bell Dr., Reston, VA 20191; 703-264-7500. See also: www.spacejobs.com.*

Engineering Technologist. Your job is to assist an engineer in designing and developing products. For example, you might test and troubleshoot electrical and computer systems. Or you may work on a survey party, calculating land areas, estimating costs, and inspecting construction projects. A two-year degree in engineering technology is the norm. *American Society of Certified Engineering Technicians: P.O. Box 1348, Flowery Branch, GA 30542; 770-967-9173.*

(Neat Niche) **Laser Technologist.** Lasers remove wrinkles, make welds, and yes, destroy oncoming missiles. While highly trained laser/optical engineers do most of the design work, you assist with the design and are in charge of building the lasers. A certificate or associate degree is required. *Optical Society of America: www.osa.org; 2010 Massachusetts Ave., N.W., Washington, DC 20036; 202-223-8130. Laser Institute of America: 12424 Research Parkway, Orlando, FL 32826; 407-380-1553.*

Industrial Designer. What should the new Toyota look like? How should a computer mouse be designed so that it's less likely to cause repetitive stress syndrome? An industrial designer provides the answers. Top training institutions are Carnegie Melon, Rhode Island School of Design, and Art Center College of Design (CA). *Industrial Designers Society of America: www.idsa.org; 1142-E Walker Rd., Great Falls, VA 22066; 703-759-0100.*

(Neat Niche) **Packaging Designer.** Your company wants to introduce a new shampoo. Of course, there already are dozens of brands on supermarket shelves. Your job is to design the bottle so that shoppers are compelled to pick yours. Working with graphic artists, marketers, and accountants, you design the most compelling packaging possible within budget. *Industrial Designers Society of America: www.idsa.org; 1142 Walker Rd., Great Falls, VA 22066; 703-759-0100. See also: www.fdp.com.*

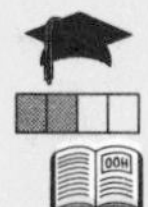

Cartographer. That's the fancy word for mapmaker. Though you still need some drawing skills, this is yet another field revolutionized by the computer. New maps are often of remote areas, only now accurately mappable thanks to computer interpretation of aerial or satellite data. Cartographers may also map seascapes to identify coral reefs, or create drainage maps to help farmers plan irrigation. *American Congress of Surveying and Mapping: www.landsurveyor.com/acsm; 5410 Grosvenor Lane, Bethesda, MD 20814; 301-493-0200.*

Road maps including directions to and from nearly any two locations in the United States are available free on the Web at *www.mapquest.com.*

Enologist. Want to make wine for a living? A bachelor's degree and internships during crush time in wineries provide the preparation. Alas, only a few colleges offer a major in enology. The best-known program is at the University of California, Davis. *American Society of Enology and Viticulture: P.O. Box 1855, Davis, CA 95617; 916-753-3142.*

Brewer. Don't like wine? How about beer? Although we're not sure the craft brewing fad will last, beer drinking will. Don't think the job is mainly tasting. It's part chemistry, part management, and okay, part tasting. *American Brewer's Guild: 800-636-1311. Seibel Institute of Brewery Technology: 312-279-0966. Brewers infosite: www.realbeer.com.*

Broadcast Technologist (sometimes called Broadcast Engineers). This is a back door into a field (TV/radio) whose front entrance is mobbed. And you don't even need performing talent. Broadcast technologists operate and maintain the cameras and other recording equipment in studios and on remotes. An utterly non-random example is going to Hawaii to cover the Aloha Bowl. The bad news is that you must often work nights and weekends, and the pay can stink. Training is less than a year at a private technical school or a bit longer at a community college. But there's an alternative. The broadcast engineer at my radio station told me that in decades past, techie kids would, like groupies, hang out at the radio stations to learn broadcast engineering. Now, few do, perhaps because most young people view radio as passé. That leaves an opportunity for you. *National Association of Broadcasters Employment Clearinghouse: www.nab.org; 1771 N St., N.W., Washington, DC 20036.*

Criminalist. He is lying dead. Near the corpse lies a tiny white hair. The criminalist picks it up. Under the microscope, it's clear that it's a pet hair. A visit to three suspects' homes finds that one of them has a pet whose hair matches exactly. Criminalists use physical evidence — a weapon, a clothing fiber, blood, drugs, even vapors — to prove a link between the suspect and the victim. It's safer than a detective job because you usually show up after the danger is over. Criminalists need only a bachelor's degree — ideally in forensics/criminalistics, but biology or chemistry is often okay. *American Society of Criminology: www.bsos.umd.edu/asc; 1314 Kinnear Rd., Columbus, OH 43212; 614-292-9207.*

(Neat Niches): **Ballistics, Fingerprint Analyst, Arson Investigator, Forgery Analyst, Forensic Chemist, DNA Analyst.**

Historic Preservationist. America has hundreds of thousands of buildings under protection of the Landmarks Preservation Commission — 21,000 in New York City alone. In many of these buildings, continuing efforts are made to restore the property to its original state. That means hiring people who can do research to find out what the building looked like way back when, and who have the management skills and/or artistic ability to re-create it. Much of this work is done on a volunteer basis, but a small number of jobs are available for the eager and well-trained. *National Trust for Historic Preservation: www.nationaltrust.org; 1785 Massachusetts Ave., N.W., Washington, DC 20036; 800-944-6847.*

Work with Data, People, and Things

Nurse. Today, whether the patient gets well depends as much on the nurse as on the doctor. As cost-cutting pressures increase, registered nurses are doing more and more substantive medical care. Bedpan cleaning is now mainly handled by medical assistants. To get the best nursing jobs, though, a two-year degree no longer cuts it. A bachelor's is fine, and if you have a master's, the floodgates open. According to the Health Resources Services Administration, by the year 2000, 400,000 nurses with master's degrees will be needed for such positions as nurse practitioner, nurse educator, midwife, and anesthetist. Yet, only 140,000 nurses will have a master's. Here is a field in which a master's makes sense. *National League for Nursing: www.nln.org; 350 Hudson St., New York, NY 10014; 212-989-9393.*

(Neat Niche) **Nurse Anesthetist.** Anesthesiologists earn over $200,000 a year, and HMOs don't like that one little bit. So HMOs increasingly prefer nurse anesthetists because they can pay them $75,000, good money for a nurse, and save a bundle. A two- or three-year program after the bachelor's degree opens the door to this prestigious, important, but stressful position. *American Association of Nurse Anesthetists: www.aana.com; 222 S. Prospect Ave., Park Ridge, IL 60068; 847-692-7050.*

(Neat Niche) **Nurse Midwife.** More and more moms-to-be and health care bean counters are attracted to midwifery's combination of lower costs and a more human touch. And midwifery can be a gratifying career. Not only do you deliver babies, you provide pre- and postnatal care such as teaching moms to breast feed. Registered nurses must complete a year of additional training for nurse-midwife certification. *American College of Nurse Midwives: www.acnm.org.*

(Neat Niche) **Obstetric-Gynecological Nurse.** Experience the miracle of childbirth on a daily basis. This niche is also wonderful because you see quick success with the vast majority of your patients.

(Neat Niche) **Transplant Coordinator.** You've drunk yourself into a stupor once too often, so your liver is kaput. Doc says you need a transplant. The transplant coordinator decides where you belong on the waiting list. (Too far back in your soused opinion.) When someone dies whose liver is the right size and blood type, the transplant coordinator schedules the team for surgery, and gives you your pre- and postsurgery education. *Center for Organ Recovery and Education: 204 Sigma Dr., Pittsburgh, PA 15238.*

(Neat Niche) **Wellness Coordinator.** Large employers hire wellness coordinators to arrange health fairs, conduct blood pressure and cholesterol screenings, coordinate noon aerobics and stop-smoking classes, and, of course, encourage employees to eat more brussels sprouts and less ice cream.

(Neat Niche) **Patient Discharge Planner.** As hospitals release patients more quickly, discharge planners help patients transition to in-home care. Planners decide if Mrs. McGillicuddy needs a home-health aide, train her or her family how to self-administer injections and other treatments, and help the family solve problems as they arise. The work is generally less stressful than direct patient care.

(Neat Niche) **Pain Resolution Specialist.** Despite the best treatment, many people must live with chronic pain. Managing it often requires psychological strategies, practical work-arounds, and trial-and-error to find the right drug.

(Neat Niche) **Case Manager.** A 90-year-old woman has been battling cancer for five years. Her cancer has now metastasized to her liver, and she is in pain. Should she receive another operation? How about painful physical therapy for her atrophying leg? Should she be in the hospital? At home? In a hospice? What should and shouldn't the HMO pay for? The case manager is the coordinator of this decision-making process and has one of the most interesting roles in the managed care movement. After reviewing the record, speaking with the patient, family, health care providers, and insurance company, and leading multidisciplinary rounds, the case manager makes recommendations that balance the interests of everyone involved: the payer, the hospital, the family, and, of course, the patient.

(Neat Niche) **Nurse Informatician.** Nurses need to access lots of data: patient records, drug contraindications, disease ins-and-outs, and insurance gobbledygook. Someone has to help the computer programmer to develop systems that are nurse-friendly and be on call to help nurses having trouble extracting information. The pay's good, the job's rewarding, and there's no blood and gore. *American Nursing Informatics Association: www.ania.org; 1656 W. Palais Rd., Anaheim, CA 92802. Training institutions for Nursing Informatics: www.gl.umbc.edu/~abbott/NIprogram.htm.*

(Neat Niche) **Clinical Trials Coordinator.** A biotech or pharmaceutical company develops a new treatment. It works on the computer and with rats, so it's time for human subjects. Nurses are routinely hired to examine potential patients, administer the experimental treatment, ensure that patients are complying, and write reports. This is a neat niche because it's little-known, in-demand, and a different experience for the nurse burned out on patient care who would enjoy being an important part of a research team.

(Neat Niche) **Menopause Counselor.** Menopause has come out of the closet, if the number of T-shirts proclaiming, "I'm out of estrogen and I have a gun" are any indication. As they enter the "change of life," some women now seek support beyond what their gynecologist can provide during the 12-minute annual exams HMOs usually pay for.

(Neat Niche) **Nurse Legal Consultant.** Law firms are inundated with people who want to sue their doctors or hospitals for medical malpractice. To evaluate those claims' legitimacy, lawyers hire nurse legal consultants to review the medical records, and if the case seems meritorious and involves nursing malpractice, to research the nursing literature to develop the case's foundation. Nurse legal consultants also testify in trials as expert witnesses. *American Association of Legal Nurses: www.mnrs.org; 4700 W. Lake Ave., Glenview, IL 60025; 847-375-4713.*

Exercise Physiologist. Athletes are learning to perform better, not just with a coach, but with an exercise physiologist. The latter may, for example, show an athlete how to improve by using slow-motion, computer-analyzed tape of exactly what his muscles are doing. Generally, a master's or even a doctorate in exercise physiology is required. In addition to consulting with teams, exercise physiologists get jobs in sports medicine clinics and corporate fitness centers. *Exercise Sciences Association: www.exercisesciences.com.*

Respiratory Therapist. We can live for days without food or water, but without air, we're dead in nine minutes. Respiratory therapists' job is to keep patients breathing — often not just the very old, but the very young. Newborns must often be placed on sophisticated ventilators. Your job is to monitor the ventilators to ensure proper oxygen, CO_2 and pH levels. You also administer aerosol medications and perform chest therapy to drain mucus from the lungs. Respiratory therapists are among the first persons called to work with doctors to treat acute asthma attacks, head injuries, and drug poisonings. *American Association for Respiratory Care: www.aarc.org; 11030 Ables Lane, Dallas, TX 75229.*

School Computer Coordinator. Schools are filling with computers, but after planting, many groves of Apples are gathering dust. The main problem is teachers who don't know how to use them effectively: which software, how to use it in a classroom setting, and what to do when something doesn't work. Enter the school computer coordinator — combination network administrator, teacher trainer, and hardware troubleshooter with a knack for figuring out how to help Johnny with whatever seems not to be working. She also has the pleasant task of figuring out what goodies to buy, and the not-so-pleasant task of telling Janie that she's lost all her work because she forgot to back up her data. *International Society for Technology in Education: www.iste.org; 1787 Agate St., Eugene, OR 97403-1923; 800-336-5191.*

Network Administrator. This is a cross between a systems analyst and network technologist, and one of the fastest growing occupations of all. You play a key role in designing an organization's computer network, supervising its installation, and coordinating maintenance and repair. *Job openings: www.computerworld.com. Job openings at colleges: www.cs.brandeis.edu:80/~zippy/academic-cs-jobs.html.*

Planner. The downtown area is rundown. What's the best plan for revitalization? A developer wants to build a housing project. What parameters should the city require? You may coordinate such redevelopment efforts or even design a new city from scratch. You conduct studies and public hearings, and before making a recommendation, you probably wear many hats: engineer, economist, sociologist, and politician. A silver tongue is essential if you expect even vestiges of your plan to survive irate community groups. Most planners specialize: urban or rural land use, transportation, housing, health and human services, historic preservation, air, water, or hazardous materials. Increasingly, you need a master's degree except in small agencies or those away from metropolitan areas. ***Tip:*** To get in, volunteer for planning committees and commissions. *American Planning Association: 1776 Massachusetts Ave., N.W., Washington, DC 20036; 202-872-0611.*

FBI Special Agent. Are you an aspiring James or Jane Bond? The reality is usually less exotic, investigating such mundane dalliances as your basic fraudulent bankruptcy, but FBI special agents do search out kidnappers, finger mobsters, catch bank robbers, and foil biological weapons terrorists. Downsides are that you travel a lot and are alone most of the time. The FBI employs over 10,000 special agents, and they prefer a graduate degree in law or accounting or fluency in a foreign language. (Doesn't sound much like the requirements we'd list if we were recruiting for FBI agents, but what do we know?) Entry-level job title: clandestine service trainee. *Federal Bureau of Investigation: www.fbi.gov.*

Are you 37 or older? Forget it; the FBI wants to hire young. So do most employers, but age discrimination laws prevent it. The FBI is above all that.

BHB

Private Investigator. You're worried that your husband is fooling around. Or that one of your employees is collecting disability and claiming repetitive stress syndrome, but is, in fact, on the golf course. Or that you'll never see that ten grand from the son-of-gun you lent it to who skipped town. Following the Louise Woodward case, you're worried that your nanny is abusing, or at least ignoring, your little munchkin. Who you gonna call? Your friendly private investigator. She'll hang out in the neighborhood, talk with some folks, hopefully without arousing their suspicion, dig through public information, and use that time-honored P.I. technique: dumpster diving. You need the ability to read people and persuade people to give you information. Remember Colombo?

Some danger exists here. For example, a wife has a husband followed, but hubby catches you, the private investigator, and wants to redecorate your face. The good news is that such mishaps are rare, especially nowadays, when many more cases are solved by a computer search than by stakeout. This is a cool career if you're clever and have a knack for not getting caught. *National Association of Investigative Specialists: www.pimall.com; P.O. Box 33244, Austin, TX 78764; 512-719-3595.*

(Neat Niche) **Credential Verification Specialist.** When one of San Francisco mayor Willie Brown's key employees was caught lying on his resume, his honor shrugged, "Everyone lies on their resume." As job and tenant applicants seem more likely to stretch the truth, and government regulations tighten about what can and can't be asked, companies increasingly turn to pre-employment checkers to verify information on resumes and to contact former employers. See Wayne Ford's *How to Spot a Phony Resume* and Ed Andler's *The Complete Reference Checking Handbook.* Andler found that one-third of all resumes contain "some level of creative writing."

Loss Prevention Specialist. The insurance industry has always been an attractive employer because of high salaries, but for many people, it's a turnoff because of the nature of the work. One of the most rewarding insurance careers is in loss prevention. Rather than, for example, being an adjustor, whose job it is to give people as little as possible after they've suffered a loss, the loss prevention specialist has the more pleasant role of helping a business develop a strategy to prevent damage to people or the environment. *Insurance Loss Control Association: c/o NAMIC, 3601 Vincennes Rd., Indianapolis, IN 46268-0700; 317-875-5250. The Insurance Career Center: www.connectyou.com/talent. See also: www.insjobs.com.*

Video Yearbook Publisher. Most high school and college yearbooks are still done the old-fashioned way: a printed book. A video yearbook can be a compelling alternative. How to get customers? Just contact high school principals and PTA presidents. Get permission to videotape the senior class in action, and then sell video yearbooks. A franchise is available: *International Video Yearbooks: 104 Suede St., Madison, TN 37115; 800-552-9103.*

Work with Data, Things, and People

Physician. We include this career partly because you'd think we were nuts if we omitted such a prestigious, well-paying profession; but listen to this: There is an oversupply of doctors, especially specialists, in most urban and suburban areas, and many experts believe that demand for doctors, especially specialists, will decrease as HMOs increasingly use nurse practitioners and physician's assistants to lower costs. Even if you can find a job, HMOs severely constrain how physicians can practice medicine: Visits are shorter, and more and more treatments are subject to external scrutiny. Meanwhile, malpractice suits climb. Perhaps the biggest minus is that a physician's life is extraordinarily stressful. Consider the typically six to eight years after college that it takes to prepare to be a physician, the enormous cost of medical school, the strain of high-stakes decision-making, and having to inform unsuspecting patients of severe illnesses, and the now prohibitive costs of starting your own practice. And there's more. Medicine is changing so rapidly that it's impossible to keep up, so many physicians practice while feeling guilty that because of their own lack of knowledge and HMO constraints, they may not be giving their patients the best possible treatment. It's no surprise that the average physician lives eight years less than the average American. *American Medical Association: www.ama-assn.org; 515 N. State St., Chicago, IL 60610; 312-464-5000. See also: www.doctorlink.com; www.edphysician.com;* and *www.nejm.org.*

We believe that for many aspiring physicians, physician's assistant (covered later) is a smarter career choice even though it obviously has less prestige and lower income potential. If, however, you want to consider the M.D. route, there are neat niches.

(Neat Niche) **Second Opinion Referral Service.** A patient is told he has six months to live. Time for a second opinion. But from whom? The patient, of course, wants the best doctor but doesn't know how to find him. You do. Using reference books, reviewing medical literature, and phoning various doctors, you can usually identify a better referral than a patient can. Market your service by making presentations to physicians and sending mailings to members of patient support groups such as cancer, heart disease, multiple sclerosis, or diabetes.

(Neat Niche) **Sports Medicine.** As the fitness fad continues, the number of weekend warriors grows, and in turn the number of injuries. Most of these are fixable, so sports medicine is rewarding. *American College of Sports Medicine: www.a1.com/sportsmed; P.O. Box 1440, Indianapolis, IN 46206; 317-637-9200.*

The evidence for the benefits of exercise is flimsy. Of course, people who exercise more live healthier and longer, but which causes which? Does a strong constitution make one more likely to have the energy to exercise, or does the exercise create a strong constitution? Before the doctors guilt-trip us into taking hours out of our already crowded weeks to sweat our fannies off, we deserve better evidence that it will be worth our while.

(Neat Niche) **Infertility Specialist.** Women working outside the home are deferring parenthood, sometimes until getting pregnant isn't so easy. Enter the infertility doctor, with an ever-growing array of fixes: in vitro fertilization, egg retrieval, and, probably sooner rather than later, cloning one of the parents. *Society for Prevention of Infertility: 875 Park Ave., New York, NY 10021.*

(Neat Niche) **Impotence Specialist.** Men's most prevalent sexual dysfunction, impotence, is in 85 percent of cases physiological. With a good impotence pill already on the market and even better ones in the pipeline, physicians specializing in this field now are able to cure a devastating disease. An estimated 18,000,000 men suffer from impotence, and until now, few sought treatment. Now, however, prospects for physicians who specialize in impotence are firm and rising. *Impotence Institute of America: P.O. Box 410, Louie, MD 20718; 301-261-2400.*

Physician's Assistant. This may be my very favorite career. It offers most of the benefits of being an M.D. with few of the drawbacks. Always looking to cut costs, health care systems, especially in urban and rural areas, are realizing that they needn't spend the big bucks on an M.D. to provide basic health care. Enter the physician's assistant. Two years of college plus a two-year training program, and you're a physician's assistant. Starting salaries exceed $40,000 and can rise to $90,000, and you get to do some of the most rewarding things that physicians do, like wellness exams (what they used to call "checkups"), teaching people how to eat and live well, curing a painful earache, and sometimes assisting in surgery. *American Academy of Physician Assistants: www.aapa.org; 950 N. Washington St., Alexandria, VA 22314; 703-836-2272.*

(Neat Niche) **Transplant Coordinator.** (See the transplant coordinator scoop a few pages back.)

Podiatrist. One of the cushiest doctor jobs, the foot doctor cuts out ingrown toe nails, performs minor surgery, sets broken bones (your feet contain one-fourth of the bones in your entire body), and uses a computer scan to fit people for custom shoes. A downside: The physician-like training is about as long and as expensive as for M.D.s. And the investment doesn't always pay off. Some podiatrists, hit hard by stingy insurance reimbursements, are closing practices. *American Podiatric Medical Association: www.apma.org; 9312 Old Georgetown Rd., Bethesda, MD 20814; 301-571-9200.*

Veterinarian. A vet is like a doctor, except you have to know a half-dozen species, none of which can describe their symptoms to you. *American Veterinary Medical Association: www.avma.org; 1931 N. Meacham Rd., Schaumburg, IL 60173; 847-925-8070.*

(Neat Niche) **Laboratory Animals Vet.** It's the easiest vet residency: Working hours are 9–5, no weekends, and you get to work in a medical school or drug company setting. There are ample jobs because most animal research must be supervised by a laboratory animal vet.

(Neat Niche) **Veterinary Cardiologist.** Demand is growing, treatments improving, earnings tops for these animal heart specialists.

Veterinary Technologist. Much shorter training than for veterinarians, yet veterinary techs get to do much of what vets do. Let's say poor Fifi isn't feeling well. You, the vet tech, might take her medical history (if you can speak dog), give her an exam, and take her blood (poor Fifi). The vet diagnoses the problem as a bladder infection and prescribes an injection that you administer. Next, even poorer Bowser comes in — he was run over by a car. The vet decides to operate. You administer the anesthetic and assist in surgery. You are even allowed to stitch Bowser up. Bowser also has an obviously broken leg. You take the X rays, the vet sets it, and you apply the cast. Finally, you educate Bowser's mommy or daddy about how to take care of Bowser during his recovery. Very cool career — and it only takes two years of education after high school. Plus you don't need to be dogged to land a job since there are four job openings for every vet tech graduate in the United States. The problem is that salaries are in the doghouse. *North American Veterinary Technologists Association: www.avma.org/navta; P.O. Box 224, Battle Ground, IN 47920.*

Paramedic. A person is having a heart attack. A woman has suddenly gone into labor. There's a bad car accident and bleeding passengers are tangled in the wreckage. The paramedic is first on the scene to try to save the day. If you thrive on adrenaline but can stay calm, be gratified by your saves but not burned out by your losses, this can be a rewarding career. Training is short. Initial certification as an emergency medical technician (EMT) is frighteningly short (just 100–120 hours!). Full paramedic status requires 750–2,000 hours and enables you to administer drugs and do all the stuff they do on *ER. National Association of Emergency Medical Technicians: www.naemt.org; 408 Monroe St., Clinton, MS 39056; 800-346-2368.*

Physical Therapist. A construction worker with an injured back, an older person recovering from a stroke, an infant with a birth defect. These are typical physical therapy patients. The therapist's job is to develop programs to relieve pain and restore function. Many of us think of a physical therapist as the person who coaches the patient through exercises, but in many cases, that's done mainly by less expensive physical therapy assistants. The PT is the patient's plan maker and instructor. Over the past decade, physical therapy had been one of the fastest growing occupations, but now, supply is meeting demand, and admission to PT School has become very difficult, only a notch easier than medical school. *American Physical Therapy Association: www.apta.org; 111 N. Fairfax St., Alexandria, VA 22314; 703-684-2782. See also: www.rehaboptions.com* and *www.rehabjobs.com.*

> (Neat Niche) **Sports Physical Therapy.** As the fitness craze spreads through the formerly sedentary, newbies to the exercise world are stubbing their toes and worse. Sports physical therapy tends to be a more rewarding, less burnout-prone niche than traditional physical therapy, which more often deals with cases in which progress is slow — for example, stroke survivors.

Acupuncturist. Insert needles, manipulate carefully, restore balance in energy fields, possibly help everything from weight loss to pain control, arthritis to upper respiratory infections. Not only is the public willing to try, the insurance companies are starting to pay. Even biggies such as Cigna, Aetna, and Blue Shield are now covering some acupuncture expenses. *American Acupuncture Association: 4262 Kissena Blvd., Flushing, NY 11355; 718-886-4431. California Association of Acupuncture and Oriental Medicine: www.acupuncture.com; 1231 State St., Santa Barbara, CA 93101; 805-957-4384.*

> (Neat Niche) **Pet Acupuncturist.** If it's good enough for people, it's probably good enough for pets. Pet acupuncture is hot in California. Can Kalamazoo be far behind?

Work with Things, People, and Words

Curator. A museum exhibition begins with your idea. You then choose the objects that best convey the idea and create an innovative way to install the exhibit. Then you work to publicize it. All in one of the more peaceful work environments imaginable. Most curators major in an academic field such as art, history, archeology, or computer science, and then join a museum, zoo, or college or government library in that field. To advance, you usually need a master's in library science. Museums are expensive to maintain, so to land a good museum job, you usually must have business expertise as well as artistic (translation: an MBA). *American Association of Museums: www.aam-us.org; 1575 Eye St., N.W. Washington, DC 20005; 202-289-1818. Independent Curators, Inc.: 799 Broadway, New York, NY 10003; 212-254-8200.*

Architect. When a filmmaker wants to create a character worthy of respect, he often makes him or her an architect. After all, architecture is the perfect blend of art and science, creativity and logic, big picture and microdetail, like ensuring that the Stage 4 wiring meets the requirements of Section 3.02.05 of the Springfield County Building Code. Alas, most beginning architects spend a lot of time on the latter, and far less on design. Insiders say that good architects must be excellent communicators: Someone who can tease out what the client really wants and can convince that Springfield County Building Department that the Stage 4 wiring deserves a variance to Section 3.02.05. One thing you don't need to be is good at drawing, thanks to CAD programs, which are now dominant in architecture. *American Institute of Architects: www.aiaonline.com; 1735 New York Ave., N.W., Washington, DC 20006; 202-626-7300.*

(Neat Niche) **Green Architect.** There is some evidence that in green buildings, employees or residents are healthier. Because these buildings make extensive use of natural light, people in them feel better, and with careful material choices for carpets and drapes and careful ventilation, people don't cough or scratch their eyes because of poor air quality. Did you know, for example, that many new carpets and particleboard emit formaldehyde, which has been implicated in causing a wide range of disorders from depression to cancer?

(Neat Niche) **Universal Architect.** Design facilities that have extensive Americans for Disabilities Act requirements.

(Neat Niche) **Senior Housing.** Aging boomers will require housing to meet their physical needs.

(Neat Niche) **Entertainment Architect.** Draft movie sets, theme parks, and museums.

(Neat Niche) **Renovation Architect.** Cost considerations mean that renovation rather than new construction is hot.

Architectural Technologist. It's a long and arduous path to become an architect. Architectural technologists get to do a lot of what architects do in a fraction of the time. You may consult with the architect on the design, create computerized blueprints, use infrared equipment to identify a site's moisture problems, meet with clients to give progress reports, and coordinate with the contractors. And unlike architecture, which typically requires as a bachelor's plus two years, plus very tough exams, plus 10 to 20 years before you get to design complete buildings, architectural techs can be involved in such matters after just a two-year post–high school community college program. *British Institute of Architectural Technologists: 397 City Rd., Islington, London EC1V 1NE, England. (Oddly, there is no American association for architectural technologists.)*

BHB

Interior Designer. What fun! Helping people figure out how to make their home or office beautiful and functional. And you get to go on shopping sprees. Trouble is, if you expect to make a living, the job usually requires much more than that: reading blueprints, developing estimates for commercial as well as residential projects, knowing whether you can knock down a wall without the building falling apart. In short, you're somewhere between a decorator and an architect. Interior *decorators* often practice without credentials, but interior *designers* must have a bachelor's degree, and to get the respected American Society of Interior Designers certification, must know building and fire safety codes and space planning. The *women.com* site explains the latter, "If a person enters a building's lobby and can't easily figure out how to get to the bathroom or the elevator, then back to the lobby, you've got a problem." One more must: You need the chutzpah to convince clients that your designs are winners. *American Society of Interior Designers: www.asid.org; 608 Massachusetts Ave., N.E., Washington, DC 20002; 202-546-3480.*

(Neat Niche) **Housing for the Elderly and Disabled.** To meet the needs of the elderly and disabled and to comply with the Americans with Disabilities Act, housing developers are turning to interior decorators with special expertise in these areas.

(Neat Niche) **Elective Medical Care Clinics.** Fat thighs? Thinning hair? Varicose veins? Sagging face? Impotence? Recent advances have made these treatable in non-hospital settings. So, free-standing clinics are popping up. These must have environments that inspire confidence. Enter the interior decorator.

OOH

Landscape Architect. Preserving Yosemite Park, designing the U.S. Capitol grounds, creating Boston's "Emerald Necklace" of green spaces tying the city to the suburbs, restoring the landscape along the Baltimore-Washington Parkway. Landscape architecture is a career for architect types who are interested in outdoor design. Projects can be mundane, like designing the spaces between buildings in an industrial park or building an artificial pond in a homeowner's backyard. Or they can be exotic like designing the landscapes of resorts, golf courses, zoos, urban plazas, colleges, cemeteries, landmark monuments, or scenic highways. *American Society of Landscape Architects: www.asla.org; 636 Eye Street, N.W., Washington, DC 20001; 202-898-2444.*

Corporate Security Consultant. Corporations have always had a problem with security, and not just with customers. Employee theft is an even greater problem — for example, stealing client lists or proprietary technology. Now with corporate property ever shrinking (genes, microcircuits, formulas) and surveillance technology ever more sophisticated (such as software that cracks encryption codes), the field of corporate security is, pardon the expression, exploding. To succeed, you must specialize — in museums or computers, for example. *American Society for Industrial Security: www.asisonline.org; 1625 Prince St., Alexandria, VA. 22314; 703-519-6200. International Association of Professional Security Consultants: www.iapsc.org; 1333 Eye St. N.W., Washington, D.C. 20005; 202-712-9043.*

(Neat Niche) **Violence Prevention/Resolution.** Workplace violence is epidemic. Over 500,000 incidents of workplace violence now occur each year. Courts increasingly find that the lack of a thorough violence prevention/intervention document is evidence of liability if a worker assaults another worker. This creates a job market for you.

Business Home Economist. For years, women have been ridiculed for going into home economics, so few do anymore. Finally, the need has exceeded demand. Business home economists are used by manufacturers of large appliances to do demonstrations and by large department stores to suggest what to buy and how to display it. Supermarket chains, food manufacturers, and trade boards employ business home economists to prepare and present information to consumers. The Egg Board, for example, may ask a business home economist to develop a booklet showing how to prepare eggs without unduly clogging your arteries. *American Association of Family and Consumer Sciences: www.aafcs.org; 1555 King St., Alexandria, VA 22314; 703-706-4600.*

Ahead-of-the-Curve Careers

Would you like to get in on the ground floor? Imagine, for example, if you had gotten into television or computers when they first came out. But what will be the blockbuster technologies of the 21st century? We have some predictions. If the leading edge calls to you even though it sometimes turns out to be the bleeding edge, keep your eyes open for developments in these areas. Newspapers and magazines often provide great clues: names of companies, what and where they're doing it.

Satellite Communications. New-generation satellites can orbit the earth at far lower altitudes. This drives costs down and increases the use of satellite communications. Within a decade, satellites will enable you to make and receive calls anywhere in the world on your cell phone, Internet connections will be 1,000 times faster than with a 56.6K modem, and most cars will be equipped with Global Positioning Systems. That will make getting lost a thing of the past. You'll simply enter your destination, and an onboard computer will give you precise directions from any location. If you somehow manage to get lost, the computer will provide directions from that location.

Commercial Space Flights. They're already booking seats on the first commercial space flights, and you can bet there will be more. There will undoubtedly be jobs at the launch pad as well as on board.

Artificial Intelligence. Scientists have touted artificial intelligence for decades, but slow computing power and crude programming languages have inhibited progress. Things are starting to change: We already have $40 software programs to diagnose medical problems, almost do your taxes for you, and design a landscape that will look great year round in your microclimate. Artificial intelligence programs help mutual fund managers decide whether to buy a stock, corporations to decide if and how they might market their new widget, and the F.B.I. to evaluate the appropriate response to a terrorist threat. *American Association of Artificial Intelligence: 445 Burgess Dr., Menlo Park, CA 95025; 650-328-3123.*

Gene Therapy. We will soon have the capability to use gene therapy not only to cure disease, but to enhance human mental and physical potential. When the science advances a bit more and the ethical concerns have been carefully addressed, we are convinced that clinical genetics is likely to be *the* field of the 21st century. As the late 20th century was the information age, we believe the early 21st century will be the genetic age.

Gene Brokerage. Scientists are now creating designer genes — for example, a replacement for the defective gene in patients with cystic fibrosis. We predict that it won't be long until we'll need brokers, as with many products, to bring together buyers and sellers of genes.

Cloning. Thousands of people die each year waiting for an organ transplant; cloning can save their lives. A one-in-a-million hybrid produces a cow that has less fat; cloning will enable us to reproduce the cow. Thousands of parents with a recessive gene for a serious disease are forced to play Russian Roulette when having a baby the regular way; cloning will ensure that their baby is born healthy. We predict that America's ban on cloning will be temporary. Does anyone prefer that only rogue nations' scientists be permitted to clone humans and their organs?

Anti-Aging Research and Practice. Initial studies have shown that certain substances may slow the aging process — antioxidants, for example. Even more exciting, we have begun to unlock what actually causes aging: shortened telomeres, the appendages to DNA molecules. As the public begins to understand that significant life extension will be possible, public demand for such research will grow, and in turn, the research opportunities. Of course as the evidence gets stronger, there will also be great demand for physicians and other health care providers who specialize in anti-aging.

Cryonic Suspension. Nanotechnology, the ability to manipulate molecule-by-molecule, means that in 50 to 200 years, it is likely that we will be able to repair age-damaged cells — for example, by lengthening the previously mentioned telomeres. More and more people are deciding to be frozen in liquid nitrogen upon their deaths in hopes of being revived when science has advanced enough that this molecule-by-molecule repair can be done. Though the odds of all this working out may be small, the alternative is absolute certainty of being eaten by worms, and an eternity of death.

Virtual Reality. One of education's few unassailable truths is that we learn by doing. Simulations allow students to do things that would be impossible to do, or at least do safely: perform surgeries, fly airplanes, be on a remote island with the challenge of figuring out how to survive. Computers already make these simulations possible, but the next level of simulation is to virtually *be* in the environment: virtual reality. Virtually land on the surface of Mars and decide what to explore and how. Be virtually transplanted to Argentina and fend for yourself in Spanish. Be virtually teleported into the Battle of Gettysburg, in the role of General Grant, deciding what to do next. The options are limitless, and all represent a monumental improvement over traditional lecture, textbook, or even conventional computer-based instruction.

Convergence. All media will reduce to one box: TV, Internet, stereo, VCR, telephone, computer, will all be one integrated unit. This will allow you to interact with galaxies of information and entertainment material. The only limit will be your ability to find what you want from all the information available. A recent prediction in a special issue of *Time* magazine: "All content — movies, music, shows, books, data, magazines, recipes, and home videos — will be instantly available anywhere on demand."

And finally, two non-techno trends that we believe will offer tremendous career opportunities:

- **Eastern Europe.** A decade after opening Eastern Europe to capitalism, some of the kinks have been worked out. Now is the time to jump in. Entrepreneurs, do what you know over there. A client set up a medical journal publishing company in Poland. Another conducts corporate training in Hungary. Both of those fields are fairly full in the United States but wide open in Eastern Europe. Both clients are now millionaires.
- **Haves versus the Have-Nots.** The decades-long trend of ever-growing differences between the society's haves and have-nots must be addressed. Well-paying jobs require ever-higher-level skills that seem unreachable by growing numbers of people. Their inability to compete renders them economically vulnerable, which reduces their chances of ever rising from poverty and increases the likelihood of social unrest. Researchers and policymakers are sorely needed to figure out a solution that doesn't require confiscatory taxation policies that would generate a revolt from the haves.

Not-So-Cool Careers

The following are all popular careers, and no doubt, there are happy people in them, but, for most folks, we think the 512 cool careers are a cut above. Lest you think we forgot about your favorite career, or wanted to know why it didn't make it into the hallowed halls of the Cool Careers Catalog, here are our excuses.

Of course, if, despite our reservations, you're excited about pursuing one of these so-called "not-so-cool careers," don't let us or anyone else stop you from pursuing it. Each person must listen to his or her own heart. We have met many people whose parents, teachers, and friends told them not to pursue a particular career and who surprised everyone by succeeding.

Airline pilot. Unless you train in the military for years, you have little chance of landing a decent-paying job. Even if you do, it's unlikely to be one of those plum commercial airline gigs. You're more likely to be spewing pesticides from an agricultural plane.

Chef. Despite the glamorous image, in the end, being a chef means lots of hours over a hot stove where tempers flare and stress is high. Creativity is rare; repetition of the same few recipes is common. Only a tiny fraction of chefs get the fame and big bucks.

Chemist. Most of the job growth in chemistry is in biochemistry. This field is covered in the "biology" scoop.

Chiropractic. Many people swear by chiropractic, and recent studies show that it is often more effective than medical approaches for lower back pain. So chiropractic can be a rewarding profession when practiced well. But for the amount and expense of the training involved, we decided that there were enough minuses to keep chiropractic out of our august group of cool careers. Chiropractic requires a two-, and increasingly, a four-year science-intensive college education followed by four years of chiropractic doctoral education (all 17 accredited institutions are private and therefore expensive) plus demanding national and state board exams. After all that training and cost, there is serious controversy over the effectiveness of chiropractic beyond treatment of lower back pain and similar ailments. Many chiropractors, egged on by practice-building consultants, claim that spinal manipulation — chiropractors' main technique — can address a wide variety of ills. But according to QuackWatch, a member of the Consumer Federation of America that focuses on health-related fraud and winner of over 20 awards as a top health Web site, "Very few health problems can be influenced by spinal manipulation. There is no logical reason to believe that regular spinal 'check-ups' and 'adjustments' provide any general health benefit." For the complete report, see *www.quackwatch.com/01QuackeryRelatedTopics/chirosell.html.* To get the chiropractic profession's side, visit the *American Chiropractic Association's Web site at www.amerchiro.org; 1701 Clarendon Blvd., Arlington, VA 22209.*

Fiction writer. Lottery odds against making even a subsistence living doing this.

Filmmaker. Lottery odds against making even a subsistence living doing this.

Fire Fighter. Too boring for days at a time, and when it's not boring, you're often in danger. Plus, you have to live in a firehouse with a bunch of other fire fighters.

Hotel Manager. It's a long road up, often with much menial work along the way.

Overseas careers. Worker permits are tough to get, especially for better-paying jobs. Also, many Americans find that living abroad is less rewarding than vacationing.

Paralegal. Although paralegal appears on the charts of fast-growing fields, we believe that this is changing. In many urban areas, there is a glut of attorneys, forcing them to work as paralegals, in turn, threatening the job security of non-lawyer-trained paralegals. And what clinched paralegal's exclusion from the Catalog is that being a paralegal is often not the most rewarding career. Although some paralegals do important research work, many function as powerless, glorified secretaries. Attorneys can be quite hierarchical, and many paralegals complain of being treated as second-class citizens. Besides, the work is often tedious. Finally, because paralegals mainly do the scut work for someone else, they don't see the fruits of their labors often enough — for example, a satisfied client.

Performance Artist (singer, actor, musician, and so on.) Lottery odds against making a middle-class living doing this.

Physicist. This is a field that requires an especially challenging Ph.D. to qualify for a substantive position, and the Department of Labor predicts a poor job market for physicists. People with physics backgrounds are more likely to find employment in engineering and geology, both of which are profiled in the Catalog.

Police Officer. Too dangerous, plus your job is basically to keep a lid on an enormous problem. You never get to deal with the core causes. Besides, there's a surprising amount of paperwork.

Politician. Although a half-million people make a living as politicians, we can't call it a cool career. The main reason is that the process of getting elected is so absurd. Your private life is made public. The process consists mainly of telemarketing, nonstop door-to-door flesh-pressing, and rubber chicken dinners, none of which reveals anything about your competence to do the job. And then there's the fundraising: taking money from special interests that will expect something in return; and no matter how much money you raise, you usually must contribute a lot of your own money to fund the absurdity.

Real Estate Salesperson. Fewer than 20 percent of real estate salespeople make a middle-class living. And those who make big money usually work big hours, including many nights and weekends. Real estate sales jobs are commission-only, and it takes months for a home to close, so you usually need at least six months of savings to support your start-up. Finally, we believe that long-term prospects for real estate salespeople are poor. In coming years, computers — for example, online house shopping — will do much of the work that Realtors currently do.

Retail Buyer. The excess of American stores portends more consolidations, resulting in less hiring of buyers and additional pressure on existing ones. Long hours are the norm. In addition, computerized ordering has eliminated many buyer jobs.

Retail Manager. Long hours, low pay, high burnout. America is over-stored.

Talk Show Host. Lottery odds against making a middle-class living doing this.

TV News Anchor. Lottery odds against making a middle-class living doing this. Besides, in many such jobs, you're basically a marionette reading off a teleprompter.

Travel Agent. The low pay and relentless telephone work with clients endlessly changing their minds are too small compensation for the travel benefits.

Chapter 3

The 20 Most Revealing Questions

In This Chapter

- Your values
- Your passions
- Your abilities
- The big picture

You meet. Your heart starts pounding. You fall madly in lust. You don't stop to think that she's married to her work. Or that his earning potential is worse than an aspiring artist's. Or that, actually, he's pretty boring. A lifetime of listening to him? Get serious.

Or the opposite, you meet the logical choice: intelligent, employed, no vices. The facts are all there, but the chemistry's not.

As in finding a mate, finding a career should involve both your head and your heart.

You've already used your heart: You picked out the careers from the Cool Careers Catalog that make your heart beat faster. Now it's time to use your head. Which of those careers (or perhaps another career), logically makes sense? Which careers offer what you really want and need? The problem is that if you're like most career searchers, you're not sure.

That's where the 20 questions in this chapter come in. Over the years, with clients and callers to our career radio shows, we've tried every approach imaginable to tease out people's *career musts:* the things people really want and need in a career. We've found these 20 questions to be of the most help to the most people.

Making the Process Easier

When a doctor takes your medical history, she knows that only a few of the answers to her many questions will reveal anything significant. She still asks all of them because she can't know in advance which questions are significant for you.

The same is true of these 20 questions. Only a few will reveal one of your true *career musts*. Questions that yield one usually elicit an immediate "Aha!" So if you have trouble answering any particular question, skip it and go on — that question is unlikely to be significant for you.

Just mark your answers directly on the questionnaire. Be sure to focus on your career *musts*. Don't pick career characteristics that would be nice but aren't *musts*. People who include all the "that-would-be-nice" characteristics end up with lists a mile long, which leaves them not much better off than when they started. So only record the things that your career absolutely, positively, must offer.

Try, too, to answer the questions with a fresh mind — don't automatically give answers that conform to your current job or to the career you're contemplating.

At the end of these 20 questions, we'll tell you how to make use of your career musts.

The Questions

We've grouped the 20 questions into these categories:

- Your values
- Your passions
- Your skills
- Your personality
- Big-picture questions

Have at them.

Your values

1. **Are any of the following values *musts* in your next career? If so, mark it or them with a star. Otherwise leave this item blank.**

High status

A minimum annual income of: (specify)

An easy job

Casual (or formal) dress code

A specific geographic location or work at home (specify):

The water, the mountains, beach (specify):

Short training time

Ability to make a difference (Be more specific if you like.)

Variety of tasks

Recognition

Adrenaline rush (competition, risk-taking activities)

Working alone (or with people)

Being your own boss

Being on the cutting edge

Little or no supervision

Work indoors (or outdoors) (Be more specific if you like. For example, a number of my clients crave working on a college campus.)

An aesthetically pleasing workplace

Opportunities for self-expression

Other: (specify)

Your passions

2. Write here any passion that must be part of your next career. Otherwise leave this item blank.

____

____

____

Want help in answering this question? Try this exercise: If you see a passion or two on this list that must be part of your next career, circle it/them.

Creating beauty
Growing things
Sports
Construction
Educating/training
Travel
Photography
Religion/spirituality
Counseling
Health planning
Health care
Fitness
Drug abuse
Foreign languages
Management/administration
Urban/regional planning
Animals
Cars
Investments
Politics
Relationships

Getting a good deal
Mathematics
Accounting/taxes
Books, magazines, newspapers
Web sites
Machines
Television/radio
Information systems
Human rights
Consumer advocacy
Landscaping
Aviation
Aerospace
Real estate
Criminal justice/corrections
Computer hardware
Computer software
Cooking
Writing
Food
Law

Music
Dance
Selling
Public speaking
Architecture
Mass transportation
Environmental issues
Science
Sewing
Law
International affairs
Labor-employee relations
Insects
Electronic equipment
Camping/backpacking
Film
Theater
Energy
History
Sex

Your abilities

3. Do you have a skill or ability or two that you are good at and *know* you want to use in your next career? If not, leave this item blank. If yes, write it here:

___

___

___

Where or for whom might you like to use that skill(s)?

Say you choose planning as your ability. If you're an artistic type, maybe you'd want to work for a company that plans traveling museum exhibits. If you're money-driven, you may want to plan events for a cash-rich industry such as software, telecommunications, financial services, or biotech.

Many people don't know what skill(s) they're good at and want to use in their career. One of the following questions may help:

- What have you always had a knack for?
- Do you have a core competency (something you do better than anything else)?
- Think about one or more instances when you were complimented on your work. What skill were you mainly using?
- What knowledge or skill do you have that few others do? Who might pay you to use it? The obvious choice is a skill or knowledge that you've used at work, but you might consider other things as well.
- What decent-paying job could you succeed at *easily?*

The following list may also help you identify your own top skills and abilities. If one or two of these are a career must for you, star it or them. Otherwise, leave this item blank.

- Generating ideas
- Laying out a step-by-step plan
- Organizing
- Making things efficient
- Problem solving
- Researching
- Evaluating
- Attending to details
- Advising
- Facilitating/Mediating
- Understanding what makes people tick
- Creating visual or performing art (specify)
- Computer skills (specify)
- Science/health care skills (specify)
- Mathematics or statistics

- Written persuasion
- Written explanation
- Oral persuasion
- Oral explanation
- Performing/entertaining
- Reading
- Making or fixing things with your hands
- Another physical skill (specify):
- Other (specify):

Many people are not sure what their best skills are. Skill assessment tests aren't panaceas, but they may be worth considering. The Johnson O'Connor Institute (800-452-1539) has branches in most major cities and offers assessments for $480. The Rockport Institute (301-340-6600) offers an at-home test with interpretation by phone for $450.

Your personality

4. Does one or two of the following characteristics truly define you? If so, star it. Otherwise leave it blank.

Leader

Entrepreneur

Caring for others

Thinker

Implementer

Artistic/aesthetic

Builder/maker of things

Solving problems by talking with others about them

Like to keep things running well

Other (specify):

5. Do you know that you want to work with a certain type of person, either as co-worker or customer? If so, circle the type(s) in the following list; otherwise leave this item blank.

Children

Teens

Adults

Older adults

The physically sick

The mentally ill

The highly intelligent

Those of average intelligence

Those of low intelligence

Arty people

Intellectuals

Happy people

People with a problem (Be more specific if you wish.)

People of a particular race, gender, or sexual orientation (specify):

Alone

Other (specify):

6. **Barbara Sher, author of *Wishcraft,* uses this technique: Walk around your living space. Does anything suggest a career must?**

   Sheila has dozens of framed photographs of family members all around her house. These photos remind her of how important family is to her. This interest can give rise to many careers — parenting coach, family therapist, genealogist, genetic counselor, to name a few.

____

____

Big-picture questions

7. **Many people's "dream career" falls into one of just the following six categories. Does yours? If so, circle it; if not, leave it blank.**

   Being a performer (motivational speaker, singer, TV news anchor, for example)

   Leading an organization that makes a difference

   Owning your own business, perhaps working from your home

   Generating ideas, planning, training/teaching, organizing, and/or writing

   Caring for others

   Any job that you can do well, pays the bills, and has nice co-workers

8. This is one of Barbara Sher's favorite questions: What is your job from hell? Now describe the inverse of that — your job from heaven.

____

____

9. Do you know of a wealthy, well-connected, or highly skilled person who likes you enough to perhaps hire you for a job more desirable than you could get on the open market? If not, leave this item blank. If so, what kind of work would you want to do for that person?

It bugs everyone. You wonder, how in the world that person got that great job? Well, she may have known someone. Especially if you're short on technical expertise, knowing someone can often help you get a better job than you could get on the open market.

____

____

10. Write your personal mission statement: one sentence that describes your life's greatest aspiration. If that suggests a career or a career must, write it here:

____

____

11. What career do your parents, partner, or close friends think you should pursue?

If you don't know, ask them! But don't too quickly accept or reject their advice because of the source. Make an open-minded choice.

____

____

12. What did you like best about each job (paid or unpaid) you've held? Do you see any common threads?

____

____

13. List at least two peak accomplishments.

These are achievements that you had plenty of drive to complete and which gave you a strong sense of accomplishment. If you can't think of two from adulthood, go back to your younger days. Does looking at your peak accomplishments suggest a career must or even a career?

____

____

14. In what career do you believe you could make the biggest difference?

Try thinking really big. For example, would you like to bring about world peace? How about becoming a specialist in biological-weapon deterrence? Rather think smaller? Perhaps your gift to the world is to be the right-hand person to someone who thinks big. One of my clients, for example, was an assistant to Galen Rowell, the environmental photographer.

____

____

15. If you couldn't fail, what would you do?

A client said, "I'd be Barbara Walters." I told her that she may or may not ever become a Barbara Walters, but trying may get her close enough — she might end up hosting a TV game show in Dubuque. Or, along the way, she might uncover a related but less crowded career such as celebrity escorting. For some people, getting partway to a dream career is better than abandoning the dream for a job at the Western Widget Waxing Company. Of course, going after a long-shot dream career, you do run the risk of ending up waiting tables.

____

____

16. What would your twin (or yourself 10 years from now) tell you to do?

A client said that he was stuck, but when I asked him, "What would your twin tell you to do?" he immediately rang out, "My twin would tell me to get off his butt and go to law school. So what if he's 35? He'll be 39 in a few years whether he goes to law school or not."

____

____

17. **If you simplified your life so that you could live on $20,000 a year, what career would you pursue?**

    Jag's most rewarding experiences came from tutoring students one-on-one, but he knew that because he hated marketing, he was unlikely to make more than $20,000 a year as a tutor. He decided to scale down to a small rental apartment and otherwise live more simply in exchange for doing what he loved.

    ___

    ___

18. **If there is anything you must avoid in your career, specify it here.**

    ___

    ___

19. **Have you or someone you love faced an adversity that suggests a career that excites you?**

    Having undergone a mastectomy, Rhonda now fits other women who have had mastectomies with prosthetic breasts and special lingerie. Rhonda meets clients in their own homes, and says, "People are very appreciative. It's so much more relaxed than walking into a cold department store with everyone hearing what your problem is."

    ___

    ___

20. **Deep down, some people know what they want to do. They simply need to be asked point-blank. Richard Bolles asks, "What job would you love to do more than any other in the world?"**

    ___

    ___

Now, what to do with all your answers? Chapter 4 can help.

Chapter 4

Integrating Head and Heart

In This Chapter

- Distilling what you discovered from the 20 Most Revealing Questions
- Identifying careers that fit your *career musts*
- A virtual career counselor
- Deciding on the final career(s) to check out

Great! You've used your head to identify your *career musts*. You've used your heart to pick out careers that feel good from the Cool Careers Catalog. Now, we show you how to integrate head and heart so that you end up choosing a career that satisfies you both rationally and emotionally.

Julie Finds a Career

For the past 20 years, Julie has been a biologist for one of the nation's largest cosmetics manufacturers. She used to like her job, but now hates it. Much of her work is now automated, so she spends half her time monitoring a machine, and the other half feeling useless. Trouble is, her biology training was 20 years ago, so she's no longer marketable as a biologist. She browsed the Cool Careers Catalog and, on gut feeling, picked out restaurant menu designer, neon sign maker, celebrity personal assistant, optician, and speech pathologist. Julie's answers to the 20 Most Revealing Questions revealed that her logical *career musts* come down to just three things: a job that required an organized, detail-oriented person, an opportunity to work with her hands, and a chance to be her own boss. In light of her career musts, she eliminated celebrity personal assistant. She tried to come up with other careers that satisfy her career musts that sounded even more interesting but could not. Even though it wouldn't involve working with her hands, Julie decided to look first into speech pathology. Join us, next chapter, for the poignant conclusion of *Julie Finds a Career.*

That's a real-life example. Now here's that career-finding process, step-by-step.

Discovering Your Top-Choice Career(s)

We're going to be straight with you. Despite our best efforts, the rest of this chapter requires concentration and could be, frankly . . . well . . . let's just say it . . . boring. It's also important. Otherwise, we would have simply pressed the delete key. Stay with us. Most of you will find the information here worth the effort. The good news is that this chapter doesn't take long.

Step 1: List your career musts

Look back at your answers to the 20 Most Revealing Questions and copy here the answers you consider most significant. These are your *career musts*.

____

____

____

If you listed more than five *career musts*, see if you can whittle down to the five most important without feeling like you're cutting off your right arm. ***Hint:*** You can often cheat by combining two *musts* into one.

Step 2: Do the careers you picked satisfy your career musts?

Look at how well each career you picked from the Cool Careers Catalog satisfies your career musts. Does that make you want to eliminate any of those careers?

Step 3: Do your career musts suggest other careers?

Look at your career musts. Do any other careers come to mind that are at least as interesting as those you picked from the Cool Careers Catalog?

If you can't come up with any other careers, see the virtual career counselor later in this chapter.

Or ask your friends to brainstorm with you. Decent party game. Here are some examples:

- When Jacque saw "sales," "romance," and "aesthetic" among her career musts, she added wedding planner to her list of possible careers.
- When Luther saw "writing," "travel," "high-income," and "fluent in Spanish," he added "marketing communications writer for a fast-growing company that does a lot of business with Central America" to his list of possible careers.

Many people's career musts are quite general — for example, "I like managing and communicating with adults." To avoid a difficult job search, you need to narrow your focus. Here's a solution: Decide *where* you might want to use those general career musts. For example, maybe you'd like managing and communicating with adults in a hospital, or in the financial services industry, or on a cruise ship to Bora Bora.

A wise client named Eric said, "Managing is managing, so why not pick an uncrowded industry, one that most people wouldn't think of?" He looked through the index of his Yellow Pages and stopped at "acid manufacturers." He read up on the acid industry, e-mailed all the local firms, and soon got a management job with a minimum of competition.

A virtual career counselor

Stuck? Can't come up with careers that incorporate your *career musts*? Try these steps. This process simulates what I actually do to come up with career ideas for clients. It's easier than it looks. Give it a shot.

1. **Come up with one career that incorporates three of your career musts.**
2. **Ask yourself what feels wrong about that career.**
3. **Come up with another career that fixes what's wrong.**
4. **Repeat Steps 2 and 3 until you make the career as desirable as you can.**
5. **Now, see if you can incorporate one or more of your remaining career musts into the career you identified in Step 4.**

To create more career options, repeat the process with the same or different three career musts.

Here's an example:

Terry's career musts include the following:

- Systems analysis in Windows NT environment
- Work with smart people

- Explain complicated things in plain English
- Work at home
- International opportunities

Here's how Terry played virtual career counselor:

1. **Come up with one career that incorporates three of your career musts.**

   Terry comes up with "train people in systems analysis." (That fit his first three *career musts*.)

2. **Ask yourself what feels wrong about that career.**

   "I'm afraid that training would get boring," Terry realizes.

3. **Come up with another career that fixes what's wrong.**

   Terry thinks, "Okay, what if I do systems analysis training in another country?" (one of his other career musts). His reaction: "No, still feels boring. Besides, the toilet paper will be worse. Okay, what if, instead of training on systems analysis, I do systems analysis *consulting*. That would give me a new challenge with each new client. Hmm."

4. **Keep repeating Steps 2 and 3 until you make the career as desirable as you can.**

   "Okay, systems analysis consulting. Not bad. What feels wrong? I'm not a good marketer. Okay. I'll get a partner who's a marketing whiz. Okay, what still feels wrong? I'm afraid it would be lonely. Okay, I'll take a part-time job so that I'll see people on a regular basis. That would also give me some income while I'm cranking up my consulting business. Okay, that feels pretty good."

5. **Now see if you can incorporate one or more of your remaining career musts into the career you identified in Step 4.**

   "Well, the international thing is the only career must I haven't incorporated. And as I look at the career I created for myself, I don't mind giving that up. I think I'll be able to satisfy my travel urges on vacations."

Additional help

Do you want more options than you have been able to come up with on your own? It may be time for a bit of professional help. Consider seeing a career counselor. To see what options your friendly authors would come up with for you, check out the "About the Authors" page at the front of the book.

Step 4: Remember what careers excite you

One or more of the 20 Most Revealing Questions may elicit not just a career must, but an actual career that excites you. If so, do you like it at least as well as those you picked from the Cool Careers Catalog? If so, add it (or them) to your list of possible careers.

Step 5: Pick one or more careers that might actually work

Look at all your possible careers:

- Careers you identified in Steps 3 and 4
- Careers you picked from the Cool Careers Catalog
- Other careers you're considering — like going into your uncle's widget business

And now, ta-dah, the moment of truth: Is there at least one career that feels like a real possibility? If yes, go to Step 6. If not, see Chapter 20.

Step 6: Find out more

Before making your final career choice, you may want to learn more about that top-choice career(s) of yours. Chapter 5 shows you how to do just that.

Chapter 5

What's That Career Really Like?

In This Chapter

- Checking out print sources
- Using the Internet
- Getting the scoop from people in the field
- Visiting a workplace
- Trying it out

You've found a career (or five) that sounds good. But what if you picked wrong? What if you fail in that career? Or you succeed but are totally miserable?

This chapter boosts your chances of picking well. It shows how to find out what a career is really like — before taking the plunge. And it's not complicated. There are just three approaches: reading, contacting, and visiting. Read about the career, and if it still sounds good, contact a few people in the field, and if it still feels right, visit a few people in their workplaces. This chapter shows you how to make the most of all three approaches.

A side benefit of all that digging around is that you have insider information about the career, which should make you *molto impresivo* in job interviews.

Julie Finds a Career: The Final Episode

In the previous episode of *Julie Finds a Career* (in Chapter 4), after browsing the Cool Careers Catalog and answering the 20 Most Revealing Questions, Julie decided to look into speech pathology. She never dreamt what she would find, right on her computer. In the online *Occupational Outlook Handbook,* Julie discovered a specialty within speech pathology that she had personal experience with: swallowing problems. Her grandmother, after a stroke, was unable to swallow, and had to be fed with a feeding tube until her death. It is one of Julie's most vivid memories. Julie got chills at the thought that perhaps her career could focus on helping people avoid the feeding tube.

And as she continued to read, Julie found out that speech pathology was even a practical career choice. Because of the aging population, demand for speech pathologists is expected to increase greatly. Even better for Julie, who wanted to be self-employed, the OOH says that demand for speech pathologists in private practice is expected to grow dramatically due to the use of contract services by health care providers. And although she would have to go back to school, the OOH says that much of the course work is basic sciences and math, all of which she had taken.

For the first time in 20 years, Julie was excited about her career prospects. Eagerly, she visited the American Speech-Language-Hearing Association Web site. There, she found dozens of articles about swallowing disorders, many of which listed authors and contact information. She phoned those contacts to ask about the more personal aspects of the job. Among other things, she learned about the field's dark side. Swallowing specialists frequently face a particularly painful situation: when a stroke patient is in an irreversible coma and has lost all ability to swallow. At this point, the speech pathologist must discuss whether to insert a feeding tube. That would prolong the comatose person's life, but it also usually means that the family must continue to pay enormous medical bills just to keep him in a coma.

Shaken but still stirred, Julie asked two local swallowing specialists if she could visit them at work. The visits clinched the decision for Julie. She saw her grandmother in the patients and could picture herself as the speech therapist helping them. Now, it somehow didn't matter that this career didn't have one of Julie's career musts: working with her hands. Now, it somehow didn't matter that she had to go back to school, or that she'd have less income for a while — the two things that had so scared Julie that she stayed for 20 years in a job in which she was so unhappy. Now, somehow, all the fears and the obstacles seemed conquerable. Julie had found her perfect work.

Researching a career may sound boring in the abstract, but for Julie, and perhaps for you, it can change your life.

Reading about a Career

Books and articles are among the most underrated products. (And college may be the most overrated, but that's another book.) If you're willing to do only one thing to check out a career, read. A good book or article constitutes access to the best, most thorough, and most carefully organized ideas. And they're available to you at any time, day or night, for the cost of a large pizza — or free at the library.

Reading an article or skimming a book, you learn what took an expert years to figure out. Consider the *Occupational Outlook Handbook* at most libraries, and on the Internet at `www.bls.gov/ocohome.htm`. The OOH includes authoritative profiles of 250 of the most popular careers, based on interviews with many people in those fields. What a treasure! Reading the OOH is like hearing what thousands of people have to say about their careers. Plus, the information is distilled for you and available whenever or wherever you want it. To us, that's cool.

Why read before phoning or visiting?

Okay, so why would you read about a career before you contact someone in that field? Simple: You don't want to sound like a dodo. Read about the career and you're more likely to impress your contacts as being worth their time. Who knows? One of them may then be willing to take you under his wing, reveal inside secrets, and maybe even help you get hired.

Also, boning up in advance means that you'll make the most of your contact. You'll only need to ask about those things you couldn't discover on your own.

Best stuff to read

"All right, so you've guilt-tripped me into reading stuff. What should I read? And please don't tell me to read something boring." We'll do our best.

Try this elegantly simple approach recommended by Mary-Ellen Mort, one of the nation's top experts on how to research a career.

1. **Call your area's central library and ask which branch has the best business collection.**
2. **Visit or call the librarian in charge of that collection, and describe the career you want to learn more about.**

   That's all you need to do. The librarian is likely to help you find the right information. It's that simple.

We'll let you in on a librarian's secret: In addition to books and periodicals, today's libraries have powerful online and CD-ROM services — too expensive for home users — that can search enormous databases for information about your target career.

But what if you live hours from a decent library? What if the only librarian you can find specializes in children's books? What if you'd simply rather we hand you some cool references? Well, okay, here they are. We think these are the best of the best.

- ***The Occupational Outlook Handbook* ($19, call 800-648-JIST to order).** Its strength is its authoritativeness. Its weakness is that it avoids any subjectivity. So it's great on the facts, lousy on the feel. For the latter, use the next two books.
- ***The Princeton Review Guide to Your Career.*** This book provides insider profiles of 165 popular careers. Each profile includes sections on "a day in the life," "paying your dues," "associated careers," "past and future," and "quality of life" in the profession two, five, and ten years after entry in that field.
- ***JobSmarts 50 Top Careers*** by Bradley Richardson contains substantial profiles on popular careers such as accounting, FBI agent, engineering, journalism, and health care.
- **Professional association publications**. We provide contact information for associations for many careers in the Cool Careers Catalog. For other careers, try the *Encyclopedia of Associations,* available in most large libraries in print. Some libraries allow you to access it online from your computer.

  From a professional association you may be able to get

  - Information for people considering the career
  - Articles for professionals in the field
  - A list of publications the organization recommends or sells
  - Membership information. Associations will at least provide that, which is often useful in itself.

  If, rather than visit its Web site, you phone or write to a professional association, be nice! The organization exists primarily to serve its members. It provides you with information out of the goodness of its nonprofit heart.
- **Dan Lauber's *Career Finder* series.** This series includes separate volumes for professions, government, nonprofit and education, and international careers. Each volume lists resources for learning about hundreds of careers. (Each volume costs less than $20 and is revised regularly; order at 888-366-5200, 708-366-5200.)
- ***Best Home Businesses for the 90s* (2nd Edition).** Written by two of us (Paul & Sarah), this book profiles 95 top home businesses.

Using the Internet to Find Out about a Career

If you do just one thing on the Internet to learn about a career, visit the Web site of that field's main professional association. Each association uses the collective wisdom of many people in the profession to select the best, most accurate information available. The previous section shows you how to locate your professional association.

Want to go a step beyond professional associations? Try one or more of the following Web sites:

- **America's CareerInfoNet** (`www.acinet.org/resource/careers`) is a service of the U.S. Department of Labor, and offers links to some of the Net's best career information sites.
- **The Riley Guide** (`www.dbm.com/jobguide`): This site links to other sites for hundreds of specific occupations.
- **Your favorite search engine.** Use the profession as the search term.

  Search engines are amazing tools. Imagine a librarian who can search every book in an enormous library to find each reference that includes the word or phrase you are interested in. Then this wonder-librarian stacks the books in order of how frequently your word or phrase is used. That's a search engine. And it's free. Plus, you have access to this "librarian" 24/7 in the comfort of your home. We love search engines!
- **The search feature at Amazon.com** (`www.amazon.com`): Simply enter your career and out pops book titles with your career in the title. The listings often include descriptions and even reviews of the books.
- ***U.S. News and World Report*'s Web site** (`www.usnews.com`): This site contains descriptions of the outlook for major professions, plus predictions of hot niches.
- **The postings on your field's online discussion groups.** There's a comprehensive list of these groups at `www.careers.org`.

To learn about an industry, try these online resources:

- For links to publications for your target industry, see `www.yahoo.com/business_and_economy/magazines`.
- For links to hundreds of other industry publications, go to `enews.com`.
- For a list of resources for learning about individual industries, visit `www.industrylink.com`.

Contacting People in the Field

You can't find out everything by reading. Talking to people lets you ask the questions your reading didn't answer. It's also a way to start building your professional network.

Many career seekers are reluctant to call people in the field. The two main reasons are "I don't want to impose" and "I'm afraid I'll sound stupid." Remember that most people like to talk about their careers. And if they don't, they're adults — they can say no. Even if you are imposing, in the larger order of things, that's okay. The time will probably come when you're in a position to help someone. If you do, you'll have squared your karmic account.

Need more prodding to pick up the phone or send that e-mail? Chapter 21 offers cures for procrastitis.

"Okay, okay, but whom do I contact?"

This list should yield you more contacts than you can stomach:

- If you have a friend or relative in your target career, you can start there. At the end of the conversation, ask for the names of colleagues you might speak with.
- Attend a local meeting of your professional association.
- Get the phone numbers of members of the professional association by phoning its national or local office or by checking its Web site.
- Talk with the editor of the professional association's magazine or newsletter. Editors often have a finger on the field's pulse, and may be willing to share some nuggets.
- Your college's career center may maintain a list of alumni who are willing to tell their career tales.
- If you have chutzpah, just open your Yellow Pages and start dialing.

Each person's viewpoint is idiosyncratic. One dentist may gush that business is booming while the next dentist moans that attracting new patients is like pulling teeth. (We couldn't resist.) So don't get too swayed by one person's opinion.

What to say

Count on getting turned down a lot in your quest for information, but the following approach works often enough, and, unlike many recommended ruses, it's honest.

When you phone, you'll rarely get your target person. The key to getting through a gatekeeper or voice-mail jail is to briefly tell your true human story. Here's a gatekeeper example:

> Hello, my name is (*Insert your name*). This may be one of the weirder (*Trust us, that word works*) calls you've gotten today, but I really need your help. I'm still trying to figure out what I want to be when I grow up. I think I may want to be a (*insert career*), but I'm not sure yet. I've read about the career, but feel I should talk with someone in the field. Can I ask you to see if your boss might be willing to answer just a few questions about what it's like to be a (*insert career*)?

If the gatekeeper can't or won't put you through, ask for your target's e-mail address. But for now, assume that you have your target person on the phone. This approach works well:

> Hello, I'm (*insert your name*). I'd really appreciate your help. I'm considering becoming a (*insert career.*) I've read a lot about the field, but I'd like to talk with someone who is actually in that career. I wonder if I could ask you a few questions about your experience as a (*insert career.*)

If the person says that now isn't a good time, ask when you can call back or whether you can meet in person.

Next, ask your questions. Of course, you may have your own, but these questions are likely to elicit useful information:

- How'd you get into this career?
- Can you walk me through a typical day?
- What do you find are the best and worst things about your career?
- What have you found to be the skills most important to succeeding in your career?
- Can you think of anything you know now that you wish you'd known when you were deciding to enter this field?
- Can you think of anything I should know about this field that is unlikely to find its way into print? (Our favorite question.)
- Any advice about the smartest way to prepare for this career?
- What kind of salary can I expect?
- Are there any particularly interesting specialties within your field?
- How is the field changing?
- Why might someone leave this field?
- Do you know someone else you think I should talk with or something else I should read before deciding whether to pursue this career?

If the conversation went well, ask if you could spend an hour watching that person at work.

Visiting a Workplace

Why visit? Because some things you have to experience to fully appreciate. Watching someone at work is the next best thing to doing the job yourself.

Craig, for example, thought he might want to be an arborist (tree surgeon), but after spending an hour on-site with a professional, he realized that needing to spend that much time on high branches, often in bad weather, outweighed the joy of artfully shaping overgrown trees.

If you won't visit at least three people in your target career, we recommend you visit none. That may seem like odd advice, but remember that a single person's version of a career is idiosyncratic. Say you're contemplating becoming a career counselor. Your visit to a chain career counseling service will likely take you to a downtown office building, where the counselors dress in suits and use a counseling style that emphasizes asking questions to draw out the client's own ideas. But, if you visit me, you see a career counselor dressed in a sweater and chinos in a home office who generates many career ideas, asks the client to react to each, and refines the next idea based on that feedback. You may love one of those career counseling modes but not the other, and if you visit only one career counselor, you'd get a limited sense of the options.

What to do during a visit?

Okay, so you're on-site. What now? Simple. Just ask the person to show you around and to let you watch her do tasks that are central to the job. If possible, get introduced to others in that career at the work site.

Use your head and your heart. Rationally, can you see yourself doing this work day in and day out? Emotionally, is it your instinct that you'd feel good in such a career?

A virtual visit

If you live on an isolated farm, it may not be easy to visit an urban planner. That's why videotapes can be invaluable. In some ways, career videos are better than in-person visits because they usually round up a variety of people in the profession, ask good questions, and give you the full tour. And a virtual visit is perfect for those shy souls who simply can't make themselves set up an in-person visit, let alone ask lots of good questions during the visit. Large libraries should have a collection of career videos.

After the phone call or visit

Even if it feels like a technique, write a thank-you letter — and not just because it's polite. Yes, recipients recognize thank-you letters as formalities, but those notes still tend to impress and, at minimum, keep you in the recipient's mind. That little note can motivate the recipient to offer you more counsel, or even help you land a job.

But, there are thank-you notes and there are thank-you notes. Here's an approach that has worked time and time again. It's more informal and open than traditional versions.

> Dear Sam,
>
> I so appreciate your allowing me to watch you make artificial limbs. I'd never have realized how psychologically demanding working so closely with an amputee can be. Helping a person to replace an arm is such a personal thing!
>
> I'm now sure I want to be a prosthetist. It balances art, science, and the need to be a real human being. If I work hard at it, I can do this.
>
> I'll follow up on your suggestion to check out Cal State University, Dominguez Hills' program. If you have any other advice, I'd love it if you'd call me. And if I have a question, I hope you won't mind if I call you. Thank you so much.
>
> Sincerely,
>
> So and So

Getting Serious

Here are a few time-consuming but potentially worthwhile activities for checking out your top-choice career. Time-consuming, yes, but much less so than making the wrong career choice.

- **A seminar or short course in your chosen field.** The professional association for that career may offer live, taped, or on-line versions. For a list of thousands of at-home courses in a wide range of fields, see *Peterson's Guide to Distance Learning*. Also, check you local college's extension catalog and perhaps even its regular catalog.
- **Conferences and trade shows.** These are excellent places to learn about a career. You have hundreds of practitioners plus their suppliers and customers all in one place. Exhibit areas sell tools of the trade, and ongoing workshops teach you the field's basics and cutting edges. Plus, the many meals, breaks, and parties are specifically designed to facilitate chatting.

- **Volunteering, interning, or project work.** Nothing takes the place of an actual tryout. A brief one is often enough to show you what you need to know about a career. Before deciding to become a high school teacher, Derrick volunteered as a classroom aide. After a week, he began to feel the draining effect of trying to keep 30 students — a different 30 every 50 minutes — motivated, let alone educated. He also quickly tired of the conversations in the teachers' lounge. Teaching wasn't right for him. Two weeks of volunteering saved him two years of training plus many more years of unhappiness in a career he did not like.

  A short-term volunteer or low-pay stint can be well worth your time — think of it as a tuition-free education. Working for little or nothing gives you power — the power to ensure that you get to do meaningful work. So, before signing on, negotiate your role. Licking envelopes for an oceanographer won't give you a good idea of what the job is like. Accompanying the oceanographer on a week stay in a bathyscaph will.

Okay. After all this digging around, your top choice should be getting clearer.

Chapter 6

Finding the Courage to Commit

In This Chapter

- Building your courage
- How the authors found the courage to commit
- A final check

No matter how much analysis you do, it can be hard to make that final decision and say: "Yes, this is the career I want!" Helping you make that decision is what this chapter is about.

When Nothing Feels Exciting Enough

Sure, maybe you just need more options. If so, Chapter 21 offers ten more sources of cool careers. But sometimes, you can look through every career compendium in the world and still have a hard time committing. Often, that's because you're holding out for a career that excites you *now*.

Fact: Many people who end up passionate about their careers don't start out that way. True, some people, early on, are aflame at the thought of becoming computer programmers, ballet dancers, or whatever, but those folks rarely use career guides. If the perfect career was going to hit you like a lightning bolt, it probably would have struck you long before now.

Here's a more likely path to career contentment. After picking your favorites from The Cool Careers Catalog and from The 20 Most Revealing Questions, select your top choice **even if it doesn't feel exciting.** As long as the career sounds better than what you're currently doing, choose it.

Start down that career trail, being sure to keep your eye out for cool side paths and ways to customize your journey to suit your strengths. That's a more likely route to career happiness than more thinking at the trailhead.

So pick a career and turn your attention to getting trained and landing a job. When first deciding on a career, you probably won't experience instant ecstasy. After all, you haven't yet experienced the career's pleasures and customized it to fit. You will, however, have chosen a path, and, in itself, that's a big step forward.

Courage Builders

Still struggling? Try the courage builders in this section.

#1: All your ducks needn't be in a row

Many people think that before starting their career, their vocational goal must be crystal clear, and they must have all the skills needed to be a smashing success. It rarely works that way.

Most successful people get their first jobs with only a general idea of their career goals, and with only some of the skills needed to succeed. They simply sallied forth asking people in the field for directions on where to turn. For example, "I like the idea of being a pharmacist, but somehow I'd like to work in a place that's a little more exotic than a Rite-Aid pharmacy." If you can't get crystal clarity about your career goal within a reasonable amount of time, sally forth anyway. In the process of looking for a job, you'll probably get clearer about what you want.

#2: The trapeze artist

Even if your proposed career goal makes sense, you'll probably be nervous at the moment of decision because it's unclear whether things will work out.

This is the moment every trapeze artist knows — the moment she lets go of the bar, not quite sure if she'll make it to the other side. She knows, however, that if she doesn't let go, she'll never get anywhere. So she looks down to be sure the net is in place, and then just lets go.

After a reasonable amount of deliberation, if you believe that the proposed change is better than the status quo, and you know you won't totally crash if the new career doesn't work out, it may be time to leap.

#3: Refine your career goal

Ask yourself what doesn't feel right about your career goal. Can you alter your career goal to eliminate or minimize the negatives? Examples:

- "Being a teacher appeals to me, but I'm concerned I won't be able to control the kids." Possible solution 1: Be sure you do fieldwork and student teaching with teachers who are terrific at controlling their classes. Possible solution 2: Decide to be a private tutor.
- "I want to run my own business, but I'm a lousy salesperson and I'm afraid I'd be lonely." Possible solution: Get a partner who's good at sales. Or team up with other businesses for marketing.

#4: Get more information

What is making you nervous about your proposed career? Sometimes, getting more information can give you courage. Examples:

- "Am I good enough in math to be an economist?" Possible solution: Talk with economists whose jobs seem to require little math. Ask them how much math they, in fact, use. Can you do that much math?
- "Is there really a market for this service I'm thinking of selling?" Possible solution: Ask potential customers.

#5: Create a less radical option

If you're not sure it's worth tackling a totally new career, choose a less radical option. Some people's need for change can be satisfied with something less than a brand new career. Maybe one of these can work for you:

- **Tweak your current job.** (See Chapter 18.) Many people who think they need a new career solve their problem by changing bosses, renegotiating their responsibilities, or improving their skills.
- **Find a new job in your current career.** Maybe a different organization's culture can cure your workplace woes.
- **Find a different niche within your current career.** Sick of being a biologist in a lab? Try field-based biology. The Cool Careers Catalog lists neat niches in many careers.
- **Stay in the same industry but change job titles.** Or change industries but keep the same job title.
- **Find more meaning outside of work.** Pursue a hobby that allows for self-expression; do volunteer work; fall in love.

#6: Compare your options against the status quo

Instead of comparing your tentative career goal to some abstract ideal, compare it to the status quo. After all, that is your other option.

On a sheet of paper, make a column for each option you're considering, including the status quo. Write the advantages of each option. To get you started, we list some common advantages of the status quo and of changing careers.

Advantages of the status quo

- You remain comfortable. Change is difficult; the only person who likes change is a wet baby.
- You avoid the time, and cost, and difficulty of training.
- You keep your friends on your current job.
- You avoid failure. If you fail in your new career, you may lose income and status, plus you probably won't get your old job back again.
- You avoid success. If you're successful, your time may not be your own anymore. That gardening you used to enjoy? No time. Those romantic weekends? No time.

Find ways to get the benefits of the status quo even if you decide to change careers. For example, if you'd feel badly about losing your at-work friends, it may help to reconnect with other friends you've lost touch with.

Advantages of changing careers

- More job satisfaction
- More money and the things it can buy
- New friends
- Get to learn new things

#7: The People's Court technique

Pretend you're a lawyer and give all the reasons why Career A is better. Then pretend you're the opposing lawyer and give all the reasons why Career B is better. Finally, be the judge and render a decision.

#8: Try out your new career as a sideline

Unsure whether your new career will work? Charlie was a customer support rep for a cable TV provider but liked the idea of producing videos of playful interviews with company employees for showing at company parties. Charlie started his video business as a sideline, not wanting to quit his job until he was sure he could make money at his new pursuit.

#9: Give yourself a trial period

Can you make it as a singer? Will that pizza-by-the-slice business be worthwhile? Reduce your risk by giving your new venture a fixed amount of time. On your calendar, circle a date perhaps six months or a year from now. If, by then, you don't see signs that you'll succeed in your new endeavor, drop it. Limiting your risk can give you the courage to give it a shot.

#10: Choose more than one career

Can't decide? Choose them all. Having more than one career at a time can be exciting, but you'd better be a fast learner, be high-energy, and enjoy long hours. For some people, this doesn't work. It's hard enough to succeed in one career.

How Marty Nemko made a career decision

I was teaching graduate students at Berkeley when I realized that I'd never be happy as a professor. I am practical at heart. I wouldn't be happy in a career in which my primary task was to publish esoteric articles in the *Journal of Educational Psychology*, but I couldn't think of a career that really excited me. The best I could come up with was career counseling, but that felt just okay.

I nevertheless took the plunge. In the beginning I was unhappy, and asked myself why. The job was too passive; sitting and listening most of the time. So I adopted a more active style. It was still too dull, so I added spice by volunteering to host a weekly radio show on careers and education. That opened the door to the other cool things I now get to do.

Molding my career to suit me converted a so-so career into a happy one. I truly am eager to get up each weekday morning — well, most weekday mornings. If I had remained as a professor until I found a career that excited me right off the bat, I might still be waiting.

#11: Realize that career contentment depends on what you do after you choose a career

If you decide that your best option is a new career, pursue it with passion even it you're ambivalent. That, of course, boosts your chances of being successful.

- Do a thorough job search: Find the specific workplaces within your chosen career likely to have good co-workers, a growing enterprise, and a product you feel good about.
- Take an off-the-shelf job and mold it to fit your strengths. Request projects that make use of your assets. You may even be able to incorporate some of the advantages of other careers you considered. For example, if you choose interior design over photography, make before and after photos a part of your service.

- Get the best training possible. Training makes you feel and be competent. The best training is often at a student-oriented college rather than at a prestigious, research-oriented one. Even more practical options include workshops, tapes, articles, mentors.

How Sarah Edwards created a cool career

My job at the federal regional office of Head Start was exciting, filled with lots of travel and responsibility. But I had a family. The stress of juggling it all put me in the hospital. Working from home as my own boss seemed like the perfect solution, but doing what?

Looking through my high school yearbook, I was struck that many people had valued talking to me about personal challenges. A counseling practice seemed like the perfect career. I'd be my own boss and I could work from home. I completed a graduate program, got my license, and opened a psychotherapy practice. At first, I enjoyed helping people, but after a time, working with unhappy people all day became depressing. I missed traveling and working to change the world. Also, I wanted to work with Paul.

We decided to write a book about working from home. It added the excitement I was missing. I was still helping people, but I help them create better career and lifestyle opportunities. We write at home. We consult at home, usually online. We even broadcast from home. We do travel to speak and do media appearances. This combination works for me.

- Recognize that your career contentment depends not just on a well-suited career and job, but on other factors as well.
  - **Accepting that work is work.** Even we, who have worklives that many people would envy, usually feel that our work is still work. Work isn't often as pleasurable as going out to eat, watching TV, walking in nature, or being with someone you love. We can gratefully accept that work is work mainly because we value being productive, feeling needed, having structure, and earning a living, even when it's not fun. If you can make this mind-set suffuse your workday, you can feel good about your worklife, even if you don't have a dream career.

  - **Your attitude toward each moment on the job.** It's easy to resent work's many moments that are too hard, too easy, too stressful, or too boring. Or we can view those moments with a Zen-like acceptance and a commitment to handle each moment with grace. For us, this is the key to happiness, not just in career, but in life: handling each moment with grace.

Additional help

If you just can't make a decision, try the chapter on procrastination cures. If that doesn't work, it may be time for a bit of professional help. Our help is offered on the "About the Authors" page at the front of the book.

How Paul Edwards found his perfect work

From the time I was four years old, my mother programmed me to become a lawyer. After 20 years of schooling and the ordeal of passing the bar exam, I achieved her dream. I was a lawyer, but I didn't like practicing law. It focuses on details and fault-finding. I only tolerate details and I love working cooperatively.

But having accepted what I was going to be when I grew up, I didn't know where to start. I tried several management jobs, but that wasn't for me either. I wanted the freedom of being my own boss doing work that would enable me to grow. So, in going out on my own, I tried different things — first political consulting, then corporate training.

What I really wanted was to work with Sarah and do something original. So I asked her to join me in writing a book about working from home. Eight books later, I've found that developing books uses the problem-solving and strategizing I liked about law and politics while speaking and doing media calls on my communication skills and challenges me to grow.

A Final Check

It's time. You've reviewed lots of careers and picked the one that feels best. Now it's time for a final check: Does your career have all five signs of being right for you?

1. **Can you, within an acceptable amount of time, acquire the knowledge and skills to succeed in this career?**

   If you're unsure, ask someone in the field to review your previous efforts. Or try to understand an introductory textbook, or find someone to teach you a bit of the field's essentials. Are you getting it? If you're unsure what knowledge or skills the career requires, find out by reading more about the career or by visiting members of the profession.

2. **Can you get the time and money to train for this career?**

   Before rejecting a career on this basis, read Chapters 7 and 8, which describe low-cost ways to get the training you need. And if you're thinking of starting a business, Chapter 19 shows ways to get the cash flowing quickly.

3. **Will this career likely sustain your interest?**

4. **Are you likely to enjoy working in this career's environment?**

   For example, at home? Outdoors? In a formal office?

5. **Are you likely to enjoy the typical people interactions in this career?**

Part II
Getting Smart

"So what if you have a Ph.D. in physics? I used to have my own circus act."

In this part . . .

Competence: It's one of life's great feelings. Getting up in the morning knowing that you're a pro, confident that when you get into work, you'll be able to handle most of what comes your way. This part shows you better ways to get competent.

Chapter 7

Degree-Free Career Preparation

In This Chapter

- Should you go back for a degree?
- How to learn more than you would in a degree program
- Getting an employer to hire you over someone with more degrees

Everyone may tell you the rule is "In order to do this work, you have to have a masters degree. . . ." But you want to find out about the exceptions.

—Richard Bolles, *What Color Is Your Parachute?*

Imagine how you'd feel knowing that you are an expert, someone who can be counted on to do the job wonderfully. Nothing is more central to career satisfaction than feeling competent.

Of course, one key to competence is good training. The next chapter shows you how to make the most of a degree program. This chapter helps you figure out whether you need a degree at all. More often than you might suspect, there are wiser ways to prepare for your career. This chapter even shows you how to convince an employer to hire you over someone with more degrees.

Lousy Reasons to Go Back for a Degree

If you have a good reason, going back for a degree can be a fine idea. Alas, many people don't. Here are the classic lousy reasons:

- **To help decide what career to pursue.** Mistake. A degree program exposes you to only a tiny fraction of the career options. Far better to choose your career using the methods in the previous chapters.
- **To postpone looking for a job.** This book helps you find a fine career and land a rewarding job without undue pain. No need to spend years and megabucks to postpone that.

- **To impress friends and family.** Aren't there less costly and time-consuming ways to do that? How about landing a good job years sooner than if you had gone for a degree?
- **To feel legitimate.** As we explain in this chapter, in many fields, you can more legitimately prepare for your career outside a university, at what we call *You U.*: a self- and mentor-selected combination of articles, seminars, professional conferences, the Internet, and on-the-job training. Don't commit years of your life and lots of money just to create the illusion of legitimacy — often what a degree mainly provides.
- **To dazzle employers.** In many fields, your boss is likely to be more impressed with a well-designed You U. education than with a diploma that both of you know doesn't mean that you're career competent. In this chapter, we show you how to prove that.

Good Reasons to Go Back for a Degree

Of course, there are good reasons for a back-for-a-degree stint:

- **For your enlightenment.** A degree program can help you become an informed citizen and to experience life more richly.
- **Some fields absolutely, positively require a degree.** For example, if you want to be a physician, the state isn't going to let you treat cancer patients just because you had a mentor. In fields like engineering, management consulting, investment banking, and at top corporate law firms, employers generally ignore applicants who aren't waving a prestigious diploma.
- **You don't believe you can find mentors or the resources to craft your own career preparation program.**
- **You need the structure of school.** To design and follow through on a You U. education, you must be a self-starter. Many people need the structure of school: Be there from 7 to 9 p.m., Tuesdays and Thursdays; read pages 246 through 384 by next Monday; write a term paper as follows; be tested on December 20 from 2 to 4 p.m.
- **You want the consistent social contact that comes from meeting every Tuesday and Thursday night from 7–9 p.m.**

Will the Piece of Paper Be Worth the Time and Money?

Many people recognize the drawbacks of getting a degree, yet insist that it's yet worth the time and money because of what the piece of paper, the diploma, can do for them. Will that be true for you?

Paul and Sarah think it's generally a fine bet. They have seen many people try to pursue a career without a degree and have to struggle much harder as a result, not just because employers insist on the degree, but because of the psychological barrier of not having a degree. Many such people feel inferior because they acquired their learning outside of school.

I am far less enthusiastic about the value of a degree. When I considered what I learned from my Ph.D., which specialized in the evaluation of education programs, my years as an evaluator of colleges and universities, and when I think back on all my clients, my sense is that, at least for motivated adults who are interested mainly in career preparation, there are usually better ways to develop career competence. Higher education may be a reasonable way to become a more sophisticated connoisseur of life, but if your goal is to advance your career, in many fields, I strongly believe that higher education is among the most overrated, overpriced products of all.

Yes, people with degrees earn more over their lifetimes than people who don't, but that doesn't mean that the degree is the main reason. They earn more mainly because degree seekers, on average, are more able and motivated to begin with. If you locked a group of degree seekers in a closet for four years, that group would likely earn more over their lifetimes than a group of people who don't pursue degrees.

The following people not only don't have graduate degrees, they don't have undergraduate ones: Seven U.S. presidents from Washington to Truman, Domino's pizza chain founder Tom Monaghan, Bill Gates, *Pulp Fiction* director Quentin Tarantino, ABC-TV's Peter Jennings (dropped out of high school), Wendy's founder Dave Thomas (also dropped out of high school), Thomas Edison, Blockbuster Video founder and owner of the Miami Dolphins Wayne Huizenga, McDonald's founder Ray Kroc, Henry Ford, cosmetics magnate Helena Rubenstein, Walt Disney, Ben Franklin, Alexander Graham Bell, zillionaire industrialist John D. Rockefeller, Malcolm X, Apple Computer founder Steve Jobs, and thousands of computer whizzes.

Of course, these people are exceptions, and it can be argued that only the exceptionally brilliant or exceptionally unintelligent can afford to forgo that diploma. But the fact is that *most* people learn more by doing rather than by sitting in university classes. Later in this chapter, we show you how, in many fields, you can prepare for a career better from outside a university than inside one. And we demonstrate how to convince an employer to hire you over applicants who got their career preparation at a university.

But first, you need to know one of higher education's dirty secrets. College catalogs usually talk about the careers possible with this major; the careers possible with that major. This misleads the reader into thinking that if he spends the years and the money, he'll land a professional job. Here's the truth: In many fields, as you will now see, there are nowhere near enough professional jobs for the number of degree holders.

Some bad news

The October 1997 issue of *Phi Delta Kappan*, a prestigious education periodical, provided this discouraging information:

> A Rand Corporation report concluded that new doctoral degrees in science and engineering average 25% *above* appropriate employment opportunities. A National Science Foundation study found a 41% oversupply of Ph.D.s in the supposedly in-demand electrical engineering and 33% oversupply in civil engineering. Rand charged that universities are oblivious to the job market. . . .
>
> Thousands from other professions face the same situation. Even graduates from America's most prestigious business schools are finding no guarantee of a job. . . . An amazing 16% of newly-minted MBA graduates of Stanford University were unable to find jobs. Less prestigious business schools fared even worse: 40% of the graduates of Ohio State's business school could not find jobs; the figure for the University of Georgia was 30%; for the University of Texas at Austin 24%; and for Tulane University 24%. . . . Experts project that of the millions of university graduates, only a mere 20% will be able to find the well-paying, challenging jobs for which they were trained.

You U., Often a Better Way

In more fields than you might think, motivated adults can make use of an approach to career preparation with a higher payoff than going back for a degree. We call it "You University."

At You U., you decide what you want to learn and then design a plan to learn it. One of my clients, Phillip, wanted to learn how to create partnerships between corporations and schools. Instead of going back for a largely misfitting master's in education or business, he did a You U. master's.

First, Phillip searched the Internet for articles on business-education partnerships. Then he interviewed, by phone, the people involved in those partnerships at the corporations. One of those people suggested things he should read and mentioned an upcoming conference on business/education partnerships. At the conference, our hero attended sessions, spoke with other experts, and found out about an on-target newsletter, and an Internet discussion group. He visited corporations with model school programs.

Now, imagine that you are a corporate employer looking for someone to develop a program with local schools. Would you rather hire someone with a master's in education, or someone like Phillip, who attended You U.? Good choice. Phillip got hired as a school liaison by one of the Baby Bells.

When Jonathon Storm decided to switch from pursuing an architecture degree to becoming a nature recording artist, instead of switching majors, he left school to learn directly from a master. He contacted the nation's leading nature recordist and asked to study personally with him. Today, Jonathon is a master.

Just look at the differences between degree programs and You U (Summarized in Table 7-1).

In a degree program , you're taught by Ph.D. types who are theoreticians, often out of touch with the basic information and practical knowledge that most students, especially most adult students, need. Worse, you're stuck with whichever professors happen to be at that college.

If you attend You U., you're taught by precisely the right sort of people. Whether you're looking to become a graphic designer, a systems analyst, an engineer, or whatever, you can probably place an ad in a trade publication, or a post on an Internet discussion group and find a master practitioner willing to mentor you for a fraction of the cost of college tuition. You can take seminars or certification programs taught by some of your field's leading practitioners. Some are offered by community colleges, university extension programs, and many by private organizations and individuals.

There's a directory of certification programs at the Alternative Careers forum within Gonyea Online Career Center on America Online (Keyword Gonyea).

Another practical approach to career training is to buy it as part of a franchise or business opportunity. Look for companies that have a proven system: have been in business at least five years before franchising, have been franchising for at least four years, and have at least ten franchisees. For a compendium of such opportunities, visit `www.paulandsarah.com`.

If you *are* looking for theoretical knowledge, a book, audio, or video allows you unlimited access, 24/7 to the world's best theorists. For example, The Teaching Company (800-832-2412) sells tapes of classes taught by some of the best professors at the most prestigious colleges. And if you want the contact of on-campus college courses, at You U., you're not bound to one campus. You can find the best professor in your locale for each course. In major cities, you have a number of universities to choose from. (There are many ways to find the good professors. For example, most colleges publish a list of its teaching award winners.)

In addition, thousands of courses are available via convenient distance learning (online, video, text, audiotape, or a combination.) Opportunities are especially extensive in engineering, business, computer science, and health sciences. Try these resources for a treasure trove of such offerings:

- The Public Broadcasting System Adult Learning Service phone 800-257-2578; `www.pbs.org/learn/als`.
- *Peterson's Guide to Distance Learning* (revised annually).
- Inabeth Miller's *Guide to Distance Learning,* for distance-based graduate classes.
- `www.a*dec.edu`, for a thorough list of distance-learning courses online.
- America's Learning Exchange is the federal government's new and growing compendium of training programs: from quick courses to full-blown degree programs. Just enter your skills, interests, or career goals, and out pop suitable training opportunities.

That's just the tip of the iceberg. When you compare degree programs with You U., there really is no comparison, but we do it anyway in Table 7-1.

Table 7-1 Degree Program versus You U.

A Degree Program	*You U.*
A massive amount of information all at one time, when you don't even have the opportunity to apply it.	Especially if you learn on the job, you learn what you need when you need it.
Many required courses. Sometimes a course is required mainly because a professor likes to teach it.	Study only what you need and want. Often, get what you need in a fraction of the time it takes to earn a degree.
Get a degree, only to find that you don't remember, let alone use, much of what you were taught. Own a sometimes valuable piece of paper.	Because you learn what you want, how you want, at the pace you want, you remember much more.
Learn when it's convenient for the professor; like Mondays and Wednesdays from 7 to 10 p.m.	Learn whenever you want to.
You are passive. You focus on learning what the professor wants to teach, fearing a low grade if you don't. Many students leave school with poor self-esteem. A cause is professors who teach material that is of little value outside the classroom yet is difficult, so students feel dumb.	You are empowered. You study what you want; to the level you believe necessary. You U. builds self-reliance and self-confidence. A key part of what makes a career feel good is the sense that you're an expert in your field. In many careers, you're more likely to feel like — and be — an expert with a "degree" from You U.
The material, especially in science or technology, is often obsolete. As long as professors keep cranking out articles in their microniche, many universities care little that they don't update their course material.	You can get up-to-the-minute information: on the Internet, from periodicals, by talking with people in your field, and from seminars offered by the leading practitioners in your profession.
Costs range from $10,000 to more than $100,000; not to mention the loss of what you could have earned had you not been in a degree program.	Costs are 50 to 90 percent less than in a degree program.

Convincing Employers to Hire You without That Degree

Imagine that you are an employer. Will you consider this candidate?

Dear Ms. Hirer,

I know that when you're inundated with applications, it's tempting to weed out those without a prestigious MBA, but I believe I'm worth a look precisely because I don't have an MBA at all.

I seriously considered going back for an MBA, but after carefully examining the courses I would have to take and their relevance (or, too often, lack of relevance) to becoming an outstanding software marketing manager, I concluded that the two full-time years could be more profitably spent.

I contacted directors of marketing at leading Silicon Valley software companies and offered to work for them for no pay in exchange for their mentoring. I figured that was cheap tuition for the on-target learning I would receive. A marketing manager at Hewlett Packard took me on. After three months, I felt I had learned about as much from him as I could, whereupon I made a similar arrangement with a director of marketing at Cisco Systems.

In these apprenticeships, I was deeply involved in a number of projects similar to those mentioned in your ad, specifically Internet marketing and managing a national consumer branding campaign. In addition, I attend American Marketing Association conferences, read the best articles and books recommended by the A.M.A., and spend much of my commute time listening to relevant books on tape. To get the bigger picture, I even read a couple of books by leading academics.

But now comes the moment of truth. In choosing a "self-directed education" over a traditional one, I believe I prioritized substance over form, but now the question is whether you will consider interviewing me?

I am hoping that you will appreciate my having developed a beyond-the-box learning plan, that I was assertive enough to make it happen, and persistent enough to see it through to completion, even though I didn't have a professor and deadlines forcing me to

> do so. Perhaps more importantly, in working at the elbow of top hardware marketing executives, I learned a tremendous amount about how to do the job well. I recently discussed my approach with an MBA holder from Stanford, and he said that I probably learned more of real-world value than he did.
>
> I'm hoping you will call me for an interview, but as any good employee, I won't just passively wait. If I haven't heard from you in a week, I will take the liberty of following up.
>
> I enclose samples of the deliverables I produced during my work at Hewlett Packard and Cisco.
>
> Thank you for your consideration.
>
> Sincerely,
>
> Christopher Wah

Again, imagine that you are the person in charge of hiring. Would you interview Christopher? Even if other applicants had Ivy League degrees?

So, before heading back for a degree at State U. — let alone Big Bucks Private U. — ask yourself whether the smart choice is You U.

Planning Your You U. Education

It's simpler than you may think. You just need to find one or more mentors, and then you and your mentors decide together what you specifically need to learn.

Finding a mentor

Start by finding a mentor who is an expert in your field, someone who can suggest resources, ensure that you're covering enough of the bases, and answer your questions. Expect to compensate your mentor either with money, or by volunteering as her assistant. The latter can be instructive in itself. Sometimes though, people, especially older people, are willing to mentor you for free. Many people fifty and older feel a strong desire to pass on their wisdom to the next generation.

Where to find a mentor:

- Someone in your field whom you already know, like, and respect.
- At a meeting of your field's professional association. Some such associations have formal mentoring programs.
- The Yellow Pages. Some people find mentors simply by opening the Yellow Pages to the appropriate category and dialing until they find the right person.
- There may be that unusual professor with enough practical knowledge to coach you.
- Post a request for a paid coach on your field's Internet discussion group.
- Call SCORE, the Service Corps of Retired Executives (listed in the Federal Government section of big-city White Pages).
- Post a flyer at the local senior center, or an ad in its newsletter.

No need to limit yourself to one mentor.

Figuring out what to learn

When talking with a potential mentor, ask this question: "I'm trying to teach myself X, Y, and Z using books, articles, the Internet, tapes, and seminars. Any suggestions?" In addition to asking your mentor(s), pose this question to other professionals in the field. You can also contact

- A respected member of your professional association.
- Your association's Web site. That site and links from it can often be a gold mine.
- Public and college libraries and their librarians — great sources on what to read and who to talk with.
- Even at You U., you don't go it alone.

A fast yet legitimate way to become a consultant:

1. **Find experts to mentor you through a You U. education.**
2. **Do a no-fee assignment for a prestigious client.**
3. **Use that designer-label client as a reference. Many prospective clients will reason, "If a high-powered client is happy, I probably will be too."**

As we said at the beginning of this chapter, as good as You U. can be, it's certainly not right for everyone. Ready for a back-to-school stint? Chapter 8 can help.

Chapter 8

Degree-Based Career Prep

In This Chapter

- Finding the right college or grad school
- Getting into a hard-to-get-into college or grad school
- Paying for your education
- Making the most of your back-to-school stint

After exhaustive statistical analysis of the national longitudinal study of the high school class of 1972, James et al. report that 'while sending your child to Harvard appears to be a good investment, sending him to a local state university to major in engineering at which he takes lots of math and preferably attains a high GPA is an even better investment.' Apparently, what matters most is not which college you attend, but what you did while you were there.

—Bill Mayher, author of the *College Admissions Mystique*

At its best, a back-to-school stint can be a blast: Taking a few years away from the real world, learning stuff you're really interested in; meeting lots of interesting fellow students, and mentoring with a wise professor who takes you underwing and lines up a cool job for you after graduation. That ideal is too rarely realized, but this chapter shows you how to maximize your chances.

Finding the Right College or Grad School

Many people choose a car more carefully than they choose a college. Would you buy a car without a good test drive? Colleges seem so difficult to judge that many college shoppers often fall back on the institution's reputation: "Harvard has a great name, so it must be good, or at least the Harvard name on my diploma will get me a good job." Not necessarily. This section focuses on less fabled institutions that, especially for career preparation, may be wiser choices. It also shows you how to find the specific program within those institutions that are of high quality and likely to do a good job of preparing you for your career.

Choosing the right type of institution

Many people simply choose the most renowned college they can get into. It's understandable. Designer-label colleges attract lots of smart students, so chances are, something will rub off. And some employers — large corporate law firms, for instance — routinely round-file resumes from applicants without a "Top 25" diploma. Even with other employers, you might ask, "If I go to Who Knows U., how will I compete in the job market against graduates of Brand Name U.?" Fact is, the job search strategies in Part III, which most people don't use, can fully compensate for the advantage of a brand-name diploma.

The same types of institutions we touted in the previous chapter are also fine choices for degree-seekers: night and weekend programs offered by university and community colleges, distance-learning programs, and colleges specializing in adult learners. For a comprehensive listing of the latter, see *Bear's Guide to Earning College Degrees Nontraditionally* ($27.95, 800-835-8535).

Choosing the right program

As important as choosing the right type of college is choosing the right program. The steps in this section walk you through making the right choice.

Be sure you've identified your career niche

Trust us: Don't make the mistake of thinking to yourself, "I'll figure it out while I'm in school." One of three bad things too often happen:

- You never find out about a specialty you could love. Let's say you're interested in psychology and simply choose a school with a psychology program. There is, however, a niche — organization psychology — that you would have loved to specialize in if you had only known it existed. Alas, your college's psychology program doesn't offer that specialization. Moral of the story: Choose your niche first and then find a program that prepares you for it.

- You take a course from a charismatic professor who loves her specialization — let's say geriatric recreation. Her enthusiasm is infectious. Now you get excited about geriatric recreation. Maybe the professor even shows an interest in you: "That was an outstanding term paper, Lucy." You find yourself deciding to specialize in geriatric recreation. It's understandable — no more anxiety about not having a career goal. And a professor's flattery can be intoxicating, precluding you from taking a hard look at the realities of a career in this field — for example, that a geriatric recreation leader usually makes less money than a welfare recipient.

- You go through a year or two of the program. Finally you find something exciting. Now you face having to spend more time and money to get trained in your new specialty.

So please choose a career niche before deciding which colleges to apply to. If you need help finding a specialty, read, and talk with people in your field.

Identify programs that train you in your niche.

Here are some ways to find the right program for you:

- Compare offerings at local colleges by visiting their Web sites or reviewing their catalogs.
- Discover whether your field's professional association has descriptions of relevant programs.
- Search for programs in the United States at `www.petersons.com`. This site picks out all colleges in the United States whose descriptions include the keywords you enter. Or browse *Peterson's Graduate and Professional Programs,* available in many libraries.

Assess the program's quality

Talk with students close to finishing the program or recent graduates. Probably no more valid way exists to assess a program's quality than talking with its customers.

How can you do this? If the college is far away, you may be able to query students through the college's Web site. If it's nearby, sit in on an advanced class that includes students who have almost finished the program. At the end of class, go up to a group of students and ask, "Do you like the program?" and "What are the best and worst things about it?"

How do you get to sit in on a class? Just phone the college and ask to be transferred to the department secretary who can tell you when and where an advanced class meets. Ask for the instructor's phone number and office hours, so that you can request permission in advance.

While you're on the phone with the instructor, ask a few questions such as, "What should I know about the program that might not be in the official program description?" or "What's the actual mean time to completion in this program?" Some programs report the "expected" time to completion, but not the time it takes the average student, which can be years longer. In my Ph.D. program, the "expected" time to completion was four years. The actual average time? Seven years!

You might also ask the secretary for the names of recent graduates. They're in a wonderful position to tell you how valuable their degree program was.

Read through the official materials

You can usually find lots of information at the college's Web site.

- Find out whether a program's emphasis matches your interests. You don't want a psychology master's program that focuses on Freudian theories when you think they're a bunch of hooey.
- How many full-time professors are in the program? A small department can mean too few choices.
- Does the content of required courses sound interesting? How about the assignments? Will the workload allow time in your schedule for respiration? To find out, check the syllabi. They're often available at the college's Web site or through the department secretary.

Assess the program's true cost

The listed tuition and fees are irrelevant. As on an airplane, passengers pay different amounts and few pay the full fare. To find out how much you'll pay, *before applying*, describe your situation to a financial aid officer at the college, and get a written estimate of how much financial aid you're likely to get that is cash, not a loan. If you don't get a satisfactory answer, contact the head of the program you're applying to.

Finding top legitimate colleges for earning a degree fast (while learning plenty along the way)

John Bear, author of *Bear's Guide to Earning College Degrees Nontraditionally*, is arguably the nation's leading consumer advocate for adult students. For 20 years, he's looked past the labels to identify the institutions that offer the best education at the lowest cost while providing the flexibility to meet adult students' needs.

Right up there is Inabeth Miller, author of *Guide to Distance Learning*. Among her many distinctions, she was a member of President Clinton's education transition team and is a recipient of the Smithsonian Institution's Award for Outstanding Educator in Technology.

We list some of Bear's and Miller's favorite institutions for getting a quality degree fast. Please know that these are not your traditional, often inflexible universities. These are universities without walls. That is, you complete most or all of your degree requirements by taking courses in your choice of format, including at local colleges, online, and on video, with fieldwork in your own community. The institution primarily serves to help you plan your program, to let you know about the courses and fieldwork available at a distance by hundreds of universities, to assess your achievements, and to award your fully-accredited bachelor's, master's, or doctoral degree.

Employers may be skeptical about such institutions, so be sure that your job application letter explains how your education was, in many ways, superior to a traditional one.

Thomas Edison State College (609-984-1150; `www.tesc.edu`): This is our very favorite institution for adults. Called "one of the brighter stars in higher education" by *The New York Times,* TESC offers a wide range of associate and bachelor's degrees, plus a master's in business, to its 9,000 students. It grants extensive credit for prior learning, including college-level learning acquired through life experience. You can complete your additional units through any combination of exams, live, or distance courses offered anywhere in the United States, or through TESC's own 100 self-study courses. The kicker is that TESC is a public college, so the price is right.

University of Phoenix (800-742-4742, 602-966-9577; `www.uophx.edu`): One of the most expensive, but among the best fully-online programs, the University of Phoenix offers bachelor's and master's degrees in business and in technology. Their programs are known for careful course design to maximize student learning and minimize dropouts. Faculty members are hired based on their ability to teach online courses, and receive ongoing coaching to ensure quality.

National Technological University (970-495-6430; `www.ntu.edu`): NTU is a smart choice for a master's in engineering. You get to choose courses from 47 prestigious universities, which are downloaded via satellite to workplaces, and now, homes, so that you can watch 24/7. NTU offers 13 engineering master's programs, plus an International MBA. An NTU degree is well respected by employers.

International School of Management (800-441-4746, 303-333-4224; `www.isimu.edu`): Three times, ISIM received top awards from the United States Distance Learning Association. It offers an MBA, an MS in information management, and an MBA in health care.

Nova Southeastern University (800-541-6682, 954-262-7300; `www.nova.edu`): Nova offers master's and doctoral degrees in business, educational technology, and computer science. Courses are skill-based, so you complete them at your own pace. They require daily online work, including online discussions. Master's programs do not require on-campus attendance, but doctoral students must attend four meetings each year on the Ft. Lauderdale campus.

Massachusetts Institute of Technology (617-253-2836; `www.caes.mit.edu`): You can get an online graduate degree from a celebrated institution. Not surprisingly, MIT uses the widest range of distance methods: videoconferencing in real time, videotape, Internet discussions, and so on.

Downsides: Only one online program is available: an MS in systems design and management. It requires an initial month in residence at MIT, plus a semester in residence at the end. The cost is an Ivyish $50,000, but not to worry. You are admitted only if your employer agrees to pick up the tab.

Keep your eyes on **Western Governor's University** (801-575-5358, `www.westgov.org/smart/vu/vu.html`). Within a decade, it stands a reasonable chance of providing among the highest quality undergraduate educations anywhere. Western Governor's is a collaborative effort of the governors of 18 states and one territory (Guam), along with major corporations such as IBM, ATT, and US West. It just started offering a online *competency-based* degree program. You progress through courses by passing built-in online projects and simulations. You go as fast or as slowly as you like, and because grading is standardized and based on substantive, real-world simulations, an employer knows that if you have a degree from WGU, it's worth something. WGU offers none of those Mickey Mouse courses where you take a regurgitate-and-forget multiple choice test, or in which the only course requirement is keeping a journal. Of course, with all that rigor, we know more than a few folks who wouldn't be caught dead at WGU.

Getting In

Sure, medical schools, many law schools, Ph.D. programs, a relative handful of MBA programs, 5 percent of undergraduate schools, and a few other degree programs, are difficult to get into. But those constitute only a tiny fraction of the offerings at the nation's 3,900 colleges and universities.

Fact is, admission levels at the large majority of college programs, especially at the undergraduate level, are virtually 98.6 — all you need to get in is normal body temperature. (We're exaggerating only slightly.)

And as we've been stressing, do not think that just because the other 150 universities are difficult to get into, that means that those schools are necessarily better. We liken designer-label schools to a Jaguar. It has a prestigious name, and costs a fortune, but, ironically, is more of a hassle (requires more maintenance, has more frequent breakdowns) than inexpensive cars with less sexy names. We must admit to feeling a certain pleasure driving along in a Toyota and seeing some fussmobile broken down along the side of the road.

The hassles with selective colleges start with getting in but don't stop there. The high concentration of academic stars instills fear in many students — inhibiting them from speaking up in class and/or turning them into studyholics. The student health center at Harvard reported that the second most common student complaint is stress and burnout. Professors at selective colleges are more likely to care about research than their students.

When you were a teenager, you may have been more likely to fall in love with someone because he or she played hard to get. By now, you realize that's foolish. Please apply that mature thinking when choosing a college or grad school. Many people aspire to be accepted to hard-to-get-into colleges mainly because they're hard to get into. Far better to fall in love with a college because of who it is, not how hard-to-get it plays.

It's a buyer's market. Because college selection is so name-driven, rather than quality-driven, many colleges, including high-quality ones, can't fill their classrooms — largely because their diplomas don't bear a brand name. The message to you is: Be picky. Most colleges — perhaps even those that will do you the most good — want you as much, or more, than you want them.

Getting into killer colleges

Despite all our warnings, let's say you do want to get into one of the most selective 150 colleges. Okay, here are the keys to gaining admission to places like Harvard and Princeton.

For starters, of course, you need top numbers. An A- average or better and a 1300+ score on The Test (GRE, SAT, MCAT, LSAT, or so on) puts you in the running. But most applicants to the selective 150 have numbers in that range, yet only some get admitted. It usually comes down to a single factor: Compared with another student with similar qualifications, will you *benefit* the college more? "Who me?" you say. "Me, benefit a college?" Yes, you. Benefits fall into the following categories:

- **The student has potential to do big things**. Remember, these colleges can afford to select only the nation's top applicants. Do your past accomplishments suggest that you have the potential to do truly big things like invent something, become a CEO, or be elected to high office? Does your admission essay convey ambitious yet realistic future plans? Are you so well connected (your father is on the House Ways and Means committee, for instance) that you're likely to be in a position to have real impact? Your application, especially your essay, must make a convincing case that you're likely to do big things.
- **The student is likely to particularly enrich the campus community.**
    - A true intellectual can invigorate classroom discussions, as well as her professors.
    - A person of color may lend a different perspective to discussions in and outside the classroom.

    Some sorts of diversity, however, count less: An Appalachian, a Vietnamese boat person, the child of a brilliant scientist, or an Israeli war veteran usually gets little or no edge in the admissions process.

- A person with the ability to play on varsity sports teams, or to perform in campus music and drama offerings, improves the quality of the college's offerings. (These talents typically give an admission edge only to undergraduate applicants.)
- An iconoclastic thinker is likely to spout unconventional but intelligent ideas in and outside of class. But be careful: Political correctness is rampant on college campuses. Writing an application essay advocating conservative ideas is risky.

- **A professor views a student as particularly desirable.** This is a perception that the applicant usually must bring about. A typical scenario is: You find a professor who specializes in a subject in which you're interested. You phone her, have a good conversation, at the end of which you both agree it would be great if you were the professor's advisee and research slave. That professor — usually in response to your request — writes a note about you to the admissions committee. No surprise, that gives you an edge.
- **Students whose family members have given a bunch of money to the college.** These students usually receive an edge in admissions proportional to the size of the bunch.
- **Students who are a uniquely good fit for the program to which they're applying.** How do those students benefit the college? If you choose a particular program because its unusual aspects are just right for you, you're likely to be satisfied, and more likely to donate money to the college. So if you're applying to Duke's Ph.D. program in biomedical engineering, explain the specific reasons why you prefer it over its major competitor, Johns Hopkins.

Some test-prep advice

A note about preparing for The Test (SAT, GRE, GMAT, LSAT, or MCAT). If you're self-motivated, use a test prep CD-ROM to prepare rather than take a course such as "Inside the GRE." Not only is it $25 versus $800, the CD-ROM provides a completely individualized approach, so you don't waste time going over stuff that's too easy or too hard. In a course, you're particularly likely to get inappropriate-level instruction if you're a non-average scorer: above 1300 or below 1000. And, of course, with a CD-ROM, you don't waste time getting to and from the test prep center.

Overrated factors in college and grad school admission

Here, we try to save you some stress. Applicants often sweat these items far in excess of their importance in the admission process.

Recommendations

These days, recommendations are almost always good, so they rarely constitute the basis for differentiating one applicant from another. Sure, if you work in the White House and the president can attest to what you've done under his watch, fine. But much short of that, recommendations rarely get much weight.

Interviews

Most prestigious colleges don't grant interviews, and those that do place little stock in them, especially interviews conducted by alumni rather than by employees of the college. Medical school interviews are, however, important: You gotta show that bedside manner.

Finding the Money

Adults, particularly those applying to graduate schools, have a particularly tough time finding aid because government financial aid formulas penalize working adults. It's worth applying because you'll probably get a government-guaranteed loan, but don't hold your breath waiting for cash aid.

Get the financial aid applications early. Some colleges' deadlines are almost a year before the enrollment date. These deadlines are firm. Meet them.

It may be worth applying for a private scholarship — you know, like the David Letterman Scholarship, which is reserved for students just like Dave: C students at Ball State University. To find private scholarships you may qualify for, use an online search program. FastWeb (`www.fastweb.com`) is a free search engine that claims to search 200,000 scholarships to find your best fits. Some experts, however, believe that it's worth paying the $35 for the search at `www.800headstart.com`. If you don't have Web access, see if a local college or bank has a computerized scholarship database. Or call CASHE, a private company with a large scholarship database, at 800-462-2743 to have a questionnaire sent to you. Return the completed questionnaire with $20 to get a list of about two dozen best-fit scholarships. Or access the CASHE database online for free at `www.cashe.com`. Apply to half a dozen of your best shots. The odds of winning are tiny, so it's a waste of time to apply for too many. If, however, you're a non-Asian minority or are an academic superstar, it's worth applying to ten or fifteen.

Harvard's money-making machine

$7 billion: Harvard's endowment in 1996

$4 billion: The jump in Harvard's endowment in 1997

4.1%: The percentage increase in Harvard's tuition from 1996-1997.

$2.5 million: The *profit* Harvard makes each year from MBA application fees alone.

Reference Service Press publishes print and CD-ROM directories of scholarships set aside for minorities, the disabled, and women: *Directory of Financial Aids for African Americans, Directory of Financial Aids for Hispanic Americans, Directory of Financial Aid for Native Americans,* and so on. These resources are expensive, but fortunately, they're available in many libraries. A portion of their large database is available at America Online (keyword RSP).

You can often wrangle some bucks with a letter, or by pleading your case in person, to your local chapter of a fraternal organization such as Kiwanis or the Rotary Club.

Money is often available for veterans. Speak to your military branch's benefits office.

If you're applying to a graduate program, don't just contact the institution's financial office, contact your specific department's office. Often, special funds are available only through the department.

Comparing the deals

If you apply to more than one college, before saying yes to one, carefully compare financial aid offers:

- How much cash will you have to come up with?
- How big a loan will you have to pay back?
- As long as your income stays the same, will your cash award be renewed each year, or once they've got you, will they pull the plug?

If your award from your top-choice college seems too low, try to negotiate a better deal with the financial aid office. The key is to provide new information that can justify a new decision. For example, you can explain that other colleges have offered you better deals. Or point out that your financial picture isn't as rosy as the financial aid form makes it appear — you have big medical expenses, or your home badly needs major repairs. Sometimes, sending an itemized budget to the financial aid officer can make your situation clearer.

Why is college so darn expensive anyway?

Colleges keep raising tuition. Four years at a brand-name private college costs $140,000. President Clinton's reaction: urge us to start saving when Junior is in the 6th grade. Plus he offers tons of new federal aid to students — which simply allows colleges to raise tuition yet higher.

Why is no one asking colleges to be more efficient? For example, should professors really be earning a full-time salary for teaching two or three classes a semester? Why aren't interactive-video-based courses, taught by the nation's best professors, used instead of large lecture classes? That would raise quality while lowering cost. But I digress.

Dealing with in- and out-of-state tuition

If you're planning to attend an out-of-state public college, you may wonder if you can qualify for in-state tuition. Probably not. It used to be easy in many states. Kal Chany, author of *Paying for College,* says, "In Oklahoma, you'd walk into the financial aid office on the first day of school and say, 'Hi, I'm a Sooner,' and you'd be declared an Oklahoma resident for tuition purposes. Now, most states are clamping down, for example: New York, Maryland, Florida, Michigan, Georgia, Vermont, and California." Nevertheless, it's worth asking the financial aid office how students can qualify for the in-state tuition rate. In a few states, all you may have to do is register your car, vote in that state, and indicate, if it's true, that you plan to live in the state after you graduate.

Making the Most of the School You Choose

A pair of identical twins could enroll in the same program at the same college, yet one twin could benefit much more than the other. This section shows how to make the most of your back-to-school experience.

Make the effort to find good teachers

Sometimes there's no choice, but you know as well as we do that a good instructor can make medieval linguistics come alive and a bad instructor can turn a course on rock 'n' roll into a snore. Be a consumer when you enroll:

- **Pick the campus's teaching award winners.** The list is in the college's catalog or available through its office of academic affairs.
- **Get picks from students who've been around awhile.**
- **Check student ratings of professors.** At some colleges, students have access to the results. Check with the student government office.
- **Ask the department secretary.** They see all the faculty evaluations and some might even give you an answer other than, "All the professors are good."
- **Check out syllabi.** Often they're on the Web, or the department secretary has them.
- **Look at the required books in the bookstore:** A great way to avoid spending $200 on textbooks you won't read anyway.
- **Over-enroll**. If you plan to take three courses, sign up for four, attend the first session of each, and drop the worst one. No need to put up with a professor so monotonic he sounds like a high school student reciting the Pledge of Allegiance.
- **Choose courses that help prepare you for your profession.**
- **When in doubt, choose the teacher rather than the course title.** European Epistemology taught by a great teacher is usually better than Human Sexuality taught by a dud.

Read first

If you do the assigned reading, you're more likely to stay awake in class. You're also more likely to participate, which also helps you stay awake. Do we sound like your mother or what?

In class, stay active

Classes may or may not be interesting, but if you just sit there, your chances of remembering much of what the professor and other students said after the course is over are about as good as of swatting a fly with a hammer. You're much more likely to remember stuff you're actually involved in, so ask a question, make a comment. Of course, you'll be hated if you talk all the time, so the next best way to be active is to ask yourself a question every minute or so. Questions such as, "What's the real-world relevance of this?" or "How might I use this in my career?" (This is one of those ideas that makes some sense to us, but to be honest, is utterly untested. If you think it's a stupid idea, no problem.)

Choose your advisor well

A bad advisor is someone whose office you want to escape from as soon as she's signed your paperwork. A good advisor can help you find good professors, sign you on as a research or teaching assistant, become your career coach, line up job leads, ponder the meaning of life with you, and make sure you don't find out three days before you expect to graduate that you're missing Statistics 203. Before settling on an advisor, chat with a few candidates whose specialization sounds interesting to you.

One-on-one

There are few truths in education, but one is that growth best occurs one-on-one. Beyond your advisor, look for opportunities for one-on-ones — even on a one-time basis. See a prof during an office hour, a peer advisor when you have a problem, or a student who said something that aroused your interest.

Adapt assignments to fit you

Want an easy way to personalize your education and ensure that your education prepares you for your specialty? Make your assignments meet your needs. Term papers, fieldwork assignments, can tie into your career plans. If an assignment doesn't turn you on, propose an alternative. You'll be surprised how often the prof says yes.

Don't take crap

A member of the orientation committee at Harvard gives the following advice to incoming students. She advises, "Fix it. If you can't, ask. If someone says no, ask someone else." If you think of this every time a problem arises, you're on the path to college heaven.

Lifelong Learning

Lifelong learning has become a cliché, and it can sound exhausting — forever upgrading yourself until you retire or drop. But there is an upside. In past generations, after years on the job, many people felt bored — like they had been there, done that. There always have been new things you *could* learn, but now, there always are new things you *must* learn to survive.

Consider staying permanently enrolled in You U. —a self-designed approach to learning what you need when you need it. That can mean one or more of the following:

- Join or form a group of your peers that gets together regularly, either live or electronically, to discuss problems and solutions.
- Don't let the monthly issues of the magazine from your professional association stack up.
- Attend at least one professional conference a year.
- Find one or more mentors. Times have changed. A mentor/protégé relationship used to be a one-at-a-time, time-intensive deal. Today, such a relationship is likely to be more fluid. You call with a question, exchange e-mails on a new development, occasionally commiserate over a cup of coffee. Ideally, you'll have a few mentor relationships, some in which you're the mentor, others in which you're the protégé.

Part III
A Better Way to Land the Job

"My sense is you're personalizing your resume too much."

In this part . . .

"Most of us hate to look for work. Period. We want the great job to knock on our front door and say, 'I'm here.' . . . It's the Job Charming fantasy. . . . Most of us also hate to market ourselves. . . . It feels sleazy."
— Cheryl Gilman, *Doing Work You Love*

Good! You've picked out a career. Now you need to find someone good to hire you. This part shows you a proven better way to do just that. It's generally easier and faster than traditional methods, and there's no sleaze required.

Plus, how to successfully negotiate salary — even if you're negotiating with Ebenezer Scrooge.

Chapter 9

The Big Picture

In This Chapter

- The pushy way to land a job or get clients
- A more pleasant way to land a job
- A little realism
- The keys to finding good work fast

Conventional wisdom says that the following is the right way to land a job. Can you picture yourself doing this?

Sally is ready to start phoning prospective employers and networking contacts at 8 a.m. because that's when they are most likely to be at their desks without gatekeepers. She checks her list of contacts, which she maintains using contact-tracking software, and begins:

> "Hello, this is Sally Jones. May I speak with Harry Hirer?"
>
> "Hello, this is Sally Jones. May I speak with Margie? We were roommates back in college."
>
> "Hello, this is Sally Jones. May I speak with the person in charge of marketing?"
>
> "Hello, this is Sally Jones. I'd like to find out more about your industry. Can we get together?"

Sally cajoles and prods gatekeepers; she leaves tantalizing voice mail messages, and diligently follows up on unreturned phone calls. Day and night, Sally is networking: "I'm looking to use my skills in planning, management, and communication. Do you know anyone in a position to hire someone with my background?"

We ask again. Can you picture yourself doing that? Although many career guides ask you to follow this regimen, we find that a lot of people don't stay with it long enough to succeed, no matter how much they are coached and prodded.

A Better Way to Land a Job

This entire part of the book is devoted to showing you our not-pushy-person's approach to landing a job. Here's an overview.

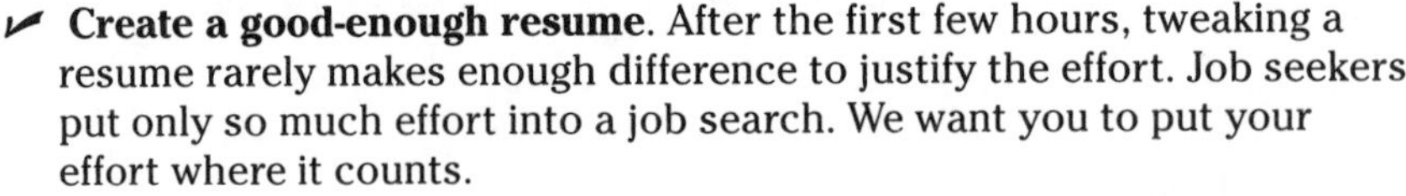

- **Create a good-enough resume**. After the first few hours, tweaking a resume rarely makes enough difference to justify the effort. Job seekers put only so much effort into a job search. We want you to put your effort where it counts.

  Next, from the following approaches, simply pick the ones likely to work best for you — we show you how to predict which ones will. And after you see which approaches are working best for you, de-emphasize the others. It sounds obvious, but you'd be surprised.

- **Find on-target want ads.** Yes, check the Sunday newspaper, but also search the Internet. One of the Internet's tools is automated job scouts that screen hundreds of thousands of jobs on the Net 24/7 to find openings on-target for you and deliver them right to your electronic door — your e-mail address. The Net offers a lazy person's approach to landing a job.
- **Identify a handful of dream employers.** We show how to find your dream employers in Chapter 14. Write to them honestly, humanly, and without overselling yourself. E-mail often works best. Gently follow up with a phone call. If they don't return the call, the heck with them.
- **Identify a small number of people in your personal network who may know someone who could hire you for the sort of job you're looking for.** If these people don't have any leads, ask them to keep their antennae out and call you if they hear of anything — you just recruited a scout. If you don't hear from your scouts, call them back once. If they don't return the call, the heck with them.
- **Write to a few search firms that specialize in your field.** If you don't hear back, the heck with them.
- **Attend one or more job fairs.** You can find dozens of employers in one place, all of whom are eager to talk with job seekers.
- **Convert your job interviews from interrogations to first dates.** We show you how in Chapter 16.

That's it. No excessive pushiness, no massive networking, no sleaze required. And with moderate effort, it works, even if you're not an aggressive person. In the following chapters, we show you the best approach to each of the seven steps. We understand that you have things you'd rather be doing than looking for a job.

When you're self-employed, you don't have to land a job, but you do have to land customers or clients. For advice aimed specifically at the self-employed, see Chapter 19.

Be Real

Many likeable people suddenly become too formal when they become job seekers. Imagine that you are an employer and an applicant says, "I believe I'm well-suited to the position." Ugh. Instead of donning this phony, job-seeker persona, talk and write humanly, honestly, even playfully in every step of your job search. Consider this excerpt from a letter to a headhunter:

> I knew I shouldn't have left New York for Knoxville. I love big-city life, from Scribners to Chinatown, but it was so tempting: sales manager for the Home & Garden Network in its crucial start-up phase. I figured that I could be happy anywhere, so I moved myself and my dog to the most Southern, backwoods small city you can imagine. Culture in Knoxville is the Star Spangled Banner at the University of Tennessee football game. After two years in the old South, I want out! Do you know anyone in New York who might throw a life preserver to an overboard sales manager?

Wouldn't you consider helping this person if you could? The standard "I-believe-I-am-well-qualified-for-the-position" approach usually creates resistance; the human approach encourages connection.

Please don't oversell yourself. If you're just a basic good hard worker, describe yourself as just that. It is a mistake to try to pass yourself off as a star. The thought of having to do all that B.S.ing will stress you out and make you more likely to procrastinate in your search for work. You'll probably sound unnatural and therefore won't be successful. And if, against all odds, you manage to bamboozle someone into thinking you're stronger than you're likely to be, you risk failing on that job, and making both you and your boss or customer miserable. So don't make a false impression. Sell who you really are. You'll enjoy your search for work more and be more likely to end up with work you'll do well. Besides — although increasingly this quality is seen to be unimportant — it's honest.

The Key to a Fast Job Search

Even though we make the process as fast as possible, to keep your expectations realistic, you need to know that fast is relative. Many people fail in their job searches because they give up too quickly. Yes, you may luck out and find your dream job right away, but realistically, you can figure on spending a few hundred hours. Actually, that's not a lot of time — only a few months to end up in a position that should keep you contented for years.

Here's the key to getting a job quickly. Successful job seekers spend only a modest amount of time on preparation. They don't need to clean their desks before beginning. They spend just a bit of time preparing for phone calls. They don't spend time primping their resume or fussing over the design of their business cards. They spend almost all their job-hunting time directly contacting target employers by e-mail and phone, responding to ads on the Internet, and asking well-connected people for job leads.

A Final Note

A number of the ideas in this part may be different from what you've heard or read before about how to land a job or get business on your own. We ask only that you read with an open mind. If you remain unconvinced, go back to the standard advice. But we have found that, especially with the sorts of people who use career guides, the approach you are about to read should land you better work faster.

The one-sentence solution

Richard Bolles, author of *What Color is Your Parachute?*, reports that 69 percent of job hunters land jobs simply by opening their local Yellow Pages, calling employers in their favorite category, and asking if those companies are hiring for the position the seeker desires.

You can be fast and even playful: Susan called all the museums and aquariums listed in the Yellow Pages and said, "Hi, I'm an experienced manager who loves museums. My company just downsized, so I'm looking for a job. I figured I'd go direct. Might you guys need someone like me?"

It can also work if you're self-employed and looking for clients. Whenever public relations consultant Michael Cahlin needs business, he simply gets out the phone book and starts calling companies he would like to work with. He asks them if they're happy with their PR. Usually they aren't, and soon he has several new clients.

This simple, direct strategy sounds reasonable to us. When dealing with a larger organization, though, a smarter method is to visit their Web site and e-mail a senior person from there.

You might try Bolles' sentence solution first, and if it doesn't work, come back and read the rest of this part.

Chapter 10
Creating Your Mind-Set

In This Chapter

- Getting that chip off your shoulder
- Making time for your search
- Shrugging off fear of rejection
- Staying upbeat

A good mind-set will make the process more successful, maybe even borderline fun.

Getting That Chip Off Your Shoulder

Many people who are looking for work are frustrated, angry, or depressed. They resent how long their job search is taking. Or they're still bitter at being downsized (a lovely term for "mass firing.") No matter how legitimate, a chip on your shoulder decimates your chances of landing a job. Even if you don't actually say "I'm angry!" people know. It may sound unsympathetic, but the best advice we can give is: Get over it.

If you just can't make yourself get over it, please try this approach before you spend a dime. Every time you become aware of a chip-on-your-shoulder thought, that *instant,* force yourself to replace it with a constructive one. Ask yourself, "What's the next one-second task I need to do to line up the work I'm seeking?" Sounds simplistic, but it works for many of my clients. Frankly, we used this system when getting overwhelmed with the task of writing this book!

Finding the Time

Many people who want to start a new career claim that their biggest impediment is lack of time. In fact, their problem usually has little to do with time. Rather, feeling a lack of time is a sign of mixed feelings about finding new work. Many people are scared of change, even if their current life is unhappy.

Nevertheless, sometimes a job search *is* hampered by insufficient time. The solution comes down to one word: *priorities.* It comes down to answering this question: "Where among my priorities is making this change? Am I willing to cut some corners at work so I can pursue this? Am I willing to tell my family that I have to spend parts of my evenings and weekends on launching my new career? Am I willing to give up golf until I land a job?" Assuming that you really do want to land a new job, and you're not finding the time to spend on your quest, it can mean only one thing: You are consciously or unconsciously choosing to do other things.

Here is the cure: Throughout the week, when you have a choice of what to do with some extra time, make it a point to ask yourself, "Am I going to work on lining up my new work or not?" If you truly want a new career, you will find enough time. Some people find more time, others find less, but if you're serious about your search, you'll find enough.

Put your job search time on your calendar. Treat that time as you would any other appointment. You wouldn't miss an appointment with the dentist (although you'd love to). Isn't your career as important?

Don't dismiss the value of five-minute snippets of time. The week is filled with them, and they are relatively painless ways to get rolling again.

People with full-time jobs are the most likely to complain of lack of time. Of course, making time to find new work is tougher for them, but it's usually doable. Phone calls to contacts are best made at the beginning and end of a standard work day and during lunch hours because that's when the folks who do the hiring are likely to be at their desks without gatekeepers screening their calls. You can set up interviews at the beginning or end of the workday, and during vacation days. At night and on weekends, you can search the want ads, the Web, or libraries for job openings and information on prospective employers. You can work on your resume, cover letters, thank-you letters, brochure, and mock interviews or presentations. And of course, you can read this book. So even if you're working full-time, there's plenty of hope.

Shrugging Off Fear of Rejection

Do you dread making contacts because you fear rejection? See if adopting any of these mind-sets helps.

It's all in how you think of it

Are you afraid you'll seem like a loser if you ask people for job leads? The key is how you think of it: You're not desperate, you're simply exploring to see if there might be a more satisfying work life for you. People can respect you for that. Many of them wish they had the guts to do the same.

The deck of cards mind-set

Think of your job search as if you're looking for the ace of hearts in a deck of playing cards. If you feel hurt or angry every time you turn over a card that's not the ace of hearts (a rejection), you'll probably burn out long before you find the ace. But if in your job search, you treat every rejection as if it's no more personal than a playing card turning out not to be that ace, you're more likely to persevere. Remember, each card brings you one step closer to the ace.

The library book mind-set

When you're at the library looking for information, you pick a book off the shelf, glance through it, and if it's not helpful, simply move on to the next book. You can think of each person you contact in your job search like a book in the library. If one person isn't helpful, simply go on to the next one with no more emotion spent than if the first person was an unhelpful library book.

The only game in which batting .050 is plenty good enough

The good news about a job search is that you only need to find one good job. It's not like baseball where you need a good batting average. I like Tom Jackson's description of a job search in *Guerrilla Tactics in the Job Market:*

NO NO NO NO NO NO NO NO NO NO NO NO NO NO NO NO NO NO NO NO
NO NO NO NO NO NO NO NO NO NO NO NO NO NO NO NO NO NO NO NO
NO NO NO NO NO NO NO NO NO NO NO NO NO NO **YES**.

The two gold miners

Imagine two gold miners. Each time the first miner tries a vein that turns out to contain nothing but rock, he gets frustrated. The other miner, knowing that he only needs to strike gold once every 50 times to make enough money, stays cool. Is there any question as to which miner ends up making more money? Any question as to who is a happier person?

Rejection as a blessing?

Look at a rejection as a blessing in disguise. It may keep you from a job that is wrong for you.

What's the worst that could happen?

Picture the worst cases: embarrassing yourself in an interview for a very cool job, sending out a bunch of job applications and never hearing from any of the employers, plugging away for six months and still not getting a job. Ask yourself, in the larger scheme of things, would your life really be that terrible? Couldn't you do something to compensate?

Staying Up

Sometimes it happens fast. Because you're brilliant, lucky, or both, you land a cool job in a matter of weeks. Alas, it doesn't always work that way. So it helps if you have staying power. The good news is that staying power is at least a partially acquired trait. Here are some mind-sets that have helped my clients stay the course.

You're going to the mall

People who enjoy shopping 'til they drop say that what makes it fun is that it doesn't require a lot of preparation, and that it's a cross between a treasure hunt and a costume party. You walk around the mall searching for treasures, asking salespeople to point you in the direction of items that you're likely to consider treasures. You try stuff on, most of which looks worse on you than it does on the rack, but it's still fun, like a costume party.

A job search is the same thing. With only a modest amount of preparation, you're exploring a "mall": your target career's milieu. You look around (by reading, searching the Net, phoning people in likely workplaces, and visiting work sites), ask people for directions to the areas within the "mall" most likely to have what you're looking for, and sooner or later, you find something good.

If you think of your job search as a visit to the mall, it helps create the right mind-set: only a moderate amount of preparation, plenty of exploration, trying stuff on, and enjoying the process, even if you don't end up buying anything for a while.

Playful yet persistent

Some of my most successful clients treat their work search like a game. Their motto: "Playful yet persistent." To acquire that mind-set, it may help to think of looking for work as a treasure hunt in an enchanted forest. Along the way, you meet obnoxious trolls, helpful munchkins, and maybe a fairy godmother or two. If you can laugh off the trolls, and take pleasure in the game itself so that you don't get frustrated even if it takes a while to find the treasure, you'll eventually find it (although it may not be the treasure you started out looking for).

Here's what we mean by "take pleasure in the game itself." Each phone call, each interview, each cover letter, can be tense or enjoyable. It's largely a matter of your mind-set. Every task in a job search, becoming self-employed, indeed in life, can either drain your energy or enhance it. Some experiences, such as a killer rejection, are unavoidable drains, but most experiences are, at least partly, under your control. For example, trying to make a cold call interesting, even playful, can build your energy, even if the call leads nowhere.

The truth option

If, during your search for work, you try to be someone you're not, you'll necessarily be nervous. But if you let yourself be your real self — yes, your best self, but yourself — you'll be more relaxed, and when you get hired, you'll be hired for who you really are. That, of course, means that you're more likely to succeed in your new work. Some people can fake it well enough to land a job, but they can't and wouldn't want to fake it forever. Better to show them the real you.

Fake it 'til you make it

This approach seems to contradict "the truth option," but keep reading. Sometimes, the key to feeling more upbeat is to act the way you would if you were *not* ready to pull your hair out. You may actually start to feel better. In psychologist's lingo, "Often, behavior change precedes and causes attitude change." In plain English: Fake it 'til you make it. To do so while still being honest, pretend that you are your best self. Think of the hour in your recent past when you were most confident, most together. Especially at key moments, pretend you are that best self.

Three balls in the air

When you have a hot job lead, it's easy to stop looking for others. Fact is, the odds of a hot lead turning into a job are much less than 50/50. Here's a useful goal: Have three balls in the air at all times. If one falls, find another. Keep three balls in the air for a while and you'll soon be able to stop juggling.

Be in the moment

We believe that the following phrase is the key to enjoying every moment, even of your job search, which is not at the top of most people's fun lists. The phrase: Be in the moment. Stop thinking ahead so much. Instead, try to get into every little task — whether it's the puzzle of deciding what to say in your resume, or the challenge of convincing a gatekeeper to let you talk with a prospective client. We are trying to enjoy the challenge we're facing right now: how to phrase this paragraph so that it's helpful but not preachy. (We're not sure we solved the preachy problem.) One moment at a time: At least in our opinion, that is the key to a successful career and a happy life.

Chapter 11

The Right Resume in Much Less Time

In This Chapter

- Resume-writing as a few-hour, not few-week activity
- A just-right resume in ten easy steps and one hard one
- Chronological, skills, or hybrid resume?
- Creating your electronic resume
- Honorable tricks
- Solutions for an imperfect work history

Creating a resume is a great first step in your job search. It usually helps you realize that you've accomplished more than you think. Plus, it distills your accomplishments into impressive sound bites that you can use in interviews and networking.

Here, we show you how to create a good-enough resume. "Good enough?" you protest, "Good enough isn't good enough. It's hard enough to get a good job with a fabulous resume. Hey, authors, I thought you said that you were going to show us the best way to land a job, and right off the bat you're compromising — a *good-enough* resume?"

No compromise. Here's why it's smarter to create a good-enough resume rather than a perfect one. Many job seekers nitpick their resumes for weeks or even months before going on with their job search, thereby delaying their hiring, which means thousands of dollars of lost income.

Worse, spending too much time on a resume can mean you don't get a job. Here's why: We've found that job seekers have only so much energy to give to a job search before burning out. Too often, they use up too much of that energy in crafting the perfect resume, leaving too little for the far more important task of contacting employers. It's like an athlete who spent so much effort in pre-race stretching that he was too tired to run well in the race.

A resume is a few-hour activity, not a few-week one. Jobs are rarely won because of the tweaking you did beyond those first few hours. Knock out a draft of your resume, get feedback on it from a couple of trusted friends, prospective employers, or headhunters, and then move on to activities far more likely to benefit you than extra weeks of resume primping.

Yes, your resume should both demonstrate competence and create chemistry. Yes, it should be formatted for easy reading. Yes, it shouldn't have errors in speling (just kiding). But no, it's not worth taking the time to craft your resume as carefully as a prenuptial agreement.

Remember, many of today's employers usually use resumes only for a quick screen — average inspection time is 15 seconds (or one millisecond if it's autoscanned). Why? In part because employers know they can't trust resumes: Over one-third of resumes contain inflated credentials, and even the honest ones can't be trusted. Thanks to rev-up-your-resume books, software, and resume ghost writers, a resume may better indicate whether a candidate got help on her resume than whether she can do the job.

So put your job search time where it counts — in putting your letter, work sample, and maybe your resume in the right people's hands.

Notice that in the previous sentence we said, "*maybe* your resume." Why? Because unless your work history is clearly superior to those of most other candidates for your target job, you're better off hitching your prospects on your letter, work sample, and perhaps a bio. And remember, if you're looking for work as a self-employed individual or small business, never use a resume. Use a bio, portfolio, or presentation kit.

Thanks to your computer, you can adapt each resume you send out so that it focuses on the parts of your background most impressive to that employer. That isn't sleazy. If you were a prospective career counseling client, wouldn't you want a counselor to describe how he helps people in your specific situation?

A Just-Right Resume in Ten Easy Steps and One Hard One

Purists may sniff, but here's our client-tested, not-too-fussy, not-too-lazy, just-right guide to creating a plenty-good-enough resume. Everything you need to know in a dozen pages.

Step 1: Write your name and contact information

This information should include your home address, phone number(s), e-mail address, and, if you have one, your personal Web site address. The latter is a good place to display your work samples.

Don't use your employer's e-mail address. It suggests that you're job hunting on company time. (You wouldn't do that, now would you?) Also, it makes it easier for your boss to find out that you're looking. All she needs to do is use the company name as the search term using a search engine. Instead, sign up for a free e-mail account at a service such as Yahoo.com or Hotmail.com.

Step 2: (Optional) Write your objective

Only write an objective if you have a specific job target and would turn down anything else.

An objective can follow this form: "A position requiring *skills* A and B and *personal attribute* Z." For example:

- Management position requiring the ability to make good decisions quickly, solid understanding of office computer systems, and unquestionable integrity.
- Psychologist position requiring successful experience with drug abusers and with diverse populations, and the ability to remain calm under stress.
- Petroleum geologist position requiring extensive knowledge of computer-based drill site analysis and Alaska field experience, and the ability to function well in isolation.
- High school English teacher position requiring successful experience in teaching advanced placement classes and the willingness to take on extensive after-school responsibilities.
- Cushy job requiring a laid-back personality, the desire for a six-figure income, and the willingness to accept it without feeling guilty that it wasn't earned.

Step 3. Choose your format: skills, chronological, or hybrid

The main headings in a skills resume are — no surprise — your skills. Figure 11-1 shows an example.

In contrast, a chronological resume's main headings are the jobs you've held, listed in — again, no surprise — chronological order, most recent job first. (See Figure 11-2.)

If your best job was not your most recent, rearrange the order so that it's listed first.

If you're concerned about your boss finding out that you're looking to leave, your resume might indicate that you're working for a major consumer products company rather than for Procter & Gamble, and that the period of employment is 1997-present rather than June 1997-present.

A hybrid resume would tack this onto the skills resume:

Professional History

1998-present, Vanderbilt & Rockefeller, Inc., New York, NY, account representative.

1996-1997, Tough Luck Casino, Las Vegas, NV, croupier.

1993-1996, Onyurbut Ski School, Steamboat Springs, CO, instructor.

Many career guides encourage many people to use a skills format when, fact is, almost all employers prefer a chronological format. Consider a skills format only if you've never held a job related to your desired position; for example, you've always been a supermarket bagger and are now seeking a job as a physics teacher.

If your work history is weak but you'd rather show it to an employer than create the impression that you've been a slacker all your life, use a hybrid resume. This is a skills resume that tacks on a plain list of your jobs. That way, after you've impressed the employer with a skill set that says you can do the job, a briefly-stated wimpy work history may matter less.

Maynard G. Krebs
9 Dobie Dr.
Gillis, MN 66696
whatmework@whitehouse.gov

Summary

Skill that would most impress the target employer:

Evidence of that skill #1
Evidence of that skill #2
Evidence of that skill #3

2nd most impressive skill:

Evidence of that skill #1
Evidence of that skill #2
Evidence of that skill #3

3rd most impressive skill:

Evidence of that skill #1
Evidence of that skill #2
Evidence of that skill #3

Education

Personal Interests

Figure 11-1: A skills resume.

Maynard G. Krebs
9 Dobie Dr.
Gillis, MN 66696
e-mail: whatmework@whitehouse.gov

Summary

Professional History

1998-present Title, employer

Accomplishment that would most impress the target employer
Second most impressive accomplishment
Third most impressive accomplishment

1996-1997 Title, employer

Accomplishment that would most impress the target employer
Second most impressive accomplishment
Third most impressive accomplishment

1993-1996 Title, employer

Accomplishment that would most impress the target employer
Second most impressive accomplishment
(Optional) Third most impressive accomplishment

Education

Personal Interests

Figure 11-2: A chronological resume.

Step 4: Pick out a specific resume to use as a model

Go to a library's career section. You'll see many resume guides, each of which contains many sample resumes. Our favorites are

- Yana Parker's *Damn Good Resume Guide* (best for relatively low-level employees)
- Don Asher's *Overnight Resume Guide* (mid-level)
- Joyce Lain Kennedy's *Resumes For Dummies* (entry- to mid-level, made simple)
- Ron Krannich's *High Impact Resumes and Letters* (a thinking-person's guide)
- Kate Wendleton's *Building a Great Resume* (excellent for mid- to upper-range businesspeople).

From a resume guide, pick one resume that

- Uses your chosen structure — chronological, skills, or hybrid.
- Has content relevant to your target job.
- Uses language and has a feel that you like.

Photocopy that resume and use it as a template. You might copy one or two more of your favorites to serve as sources of phrasing.

This next step is the hard one. We do our best to make it as easy as possible.

Step 5: Draft a resume that follows the structure, language, and feel of your model resume

What to put in that structure? Your accomplishments.

Pull out all the accomplishments from your work experience, including unpaid work or school activities if necessary, *that will most impress your target employer*. To figure out which of your achievements to include, put yourself in the employer's shoes.

Of course, quantitative achievements are easy to cite and are powerful, for example:

- Ranked second of 15 salespeople in net profit generated. (Of course, you don't have to mention that the other 13 were part of an early-release program from the state mental hospital.)
- Developed proposal that received $1.5 million grant.
- Isolated gene marker L78PS.
- Conducted study that resulted in a 20-percent decrease in company phone bills and earned me a cash bonus (which only partly compensated for the personal phone calls you made to your girlfriend in Shanghai).
- Only one accident in two years as operations supervisor. (Of course, that one accident was a doozy: A worker slipped on the wet floor you created, fell down a chute, and landed in the company's new high-powered meat grinder, which, natch, was running full-tilt.)

Less quantifiable accomplishments are also fine:

- A quote from your performance evaluation or letter of recommendation: "Tawanda is one of our brightest and most easy-to-get-along-with employees."
- Successful projects: "I developed a new system for assaying immunosuppressants."
- Increased responsibility: "Within three months, was given sole responsibility for the agency's largest graphic design projects."
- Compliments you've received from co-workers or satisfied customers. (Do not mention the time you were complimented for finally getting something right.)

Get letters of reference early in your job search. Not only will they be useful for your resume, they're great for sending along to prospective employers.

Some accomplishments can be particularly powerfully stated as PAR stories. In a *PAR story*, you describe the *p*roblem you were faced with, how you *a*pproached it, and how it was *r*esolved. Take the accomplishment, "Only one accident in two years as operations supervisor." By itself, it sounds okay, but here's what it looks like as a PAR story:

> "When I was hired, there had been three serious accidents in the past year. One man lost part of a finger. I observed and interviewed all the assembly line workers and the former supervisor, and we developed a new plan for reducing accidents. In my two years as supervisor, there has been only one accident: a slightly twisted ankle." (We were only joking about the meat grinder.)

Remember, to get a job offer, you must prove three things:

- You can do the job.
- You will do the job.
- Your personality fits the organization.

So don't forget about "soft" accomplishments such as people skills and boy/girl scout attributes like reliability and hard work. If true, include such accomplishments as

- Voluntarily worked, on average, a 55-hour work week. Took only four sick days in three years.
- Well-liked by co-workers. If they gave an award for employee most likely to be asked out to lunch, it would be me. (Of course, as a result, I now weigh 430 pounds.)

Still can't think of enough accomplishments or PAR stories? Think of all the people who benefited from your efforts. What would they say about you? Any statistics you can cite?

There's no need to list a zillion accomplishments. All you need are the half-dozen or dozen that will most impress the people with the power to hire you for your target job. If you have more than a dozen, fine. Keep them on a separate page in your word-processing file containing your resume. For different employers, you may choose to include different accomplishments. For example, you can save that time you managed to cram 17 people into your Toyota Tercel for that job opening as an efficiency expert.

Yana Parker, author of *Damned Good Resume Guide,* warns, "Don't mention activities you never want to do again or you may end up with a job you don't enjoy." (Like tending that meat grinder.)

Honorable tricks

If your employers are more impressive than your titles, list those first, and vice versa. Perhaps bold face the impressive part.

IBM, clerk.

Product manager, Dewey, Cheatham & Howe, Inc.

Some more tips and tricks:

- If your firm is impressive, describe it. If not, simply list it.
- If what you did is more impressive than your official title, use that. For example, if your title was administrative assistant but, in truth, you mainly coordinated projects, it is more honest, as well as to your

advantage, to list your job title as project coordinator. (You may want to keep it to yourself if your title was president and you mainly played golf.)

- If your employment chronology isn't perfect, put the dates on the right side where they draw less attention.
- Throughout the resume, boldface and/or underline phrases that are particularly impressive. Remember, your resume may get only 15 seconds. It would be a shame if your best accomplishment would have been read in the 16th second.

Solutions for an imperfect work history

Here's how to present flaws honestly without killing your chances of landing a job.

Problem: You're unemployed.

Solution: Consider getting a volunteer or temp job for a prestigious employer in your desired field. Or set yourself up as a consultant. Before putting consultant on your resume, do have at least one consulting assignment (even if unpaid), so you have an answer when the interviewer asks, "Well, Binky, tell me about one of your consulting assignments."

Problem: You've job-hopped.

Solution: Give reasons for leaving; for example, it was a temp position, or you had to move because your spouse got a job offer she couldn't refuse. You might want to omit your reason for leaving if you were fired for grand theft.

Problem: Your have little or no work history.

Solution: You haven't been catatonic all this time (we hope). Even most party-hearty, kick-back, down-a-brew types have done enough constructive things to fill a resume, at least a one-pager with lots of white space and wide margins. So make a list of your accomplishments: classes you've taken, projects you completed, volunteer work, and so on.

Your accomplishments still look skimpy? Create them. For example, volunteer to do a project for a friend, or even better, for a prominent company.

If you include volunteer work, call the work section of your resume "Experience."

Don't use vague language to hide what you were doing, like the homemaker who wrote: "Operations manager for multi-dimensional enterprise." Such creativity appears deceptive, which is the last thing you want an employer to think.

Yana Parker suggests that parents who stopped working to raise their kids be honest, and be sure to include any out-of-home paid or volunteer work. For example:

> 1988-1998, Full-time parent. Plus community work involving fund-raising, voter registration, and community service committee work.

Problem: A gap in your work history.

Solutions: List your resume in years rather than months. Fill in the gaps with any education or volunteer work.

That solution, however, doesn't solve David's problem. He worked for a firm that took on too much work with a too small budget, so David burned out and took a year-long vacation.

Our recommendation: Tell the truth. In addition to being honest, the truth often works wonderfully. For example:

> June 1997-June 1998, Bum.
>
> I have never had a break, and figured while I was still plenty young enough to enjoy it, I would spend a few months on pure pleasure: traveling in Europe for two months, helping my brother remodel his kitchen, taking golf lessons, even cleaning out my basement! And lest you think I was a total slug, I attended a landscape architecture conference, and during a drive through California, I visited a half-dozen award-winning landscape architecture projects.

Are you surprised? A narrative in a resume? And so informally written? Not to mention that David described his occupation for a year as "bum." Yes, yes, and yes. If there's one key to landing a job that you'll be happy and successful in, it is to tell your true, human story throughout the process: in resumes, cover letters, cold calls, and interviews. In today's era of the oh-so-primped job applicant, a candidate who tells his or her true story often stands out as the sort of person the employer wants in her organization. And if the employer thinks not, it's a sign that you don't want to work there.

You may ask, "Shouldn't a story like that go in the cover letter, not the resume?" Answer: It should go in both. It's wise to repeat crucial material that explains away problems and creates positive feelings about you. Besides, resumes and cover letters have a habit of separating from each other; as when the recipient of your resume and cover letter forwards only your resume to his boss.

Problem: You're older.

Solution: Ignore the conventional advice to hide your age by listing only your ten most recent years of work history. During an interview, your age will be apparent. Better they should know sooner than later. If they have their heart set on a young sprout, they're not going to hire you anyway. Better to get screened now than to get your hopes up, do a great job in the interview, and still not get the job. In Chapters 15 and 16 we show how, in a cover letter and interview, an older person can actually convert gray hair into a plus.

Step 6: Write the education section

Normally, the education section follows the employment section, but list your education first if it's more impressive than your work achievements. This is true of most job seekers just starting out.

Include your grade-point average if it exceeds 3.0 in your major or overall. Also include any honors, like Dean's List or cum laude. (No, second prize in your fraternity's belching contest doesn't count.)

If you started but never finished college, simply list the years of attendance and your major. For example:

> 1996-1998, Kegger College, major in sociology.

If you're still working on your degree, write your expected graduation date.

If not obvious from your major, list courses that are particularly relevant to your career goal. Include education outside of school, such as seminars.

For example, David wrote:

> 1998 Continuing education:
>
> Geohydrology issues in shoreline foundations. University of California, Santa Barbara Extension.
>
> TrackIt: advanced methods. Computer Attic training seminars.
>
> 1997 B.S. in Landscape Architecture, California State Polytechnic University. Cum Laude. 3.5 overall grade-point average, 3.7 landscape architecture grade-point average.
>
> Special career-applicable courses:
>
> Three years of college-level Spanish. (moderate fluency)
>
> Business courses in project management and finance.

If most of your career-relevant learning occurred outside of school, describe it. Figure 11-3 shows the education section of an aspiring curator with a career-irrelevant major and lots of out-of-school education.

If you learned things that may impress an employer, you might add ". . . which taught me XXXXXX." For example: "BA in political science, which taught me survey methodology, database management, and statistical analysis."

EDUCATION

Academic Education
1998, Williams College, BA in political science

Curating-Related Education
1996-1998 Apprenticing/coaching by:

Miriam Weinstein, curator Williamstown Art Museum

Dave Murphy, curator, Kansas City Museum of Art

Sharon Presley, curator, Chicago Museum of Science and Industry

Professional conferences
American Association of Museums, each annual conference from 1995 to the present

Seminars

The Business Side of Curating: three-day pre-conference workshop, American Association of Museums, 1996

Exhibit Traffic Planning: Williamstown Museum symposium

1994-present Independent reading: 7 books, 50+ articles (titles on request)

Figure 11-3: The education section of a resume for a person with plenty of experience.

Step 7: Optional sections

List awards, community involvement, professional affiliations. Only include these if they're likely to impress your target employers. Fellow of the American Academy of Sciences, yes. Member, Hell's Angels, no.

Step 8: The personal section

Here, you list volunteer activities, personal interests, hobbies, and so on. This section can sometimes be a door-opener. Seeing a resume from a fellow backpacker can move an employer to pick up the phone.

Step 9: List your highlights at the top of your resume

This is the most important part of your resume. Here, spend time. In the 15 seconds your resume may get from its recipient, this is the only part you can be sure will get read.

You have three options: Most people will choose just one, but if two are more impressive in your case, include them both.

Option 1

In one line each, list the accomplishments that will most impress your target employer. Call it a summary.

> **SUMMARY:** Received A.S.L.A. Award as landscape architect on U.S. Highway 1 shoreline restoration project.
>
> Top evaluations from supervisor: "Gets the job done right, plus he's fun to be around!"
>
> Seventeen completed projects. Excellent customer satisfaction (many references available).
>
> Solid knowledge of AutoCad version 15, and TrackIt project management software.
>
> Led 12 friends on a trip down the Amazon.

Option 2

A short paragraph describing the things about yourself most likely to impress your target employer. This is a good option if you are a good employee who can't point to specific achievements. The key here is to imagine yourself as the employer. What attributes would she most want that you can honestly claim? Let's say it's a nursing position.

> **SUMMARY:** Seven years as general medical-surgical nurse, known for exceptional concern for patients; absolute accuracy in treatment and in providing emotional support. Supervisor wrote, "Jan is thorough and remarkably helpful not just to patients, but to all of us."

Option 3

A short paragraph that quickly tells your human story — what brings you to wanting this job. Weave in the best thing(s) you bring to the table. This is the preferred option if your best shot at the job is making a human connection rather than selling your previous experience.

> **SUMMARY:** I was able to work with a number of patent examiners as an engineer at Loral. As time went on, I became fascinated with what they do. That is what I am meant to do! After a year of intensive preparation, I now am eagerly seeking a position as patent examiner.

Step 10: Get feedback

Show your resume to a respected friend and then a potential employer or personnel recruiter. Make any recommended changes.

John Sullivan, Professor of Human Resources at San Francisco State University suggests that you have your reviewers circle all the items in the resume that impress them, put an "X" through all items they don't like, and a question mark by all items that confuse them or slow them down.

Step 11. Stop obsessing and start celebrating

You're done!

Your Electronic Resume

Today, many job seekers need an electronic version of their resume. Even newspaper want ads may request one. And an e-resume is a must for posting online or responding to an online ad. Your computer skills would look rather thin if, to respond to an online ad, you had to print out your resume and fax it rather than just click and send. Here's how to convert your resume into an electronic version:

- Describe your job using nouns rather than verbs: manager rather than managed, programmer rather than programmed.
- If you have experiences and accomplishments you're unsure of including, add them to your electronic resume. Increasingly, employers electronically scan resumes to find words that match keywords in the job description. Because computers don't get bored with resumes (unlike humans), you can make your for-scanning resume longer. The more you include, the better your chances of matching a job announcement's keywords. (Don't try appending a copy of an electronic dictionary to your resume!) If you plan on adding a lot of stuff, consider having two electronic versions: a shorter one for manual screening and a longer one for electronic screening.
- Keep it simple: no fancy fonts or bullets — even centering is risky. Keep everything left-justified. Use asterisks instead of bullets. If you need to indent, use spaces, not tabs. The plainer your resume, the more likely the recipient's system will be able to read it. Do, however, add a line to the end of your resume: "A printed-out fully-formatted version of this resume is available on request." You might want to fax that printed-out version along with your e-mailed one.
- Use hard carriage returns rather than word wrap.
- Avoid bells and whistles such as a scanned-in photo of yourself.
- Save your file as plain text (usually called plain-text, ASCII, or text-only, depending on your word processor) so that you can cut and paste it in an e-mail to a prospective employer or onto a resume site.

Do not send your e-resume as an attachment because many recipients have difficulty opening attachments. Cut and paste it directly into an e-mail or onto a resume site.

Want an electronic hand holder as you develop your resume? Visit `www.ucla.edu` and click on the Jobs links, or try `tripod.com/work/resume` or `eresumes.com`. Or try a software package such as Winway Resume ($40, 800-4-WINWAY). It walks you through the resume development process and suggests hundreds of "job-winning phrases." It also includes hundreds of sample resumes, plus a variety of templates.

Chapter 12

Just What Sort of Organization Do You Want to Work For?

In This Chapter

- Myths about working in the private sector
- Why working for a nonprofit is overrated
- Why working for the government is underrated
- Who's happiest working for a large organization
- Who's happiest working for a small organization
- Who's happiest being self-employed

Do you want to work for a large company, a small company, a nonprofit, the government, or for yourself? In a way, it's a stupid question. It's like asking if it's better to eat at a restaurant or at home — it depends on who's doing the cooking. In every category, there are wonderful jobs and jobs that could depress a pollyanna. Any statement we make about an entire employment sector is an overgeneralization, but there are enough grains of truth to justify this chapter.

The Private Sector

UNCONVENTIONAL WISDOM

There are many myths about jobs in the private sector:

Myth: Compensation is better.

Truth: That's true only for very senior positions. Otherwise, salaries are generally comparable with government positions, although higher than in nonprofits.

Myth: The private sector is the most efficient.

Truth: There are too many exceptions to this. You really must assess this on an employer-by-employer basis: Ask your contacts to recommend good organizations and individual bosses, and probe during your job interviews. ***Note:*** Talk with potential co-workers before accepting a job offer. Those faces that smile when recruiting you may turn into gargoyles on the job.

Myth: Beware the private sector. Companies are ruthless, caring only about the bottom line, and are downsize-crazy. The same company that says "We care about our employees" will downsize you if it thinks it can save a nickel.

Truth: Yes, companies worship the bottom line, but nonprofits and even government agencies are also under financial pressure and often resort to downsizing.

Whereas the for-profit sector tends to be a mixed bag, in the nonprofit world, the picture is clearer.

The Nonprofit Sector

People have a romantic vision of the nonprofit sector. It *is* wonderful to work alongside people willing to volunteer or work for peanuts because they believe in a cause. Yet turnover in the nonprofit sector is very high. Why?

- It's easy to lose sight of those cute harp seals you're trying to protect amid your day-to-day routines. Most tasks in non-profit organizations are the same as those in the private sector: managing employees, writing reports, and so on.
- Budgets are often too tight, which can mean spartan surroundings. It can also mean that you may have to do without things that private sector employees take for granted — like a computer that gets repaired before the next generation of computers comes out.
- Nonprofits are run largely with volunteers, the quality of whom is variable.

Frankly, we wish that salaries and working conditions were better in the nonprofit world. These organizations address valuable goals that would be well served by attracting our best and brightest, but we would be remiss in encouraging you to give all for The Cause without providing full disclosure.

For a clearinghouse of Web sites on nonprofit careers, see `www.impactonline.org`; and `www.tripod.com/jobs_career/goodworks`.

The Government

Working for the government is an underrated option.

When you think of a government job, what do you think of? A postal worker? A pencil-pusher? The fact is, the government employs millions of professionals: doctors, lawyers, economists, engineers, scientists, accountants, planners, and managers.

Indeed, the U.S. government is America's largest employer, with 17,000,000 employees. One in seven Americans works for the federal, state, or local government. And despite the much-reported downsizing, the federal government alone *hires* at least 1,000 new workers *every day*.

Today, many people shun government jobs because they hear that government is shrinking. We believe this is a mistake. Although still in downsizing mode, we believe that government employment will increase greatly as Democrats gain more power. Democrats, of course, believe in bigger government. To convince you to consider government employment, we better explain why we're so certain that the Democrats will gain more power:

- We haven't yet seen the full impact of motor voter registration. People yet unregistered are more likely to be low-income, a group that votes heavily Democrat.
- The new census-taking method will increase the number of counted minorities. That is the demographic group that votes most heavily Democrat.
- Birthrates in the past 20 years have been much higher among minorities.
- The schools, media, and colleges, which are the major influences on our thinking, are more liberal and activist than ever.
- Increased immigration over the past decade is resulting in new voters who vote heavily Democrat.

Not only does the government employ millions of people, it pays them well. Except at top levels, government pay is as good or better than in the private sector. And unlike the temp-happy private sector, a high percentage of government employees hold full-time positions with full benefits and exceptional legal protections.

Another stereotype is that government jobs are so bureaucratic that it's tough to get anything changed. In fact, most government jobs are no more bureaucratic than in the private sector. Individual government departments are being given more authority to make changes than in years past. You won't have to massage five egos and fill out four forms to get an extra ration of fax paper.

Yet another invalid stereotype is that government employees are apathetic because the government lacks the profit-making incentive. In fact, in many government offices, there's a different, sometimes equally powerful motivator: The recognition that government's purpose is to serve all the people, not just the company's owners.

Getting Hired by Government

You use the same strategies to land a government job as any other — for example, make direct contact with specific persons with the power to hire you, even if a job isn't open. That way when something does open up, you have an inside track.

There are, however, a few bits of little-known information that can put you ahead of the pack when trying to land a government job:

- The government mainly hires from within, so if you're attracted to a government career, it's easiest if you start your career in government service.
- Don't think you need to move to Washington, D.C., to work for the federal government. Only ten percent of federal employees work there. California alone has as many federal employees as D.C. Thirty-five percent of federal employees are clustered around the ten regional centers: Atlanta, Boston, Chicago, Dallas, Denver, Kansas City, New York City, Philadelphia, San Francisco, and Seattle.

- You can speak to someone at the Federal Office of Personnel Management to find out where you might fit. (See the front of your White Pages for a local phone number.)
- Don't forget about local government. Ten million people, over half of all government workers, are employed by local governments, and the annual turnover rate is 14 percent. Translation: lots of job openings.

Segments within local government that many job seekers forget about are: county government, school districts, fire districts, and park districts.

Top Four Reasons to Work for a Large Company

- **More stable employment.** Despite the relentless downsizing and mergers, large employers are more likely to retain employees than small ones. Small businesses may struggle with inexperience, undercapitalization or market changes, and even go out of business. Of course, this could mean no job for you and worthless stock options. For every employee who got in on the ground floor of Yahoo!, there are thousands who are holding sexy-sounding but worthless pieces of paper.
- **More advanced technology.** It's expensive to keep up with the latest and greatest. That's a luxury that mainly large companies can afford.
- **More likely to provide sophisticated training**. If you have 1,000 employees who need the same training, you can justify the cost of developing a first-class program.
- **Status.** It feels better and looks better on your resume to say you work for Hewlett-Packard than for the Western Widget Company.

Top Four Reasons to Work for a Small Company

- **More control.** It's been said that at a large company, you need approval to blow your nose. In a small company, you're more likely to have the authority to blow some money; that is, to take an idea and run with it.
- **More job opportunities.** Small companies are creating most of the jobs. Recently, however, large companies started to do more hiring, even of middle managers, who were thought to be on the path to extinction.
- **Variety.** You get to wear many hats. For example, a scientist may be part-time salesperson, marketer, and manager.
- **Easier to get hired without formal credentials.** Many small companies are less concerned about whether you have that piece of parchment. They just want to know if you can hit the ground running.

Unless you're a risk-taker, focus on companies that have been around a little while and are in growing industries. Helping a start-up sounds romantic, but many of them struggle and die. That's not romantic.

Self-Employment

Self-employment is a wonderful option and a terrible one. It depends on who you are. You don't need a lot of money to stake your business. You don't need an MBA. You don't even need a new idea — we've seen many people succeed with copycat businesses. In fact, it's often easier to succeed when you can learn from pioneers' mistakes. What must you be to be successfully self-employed? It comes down to two things: having practical smarts and being a self-starter.

If you have those two qualities, here's why we're high on self-employment despite the long hours and the worries that come with running your own business:

- **Control.** Many of us enjoy control. When you're self-employed, you're the president. Want to try to sell a new product? Anytime you want. Want to hire someone? No six-month approval process. Want to reduce your record-keeping? No boss warning you that you need to be held accountable.
- **Perfect for the uncredentialed.** Try convincing a company to let you be the president without a decades-long climb up the organizational chart. If you're self-employed, you can instantly go from gofer to CEO.
- **Reasonable job security.** Sure, half of new businesses fail during the first five years, but you can cut that risk in half by operating your business from home. And, among smart self-starters who follow the advice in the self-employment chapter, the odds of staying in business are probably as good as those of keeping a job. You can't lose your job due to a personality conflict, a change in management philosophy, a boss who decides she needs someone with a different skill set, a merger, an acquisition, or a downsizing.
- **You get to keep all the profits.** How many employees save their employers sheaves of money and get nothing for it? Many employees are grateful for an attaboy and a cost-of-living raise.
- **The pride of creating something.**
- **Flexibility.** Yes, you're going to work your butt off, especially in the early years, but on your own terms. Want to work 'til midnight on Tuesday and play golf on Wednesday? Your call. Want to be home for your children after school? You're the boss. Want to work at home, in your pajamas, with hard rock blasting? Whatever you want.

Chapter 13

A Better Approach to the Want Ads

In This Chapter

- How much should *you* use the want ads?
- Using the Internet to instantly screen thousands of ads to find the ones *you* should respond to.
- The very best ads to respond to
- The best way to respond to an ad
- Want-ad stress savers

We know, We know. You've probably been told, "Don't spend much time answering want ads. You'll answer a thousand before getting one job offer."

That's true for people who don't know how to use the ads — but *you* will. This chapter shows you how to make the most of want ads — a better job search tool than you may think.

Ode to the Want Ads

Oh want ads, oh want ads, come to me oh want ads.

You give me succor in the night, inspiration by day.

All right, enough poetry. In plain prose, here's why the want ads make more sense than you've been led to believe.

- With thousands of job openings to choose from, you can focus on those that really fit. The odds of a networking contact leading to a good-fitting job are much smaller.

- Unlike with networking or cold-calling, you usually know exactly what the employer is looking for — the job requirements are right there in the ad. So you can tailor your resume, cover letter, and interview to the company's needs — ads are a legal cheat sheet for job applicants.
- Responding to want ads is more psychologically rewarding than networking because
  - You know you're probably applying for an actual job opening.
  - Responding to want ads is less stressful than asking people to help you find a job, let alone trying to convince an employer who hasn't listed a job opening that she should hire you.
  - Networking and cold-calling often involve trying to convince someone to buy something they're not looking for — not fun unless you're a real sales type.

You have to expect a high percentage of nonresponses and rejections, even if you craft excellent responses to ads. An appealing want ad can draw dozens, even hundreds, of applicants. The good news is that you only need one job.

- Using the want ads is an ideal approach for people who work during business hours. "When will I find the time to network and make cold-calls?" is a frequent cry of working stiffs. In contrast, you can search for and respond to want ads at night and on weekends, so you don't have to take time off work.
- Using the want ads is ideal if you're looking for a job out-of-town. The Web contains sites you can search quickly, with literally millions of jobs all over the world. In fact, want ads are an especially large part of an out-of-town job search because you probably don't have many faraway networking contacts.
- Responding to want ads is ideal for people who write better than they schmooze.

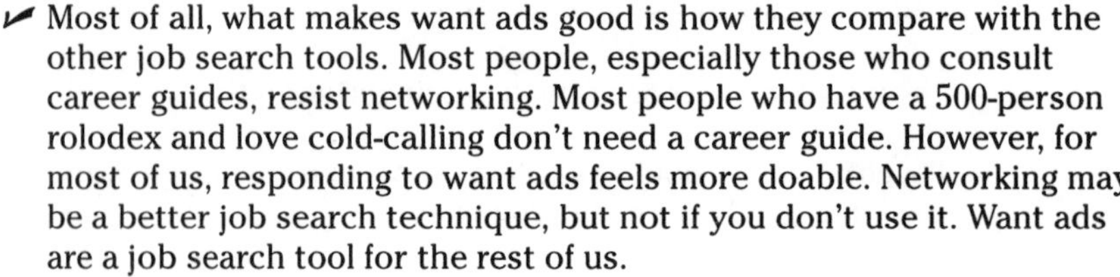

- Most of all, what makes want ads good is how they compare with the other job search tools. Most people, especially those who consult career guides, resist networking. Most people who have a 500-person rolodex and love cold-calling don't need a career guide. However, for most of us, responding to want ads feels more doable. Networking may be a better job search technique, but not if you don't use it. Want ads are a job search tool for the rest of us.

Want ads have long been underrated and networking overrated, but today, that's truer than ever. In the 1980s, when networking first got hot, employers didn't mind getting networked. It was a bit flattering to be asked for advice. Also, employers hadn't yet figured out that a request for advice was often a ruse to land a job interview. But now, almost 20 years later, employers are busier, tired of being networked, and increasingly seeing informational interviews as ploys, even when they're not. So networking, while it still often works, is less potent than it used to be.

Meanwhile, thanks to the Internet, answering want ads is a job-search method on steroids. Well over a million job openings are posted on the World Wide Web. You can search through them to find tailor-made jobs from the comfort of your home. You can even have personal electronic job finders scour the Net for you 24/7, searching through hundreds of thousands of jobs each week and delivering the few perfect fits on a silver platter right to your electronic door. All free to you! Now tell us that's not cool.

How Much Should You Use the Want Ads?

Other career guides give everyone the same advice: Use want ads sparingly. But one-size-fits-all advice rarely does fit all. So how much should *you* use want ads? Some people should devote no time to scanning the want ads; others should devote more than half of their job search time. Here's how to tell what's right for you: The more of these questions you answer yes to, the more you should use want ads.

- Are you better at writing resumes and letters than at networking?
- Are you more likely to answer ads than to network?
- Do you know only a few people in your field?
- Are you expecting a salary under $70,000?
- Is your target job in demand?
- Are you currently employed in or near your target field?

If you're trying to break into a new field, don't waste your time responding to ads. Employers don't have to advertise to find someone with no experience. They can ask their cousins, friends, or employees. Career changers, focus on cold-contacting your dream employers and on asking your personal network to put you in touch with them.

Not sure whether the want ads will work for you? Craft good responses to perhaps twenty carefully selected ads. If you get no positive responses, you have your answer.

Want ads can even be useful when you're self-employed. Use them to identify organizations that are looking to hire someone to do work that's up your alley. Propose doing the job on a project-by-project basis.

Making Want Ads Work for You

Okay, here's the meat. This section lifts you from the madding crowd into the elite minority that might actually land a job using the want ads.

A computer really helps

Access to the Internet is key. If you don't have a computer or Web access, most libraries do, and librarians can help you get started. Commercial firms like Kinko's also rent computer time. But think about buying a PC — you'll need it in every aspect of your job search (and the games are cool). Prices have dropped like a stone. High-quality base-model computers, plenty fast enough, complete with printer and monitor, can now be had for under $1,000.

An easy record-keeping system

Keep records of all ads you reply to and the cover letters you send. They'll be helpful at interview time. The simplest approach is to tape each ad to a separate 8½-x-11-inch piece of notebook paper, and put it in a three-ring binder along with your cover letter (if customized). Note any materials you included.

The very best ads to respond to

For the next couple of years, you have a rare opportunity. There are ads out there for real jobs, good jobs, that *don't* generate 500 responses per ad. These are the internal postings that, in years past, only company employees knew about. Where are they? They're at individual employers' Web sites. Most job seekers respond to ads in newspapers and at Web megasites, but don't bother with individual employers. This is a huge mistake. Here's why.

The first place many employers post their job openings is on their own Web sites. Why? Because it's easy, it's free, and respondents to ads at individual sites tend to be high-caliber and specifically interested in the company. Because employers don't get inundated with responses to such ads, your e-mail response to their Web site ad is likely to get a careful look. Later in this chapter, we show you how to craft a great response to a Web-site ad.

Perhaps best of all, targeting certain Web sites enables you to focus on the employers you'd really like to work for. Don't know who they are? Go to your friendly business-section librarian, describe the type of organization you want to work for (like a small, growing, biotech firm in Boston), and he can usually dig up a targeted list of employers and their Web sites. No such librarian? The following sources can often lead you to good organizations that might be hiring:

- Your favorite search engine. Use search terms such as "fastest growing Boston biotech."
- Attendees at a local meeting of the professional association for your field.
- The Chamber of Commerce.

A few years from now, most employers will immediately post their job openings on megasites such as `monsterboard.com`. Applicants will then have to compete against the entire world. But we're not quite there yet. So visit your target employers' Web sites and see if they list any openings for you.

While you're at the Web site, even if there's no appropriate job opening, send an e-mail to a senior official, saying something like "I am a software engineer with skills A, B, and C. My current employer is happy with my work, but I'm moving to your area for family reasons, so I'm looking for a new job. Attached is my resume. Let me know if you're interested."

Most job seekers think the Net is mainly for tech jobs still. This is no longer the case. Hundreds of thousands of non-technical job openings are on the Net, and not enough job seekers know about them. The Net is an unexplored gold mine for non-technical jobs of all sorts.

Developing an efficient way to screen a large number of ads

Another good strategy is to efficiently screen large numbers of ads to find good fits.

Going low-tech

You can scan your local Sunday newspaper regularly.

You can consult professional periodicals. You'll find more on-target ads than in general newspapers. If you don't know the professional association for your field, check the Encyclopedia of Associations which lists periodicals for most fields. Some libraries offer it online or on CD-ROM.

You can look at your current employer's internal job postings. It should be fairly easy to convince your current employer that you understand your organization's needs.

You can phone your field's job hotlines. For example, there's a touch-tone system that lets you home in on suitable job openings in the U.S. federal government. It's the Career America Connection: 202-606-2700. For a master list of hotlines, see Dan Lauber's *Job Finder* series.

Using the Internet

The low-tech stuff is all well and good, but, oh the Internet. It contains over a million job openings. And though you may be competing against many applicants, the beauty is that you can identify your best fits almost instantly. At many job Web sites, you can answer multiple-choice questions about the kind of job you're looking for. Then, the site not only searches its thousands of job openings and lists the perfect fits, but, if you take a few minutes to sign up for this service, whenever an employer lists a job on that site that fits your answers, you get an e-mail inviting you to apply for the job. Sign up for this service at a bunch of sites, and you essentially recruit a team of electronic scouts searching 24/7 through hundreds of thousands of jobs each week and delivering the few perfect fits to your e-mail address, all for free. Amazing.

Here are major sites offering these electronic scouts. They're sometimes called push sites because they push appropriate job ads right to your e-mailbox.

- `www.4work.com`
- `www.careerbuilder.com`
- `www.espan.com`
- `www.jobbankusa.com`
- `www.monster.com`
- `www.nationjob.com`

Another type of job site worth checking out is resume-posting sites. At these, job openings are matched not against your answers to multiple-choice questions, but against your resume. When employers place a job opening at a resume-matching site, they list the words they most want to see in an applicant's resume. If you register your resume at the site, and it contains enough keywords, you're invited to see the job announcement and to apply for the job.

Using these resume-posting sites is the modern-day equivalent of mass-mailing your resume. For minimal effort and little or no cost, you can post your resume at online resume-matching services, thereby reaching not just 500, but hundreds of thousands of employers. Chapter 11 describes how to create an electronic resume.

Unlike push sites, resume-matching sites aren't on autopilot, but they're the next best thing. You can search tens of thousands of openings in minutes. In fact, these sites offer an advantage over the autopilot ones: immediacy. These jobs on these sites are fresher. Sometimes, it can take an automated site a week or longer to send the job listings to your e-mail.

At other sites, you have to visit to see the listings, but it's worth the effort. There are a million job openings on these sites alone:

- America's Job Bank at `www.ajb.dni.us` has 300,000 listings from 1,800 state employment agencies, mostly in the private sector.
- CareerPath at `www.careerpath.com` carries more than 260,000 fresh ads per week from 60 of the largest newspapers in the United States.
- The Job Factory at `www.jobfactory.com` links to 250,000 listings
- Career Mosaic at `www.careermosaic.com` has 70,000 heavily technical listings.
- Federal Job Announcement Search at `www.fedworld.gov` posts and updates more than 1,500 new U.S. government openings *daily*.
- Career Magazine at `www.careermag.com`.
- JobTrak (`www.jobtrak.com`) offers 3,000 job listings aimed at new college graduates. To access them, you must be a student or alum at one of 700 participating colleges.
- Action Without Borders (`www.idealist.org`) lists openings at 9,000 nonprofit organizations.
- Online Career Center at `www.occ.com`.

For links to and descriptions of 22 general-interest places to post your resume, visit `www.tripod.com/jobs_career/resume/linklist.html`.

There are a number of sites that focus on the health professions: www.medconnect.com, www.medhunters.com, www.medsearch.com, www.medjob.com, and www.chemistry.com. The Cool Careers Catalog in Chapter 2 lists Web sites devoted to individual careers. You may find other career-specific sites through a professional association.

After you land a job, take your resume off the Net, and not just to keep from getting calls from employers dying to hire you. Your new boss may find it on the Net and think you're already looking to leave.

Posting position-wanted ads

Post a "position wanted" request on an Internet discussion group visited by target employers. To find on-target groups try www.dejanews.com, www.liszt.com, and www.forumone.com. As always, don't be afraid to be informal, even playful. Imagine that you are the head of a biotech lab and see the following post on your field's listserv, an electronic mailing list:

> POSITION WANTED
> Hot cellular biologist
> Will clone for food

Mightn't you bite?

Before posting your ad, check the discussion group's Frequently Asked Questions (FAQs) to be sure you won't get flamed, the Net term for "yelled at."

A low-tech option is to place a "position wanted" ad in your professional association's publication or on its Web site. If you're concerned about your boss seeing the ad, place a blind ad — one that omits your name. Respondents send inquiries to the association which, in turn, forwards them to you.

It's rarely worth placing "position wanted" ads in general-interest newspapers. Employers rarely read them.

A special way to use the want ads

Most job seekers want to find growing organizations because they hire more people and downsize fewer. Besides, it's fun to work for a place on the upswing.

The want ads are a good way to find growing organizations. If an organization is advertising a number of openings, it's probably growing. Even if none of the openings fit you, contact someone there with the power to hire you. For example, if you're looking for a sales manager position, contact the vice-president of sales. Don't know how to find that vice president? Phone the switchboard and ask for the name, phone number, e-mail address, and snail-mail address of the most senior person in charge of sales.

Want-ad stress savers

Amid all those ads, all those applications, and yes, all those rejections, it's easy to feel like you're drowning. This section helps keep you swimming so that you can make it to shore.

Avoiding intimidation

Intimidating things: Arnold Schwarzeneggar, gangs, the want ads. The want ads? Absolutely. Many job seekers *are* intimidated by the want ads: It seems that every job either is for a dishwasher or requires umpteen esoteric skills. The good news is that the ads are misleading.

It's no fun screening letters from 500 applicants, each of whom claims to be uniquely qualified. So when writing job ads, many employers deliberately beef up the job requirements to hold down the number of applicants, knowing full well that they'll hire someone without all those qualifications. Ken Elderkin, author of *How to Get Interviews from Classified Job Ads*, laments, "It seems that for even the lowliest of positions, applicants are required to leap tall buildings in a single bound." The reality is that most real-world jobs are less demanding than those described in want ads. So relax. Even you can probably land a job.

Remember also that the want ads represent less than 20 percent of all available jobs. The jobs that are advertised tend to require lots of arcane skills — only God has them all. Why? Because an employer can usually fill less-demanding positions without having to advertise them. You can access these easier-to-qualify-for jobs by cold-contacting hirers and by networking — how-tos in Chapters 14 and 15. So don't let those want ads intimidate you.

Should you respond to ads for non-professional positions?

Don't expect to walk out of your graduation ceremony and into a company car. The everyone-goes-to-college trend, produces an ever-growing surplus of college degree holders. So you may well have to respond to want ads for non-professional jobs. Don't worry, they can be launch pads for your professional career. One of the best entry-level jobs is in customer service. It's a great way to learn about the products and customers' needs. Beware of jobs that may not teach you much — like receptionist positions.

What about part-time and temp openings?

Even if your first choice is a full-time permanent job, don't ignore ads for part-time or temporary work. These days, employers are increasingly reluctant to hire full-time employees. Full-timers get benefits, vacations, government-mandated perks and leaves, and — most frightening to employers — strong rights in case of termination. Today in the United States, almost half of full-time permanent terminated women and minorities file wrongful termination claims. Hiring a temp or part-timer allows an organization to employ people only as long as they're needed, and to try out employees before taking the risk of hiring them full-time. What does this mean to you as a job seeker? That if you limit yourself to full-time positions, you'll eliminate lots of jobs, including many that are tryouts for full-time positions.

Temp and part-time jobs may offer you other advantages. They enable you to sample a number of industries quickly. They're easier to get hired for, so you may land a position you couldn't get if you were competing against applicants for a full-time position. Temp and part-time jobs can even be a smart choice, long-term. They're more likely to allow you to avoid the long hours and permanent commitment that a full-time job often requires. Temping isn't for everyone, but because it offers advantages both to some employers and some employees, it's no surprise that the number of temps has doubled in the past decade. Don't reject, out-of-hand, openings for part-time and temp jobs.

When you don't quite fit the job requirements

If you're lacking one job requirement listed in a want ad, go ahead and apply anyway. If you're missing more than one qualification, go on to the next ad. Your chances of landing an interview, let alone the job, are tiny. Besides, even in the unlikely event you somehow get the job, lacking more than one of the job requirements makes you likely to screw up.

Sometimes, want ads say little about the job requirements. If a phone number is listed, call and ask for details. If you can't get any, but the ad's few words sound appealing, give it your minimum effort: your generic letter and perhaps your work sample (discussed later in this chapter). If they don't like those, they're unlikely to like you.

Blind ads

Ken Elderkin suggests that you not be turned off by *blind ads* — ads that don't specify the employer. Employers use blind ads mainly to avoid being bombarded with 500 people phoning to find out the status of their applications or to beg for interviews. They're usually real jobs. Don't, however, respond to a blind ad if you're afraid that your employer might have placed the ad.

Whenever you respond to a blind ad, protect yourself against unscrupulous headhunters who want to broadcast your resume to every employer in town. Headhunters add 20 to 30 percent to the cost of hiring you. You get some protection by adding this to your cover letter:

> "If you are a recruiter, please show my resume only to the employer for this job opening. Contact me before approaching other employers."

Protecting yourself

These caveats are compliments of JobSmart webmistress, Mary-Ellen Mort.

These days, job hopping is expected in many fields, so it may be no big deal if your boss finds out you're looking to take a hike. If, however, you're afraid that your boss's finding out you're looking could cost your job, think twice before asking job-search questions on a Net discussion group. Also, before posting your resume on a site, be sure the site guarantees confidentiality. This usually means that the site agrees to store your resume. When your resume fits an employer's criteria, the site e-mails you, and invites you to apply. If you post your resume without such guarantees, your boss need only crank up his search engine and search on your name to discover your wanderlust. If you do decide to post your resume, don't e-mail it from your employer's e-mail address. Many companies routinely search the Net on its own name. No need for paranoia, but if you're worried about your boss knowing, send your queries to individuals and request anonymity.

Don't overestimate the Net. Yes, it's cool, yes it's easy, but remember that you're competing against seven continents of applicants. Mary-Ellen warns, "I get letters from people who sent 6,000 electronic submissions, signed up with every resume site on the Net, got no responses, and feel there's no reason for living. Technology has told them that they're worthless." The reality is that there are zillions of people trying to find jobs by using the Net for the same reason you are — it's easy.

So use the Net, but don't rely on the Net. Spend the small amount of time it takes to see if your dream employers have good-fitting job postings at their sites. If you're not afraid of your boss finding out, sign up for some push sites. Once a week, check a few non-push job sites. But think of the Net as only one part of your job search.

When to respond to a want ad

Respond either to fresh ads or to those two or three months old.

Fresh ads are good because sometimes employers want to act fast; they hire the first good person they can get. Generally, these are positions that pay under $40,000. For such positions, respond the first day the ad comes out. For higher-level positions, you probably have a few days — they usually won't start screening until a week after the ad runs or until the advertised deadline.

Two- or three-month-old ads are good because, more often than you may think, the hiring process stalls. Perhaps the employer can't decide on a candidate, gets busy with more urgent matters, or already fired the new hire. The employer may be reluctant to call candidates back months after the ad was placed — she's embarrassed that so much time has passed, or imagines that the top candidates have found other positions. Then suddenly, your fresh, new application appears. Sometimes, the easiest thing is to interview you and if you sound good, offer you the job. Rather than appear like a procrastinator who's just now getting around to responding, send the sort of letter you'd write to one of your target employers who did not have a job opening.

The best way to respond to an ad

Above all, your application must make clear that you fit the stated job requirements. You must also convey your humanity so that you have a chance of making that oh-so-important human connection. Finally, if possible, include a *work sample* — something that demonstrates that you can do the job better than other applicants; a copy of your stellar performance evaluation, or the article you wrote (perhaps just for this job search) on the seven keys to success in your profession.

Here's how David, a landscape architect, responded to a want ad:

> Hello,
>
> I searched through literally thousands of want ads to find the few that really excite me and seem to fit me. Yours, Position 4235J, listed at the Online Career Center, is one of those ads.

Always identify the ad. The employer may be running many.

> Your position excites me because I've been wanting an opportunity to do more scenic highway restoration. I've done one such major project (restoring the Highway 1 shoreline) and we received an ASLA award for it.

Touting his biggest achievement upfront.

> Now, I've been bitten by the big-project bug, and would like to do more. That's why I was excited by your job opening.

Again, the informal tone conveys good things: enthusiasm, honesty, and that he'd be a nice person to work with.

> Not only am I excited about the position, I believe I'm well suited to it as the following table indicates:

The following structure makes it easy even for a clerk to see that you meet the job requirements.

Job Requirement Listed in Ad	*Me*
Two years experience as landscape architect.	Two years experience as landscape architect.
Experience with technical aspects of shoreline restoration.	Yes, see above.
Knowledge of X-Pro project management software.	Extensive experience with similar project management software.
Negotiating local and regional environmental regulations.	This was a key part of my position.

Note that although David didn't meet one of the requirements (knowledge of X-Pro software), he put the best face on it rather than ignore it.

> Beyond the specific job requirements, my co-workers and boss say that I'm enthusiastic and fun to work with. Of course, those are just words, so I'll be happy to give you my boss's and co-workers' phone numbers.

The previous paragraph again recognizes that personality is as important as skills.

> To give you a sense of what I can do, I'm enclosing a copy of one of my drawings for the shoreline restoration project, the Environmental Impact Statement I wrote, and the before-and-after photos of the project.

That all-important work sample puts him ahead of the pack. Don't just tell them; show them.

> My salary requirement is $45,000 to $55,000 depending on the scope of responsibilities.

This is in response to the ad's request for a salary requirement. The best way to respond is with a fairly wide range plus "depending on the scope of responsibilities."

Of course, it is difficult to see if this position truly is a good fit for me from an ad, but it sounds right. I'm hoping that you will choose to interview me, so we can both see if we're right for each other. If we like each other, I'm even willing to volunteer for an evening or a weekend as a tryout.

The previous paragraph strikes a good balance between sounding interested but not desperate. It also makes a tough-to-refuse offer.

Sincerely,

David Michaels

Wouldn't you interview David? Even if he didn't include his resume? As it happens, David has been unemployed for a year. By sending a letter, and a work sample, but not his resume, he increases his chances of landing an interview — even if the ad asked for a resume. Had he submitted the resume, his unemployed status might have nixed him.

More ways to boost your chances

As we said at the outset, our goal is to give you every possible edge that's ethical so that you can triumph over the zillions of others who respond to want ads. Here's a final set of ahead-of-the-pack strategies.

The hide-the-resume game

If, like David's, your employment history is unlikely to be top-of-the-heap, you may want to defer showing your resume to employers as long as possible. A surprising number of people get jobs based on a letter, a work sample, an interview, and references, without ever submitting a resume.

Your second-best option is to hold off sending the resume until after your interview. That way, you can customize your resume in light of what you learn in the interview. A third possibility is to bring your resume to your interview. That way, you can explain any weaknesses. So think of it as a game: Hide the resume. The longer it takes an employer to see your resume, the better.

Remember that a resume is a sales tool. If you sense that your resume won't elevate you over other candidates, don't send it, even if you're asked for it — you don't want your supposed sales tool to kill the possibility of a sale.

Of course, many employers will dump your application if you don't include your resume, but when the day is done, your chances of landing a good job are better if you show employers only the stuff that makes you look better than the competition. Consider omitting your resume especially if you're changing careers or have a significant gap in your employment history.

If your resume is weak, consider using a *bio* instead of a resume. A bio is a less-than-one-page sheet summarizing who you are. Traditionally used by authors (ours are at the beginning of this book) and senior executives, a bio often works beautifully as a resume alternative — because of its cachet, because it doesn't mention gaps in work history, and simply because it's not a resume. Remember, resumes are considered among the least truthful of documents.

Don't just tell 'em, show 'em

If resumes are among the least trusted documents, work samples are among the most.

Don't have a work sample to send? You probably do but don't realize it. Teachers can use sample lesson plans; managers, the planning document they created; nurses, a performance appraisal; programmers, a disk; artists, photos of their work. None of these applies to you? How about this? Write a short report titled, "Seven Lessons I've Learned About (a topic that might interest the target employer)." Include your bio as the last page. The report conveys your expertise in a way that no resume can.

Preempting objections

Letters of application are great places to deal with potential objections to your qualifications. Maybe you're concerned that you'll be viewed as too old. Here's what 50-year-old Chava wrote:

> If you're looking for a 25-year-old, I'm the wrong woman. I'm 50, and believe that's a plus. I've had the time to learn what works and doesn't work in managing people. And unlike some younger workers, I don't plan on job hopping. If I'm as happy here as I think I'll be, you'll have a loyal employee. I might also mention that I'm in perfect health and am one of those old dogs who loves to learn new tricks.

Many job seekers make the mistake of hiding their age, race, or physical disability in their job applications. If an employer wants to hire a young employee, then, even though it's illegal, she'll probably find a way to hire one. Better to let the employer know the truth up front, and save both of you time and energy. And by writing about any potential problem up front, you can make your case for why the perceived problem isn't a problem.

Saving emotional energy

Because advertised jobs generate many responses, it's not worth spending much time on each ad. Crank out your letter, stick in your work sample, perhaps your resume, and send it. Sure, if the job opening is your dream come true, do a bit of research on the employer first. For example, visit the company's Web site. (An easy way to find a Web site is to use a search engine using the company's name as the search term.) Then add a sentence or two to your application letter explaining why you're a good match for the company. But in responding to most ads, it's not worth your time to do much research, or to follow up your want-ad response with a phone call asking about its status. If you haven't heard, the heck with them.

Ads may sound like the employer wants to hire someone yesterday, but the process often takes months. Don't invest yourself emotionally in any ad. Trust us, you'll lose more than you gain if you do. Respond to an ad and forget about it.

Okay, for the few ads you're most excited about, follow up in three weeks with another letter or phone call. Explain that you are excited about the job and wonder if they have had an opportunity to review your application. (Do not say, "Jerk, how come you haven't responded?" Blame is unacceptable in the job search game.) You may also ask, "Is there any reason you're hesitant to hire me?" If there is, you may be able to counter the objection.

Don't spend a lot of effort on follow-up — just a quick note or phone call. The odds of such efforts resulting in a job are tiny. Conserve your energy for the important things.

Rejections are tough, but no response is even more painful. Don't take it personally. It's a sign of the times: Many bosses think, "If it doesn't contribute to the bottom line, don't do it." Sending out rejection letters doesn't contribute to the bottom line.

And remember that rejections don't mean what you think they mean — that you are lower than pond scum. A rejection more likely means the job was filled by an insider or an insider's aunt; that affirmative action was a factor; or that the employer decided not to fill the position. And worst case, let's say they do think you're pond scum. You don't want to work there anyway. The heck with them.

Have realistic expectations. For every 25 well-done responses to carefully selected want ads, expect a few rejection letters, 20 no-responses, and one or two requests for interviews. Those two interviews are enough to make responding to want ads well worth your time.

Chapter 14

Contacting Your Dream Employers (Even If They Aren't Hiring)

In This Chapter

- Finding your dream employers
- Learning about your dream company
- Getting in touch
- Going to the (job) fair

Personally speaking, if we were looking for a job, this would be the first method we'd use: directly contact our dream employers, even if they didn't have a job opening. It should work something like this:

1. **You identify your dream employers.**
2. **You get them to like you.**
3. **They create a position for you or give you the inside track when a position becomes available.**

This chapter shows you the best, easiest way to take these three steps, but if, after reading this chapter, contacting your dream employer without knowing if they have an opening still gives you the shakes, drop it. You'll do better with job-search approaches that don't feel like torture.

Although this chapter mainly talks about finding a salaried job, the same three steps apply if you're self-employed and looking for customers. Remember, the same companies that hire salaried workers often also hire self-employed people to work on a per-project basis.

Creating Your List of Dream Employers

The standard advice is to develop a long list. Bad idea. It's tough to convince 50 employers that each one is the ideal one for you. Besides, why not put your effort into the few that really are most likely to make you happy?

Is there a cool employer or two you'd die to work for? If so, stop reading and start writing, e-mailing, or dialing. Do it now.

"But I don't know who my dream employers are!"

No problem. The simplest and perhaps best approach is to find the library with the best business section and tell the librarian that you want a list of employers that meet your specifications (environmental nonprofit organizations in Westchester County, for example).

Or if you're a do-it-yourselfer, the following information can help you find your ideal employer, no matter what interests you. You can discover small telecommunications firms in San Diego, large fashion houses in New York, or fish farms in Dubuque. (Well, you may have trouble finding the fish farms.)

Sources of local dream employers

There are lots of ways to find your best bets:

- Ask friends, colleagues, competitors, suppliers, customers, headhunters, and counselors at local college career centers.
- Check out the "best" lists: Big-city general newspapers and business newspapers such as *Business Times* (`www.amcity.com`) and *Crain's* (`www.crainsny.com`) regularly list the best, fastest-growing, and largest organizations. Many of these publications have online sites, where you can search on such terms as "best companies," top biotech," and "fastest growing."
- Ask attendees at a local chapter meeting of your field's professional association.
- Consult the *Adams Job Bank* series of books, available for more than 20 individual metropolitan areas. They list thousands of local employers by category and company size.
- Try the chamber of commerce. To avoid the party line: "All our members are good companies," ask a specific question: "I'm looking for a job as an economist. Do you know of any good, fast-growing small companies (small companies are where much of the job growth is) that might be good places to work?"
- Ask industry insiders. An easy way to do this is to visit the Web site of an employer in your target field. Often those sites let you send e-mail to some of their employees. Sometimes, the big shot you could never reach by phone answers your e-mail the same day.

- Check out features in local magazines and newspapers about fast-growing companies, new product introductions, and profiles of notables.

- Look for interesting company T-shirts. We're only half-joking. It's a good sign if an employer creates cool T-shirts for its employees.
- Call your favorite government agencies (see the front of your White Pages), and ask the procurement department for the names of outside contractors who employ people in your target job. Many government agencies outsource much of their work to contractors.
- Check out your field's category in the Yellow Pages. Sometimes the employer's description in the ad calls out to you.
- Check the "associations" listing in your Yellow Pages for a list of local nonprofit organizations.

- Don't ignore your current employer. It's usually easier to have your present job tweaked to fit, get a transfer, or even get an in-house promotion than to convince some stranger to give you the perfect job. If you trust your boss, have a heart-to-heart chat and describe your dream job. If you're skittish, try the human resources department; it may guarantee confidentiality. But be sure to ask before spilling your guts.

Sources of dream employers farther away

It's even easy to find on-target employers thousands of miles away:

- See *Who's on Top?* (at `www.hooversonline.com`). From among 13,000 companies, the Hoovers' business database company offers its picks of top companies in categories such as "most admired," "fastest growing," and "best companies to work for."
- Check out a book called *The Job Vault,* which contains inside information such as strategic direction and corporate culture on over 500 of America's largest employers.
- Use the CD-ROM or online services found at many libraries, plugging in search terms such as "best aerospace companies."
- See "The Hundred Best Companies to Work For," in the January 1998 issue of *Fortune* Magazine. An expanded version is available online at `www.pathfinder.com/fortune/1998/980112/int.html`.
- Ask on Internet discussion groups. To find on-target ones, visit `www.dejanews.com`, `www.liszt.com`, and `www.forumone.com`. Once you find an appropriate group, just post this question: "I'm looking for a job as an *(insert desired job)*. Can anyone recommend good places to work that might be hiring?"

- Read Kathryn Petras's *Jobs* (revised annually) for profiles of top businesses in dozens of industries.
- Browse through www.thomasregister.com. This contains the mammoth Thomas Manufacturing Register, which is product and contact information on 155,000 companies. You can search by company name, brand name, or type of product.
- Consult the *U.S. Government Manual* (www.access.gpo.gov/nara/nara001.html) and *The Budget of the United States Government* (www.access.gpo.gov/su_docs/budget/index.html) for indications of which federal agencies will be growing. Petras explains, "This is a clever way to get a real head start on everyone else. Every year, *The Manual* . . . tells the policies and priorities of each federal agency or department. *The Budget* goes one better: it tells where the money is going. Often agencies with increased allocations will be hiring."
- Check Dan Lauber's *Job Finder* series for lists of hundreds of field-specific directories.

Do you know the organization's name but need the phone number? Try an Internet phone book such as www.bigyellow.com, or www.bigbook.com. AOL subscribers, use aol.com/search/html2/business.html. Or go low-tech: the toll-free phone directory: 1-800-555-1212. Hundreds of thousands of organizations have toll-free phone numbers.

Are you unsure whether you'd be happier in the private, government, or nonprofit sectors? A large or small company? Just you and Bow Wow? See Chapter 12.

A tip for techies. Consider non-technical companies; you'll have less competition. For example, a client who was a so-so database manager focused his search on art-related businesses, and had an easy time of landing a job at one of the world's leading art auction houses.

A word about employment agencies

What's the word? Iffy. Yes, employment agencies can give you access to some jobs you might otherwise not know about, but you pay a price. Agencies typically take 30–40 percent of what you'd make if you contacted the employer directly. And the employer pays, so the agencies are more concerned about satisfying the employer than ensuring that you find a rewarding job. Sure, if you're well-qualified for an in-demand field, it doesn't hurt to include a few employer-paid employment agencies on your list of contacts. But focus on going direct to employers and jointly deciding what you could do to meet their needs and yours. You'll find a better job and be paid more for it.

Finding the right hirers in each organization

What do we mean by *hirers?* They are the people with the power to hire you. They are almost never the human resources department. They are

- The big enchilada at the small company you want to work for.
- The department head in the large organization you crave. To boost your chances of getting a response, write to the potential hirer and send a copy to that person's boss(es).

"But how do I find the name(s) of the people to contact?" you ask. Phone the organization. This is the best way, because unlike with directories, you get a currently accurate name, title, address, and, if you're lucky, a direct phone number.

Don Lussier, author of *Job Search Secrets,* recommends the following approach. Call the company's general number and say, "I'm updating my mailing list (which you are). Who's in charge of XXXXX (marketing, sales, or research, for example)? How's that spelled? And her title? Her phone number? If the receptionist asks what this is for, tell the truth. The worst case is he sends you to Human Resources, which isn't the end of the world. HR may even have a suggestion for you. Besides, you can always hang up.

If you don't get anywhere with the receptionist, call back and ask for the organization's mailroom. It doesn't have gatekeeping responsibility, does have the organization's directory, and often will surrender the information.

Internet approaches:

- Check the organization's Web site. It may include contact information for its employees.
- `Hooversonline.com` lists contact information for senior officials at 13,000 organizations, plus company overviews.
- `www.americasemployers.com` profiles 50,000 companies.
- `www.house.gov/reform/plumdata.htm.` provides contact information for hundreds of the most influential people in the federal government. (Maybe Vernon Jordan can get you a job?)

If you have a name but no contact information, use one of these Web phone directories. They list addresses, phone numbers, and e-mail addresses for millions of individuals.

- www.bigyellow.com.
- www.bigbook.com.
- www.555-1212.com.
- AOL subscribers can use aol.com/search/html2person.html.

Keeping track

Pull out that 8½-x-11-inch three-ring binder you're using to keep track of the want ads you responded to.

Have a separate page for each potential hirer and each networking contact. At the top, write the person's name, contact information, plus need-to-remember information from conversations and from your research on the organization.

Now get 31 divider sheets, the manila ones with the colored translucent tabs attached. Number each divider from 1 to 31, one for each day of the month. Put them into the three-ring binder.

Place each hirer's page in the correct day's section. For example, if you spoke with someone today and it's the 10th of the month, and you're supposed to follow up in a week, put that page in the section labeled "17."

Finding Out What That Organization Is Really Like

A benefit of targeting just a few organizations is that you have the time to bone up on them before contacting them. An employer likes to see that he's not just one of the 1,000 resumes you scattershot. "I want to work for you because you are a dynamic company," just doesn't cut it.

On the other hand, there's no need to go overboard. Not only is it time-consuming, it can make company officials feel like they've been snooped on. They might, for example, wonder, "Will he be snooping around on us after he's hired?" Doing too much research can also create the impression that the job seeker is so desperate for a job that he has nothing better to do than research companies. So just do a moderate amount of research. We include lots of research sources here so you have plenty to choose from, but just pick your favorite one or two.

The public info

Here's information that's just waiting for the taking:

- Visit the employer's Web site.
- Use one of your public library's huge online databases, like *First Search,* which allow you instantly to identify every mention of the employer in any of thousands of periodicals.
- Read the CEO's articles or speeches (call her assistant and ask for copies).
- Phone or e-mail a large company's public relations or shareholder relations department and request a packet of information on the company, an annual report, product catalog, and any articles on the organization's current operations or future plans.
- Check out the organization's 10K report, a souped-up annual report that the Securities and Exchange Commission requires large companies to file. Every company's 10K is available at a single Web site: `www.secgov/edgarhp.htm`.
- Tell the receptionist of a small company that you're looking for a good organization to work for, have heard good things about this one, but want to learn more about it before contacting the company. Can she send you some information on the organization?

The inside info

John Sullivan, Professor of Human Resources at San Francisco State University, wisely advises that reviewing a 10K and visiting a company's Web page is now so easy that it doesn't give you an advantage over many job applicants. What does is knowing something about the organization's needs, culture, strengths, and weaknesses — the stuff that doesn't get into print. Here's how to access that information.

- Use your favorite Web search engine (you might try `www.metacrawler.com`), using the name of the employer as your search term. That may yield unauthorized discussions of the employer: independent product reviews, even rants from disgruntled employees or customers.
- Ask about the company on an Internet discussion group for that industry.
- Call or e-mail employees, especially those in your target job, plus salespeople and competitors' salespeople.

Making Contact

Most people should write a letter first and follow up with a phone call to hoist their letter off the bottom of the hirer's priority list. Writing first allows you to neatly lay out your case for being hired and boosts the chances the hirer will not have his secretary say that he's in a meeting when you call.

If, however, you're a better talker than a writer, call first and follow up with a thank-you note. A side benefit of that approach is that your thank-you note can focus on the things the hirer cared most about in the phone call.

Don't include your resume with the letter unless it will knock their socks off. Just send your letter and a sample of your work: a report, computer program, videotape of you in action, for example. Not only do these present the best of what's in your resume, including a resume is an immediate tip-off that you're a job seeker. Often, a busy recipient will open an envelope, see a resume, and simply round-file it without even reading the cover letter.

Joyce Lain Kennedy, in *Resumes For Dummies*, recommends that if you fax or e-mail your letter or resume, follow up with a regular copy. It both demonstrates the seriousness of your interest and reminds the employer about you without your having to nag with a phone call. If feasible, hand-deliver the hard copy. If you do, ask the receptionist, "Might I give it to him now in case he has any questions I could answer while I'm here?"

What to write

Here are three approaches that work.

Approach 1: When you have directly relevant experience

Here's how David, the landscape architect who was burned out from overwork and trivial jobs made his case to Mr. Hirer:

> Dear Mr. Hirer,
>
> I'm a landscape architect who has won an ASLA award for a shoreline restoration project for Highway 1, and who would really enjoy doing more highway projects.

Sells his best feature before Mr. Hirer has a chance to toss it in the trash.

> The problem is that my current firm is doing mainly small projects, such as installing artificial ponds in people's backyards. Having been bitten by the Big Project Bug, I'd prefer to find a job where I can do more of them.

Off-the-wall ways to make contact

Often, being cutesy bombs, but especially in fields such as sales, public relations, and in the entertainment industry, one of the following ways to make contact may be worth the risk. They're adapted from Brandon Toropov's *303 Off-the-Wall Ways to Get a Job* (Career Press).

- Send nothing but a hand-written Post-it that says, "You should hire me and I can prove it. Call me at (insert number.)"
- Send a verbal resume: an audiotape in which you recount your accomplishments, and conclude by explaining why the employer should hire you over other people with a similar background.
- Attend the company's annual meeting. During a coffee break, introduce yourself to bigwigs you'd never otherwise get access to.
- For the truly gutsy: Blow up your resume until it's three feet tall. Get two such enlargements and make them into a sandwich board. From 8-9 a.m., stand in front of your dream employer's headquarters wearing the sandwich board, and hand out regular-sized resumes to the employees coming into work. You might even invite the media.

The informal language conveys honesty, enthusiasm, and a good personality.

> That's why I'm writing to you. I've learned that your firm specializes in highway projects.

This shows the hirer that David has done his homework, yet it took David very little time.

> I'm wondering if you need someone with my background, or if not, are willing to offer me a few words of wisdom on how I might hook up with a firm that does larger projects? I, of course, would be happy to tell you all about the Highway 1 project. It really was fun.

David's request sounds easy and pleasurable. Again note the informal language — more appealing than "how I might find a job." These sentences again convey enthusiasm and give the hirer a reason to meet even if he has no job openings. Also, David was wise to be candid that he's looking for a job, not just advice. Not only is that honest, it's pragmatic. By now, many bosses are wise to the ploy of asking for "advice" when, if a job was offered, the job-seeker would probably jump at it.

> To give you a sense of what I can do, I'm enclosing one of my drawings for that project, the Environmental Impact Statement I wrote, and, my favorite: the project's before and after pictures.

Again he shows enthusiasm.

> As I reread this letter, there's something missing. Somehow, I want to convey that my co-workers say I am enthusiastic and fun to work with.

Again informal and therefore attractive and candid. Richard Bolles says that a key to getting hired is telling hirers "what makes you different from the nineteen other people who can do the same thing you do."

> Of course, those are just words so I'll be happy to give you my boss's and co-workers' phone numbers.

Shows he's enthusiastic and forthcoming.

> If you and I think it's worthwhile, I'm even willing to volunteer for an evening or a weekend as a tryout.

This sentence is powerful. David's willingness to prove himself by volunteering can be persuasive.

> I'm hoping you'll phone me. My number is 510-655-2788, and the best times to reach me are from 8 to 10 a.m. and 5 to 6 p.m.

Always include best times to reach you.

> But I know you're busy, so like any good employee, I won't just passively wait for your call. If I haven't heard from you in a week, I'll take the liberty of phoning to follow up.

The previous two sentences have worked wonderfully for my clients.

> Sincerely,
>
> David Michaels

Approach 2: When you don't have relevant experience

Ellen has never sold anything, let alone cable TV programs to cable media system operators (MSOs.) But she wants to try it, and here's how she makes her case for why the hirer should let her.

> Dear Ms. Hirer,
>
> After quite a bit of research, I picked out the handful of companies I would most like to work for. Yours is one.

Everyone wants to feel special.

> I'm impressed by your relationship with the MSOs, the premium packages you've developed, and the innovative promotions you do, such as inviting buyers to guest-host. The question is, "How do I get you to find a job for me?"
>
> I thought you might get a sense of what I know and how I think by sending you a White Paper that I wrote on a topic you might be interested in: *Seven Lessons I've Learned About Selling to MSOs.*

Ellen wrote it specifically for her job search.

> Also, in a recent article about you in an industry magazine, I read that you are trying to decide whether to develop your own cable modem or to keep selling an OEM product. I'm enclosing a one-pager that describes how, if I were hired, I would go about trying to come to a wise decision.

Many employers appreciate people who can solve their problems.

> Of course, I have only limited information, and no doubt, if I were actually working for you, my plan would change based on additional data, but this may give you a sense of how my mind works.
>
> I'm hoping that you'll phone me. My number is 319-487-2578, and the best times to reach me are from 8 to 10 a.m. and 5 to 6 p.m. But I imagine that you're busy, so like any good employee, I won't be passive and simply wait for your response. If I haven't heard from you in a week, I will take the liberty of following up with a phone call.
>
> Sincerely,
>
> Ellen Neiman

When showing an employer that you know something about the organization, be sure to sound like a conscientious job searcher, not a muckraker. This is especially important if you've dug up a lot of stuff. Here's an example of wording that works:

> Where do I want to work? Of course, that's an important decision, so before contacting anyone, I've taken the time to identify divisions in companies in which I might fit best. I talked with a few folks, visited company Web sites, even occasionally called a president's secretary and asked for copies of his or her public domain articles or speeches. I've been particularly impressed with Cocoon Research Labs. Not only does your new focus on telomere attenuation (the actual cause of aging) fit my background and

interests, but I hear that in your telomerase department, people are pretty much left on their own. If they produce, terrific, if not, adios. That attitude fits me to a tee.

In some fields, you can argue that your lack of experience is actually a plus. For example, a former teacher who wanted to join an ad agency's creative team successfully argued that *because* she came from outside the world of advertising, she would bring a fresh perspective to ad planning meetings.

Approach 3: When you have some nerve

This approach is a bit slick for my taste, but it has worked well for positions where assertiveness is a plus — investment banking, for example. (This letter was not one of my concoctions, and I was stymied in my search for the source. Our apologies to the author.)

Dear Mr. Hirer,

I am writing to you and to *(name his three bosses)* to find the most appropriate person to meet with for a 30-minute job interview. I offer these main benefits *(name three).* When I follow up with your assistant in the next couple of days, please let them know whether you wish to schedule the 30-minute appointment and what times are good for you. Otherwise, please direct me to the appropriate person you want me to deal with regarding getting together.

Thank you. I look forward to meeting you.

Sincerely,

Joe Nervy

Before calling

Some successful job seekers do almost no preparation before picking up the phone. They just dial the number, think about their opening line while waiting for the phone to be answered, and wing it from there. It works because it's spontaneous, natural, and doesn't sound prepared. Of course, try this only if you think well on your feet.

Most successful job seekers, however, do some prep work. Three bits of writing can greatly improve your phone calls, not to mention keep you calm. And because you're on the phone, you can keep those three bits of writing in front of you — a good crib sheet. (No videophones, please.)

Your quick human story

What we call your quick human story is your sound bite, what you most want prospective employers to remember about you. It includes

- The job you're seeking
- The best thing(s) you bring to the table
- Why you're looking

How can you cram all that into a few sentences? Here's David's quick human story:

> I'm a landscape architect who recently got to work on my first big project: the restoration of Highway 1, and we won an ASLA award. I got really hooked on big projects and would love a job where I can do more of them. Might you need someone with my background?

Once you have your story, you need to present it well. Here are four steps to a great delivery:

1. **Write out your quick human story as a script.**
2. **Write just enough words, perhaps twenty percent of your script, to remind you of its main points.**

   For example, David might have written: landscape arch., first big project, got hooked, want more. Need my background? These are your *cue words*.
3. **Practice telling your quick human story with just the cue words in front of you.**
4. **On the phone, keep just the cue words in front of you.**

   Tell your true human story without looking at them, but if you're stuck, use them to get you back on track.

This approach not only leads to a natural-sounding presentation, it prepares you for telling your quick human story when you can't have your cue words in front of you — during interviews and in networking. If you're bound to a script, it will probably leach any chemistry from your presentation. Remember, chemistry is key.

PAR stories

PAR stands for Problem, Approach, Resolution: You describe a problem, how you approached it, and how you resolved it. (See Chapter 11 for more on PARs.) Here's one of David's:

> **The problem:** We had a problem with the pilings. Although the geologist's report claimed that the earth was solid down to 60 feet, we hit soft stuff at just 18 feet. Everyone thought we'd have to use a drop hammer all the way down to 60 feet, which would have cost an extra $45,000 plus two days of intolerable noise for the workers, freeway users, and residents.
>
> **The approach:** But I checked some print and online resources and found that a project in Maine ran into a similar problem. They were able to solve the problem by lining the piling with a special sleeve down to just 18 feet.
>
> **The resolution:** That little bit of research saved us $35,000 and a heck of a lot of noise. It felt pretty good.

You may use only one or two PAR stories, but it's good to have at least three ready so that you can pick ones that fit naturally into the conversation.

Objections

Here are common objections encountered in a phone call and sample answers. Again, don't use a script. Unless you're a professional actor or TV news anchor, it will sound read. (Think of those telemarketers who call you and sound like they're reading. Would you buy from them, let alone hire them?) As with your quick human story, start by writing a script of responses to likely objections to you, then write cue words, practice responding using your cue words, and keep your cue words in front of you while you're on the phone in case you draw a blank.

Objection: I'm very busy. I'm going into a meeting. Can't talk with you.

Answer: I understand. When is the best time for me to call back?

Objection: You were self-employed. Why would you want to work for a company and lose all that autonomy?

Answer: I've enjoyed it, but as you know, the cost of providing good veterinary services is exploding. So I realize that to compete, I need more resources than a one-person practice can provide. I know I'll be able to do more for my patients and bring in more business with the resources of VetCare behind me.

Objection: We don't need anyone with your background.

Answer: I understand. Do you have any idea of what you'd do if you were in my shoes?

After he responds, ask, "Would you be willing to keep your ears open and call me if you hear of anything?" He usually says yes just to get you off the phone. That's fine. If only subconsciously, he will keep his antennae out. You've recruited a scout! If he agrees to be your scout, put his record sheet into your three-ring binder's slot for a month away.

Remember, the odds are tiny that, at a particular moment, a hirer will have a job for you. However, if you can recruit the hirer as a scout, you'll have months of moments in which the hirer could create a job opening or hear of one. So take heart. Even if an employer says "No jobs available," as long as she's willing to be a scout, you've had a big success.

When Martin Schwartz, one of the world's most successful stock traders was looking for a job and a prospective employer said, "Nothing is available," Schwartz responded, "Well, someone must have given you your first break." We're not sure that one-liner was the cause, but Schwartz got six job offers within a week.

Objection: If you're so good, why are you looking for a job?

Answer: (These are the most widely acceptable answers. If true, choose one):

- Want to make more money
- Tired of the long commute
- The job ended
- Looking for more responsibility
- Looking for the opportunity to learn new things

For additional objections and possible responses, see Chapter 22.

One other area to prepare is your voice. You make a hard-to-change impression within the first few seconds of a conversation. Your tone of voice must be friendly and confident without coming on too strong. Yet you must be yourself. Sounds paradoxical, but it's not. At different times, we all use different voices. Avoid your depressed, I-hate-looking-for-a-job voice. Record your friendly, confident-sounding voice, listen to that tape, and start using that voice more, especially when talking with a prospective hirer.

Cold feet?

Before calling an actual employer, you might role-play a call with a friend. Next, if possible, call a hirer who was referred by a friend. Then call your lowest-priority potential hirers, your throwaways. You are going to mess up on your first few. The first few sheets of a print job are inevitably throwaways, so the printer uses crummy paper. Only when the copies are coming out well, does she put the good paper in. Only when you've had a couple of good phone calls should you move to your top-choice employers.

Afraid you're going to stumble on the phone? A few mess-ups may actually make you *more* credible. When I started out on radio, to avoid stumbling, I scripted much of what I said. Boy, did I sound perfect — too perfect. Reading a script stripped away the human connection that is so key to a successful interaction. Now, I simply start talking, and only when I get stuck do I look at the few phrases I've written down to remind me of my main points. Now, after ten years on the radio, I stumble more than I did when I started, which makes me seem more human, and in turn, actually connects me better with my audience. So relax. Keep your few talking points in front of you to help you when you're stuck, and when you stumble, know that it probably won't hurt you.

The first call is the hardest, so don't just make one call per sitting. Set a goal, for example, "I'll take a coffee break after I've made ten calls." I can hear you protesting, "Ten calls! That will take all day." Remember, if you make ten calls, you'll probably only get through to a few people, so the coffee break will come sooner than you think.

The call

Your letter to the hirer already laid out all the great stuff about you. You're way ahead of the game. The only reason you're following up with a phone call and not simply waiting for the employer to phone you is that unless the hirer happens to instantly need someone just like you, you will likely be lost in the swamp of his million other higher priorities. For you, your new job is priority one, so it's your place to call.

Getting through to the hirer

One of job seekers' greatest frustrations is being unable to get through to the hirer. They can't get past a gatekeeper or through voice-mail jail, and they leave messages that never get returned.

No method always works, and prepare to get turned down at least half the time (no big deal), but each of these strategies increases your chances of getting to speak with the Great and Powerful:

The most important phrase to keep in mind in every contact: *Be persistent but likable.* Please remember this. Those two words are the keys to a successful job search: *Persistent. Likable.*

Getting out of voice-mail (or e-mail) jail

If you get Ms. Hirer's voice mail, unless your story is so compelling that she's unlikely to resist returning your call, don't leave a message. Few bosses return messages from job seekers. Besides, you want to be prepared with your notes when she calls. With your luck, she'll call back while you have your hands wrapped around a drippy burrito.

Usually there's an option within voice mail such as, "Press 0 for the receptionist." Do it. We show you how to deal with the receptionist in the next section.

If you do decide to leave a message, try this: In your natural, pleasant, not-stuffy voice (Remember: your first few seconds are key), leave a message with your quick human story. Leave the best times to reach you. Here's David's version.

> Hi, this is David Michaels. I'm following up on the letter I sent you last week. I'm the landscape architect who worked on that shoreline restoration of Highway 1 that won an ASLA award. As I mentioned, having gotten a taste of big projects, I'd love to do more. I understand that your firm specializes in large highway projects. If you think I might be of help to you or have any words of wisdom on how I might find a job doing more large projects, I know you're probably busy, but I'd love a call back. My phone number is 317-636-2740. (Say it slowly.) That's 317-636-2740. The best times to reach me are today until 5 p.m. and tomorrow from 10–12. Thanks so much.

Getting past a live gatekeeper

Here's a tough scenario. In this case, David didn't write first, so it's a total cold call, and he got the gatekeeper from hell. Here's how he handled it:

Gatekeeper: Mr. Hirer's office.

David: Hi. Is he available?

The brevity and informal tone make it clear he's not an interloper and increases the chances that the gatekeeper will put him through without an interrogation.

Gatekeeper: Who may I say is calling? (*So much for no interrogation.*)

David: David Michaels.

Gatekeeper: May I ask what this is in reference to? *(The dreaded question.)*

David: I could really use your help. *(An opener that has been known to calm even dragon-like gatekeepers.)* I'm a landscape architect who's won an industry award for my work. I'm looking to do more large projects and I heard that your firm specializes in them. I'm sure Mr. Hirer is busy but could I ask you to see if he might speak briefly with me? Even if he can't use someone like me, maybe he might have a few words of wisdom about where I might turn.

Gatekeeper: I'm sorry, Mr. Hirer is unavailable. If you wish, you can leave a message, but there are no positions available.

David: Could you recommend someone else it might be wiser to speak with?

Gatekeeper: No. Would you like to leave a message? I really must go now.

David: Thank you, no. I'm tough to reach. When's the best time for me to try back?

Leaving a message, especially with this gatekeeper, is unlikely to bear fruit. Besides, you want to be sure the call happens when you have your notes in front of you. Better to retain control and call back.

Gatekeeper: I don't know. He does stay late occasionally. *(Finally, a morsel.)*

David: Thank you very much.

At least half of gatekeepers are this useless to you — it's their job to protect their boss's time. That's okay. The key is to not let the grinches get you down. Laugh him or her off as you would a troll in a video game, and move on. Sooner rather than later, a guardian angel is likely to descend.

When to phone back? If the gatekeeper doesn't recommend a specific time, try a *prime time:* a time when the hirer is likely to be at the desk, not in meetings, and without a gatekeeper to cajole. Prime times are 8–9 a.m. and 5–7 p.m.

If you leave a voice-mail message and the hirer doesn't call you back within 48 hours, she probably never will. So call back, but after that second message, the heck with her. If there was any real interest, your mailing and two phone calls would probably have evoked it. Yes, there are stories of people who impressed a boss because they were persistent enough to call ten times, but those are rare. You're better off allocating your time to efforts that are more likely to pay off.

However, give any dream employers an extra shot: Try again in a month. Things change.

Try e-mail. Many people who ignore your phone messages respond to an e-mail because they answer their e-mail at night when they're not as pressured.

You're finally speaking with the hirer. Now what?

David has finally gotten Mr. Hirer on the phone. Unfortunately, Hirer isn't much easier to deal with than his gatekeeper from hell:

Hirer: Harold Hirer here.

David: Hi, this is David Michaels. I'm that probably too-eager sounding landscape architect who's interested in doing more large projects. *(A bit of mild self-deprecating humor is refreshing, especially from a job seeker. As in every interaction in the job search, the key is to establish a human connection quickly.)* Thanks so much for taking my call. As I mentioned, that ASLA award-winning project really hooked me on big projects, and I'd love to find a job in which I can do more. I understand that your firm specializes in that sort of work. Might you need someone with my background?

Some career guides advise you to instead ask, "Might you know someone who needs someone with my background?," but that is disingenuous and appears so.

Hirer: Mr. Michaels, I really have only a minute. We don't anticipate any openings for the foreseeable future. If you wish, you may send us your resume.

Unfortunately, Mr. Hirer isn't biting.

David: I'll do that. Any words of wisdom on what I might do to get to work on some larger projects?

Although his heart sinks, David makes the effort to be pleasantly persistent.

Hirer: I can't think of anything.

David: Anyone you think I might want to talk with, or anything you think I should read?

Hirer: You should get the quarterly *Grants Awarded* report from the State Highway Commission.

Cool.

David: Thank you. Would you kill me if I asked you to keep your ears open for any other possibilities, and to call me if you hear of anything?

Again, humor helps.

Hirer (Deep breath): Well, I'll see.

David: I know you're busy. So if I'm still looking for a job in a month, I'll call you to follow up. Thank you so much.

Hirer: Good-bye.

Hirer has to admire his persistence.

David: Good-bye, Mr. Hirer.

This is far from the best conversation. None of the best outcomes happened: Hirer had no interest in considering David for a job, he did not invite him to come in to see how the office operates, nor he did refer him to a specific person. David got just one possibly useful tidbit. Just as in a good treasure hunt, you get a little clue here, a little clue there, and eventually, if you don't give up, you usually hit paydirt.

Of course, every conversation is different. That was an attempt to show you a tough one done well.

Secrets to success in that first conversation

Beyond what David did, here are some other tips that can put you ahead of the pack:

- Look for opportunities to build a connection. If the person says something a bit personal, follow with a related comment or question. Typical door openers:

  "We're just finishing up a big project." Follow-up: "Would you mind telling me a little about it?"

  "I'm ready for the weekend." Follow up: "Me, too. I'm going to Stone Mountain."

  "I loved Jamal Washington's speech. It was brilliant." Follow up: "I missed it. What did he say?"

- Share interesting information such as recent research findings or war stories. "That reminds me of the time. . . ." If you get a positive reaction, share a bit more.
- If Ms. Hirer starts talking about the challenges she's facing, that's a golden opportunity. Play consultant. Ask questions to better understand the problem, perhaps guiding the hirer to gaining clarity about her situation. You might even gently offer a suggestion, worded like, "Obviously, I know just a bit about your organization, but in light of what you've just said, I'm wondering if it might help to *(offer solution)*.
- Try to get a sense of whether you'd really like to work there. You're not desperate, you're looking for a good match. So if it appears that Ms. Hirer might be interested in you, ask a couple of questions to see if you'd be interested in working at her firm. For example, "What sort of person fits best in your company?" or "What have you found to be the best and worst things about working at your firm?" In addition to helping you decide if you'd like working there, Ms. Hirer's answers offer valuable information to use if you ever get invited for a formal job interview.

- A face-to-face interview is more likely to yield a job offer or substantial help in landing a job. And a workplace visit can teach you a lot. If after a few minutes, the chemistry is good (for example, if you've just offered a well-received suggestion), or you'd like to visit that workplace, stop the conversation and say something like, "You know, I'd be happy to continue this conversation in person. I could be available any time Wednesday morning or Friday afternoon. Do you have a 15-minute block on either of those days?" (Always give two choices.) This approach is subtly but importantly different from the standard one that implies that you should *always* try to get an in-person meeting with a hirer. Unless an initial conversation gives good reason for optimism, it's not worth your time.

Walking in: Not for the faint-hearted

Walking in unannounced to prospective employers can be very effective. When I'm in a TV studio, nervously waiting to go on the air, I often chat with the producers and camerapeople. I usually ask them how they got their cool jobs. Frequently, they say that they went door-to-door, from studio to studio, until someone said yes. Similarly, when my wife and I came to California, we got in the car and drove from school district office to school district office. She got three job offers within seven days. Colonel Sanders started selling his chicken by going from restaurant to restaurant asking the owners to try his chicken.

Richard Bolles advises that walking in without an introduction works best for entry- to mid-level jobs; and for blue-collar jobs, walking in is *the* most effective job-search method.

Always start by telling your quick human story and seeing if you can make an appointment for an interview, or if you're really lucky, get an interview on the spot.

If the gatekeeper says no and you're really gutsy, sit and wait until the boss walks past you. That can easily result in wasted hours, but it has worked. (Or maybe that was a movie.)

"Do I really have to write a thank-you letter?"

It may feel disingenuous to thank someone for putting you through a stressful tryout, but thank-you letters work. In addition to demonstrating that you are thorough, a thank-you letter, done right, can accomplish a lot:

- The half-life of being in Mr. Hirer's mind is short. A thank-you letter extends it.
- It allows you to correct screw-ups. ("You asked me about that circuit. On further reflection, . . .)
- You can say more about things he cares about. ("There is one more thing I think may interest you . . .)
- You can remind Mr. Hirer of things you said that he liked. ("I'm pleased that you liked my analysis of the trend in optometry away from sports-vision therapy.")
- You can remind him of your strengths. ("It's a relief that you think my ability to program in CGI is a plus.")
- You can remind Mr. Hirer that he committed to being your scout. ("Thanks so much for agreeing to keep your ears open and letting me know if you hear of anything. I know you're busy, so if I haven't heard from you in a month and I'm still looking for a job, I'll call to follow up.")

A model thank-you letter

Here how one job seeker put it all together.

Dear Marilyn,

Thank you for taking the time to talk with me. I know how busy you are.

I really appreciate your suggesting that I speak with Carol Lloyd over at Western Maryland High. I've left a message and hope she'll call back.

I thought a bit more about your question, "Why do you use phonics so much even though it seems so boring?" You're right, it's boring to us, but when I watch kids, especially the slow kids who have trouble learning to read using whole-language, they actually aren't bored at all by phonics — they like it because it's very concrete.

Most of all, I appreciate your willingness to keep your antennae out and letting me know if you hear of a teaching position I might be interested in. As you may recall, I'm especially interested in a high school English position at a school with lots of bright kids.

I know you're busy, so if I haven't heard from you in a month and I'm still looking for a job, I'll call to follow up.

In any event, thanks so much for taking the time to talk with me. Say hi to Sandy for me,

Diana Sawin

The worst-case thank-you letter

Even if an employer totally blows you off, it's worth a brief thank-you note.

Dear Mr. Brusque,

I'm sorry I imposed on you with my phone call last week. I understand that you are busy, and the last thing you need is to be interrupted by some job seeker.

Sometimes circumstances change, so here's my resume and a work sample. Don't worry. I won't bug you again, but if, in the future, I might be of help to you or one of your colleagues, I'd welcome a call.

Sincerely,

David Michaels

Going to Job Fairs

Imagine a hotel ballroom with dozens of employers, all of whom are happy to talk with you. That's a job fair. You almost certainly won't get hired at a job fair, but it's the only way to get dozens of face-to-face screening interviews within a few hours.

It's also a terrific way to learn about your field: what's new, who the players are, what employers are most looking for, what salary ranges are, and the best places to train.

Trade shows can serve the same function when you're self-employed and are seeking customers.

Preparing

In advance, see which companies will be attending and do a bit of research on at least some of them: Visit their Web sites, call the company and ask for the information they send to prospective customers.

Come with lots of letters (and copies of your resume if you think it's strong enough). Certainly have your quick human story ready to fall trippingly off your tongue.

Come with your ego well-protected. Job fairs are usually crawling with job seekers, so employers have to screen you as quickly as possible.

Avoid job fairs if you don't want your employer to know you're looking and if there's any chance she'll find out.

At the fair

Show up early. Things aren't so crowded, and the interviewers eyes aren't glazed-over. If things are jammed up front, head to the back and work your way forward. (This also works in avoiding long lines at amusement parks.)

No matter how promising the conversation, don't spend too much time with one person. No one job fair contact is likely to be worth giving up the many other contacts you could be making. Besides, in excusing yourself after a reasonable amount of time, you come off as confident, not desperate.

To avoid confusion, right after you leave one prospect, make notes — perhaps on the back on their business card — on what you learned, for example. If it was a particularly fruitful conversation, jot down what to put in your thank-you note. The thank you note you'll mail that day, right?

In the next chapter, we turn to the vaunted personal networking. Are we having fun yet?

Chapter 15

Networking Made Easier

In this chapter

- How much networking is right for you?
- How to network well
- How to persuade yourself to network
- Less obvious networking opportunities

Here are the opinions of networking cited in a November 1994 *Wall Street Journal* article:

> Networking is dead.
>
> —William Morin, chairman of Drake, Beam, & Morin, one of the nation's largest outplacement firms.
>
> Networking is a bankrupt concept.
>
> —Michael McGill, chair of the Southern Methodist University Business School
>
> Informational interviews are a pain in everyone's butt.
> —Susan RoAne, author of *What Do I Say Next*?
>
> You get a call at work that feels like networking and you want to throw up.
> —David Opton, executive director, Exec-u-Net.

In the previous chapter, we said that a great way to land a job is to directly solicit your dream employers. Many people think that's networking. No. When you network, you're asking your personal contacts for job information, especially referrals to other people who could hire you.

Back in the '70s and '80s, networking was a highly effective job search technique, but by now, people are sick of getting networked. Yet career guides continue to urge job seekers to network, network, network, invoking that out-of-date statistic: "70–80 percent of jobs are obtained through networking." Times have changed. People are much more resistant to getting networked.

Today, networking has a good chance of leading to a salaried job mainly when:

- Your contact likes you a lot *and*
- Knows your work well *and*
- Is close with someone with the power to hire you at an employer you want to work for *and*
- That hirer is willing to hire you for your target job.

The chances of all four occurring simultaneously are about as good as the chances of the publisher of the *...For Dummies* books changing the color of its books' covers. Even when networking works, it usually takes months — somewhere down the line, your networking contact hears of an opportunity for you that pays off.

Unless you have a terrific personal network, you're better off devoting more of your job search time to contacting dream employers on your own. Not only are your chances better of hooking up with an ideal employer, you're more likely to impress the boss if you get in on your own merits than if you rely on contacts. In addition, many job seekers cringe at the thought of having to network, so they procrastinate.

Then why a chapter on networking? Because it still is useful under some circumstances. This chapter shows you when networking is worthwhile, and how to make the most of it.

How Much Should You Network?

Most people should devote no more than one-third of their job search time to networking, and probably less. The more of these statements that you can answer "true" to, the more you should network:

- You enjoy networking.
- Your personal network includes people who can hire you for your target work or refer you to someone who can.
- Your best skills are common ones — for example, planning, communication, organization, or management. With just those skills, networking is usually a must. Because many people have those skills, employers often offer jobs requiring them to people they already know. So if your best skills are commonly held ones, go forth and network so that you can get to know lots of hirers.
- You're looking for information about the career, not just job leads.

In self-employment, networking probably still is the most effective way to build a clientele — if it's done right. That usually means joining groups and organizations and developing *ongoing* relationships with people who could use your product or service or refer you to others who do.

Making the Most of Networking

Basically, all you need to do is trot out your *quick human story* (that 10-second explanation of why you're looking and what you're looking for) and ask a few questions of perhaps a dozen people in your personal network. Here are your top-choice contacts, in approximate order of desirability:

- People you know who could hire you for your desired work
- People you know in your target occupation
- People you know who deal with people in your target occupation (customers, colleagues, consultants, and so on)
- People you know in your field's professional association
- Wealthy or well-connected people you know (they know lots of hirers)
- Co-workers or supervisors in your current or previous jobs
- Family
- Lovers, past and present (be careful)
- People in the media: journalists, radio/TV, and so on
- College professors, especially those who might know hirers in your chosen field
- Your college's alumni working in your desired career
- Friends
- College buddies
- Lawyer, doctor, financial planner, Realtor, accountant, fitness trainer, landlord, haircutter, and so on (they know lots of hirers)

Seven things you can get from a networking contact

What are you looking for from a contact?

1. The name of someone with the power to hire you
2. Information about the field or the local situation
3. A suggestion of something to read
4. A suggestion of an organization to join
5. A suggestion of a meeting to attend
6. A promise to keep their ears open for job leads (important)
7. A job interview

Secrets of successful networking by phone

Later in the chapter, we suggest networking methods for people too shy to phone, but if you can muster the courage, phoning is usually better. You'll be surprised: A reasonable percentage of the people you call will be willing to give at least a bit of help to a job seeker.

An example

Let's make it tough. In this example, David hasn't spoken to Marsha, a fellow student in his landscape architecture program, since college and she wasn't exactly a bosom buddy back then, nor does she have much time for David now.

David: Marsha, hi, this is David Michaels. I imagine that I'm the last person on earth you expected to hear from.

As important as what you say is how you say it. Your tone should be informal, even playful. A radio veteran's tip: Even if you're on the phone, smile. It makes you sound better.

Marsha: Well, that's true, David.

David: I imagine you're wondering why I'm calling. No, I don't need a place to stay.

Again that humor thing. It also subtly makes Marsha grateful that whatever it is David will be asking for it won't be as invasive as him in a sleeping bag on her living room floor.

Marsha, I've just finished a project restoring part of Highway 1, but it was a one-time opportunity. I can live with going back to artificial ponds in people's backyards, but it would be fun to find a job where I could do more big projects. Any suggestions for where I might turn?

Many experts still suggest requesting an in-person meeting but often, the additional benefit isn't worth the time and effort. Unless, in a particular situation, you think otherwise, the phone is fine.

Marsha: David, I don't have any connections like that.

David: Oh well. Would you mind keeping your ears open and letting me know if you hear of anything? If I'm still looking a month from now, I'll give you a call to follow up.

Marsha (with the enthusiasm of a dental patient being asked if she's ready for her extraction): All right.

That recruits Marsha as a scout.

It's hard for Marsha to say no because keeping her ears open requires no effort. Obviously, Marsha is cool to all this, and unlikely to beat the bushes for David. But if you select the people on your networking list well, they're the types who do hear about lots of things. If Marsha does hear of something, she'll call David, or at least, when he follows up a month later, will pass along the information.

The main purpose of a first networking contact is not a referral to a hirer. The odds of the person having one at that moment are small. The main purpose is to recruit that person as a scout. Once you tell someone, even a casual acquaintance, that you'll be following up with them in a month, they'll be keeping their antennae out for you, if only subconsciously. The result of Round 1 of your networking calls is that you recruited a good number of scouts. Invaluable.

Of course, in his record-keeping three-ring binder, David puts Marsha's page in the section for 30 days hence. For example, if he made the call on the 8th of the month, he puts her page in the "7" section.

David: Now that the yucky business part of this call is taken care of, how are you?

Saving the chit-chat for after business is taken care of has two advantages: The chit-chat no longer seems like a ploy to warm Marsha up, and if she's too busy for chit-chat, she can say so and you've already gotten the important part of the call taken care of.

If Marsha had been at all open, David would have looked for opportunities to help her, so it wasn't just he who benefited from their talk.

Marsha: David, I'd enjoy chatting with you, but frankly, I've got five things going on here at once. I gotta run.

David: I understand, thanks a lot.

Marsha: Okay, David.

The payoff

If Marsha had given David a little encouragement, he would have tried to make more of the conversation, for example:

- "Here's what I'm planning to do to find a job. Whaddya think?"
- "What do you think of my resume?" (or cover letter, or work samples)
- If Marsha gave him the name of a lead, he would ask, "Any others you can think of?" (If Marsha has one lead, she's likely to have others.)

Of course, as with direct contacts with potential employers, it's worth sending a thank-you letter. (We talk about thank-you notes in Chapter 14.)

Are You a Reluctant Networker?

L. Michelle Tullier, author of *Networking for Everyone,* offers tips for reluctant networkers:

- Don't assume you're being a pest. Introverts tend to assume they're bothering others if they contact them. In fact, most people enjoy being asked for help and advice.
- If you're afraid, remind yourself of previously successful conversations. Those recollections may give you the courage to make the next contact.
- Don't underestimate the power of listening. Networking may seem like it's all about talking, but listening is as important, and it's easier for the introvert.

If you can't get yourself to pick up the phone, write. Here's a letter to a colleague and friend:

> Hi Jean,
>
> After we finished physical therapy school, I took some time off to play, but now it's time to grow up, so I'm looking for a real job. Any ideas on a cool place to work or who I might talk with?
>
> I've enclosed my resume and cover letter in case you have any suggestions on how I might primp it up a bit.

Last time I saw you, we were interning together in the hospital. You're not still seeing that guy are you?

Anyway, if you have any ideas, I'd really appreciate your letting me know.

Thanks,

Chris Hirsch

Extra Credit Networking Opportunities

Taking advantage of one or more of these opportunities will earn you an A in networking, and more importantly, should help you find good work faster.

Leading a workshop

If you're a good presenter, this is powerful: Offer to teach a seminar attended by people with the power to hire you, or even at a local Rotary Club or Chamber of Commerce meeting. At the end of your presentation, if you're looking for a salaried job, announce that you're looking for your dream job, and describe it. If you're seeking clientele, describe what your business offers. This is the equivalent of showing your best stuff to a bunch of potential employers or clients so that they can hire you for your dream career. Not bad.

Attending conferences, trade shows, and workshops

These are one-stop-shops for workshops that introduce you to the field, for products that serve the field, and for meeting people in the field. You meet potential contacts everywhere: next to you in a session, in the lobby, in the open hospitality suites. At conferences, don't forget about the vendors. They can be as useful as attendees. Start by asking about their businesses and themselves. Soon enough, you'll be able to ask for their advice about your career.

Get active in Internet discussion groups

Start by just reading the group's postings so that you learn its culture and what's important to the group's readers. Then get active by responding to postings and placing your own. Be helpful. After you demonstrate that you know your stuff and have made substantive contributions to the group, post a message such as, "I'm looking for a new position. Does anyone know someone who might need an employee with skills A, B, and C?" Or if you're self-employed and seeking customers, and the group doesn't prohibit such appeals, gently describe your product or service.

Getting active in your professional or trade association

Joining isn't enough. To pay off in a job or paying clients, you must become an insider. Volunteer for committees, present at conferences, or exhibit at a convention or trade show. Get knowledgeable and meet people in one of your field's hot areas. Speak with the editor of your association's magazine or newsletter. All these contacts can be leads.

To find the right professional association, check the *Encyclopedia of Associations,* found at most libraries. Some libraries make it available online to patrons so that they can use it at home or work. Find the association in your field with the largest membership and visit its Web site or phone the national headquarters to get the name and phone number of the president of your local chapter.

Nicholas Lore, author of *The Pathfinder,* suggests that you write an article on a hot topic in your field for your association's periodical. Do some reading first so that you don't sound like an idiot, and then interview a few of your field's heavy hitters, especially those with the power to hire you. Make sure the interview is more of a dialogue than an interrogation. When the article is published, call your sources, ask if they'd like a copy, and while you're on the phone, ask for a bit of career advice.

Striking up a job-finding conversation at a meeting or party

Gather up a little courage and try this approach when the appropriate situation presents itself:

- Prepare a five-second introduction, such as, "Hi, I'm Jane Jones. I'm a programmer in the edutainment field." Also, be sure you have your quick human story ready to tell, and any PAR story that might be entertaining.
- At the meeting, smile and approach the person you'd like to talk with.
- After exchanging introductions, ask about the person: "What do you do?" Listen well and then dovetail onto something he said. When you're stuck, tell your quick human story, and later perhaps a PAR story.

Joining networking groups

These local groups are formed explicitly for networking, usually among businesspeople. They're often sponsored by a professional association, groups such as the Chamber of Commerce, or a minority or women's advocacy organization. (We're still waiting for men's advocacy organizations, and, yes, we do need them.)

Build alliances, not shallow networks. *New York Times* career writer Sabra Chartrand advises that instead of chit-chatting and wholesaling your business cards when you meet people who impress you (for example, a speaker at a conference or someone you meet a charity event), ask them to join you in a project or volunteer to join theirs.

A good way to get to know someone is to work with them. Volunteer boards are a particularly good place to build alliances, but they can be formed in much less august circumstances — one woman invited all her potential allies to a house painting party.

At group networking activities or online boards, keep in mind that other people are there because they, too, want to network. They may be as uncomfortable as you. So if you smile and extend your hand, you'll probably be doing them a big favor.

Chapter 16

The Job Interview: Converting an Interrogation into a Date and a Demo

In This Chapter

- Preparing for the interview: Six smart things you can do
- There really are only three interview questions
- Fourteen ways to create chemistry
- How to prove — right there in the interview — that you can do the job
- Ask the three power questions
- After the interview: Where the job is often won or lost

At its best, a job interview is like a first date: a pleasant discussion in which you're both trying to see if you should get involved with each other. Unfortunately, many interviews are more like The Inquisition.

This chapter shows you how to keep things pleasant, maximize your chances of making a good impression, and find out whether you should pursue a relationship.

Online interviews are becoming more common. Many of the ideas in this chapter apply to them as well as to traditional interviews.

How Chava Triumphed over the Interview from Hell

Chava was applying for her first professional job, but the principles she used apply whether you're a clerk or a CEO.

Chava had been selling women's clothes at Macy's and liked selling, but eight bucks an hour and a 20 percent discount on overpriced merchandise was no life. So she figured she'd try to jump on the Internet bandwagon and sell ads for Web sites. She made a list of dream employers and NanoNet (not its real name) was at the top. Chava wrote to each sales manager explaining why she'd love to sell Internet ads, and followed up with a phone call to each. She got through just once, to a sales manager at Netscape who blew her off: "Send your resume to Human Resources."

Then the phone rang: "Hello, Chava, this is Sandy from Justin Crasdale's office at NanoNet. Justin would like to interview you for a sales position here."

Chava: Wonderful! What interview slots are available?

Sandy: We'll be interviewing each afternoon next week.

Chava: Could I possibly get the last slot?

A study by Robert Half & Associates found that the last person interviewed gets the job 55 percent of the time. (This sounds too good to be true. Other studies might not yield such clearcut results.)

Sandy: Okay. How's next Friday at 4 p.m.?

Chava: Great. Of course, I want to be prepared. Can you send me some information on NanoNet and a written job description if you have one?

Sandy: Okay. *(She takes down Chava's address.)*

Chava: I haven't been to NanoNet's offices. What's appropriate for me to wear for an interview there?

Sandy: A nice sweater and pants or skirt will be fine.

Chava: Anything I should know about the company culture that might keep me from putting my foot in my mouth?

The first of many examples of informality. Being informal and natural is key to job interview success. You may say, "But this is only the receptionist." Don't kid yourself. Many receptionists are not shy about telling their boss, "That Chava seems like a snob."

Sandy: Well, people work pretty hard around here, so you might want to hold off asking about vacations.

Chava: Thanks a lot. Can I get directions? And is parking difficult?

Sandy: *(Gives directions and parking info.)*

Chava: Thanks. I'll see you Friday at 4.

Chava got off the phone and yelled, "YESSSSSSSS!" Her next emotion was fear. "God, I want to do well." She channeled her fear into energy to prepare. (No obsessive preparation, though — a few hours, wisely spent, is enough.)

"I better learn something about the company. I don't want to be like the applicant for a job at IBM who couldn't answer, 'What does IBM stand for?' Of course, I'll read the stuff that the receptionist will send me, but I'll also visit NanoNet's Web site and find a relevant newsgroup. I'll call the company back and ask to speak with an ad salesperson. Maybe he or she will tell me what the company's like and what they look for." (This may sound like a lot of work, but it really takes only an hour.)

To calm her nerves, Chava wrote down the best answers she could think of to the questions she was most afraid of: Why have you been unemployed for a year? Why should we hire someone with no experience in the field? In the interview, she won't use the script, but it helps to craft a good answer in advance.

She wrote her ten-second *true human story* (a not-stuffy explanation of what she's looking for and why). It's a good answer for some common interview questions, like: "Tell me about yourself," "Why do you want this job?" or "Why should we hire you?"

Here is Chava's true human story:

> I've done very well as a salesperson at Macy's, but now I've graduated from college and I'm ready for a real sales job. I've gotten very excited about the Internet — I love NanoNet. And I've spoken with one of your salespeople, Jerry Rosoff, and the job sounds perfect for me. I think I could be a great salesperson for you.

She wrote a one-minute version which added an example to back up the claims in the ten-second version.

> When I was in college, I worked in retail sales at Macy's, and did very well. A customer would come over, ask to see a dress, and often, by the time I was through, I had also sold her a blouse and jacket. I just have a knack for sales. As you might imagine, sales clerks at Macy's make very little, so I asked myself, "What would I like to sell that could earn me a good income?" That's why I'm here. I love the Internet, I use NanoNet all the time, and when I spoke with Jerry Rosoff and he told me how you go about generating leads and the sales, I said to myself, "Chava, this is you!"

Chava tried to put herself in the shoes of the *hirer* (the person with the actual power to hire): "What attributes does Crasdale most want in the person he hires?" "Which of those can I honestly claim?" Throughout the interview, she'd stress those things. She decided on

- Can think on my feet
- Persistent
- Can explain complicated information in plain English
- Good at closing the sale

Chava wrote a few *PAR stories* that prove she has these attributes. PAR stands for a *p*roblem she faced, how she *a*pproached it, and how it *r*esolved. What PAR stories could convince Crasdale that Chava had one or more of the attributes he wanted? Here is one:

> It was just before Christmas. I was working the cash register with a long line of customers when a woman cut to the front and asked me if we had a dress (a $700 St. John's!) in another color. Dilemma! If I told her to wait her turn, she probably would be angry, but if I took care of her, the other customers would be rightfully annoyed. So I compromised. I told her where she could look for the dress, and asked her to come back if she couldn't find it and I'd do everything I could to track it down for her. As it happened, she couldn't find the dress, came back, and again cut in front. I tried to stay calm and said. "I'll be happy to check with the other Macy's stores. If you like, get in line, and I'll help you as soon as you get to the front, or if you prefer, try to find another salesperson who isn't chained to the register." She decided to wait for me. I checked the computer, found it, called the store to verify it was there, and had them ship it to her home. One $700 dress sold, one customer happy.

Of course, Chava didn't want to sound scripted. So, after writing all of the items, she pulled out an index card and wrote a few words to remind her of the key points in her company research, answers to tough questions, true human story, and PAR stories.

Finally, Chava invited a friend over to role-play an interview, including these questions she was most scared of. Chava even videotaped it. Afterward, Chava and her friend watched the video, putting themselves in the shoes of the employer, looking for chemistry as well as content, asking themselves throughout, "Is this making me more or less likely to hire Chava?"

The big date

Chava stood in front of her closet, talking to herself. "I really like this dress, but maybe it's too flashy. Hmm. I'll feel confident in this, and it's safer. Oops. I wore it once already. Better be sure it doesn't smell. No faster way to a bad impression! It's okay."

"Easy on the perfume. I know I'm supposed to think of this as a first date, but I don't want to smell like a hooker." (It's safest to pass on fragrance altogether.)

"I'm not going to be compulsive and drive there three hours ahead of time to be sure I don't get lost. If I get there that early, I'll just stew and get more nervous. I'll just leave an extra half-hour.

"All right, let me make sure I have all the stuff I might need:

- My 'cheat sheet' index card.
- Copies of my resume. I'll only show them my resume if they ask for it — my resume is unlikely to stand out compared with the competition. Besides, I want to focus on what I'll do for them in the future, not look at what I've done in the past. If they have my resume in front of them, they might ask me mainly about what I've done in the past.
- Copies of my transcript. Same story here. I'll have it if they ask for it, but I don't want that to be the focus of the interview.
- My work samples: I will bring copies of the evaluations from my supervisor, and a copy of those two nice letters I got from customers."

Chava walks in

She approached the front door of the building. "I know that from the minute I walk in here, I have to have a good mind-set. I'm going to be myself — my best self — but myself. I'm going to be informal, even playful if it feels right. I have to find an employer who wants me for who I am.

"I am going to try and have a good time in there. All applicants are nervous, but if I try to enjoy it and create some chemistry, it will help my chances of getting the job because I won't appear stiff, and who knows, it might actually be sort of fun."

"I am going to think of this interview, not as an interrogation, but as a date: We're *both* trying to figure out if we should get serious. That means it's okay that I ask questions throughout the interview, so it's more of a conversation than an interrogation. Besides, if I'm asking questions, I don't have to do all the talking. Much better than sitting there the entire time getting bombarded with questions that will make me squirm."

"Actually, all we need to know about each other are:

- Can I do the job?
- Will I do the job?
- Will we like each other?

"My job in the interview is to help us both answer those questions."

The interview

Chava reached the oak door that read, NanoNet: Technology Made Human. "Remember, be real." She opened the door, saw the receptionist, smiled, and said, "Hi. I'm Chava Merideau. I'm here for an interview with Justin Crasdale. Are you the person I spoke with on the phone?"

Sandy: Yes.

Chava: Thanks for the material you sent me on NanoNet. Very helpful.

Sandy: You're welcome. I'll see if Mr. Crasdale is ready for you. Have a seat.

She phones him. Meanwhile, Chava reviewed her index card to remember just the big things: "Blue dress PAR story, Chinese customer PAR story. It's a date: We both size each other up; I ask questions, create chemistry."

Sandy: Mr. Crasdale will see you now. This way, please.

Chava entered, unaware that she was about to face the interview from hell. She walked in to find four interviewers.

Chava: Hi, I'm Chava Merideau.

Crasdale: Yes, and I am Justin Crasdale, the sales manager, and these are Esmeralda Gomez, one of our salespeople, C.J. Fong from marketing, and Antoine Jackson, our affirmative action officer who will be observing the interview. Ms. Merideau, please sit down. Tell us about yourself.

No chit-chat, no warming up, no chance for Chava to ask Justin about that football on his desk. Just that vague: "Tell me about yourself." Her heart raced but she calmed herself by reminding herself, "If this is a sign of what they're like when they are trying to recruit someone, I don't want to work here. Remember, Chava, this is a date, and if he's a loser, you can dump him. Okay, Chava, no biggie, but don't prejudge. Try!"

Chava: *(Gives her one-minute true human story):* When I was in college, I worked in retail sales at Macy's and did well. A customer asking me to show her a dress often left with a blouse and jacket too. I think I have a knack for sales. As you might imagine, you can't earn a living on the sales floor at Macy's, so I asked myself, "What would I like to sell that could earn me a good income?" That's why I'm here. I love the Internet, I use NanoNet all the time, and when I spoke with Jerry Rosoff and he told me how you go about generating leads and closing sales, I said to myself, "Chava, this is you!" But, as you know, I don't have direct experience selling ads. Do you see that as a serious problem?

Chava's question demonstrates the essence of a good interviewee. Rather than just selling herself, Chava, as on a first date, is trying to determine if there's a match. That question also changes the dynamic from adversarial — she's trying to sell us and we're trying to find out what's wrong with her — to collaborative. We're both trying to figure out if we're right for each other.

Crasdale: We're not sure, that's why we're interviewing you. *(These NanoNetters are as warm as Fairbanks in February.)*

Chava: Might I ask, what characteristics really make for a successful salesperson here at NanoNet? *(Great question. This helps Chava focus all her subsequent responses, and give her a sense of whether she could do this job well.)*

Gomez: In the end, selling is relentlessness and a thick skin. *(Chava cringes. Another sign that this job won't be right for her.)*

Crasdale: May I see your resume? *(Chava gives it to him. Her heart is racing again.)* I see that your resume indicates that you have been unemployed for over a year. Why is that Ms. Merideau?

Chava *(Tells her human truth while trying to weave in proof that she has at least one of the desired attributes):* After graduating college, before starting my career, I figured it was a perfect time to do some things I wouldn't be able to do while working. So, a friend and I drove across country. It was quite an adventure. Mind if I tell you a brief story? *(Half-hearted nods.)* When you're on the road, there are many times you really have to think on your feet. *(One of the attributes Chava thinks is important in a salesperson.)* Our car broke down in the middle of nowhere and when we finally got the car towed to the nearest garage, the guy said it was a broken timing chain and it would cost $1,000. We somehow didn't trust that, so I phoned the nearest Toyota dealer, described the problem, and he said that it didn't sound like a timing chain problem. We had AAA tow it to the Toyota dealer. It turned out to be a clogged gas line which cost us $75. That's the sort of problem I faced then. Can I ask you, what's a typical problem I might face as a salesperson for NanoNet? *(Ending some, though not all, of your statements with a question is a great way to convert an interview from an interrogation into a conversation.)*

Crasdale: Companies can advertise on millions of sites. So, customers are always saying, "Gee that's expensive. This other site is charging much less." It's tough to stand your ground on pricing without losing the customer. *(This warns Chava that perhaps NanoNet ads are overpriced and she might have a hard time selling them. She stores that information away.)*

Chava: I understand. I imagine that you'll teach me some strategies for dealing with that sort of problem, but maybe this will give you a little sense of the way I think. If a customer said, "This other Web site promised me a lower rate than yours." I'd say something like, "I certainly understand why that would be tempting, and maybe that's what you want to do. But our many customers have found that the quality of the ads and the quality of the hits you get on our site actually make us a bargain. Why don't you try us for a trial period, and then reassess? We offer special pricing for new trials. Does that make sense?" I was just winging it, but do you think that sort of approach would have a chance of working?

Chava has just done the very best thing a job seeker can do in an interview: Project yourself into the job and demonstrate how you'd handle a problem. Nothing is more important than moving from describing your past accomplishments to describing what you'd do for the employer in the future. This is especially true if your past accomplishments aren't terrific — and Chava's certainly aren't: Unemployed for over a year, retail sales clerk before that. Note also that Chava again ended her statement with a question. Not only does this convert an interrogation into a dialogue, but that particular question also ensured that she didn't sound like a know-it-all.

Fong: It could. Nothing works all the time. *(Negativity oozes from this place.)*

Chava: You know, before we get too far, I should get a sense of whether the compensation is in a range I could accept. The job announcement didn't include a salary. What have you budgeted for the position? *(See the following sidebar for why this is a good question.)*

Avoiding uncomfortable questions about salary

Standard advice is to never bring up salary until the job is offered, let alone early in the interview. My clients find the conventional wisdom to be wrong. Typically, somewhere in the interview, the interviewer asks, "What is your current salary?" or "What is your salary requirement?" There are lots of answers to such questions, none of them very helpful to you. It may be better to preempt the problem by striking first with a question like, "What salary range have you budgeted for the position?"

If they respond, "Well, how much are you looking to make?" Respond, "I'm looking to be paid fairly. What have you budgeted for the position?" If they continue to hedge and insist on dealing with you as a Middle Eastern rug dealer might, that's a sign you don't want to work for them.

If forced to, offer a wide range, for example, $40,000–50,000 depending on the scope of responsibility.

The rules are slightly different if you're negotiating as a self-employed person or independent contractor. You don't ask the hirer what he's budgeted. You gather information about his needs, describe what you can do to meet them, and then give the cost. If you've done a good job of this, and priced yourself fairly, the hirer will usually agree to the price.

At this point, Chava had asked a number of questions in a short time, so she let the interviewers ask a number of questions in a row. (Such lovelies as, "How committed would you be to our firm?") She didn't want to appear too aggressive even though she was applying for a sales position. Despite the rigors of this interview, she worked hard at staying her best self, confident, informal, human. Let's fast-forward to the end.

Crasdale: Do you have any other questions, Ms. Merideau?

Chava: Yes. Could you tell me why the position is open?

Crasdale: The other person didn't work out.

Chava: May I ask why?

Crasdale: He just didn't make his number.

If Chava is offered the job, before accepting it, she would insist on speaking with her predecessor. It's appearing ever more likely that the problem is the product and, perhaps, Crasdale.

Chava: Mr. Crasdale, would you be my direct supervisor?

Crasdale: Yes.

Chava: What sort of person ends up being happy working for you and vice-versa?

Crasdale: Someone who's a real self-starter. I'm very busy and don't have a lot of time for hand-holding.

Chava: Thank you. I understand. *("I understand you're a bad boss," she thinks. But because she is still not ready to rule this job out, in her best-self voice Chava wraps up.)* Well, I am interested. In light of our discussion, I think that my ability to think on my feet, be persistent, and be honestly enthusiastic about your site would mean I can do a good job for you. But of course, you have to make that call. Do you think I can do the job?

"Do you think I can do the job?" is the best concluding question. If the answer is yes, you can follow up with, "Are you ready to offer me the job?" If the answer is no, you can counter the objection before leaving, in your thank-you letter, or through your recommenders.

Crasdale: We will inform you of our decision within two weeks. (He rises. They all rise.)

Chava: *(Friendly tone as always.)* Thank you. I look forward to hearing from you.

Out the door

She keeps her game face on as she says good-bye to the receptionist. When she leaves the building, she finally can relax. "Oh, man, I can't imagine working here!"

That is indeed a triumph. Many job seekers are so hell-bent on impressing the interviewer that they don't get enough information to decide if an employer is right for them. Too often, the result is accepting a job they'll be unhappy in. Chava's first-date approach to a job interview prevented an unhappy marriage.

She both asked and answered enough questions to help all of them assess the three core issues: Can she do the job? Will she do the job? Will they like working together? Given the information Chava got, if she were offered a job, before accepting, she would have to get some pretty encouraging words from other NanoNet salespeople and customers.

The Key Interviewing Principles

Before, during, and after the interview, there are things you can do to put yourself ahead of the pack.

Fourteen ways to create great chemistry

Don Lussier, in *Job Search Secrets,* laments that, too often, the candidate who wins the job is not the most qualified, but the one who gets along best with the interviewer. Here are potent ways to ensure that you get along.

#1: Body chemistry

Let's start with the basics. We wouldn't mention it if it weren't a frequent problem. You can't have chemistry if you have bad breath or body odor. You'd be surprised how many people do.

#2: Stumble a bit

Talk too smoothly and you seem glib. Interviewers *expect* you to be a little nervous and to struggle with some questions. So take time to think, hesitate, even backtrack. You'll seem human and not overly coached.

#3: The first-date mind-set

Many people think of a job interview as somewhere between an interrogation and the Inquisition. You're sitting there under a bare light bulb, bombarded with questions, many of which you can't answer. After an interrogation-type interview, you're unlikely to know whether you'd like to work for that employer. Not to mention, you've had your worst experience of the week.

It doesn't have to be that way. An interview can be more like a first date, in which each of you has a chance to decide if you're well-matched, logically and chemically, just as in a romantic relationship. A first-date mind-set also discourages you from assuming that too-formal, phony-appearing job-seeker persona: "I believe I am well qualified for the position."

You make an interview more like a date than an interrogation by asking questions throughout the interview. Most of the questions can come from your pre-interview research about the employer or as follow-ups to what the interviewer said, but here are a few generic ones:

- What would people say they like best and worst about working here?
- What should I know about working here?
- Who would I be reporting to? What sort of person gets along best with him?
- What do you like best and least about your products?

Most interviewers are glad to answer your questions — indeed, they view questions as signs of intelligence and indicators that you're interested but not desperate.

Treat the interview as a first date and you'll both decide more wisely whether or not you should enter a relationship.

#4: The most important ten seconds

You make a hard-to-change impression in the first ten seconds you meet someone. How to make a good first impression? It's a sad commentary on human judgment, but all you have to do is follow the advice offered by Gary Ripple, author of *Campus Pursuit:* Smile, offer a firm handshake, look the person in the eye, and pleasantly say, "Hi, I'm Joe Blow." Wait to be invited to sit down, then lean slightly forward, keep a pleasant look on your face (I said pleasant, not psychotic), and maintain eye contact most of the time. Believe it or not, in just those few seconds, you've given yourself a big boost.

End an interview using a similar approach. Smile, look the interviewer in the eye, shake his hand, and, if true, say that you actually enjoyed the interview. If not, thank him for an interesting experience.

Think of the interview as beginning the moment you walk into the building and ending only when you're back out on the street again. Why? Walk in the building slouched over and the person walking next you could be the interviewer coming back from lunch. After the interviewer says good-bye, many applicants blow it by letting down their guard, changing their demeanor, and saying something stupid.

#5: Try to have a good time

A good time and a job interview seem to be mutually exclusive, but not necessarily. Enjoy the decor in the reception area. See if you can figure out if the interviewer is nervous. Does her office give clues to what she's like: the family pictures, the golf clubs in the corner, the desk that looks post-tornado. Listen well to the interviewer. Does it sound like she'd rather talk about her upcoming vacation than "What is your greatest weakness?" When you get asked a killer question, see if you can answer it quickly and move the conversation to a more pleasant area. Ask the questions you're curious about, the serious and the playful. After you establish some credibility, it can only enhance your image as a nice person to ask a human question such as, "Do people around here read Dilbert?"

#6: Be your best self, but be yourself

The standard advice is to be enthusiastic. If you're one of the many quieter job hunters, who has a hard time showing enthusiasm, this is poor advice. Trying to be someone other than who you are tends to make you feel extremely nervous in interviews. If you're a quiet person trying to be enthusiastic, you may come off as unnatural, which won't lead to success. Interviewers have their noses out for even a whiff of dishonesty.

More important, even if you manage to snow them in the interview and get hired, it's a hollow victory. You can't and certainly don't want to keep up an act forever.

By being your real self, you're not that sanitized middle-of-the road personality that most job seekers try to be. You're uniquely you and are therefore more likely to be at the top or bottom of the heap than in the middle. Sure, if you're not what they're looking for, they'll turn you down. Fine! Better to show them the real you before you commit to each other than after — just like marriage. We believe that this paragraph is one of this book's most important. It offers a key to finding happiness in your career.

Having said that, we recognize that there are many "real yous": the you drinking beer in front of the TV is not the same as the you working on your greatest accomplishment. Be yourself, but be your best self.

#7: Really listen and watch

Especially in an interview, most people don't listen well. We're so worried about what the interviewer will think of us, and are planning what we're going to say next, that we don't listen to what the interviewer is saying. We're even less likely to listen for the meanings behind the words and to pay attention to body language. That's a shame because so often there are crucial hidden messages:

- The interviewer's reactions may reveal what he likes and dislikes about you.
- The interviewer may be empathic with you. In today's world of frequent job hopping, it probably hasn't been long since your interviewer sat on your side of the desk. Looking out for signs of empathy might relax you.
- Perhaps he's nervous because he hired someone before who didn't work out. It took three years to get rid of her, and now she's suing the company for wrongful termination. Your interviewer may be scared of making another mistake — it could cost *his* job. Being attuned to his nervousness may make it easier to stay positive when he's grilling you.
- When you're really listening, you're able to ask questions that follow up on what the interviewer is saying — a great way to create chemistry.
- The interviewer may be insecure. She may be embarrassed that she's unclear about what she wants the new employee to do. Putting yourself in her shoes can make you realize this. Then you can lead a discussion to see if the position can be molded to fit your strengths.

All these clues are available — but not if you're so caught up in making a good impression that you're unable to read between the lines of what your interviewer is saying.

#8: Talk the right amount

A useful maxim for interviewing is to talk 40–50 percent of the time. And each comment should generally be 15–60 seconds long. More than that and you risk sounding egocentric or putting your interviewer to sleep. If the interviewer wants more information, she can ask a follow-up question.

#9: Ask the power questions early in the interview

"What are you most hoping to find in the person you hire?" "Anything else?" and "What are the most important things you'll want me to work on in the first few weeks on the job?" The sooner you can ask these questions, the sooner you can start tailoring your answers to what's important to the employer.

Mid-interview, ask, "Do you think I could do this job well?" That can elicit any concerns about you, which you can go on to address in the rest of the interview. That question is also an excellent final query.

#10: Bring up one weakness early on

Bringing up a weakness can help both you and the interviewer assess if you're likely to be successful on the job. Chava brought up her lack of experience in the Internet field. In bringing it up herself, not only did it demonstrate her candor — unusual in a job candidate — it allowed an open discussion of how serious a liability that would be. That's good for both interviewer and interviewee.

It's especially advisable to bring up a weakness the interviewer is likely to bring up anyway. One of public relations' basic truths is that when there's bad news, get it out early. If you withhold, and each bit of questioning reveals a little more dirt, it encourages more digging, lowers your credibility, and makes the exploration last longer and seem more serious.

#11: Mirror the interviewer

If she's strictly business, you should be too. If he's social and playful, show that side of yourself.

#12: Reveal a bit about your personal life

Talk a little about your family, hobbies, and so on. If you get a good response, reveal a bit more.

#13: Know the secret to video interviewing

To save travel costs and reduce scheduling hassles, employers increasingly use video (also phone and online) interviewing instead of face-to-face. Typically, the applicant need travel no further than the nearest video-conferencing facilities (for example, a Kinko's). There's only one special thing to remember: There is a lag between the video and audio transmission, so voices can seem out of sync. So before answering a question, wait until you hear the interviewer finish. Don't rely on the video or you risk interrupting the interviewer.

#14 (Highly optional) Bring cookies

For most jobs, employers interview many candidates, and after a while, the applicants begin to blend together. Brandon Toropov, author of *303 Off-the-Wall Ways to Get a Job,* offers a way to make yourself memorable: Offer home-baked chocolate chip cookies to the interviewers at the end of the interview. "I thought this might be a nice way to end the interview."

Don't just say you can do the job; prove it

Standard career guides tell job interviewees to focus on their accomplishments — what they did in the past. We find that job candidates are more likely to score by focusing on the present: by demonstrating right there in the interview what he can do to solve that employer's problem.

Imagine that you are director of sales for a publishing company and you're interviewing two candidates for a sales job. Candidate A talked about his previous sales experience, while Candidate B pulled a book off your shelf, pretended she was on a sales call, and sold the book to you. Assuming the candidates were otherwise equal, which would you hire?

Good interviewers ask you to demonstrate what you can do. They might, for example, ask what-if questions. But many interviewers aren't good. So ask if you can demonstrate — right there in the interview — that you can do the job. If that feels inappropriate, show how you might approach a problem the employer wants solved. At a suitable moment in the interview, you might say this: "Can you give me an example of an important problem or project you envision me tackling on the job?" *(Hopefully, you get an answer.)* I wonder if it might help us all get a sense of whether we're a fit if I show you how I'd approach a problem like that." Start by asking the interviewer(s) questions about the problem to give you the information you need to craft a plan for addressing it. Then say, "In light of what you've said, I'm wondering if the following approach to the problem makes sense. *(Outline your approach.)* Of course, I'd know a lot more if I were actually working on the project, but I hope this gives you a sense of how I might approach things."

You want the interviewer to picture you doing the work. Nothing does it like a demonstration. Sometimes, alas, you won't be allowed to do a demonstration. Some organizations, for example, require that all interviewees be asked precisely the same questions.

Maximize the good part of the interview

Give longer answers to questions you like. Give shorter ones to questions you don't. Job seekers frequently do the opposite. They keep trying to dig themselves out of trouble and often just dig themselves deeper, and at minimum, ensure that a larger proportion of the interview is spent on their weaknesses.

Also remember to ask questions to redirect the interview to areas you want to talk about — for example, about the new job and how you'd approach its challenges.

Golden opportunity: Is the employer unsure of the job description?

Often, the employer knows she needs to hire someone but isn't sure how to best use the person. If, in the interview, you can help clarify that the employer really needs someone with your strengths, you may well talk your way into a perfect-fit job. In the process, you may also be able to get the hirer to upgrade the position's responsibilities and, in turn, its salary.

Early in the interview, ask, "Are the tasks you'd want me to focus on mapped out at this point or do they depend on the candidate?" If there's some play, it's a golden opportunity for you to mold the job in your image. And the interviewers may be grateful for your help. Ask them to tell you about some of the organization's needs. Then gently propose how the position might be structured to meet those needs and how your strengths would be well suited. Example:

> "It sounds like, at least in the short run, you've identified two key problems: getting the staff more comfortable with the new computer programs and reducing the backlog in processing claims. That would be fun to tackle. My software training background will help me in getting the staff comfortable with the computer program, and I know I'll enjoy figuring out how to streamline the claims process."

If you sense you're a poor match for this job

Sometimes, you can turn the lemon into lemonade. Try this:

> "In listening to you, it doesn't sound like I'm a very good fit for this position, but I'm wondering if I might be of use to you in another way. What I bring to the table are *(insert your best skills/attributes)*. Might someone with that background be of help to you?" This can sometimes convert a rejection into your perfect job. This is a good example of industrial magnate Henry Kaiser's famous advice to job seekers: Find a need and fill it.

After the interview: Where the job is often won or lost

If possible, right after the interview, head for a coffee shop, and while everything's fresh in your mind, grade yourself on the Interview Report Card, and draft a thank-you note.

Interview Report Card

Did your face, voice, and body language convey interest?

Did you create a good impression in those crucial first few seconds?

Did you share a weakness early in the interview? Did it seem to help or hurt you?

Did you listen well or were you too focused on what you were going to say next?

Did you describe the accomplishments most likely to impress the interviewer?

Were you able to not just tell but demonstrate that you could do the job?

Did you ask questions throughout the interview, not just at the end?

Did your questions help you get clearer about whether you want this job?

Did you talk roughly half of the time?

Did your comments rarely exceed one minute in length?

Did you show caring about the people, asking personal questions as appropriate?

Did you show that you care about the organization's product or service?

Did you reveal an appropriate amount about your personal life?

Did you mirror the interviewer's style?

Were you honest enough?

Were you your best self?

Were you able to have a reasonably good time?

Grade yourself

Grading yourself on this report card will help you in subsequent interviews. It's easy to deceive yourself into thinking that you did better than you did.

Ahead-of-the-pack thank-you letters

UNCONVENTIONAL WISDOM

There's something slightly disingenuous about writing a letter to thank someone for an interrogation. But done right, a thank-you letter can boost your chances of landing the job, so the bit of artifice is probably justified.

If you can draft the darn thank-you letter right after the interview, it's best. Then let it sit overnight, review it with fresh eyes the next day, and mail it out.

A thank-you letter is an opportunity to do a lot more than say thank you. It allows you to:

- Remind the interviewer of the things she was most impressed with. "I'm pleased you think my experience managing stevedores would be valuable."
- Give a better answer to a question you flubbed. "I've given further thought to that question you asked about retrograde transmission."

- Say more about things the interviewer cares about. "There was one more thing I thought you might be interested in."
- Reiterate your interest in the position.

Here's a letter that accomplishes all of the above:

> Dear Nadine,
>
> I really enjoyed the opportunity to interview with you. The dyslexia project is revealing some solid results. I am pleased that you think my background in pathology would be helpful and look forward to the possibility of joining your staff.
>
> You asked a question that got me thinking. You asked what sort of study I think would be the most valuable next step. On reflection, I think we'd get valuable information from doing PET scans of dyslexic children of different ages to better understand how cerebral structure and function change developmentally. That could point us to the best times to provide educational as well as physiological interventions.
>
> I'm looking forward to hearing from you.
>
> Sincerely,
>
> Allan Gold

References

Don't get too compulsive about your references. Many employers treat references cursorily. They know that, for a variety of reasons, recommendations can be invalid. A boss can sing the praises of a lousy employee to avoid the risk of a lawsuit. Or she can sound lukewarm about a top employee to avoid the new employer suing her if perchance that employee doesn't work out. Don't sweat recommendations much.

However, do ask people you're planning to use as references if they're willing to serve. That can avoid surprise bashings. Try this wording: "I was hoping to use you as a reference. Do you feel you're in a position to provide a strong one?"

When a prospective employer is ready to call your references, you call them first. Explain the ways that you're well suited to the job and the issues you'd like your reference to address.

If you are employed, ask hirers to defer contacting your references, especially your current employer, until ready to hire you. You don't want your current boss to find out you're looking if you don't actually get a job offer.

Even if you're excited about a possible job, be careful not to tell anyone who may tip off your current employer. Hot prospects often turn cold. The career battlefield is littered with people who talked about their next job too soon and got shot down by their current boss who didn't want an employee he couldn't count on. Hold off until you and the new employer have actually signed a job offer. Trust us on this one.

The end game

Often, this is where the game is won and lost. Most employers appreciate polite persistence.

A few days after you mail your thank-you letter, call to ask where you stand. If you're not the front runner, ask, "Is there anything that makes you hesitant to hire me?" If a concern is raised, explain why it is unjustified (if it is), have a reference do so, or offer to provide a work sample — a piece of writing or a one-day trial, for example. End the call by affirming that you're eager and confident that you can do the job. Offer to continue the discussion by saying, for example, "Of course, we only scratched the surface in our discussion of *(insert topic)*. If you might find it useful, I'd be happy to explore *(insert topic)* with you further." Send a follow-up note reiterating all of this.

If it's a job worth using up the good will of one of your references, ask her to phone the employer to say how wonderful you are.

Two weeks later, if you haven't heard, you might send a letter such as, "You and I discussed *(insert topic)*. I came across this article and thought you might be interested. Speaking of interested, I still am interested in the position and hope to hear from you soon."

Today, when it has become extraordinarily difficult to dismiss a full-time employee, expect multiple interviews and possibly employment testing. Three or four rounds of interviews are common for mid-level positions.

You Got the Job Offer!

Congratulations. It's a great feeling to be offered a job. But don't sound too anxious. At minimum, it will hurt you when negotiating the terms of your employment. We've even heard of cases in which excess enthusiasm resulted in a retracted job offer. The employee demonstrated so much excitement that it made him appear desperate. That motivated the employer to check his references more closely than he otherwise might have, whereupon he developed buyer's remorse, and offered the position to another candidate.

The right response to a job offer is, "Very good. Can we set up an appointment in a couple of days to discuss salary and other terms of employment?" Then it's homework time. See Chapter 17.

Someone Else Got the Job: All's Not Lost

If the job is offered to someone else and you're in mourning about it, phone the employer and say something like, "I'm disappointed. I know I could have done a good job for you. Might I ask what made you hesitant to hire me? Anything else? (That follow-up often generates something valuable). I want to know if there's something I need to work on." Close with, "If by any chance your situation changes, I hope you'll keep me in mind. Would you mind if I phoned you back in a month to follow up? And is there anyone else you think I should talk with?"

Sometimes, the employer may like you, but not for that position. Don Lussier, in *Job Search Secrets,* suggests that you propose one or more of the following:

- Placing you in an existing opening
- Slotting you to fill an upcoming opening
- Finding a temporary opening
- Creating an opening by releasing a problem employee
- Offering you a consulting assignment
- Recommending you to another employer
- Doing a project as a volunteer. Even if that project doesn't turn into a paying job, you can still list that first-rate organization on your resume as your most recent work experience.

Facing Rejection

Despite all efforts, even the best candidates get rejected a lot. The successful job seeker learns from it, if possible, and then doesn't allow himself to get frustrated.

A rejection after you've told your true human story is often a blessing. Wouldn't you really rather hold out for someone who wants you for who you are?

Chapter 17

Negotiating a Cool Deal (Even If You're Dealing with Scrooge)

In This Chapter

- The argument for and against negotiating
- Preparing: where the battle is often won or lost
- Getting the boss excited about you
- When to pop the question: What will you pay me?
- Ten things every negotiator must know… and most don't
- Negotiating tips for the self-employed
- When to say yes
- The Negotiation Test

Negotiating is really worth the effort. The minutes you spend negotiating the terms of your employment can not only earn you more money but also gain you more respect. Employers often admire people who value themselves enough to hold out for what they're worth. If you accept the first offer, you may make the boss think that you're desperate, which lowers your perceived value.

So read this chapter even if you're not ready to negotiate. Remember, life is a negotiation — from who gets the bathroom first in the morning to reacting to your mother's lament that you don't phone home often enough.

Chava Negotiates with Scrooge

In Chapter 16, Chava was savvy enough to triumph over the interview from hell. Well, at the end of her next interview, she heard the magic words: "We'd like to hire you. Let's talk compensation." Here's the story of Chava's next triumph: negotiating the terms of her employment.

The end of the interview

To protect the guilty and to make sure we don't get sued, we'll just call the boss Scrooge.

Right there at the end of Chava's interview, Scrooge wanted to sew her up.

Scrooge: Chava, we'd like to offer you the job. Let's talk turkey.

Chava wasn't biting.

Chava: Thank you. Can we set up an appointment a couple of days from now to do that? *(That lets Scrooge know, in a non-confrontational way, that she won't just accept any offer. It also gives her time to prepare.)*

Scrooge: Are you sure you wouldn't like to talk salary now?

Chava: Thanks, but if it's okay with you, let's do it a couple of days from now. By the way, do you have any written material to help me learn more about the company or the projects I'll be working on?

As you'll see, these reading materials will help in her negotiations later.

Chava does some research

The next day, Chava called the company's human resources department to find out if salary range for the position was made public. No dice. Next, she called the company's sales department and asked to speak with a salesperson.

Chava: I've just been offered a sales job at Scrooge Online and am meeting with Scrooge himself tomorrow to discuss salary. Any advice?

Salesperson: I really don't feel comfortable saying much. Don't say it came from me, but watch out for a lowball offer *(a very low first offer designed to make the employee grateful for a subsequent offer that is slightly higher but still wretched).*

Chava: Thanks.

Chava then went online to JobSmart (`www.jobsmart.org`), where she found more than 150 salary surveys. That gave her a sense of what fair pay would be. She printed out the relevant information to bring to the negotiation.

As part of her preparation, Chava came up with a higher-level responsibility that she could take on that could convince Scrooge to boost her salary.

Finally, she role-played the negotiation with a friend so that she wouldn't feel like a total novice going up against a pro.

The negotiation meeting

Scrooge: Come in.

Chava: Thank you.

Knowing that even Scrooges may soften a bit when there's a human relationship, Chava starts with a bit of chit-chat.

Chava: I was thinking about you. I imagine you must have done dozens of these salary negotiations.

Scrooge *(Smiling wryly):* More than dozens.

Chava: Do you like doing them?

Scrooge: To tell you the truth, I don't.

Chava: Well, let's see if we can do this one with minimum pain for either of us.

Scrooge: As long as you give in on everything.

Scrooge knows that humor doesn't cost him a dime and often softens up the opposition.

Chava laughs. And then, before turning to the actual negotiation, she did one more important thing.

Chava: I read the material you gave me and have been thinking about what I've learned from our interviews. I'm wondering: If I were to accept the position, might it be helpful if I set up a database that merged all the sales reports? That way, we'd all have access to great data on what works with what kinds of customers.

Scrooge: That does sound like it might build the bottom line. We'll see.

Chava has now raised her perceived value. This is the time to pop the question.

Chava: So what do you think is the highest salary that's reasonable of me to expect?

Scrooge: I expect you to pay us for the privilege of working here.

Chava: Okay, no problem. Scrooge, what do you really think?

Scrooge: It's commission only. No salary. Take it or leave it.

There's the lowball offer.

Chava *(Chuckling):* Scrooge, one of your salespeople said that's how you start but that if I held out for what I'm worth, you'd be fair. Besides, I checked a Web site that reports salary surveys, and here are the averages. *(She shows the comparable salaries she had printed out.)*

Scrooge: Well, what's the least you're willing to take?

Chava: Well, what's the most you're able to give?

It's generally better to try to let the number come from the employer.

Scrooge: I don't play those games. Let's hear your bottom line.

Chava: Okay. As you can see from the comparables, the average salary for a new salesperson is $40,000 base, with a commission structure that yields the average salesperson $60,000. You chose me because I'm above average, so I want a $50,000 base.

Scrooge: Over my dead body.

Chava: I deserve every penny, but we want you to live, so what's your best offer?

Scrooge: I'll tell you what I'm going to do. I like your style. I'll see if I can get you a $40,000 base with a commission structure that, if you're any good, should yield you $60,000. I'll talk with the sales manager. If he says okay, you've got a deal.

Chava: I'll consider that.

Unfortunately, naive Chava doesn't realize that Scrooge is using two hardball techniques on her. First, he's icing her: He raises her hopes of getting at least an average offer, and then puts her on ice while he ostensibly consults a higher authority. Scrooge deliberately waits a week before calling her back, knowing that will make her antsy and more likely to accept a low offer. And at the meeting, he pulls hardball technique number two: the higher authority ploy, the oldest trick in the book.

Scrooge: Chava, I am so sorry. I'm shocked. I did everything I could to convince the sales manager, but he absolutely refused. He said that giving you that much would alienate the other salespeople. The best I can do is $20,000 base. With commission though, you should end up over $40,000.

Chava must now summon her courage. She reminds herself that most employers (perhaps not as doggedly as Scrooge) try to get employees to work for as little as possible, but if pushed, will pay market value. Otherwise, a company is left only with employees willing to work for peanuts — which usually means a weak workforce. And Chava must remember that if Scrooge Online is one of those foolish companies, she doesn't want to work there. She must retain the power to walk away. This is the time to be tough. She remembers the old negotiating maxim: Be tough on the numbers, easy on the person. That means be nice, even playful with your opponent, but stand quite firm on the terms. Chava also knows that, if possible, she shouldn't make a specific counter to his $20,000 offer. That would be a concession without getting anything in return. Here's how Chava puts it all together:

Chava: This may not work. I need to be paid fairly. You chose to offer me a job because I am above-average. It would feel wrong to accept below-average pay. Scrooge, you've been very successful, and I'm sure that while trying to get a good deal, you also want to be fair. You can count on my giving you more than your money's worth. For example, I am open to doing projects like developing that database. *(Now you see why it's important to propose a high-level project?)* Do we have any chances of working this out or do we need to part company here?

Scrooge: Well, I'll tell you what. $30,000 it is.

Chava: Let's put salary aside for a moment and discuss benefits?

They discuss benefits, and Chava is able to extract a couple of things that benefit her yet actually net Scrooge Online a profit. She gets permission to work at home two days a week. That saves her commute time and Scrooge office expenses. She also gets Scrooge to spring for $1,500 a year in continuing education. Chava benefits because she gets to stay up-to-speed and Scrooge gets an employee better able to build the bottom line. Now, having come to some agreements and having had a tension-reducing break from the salary negotiation, Chava returns to the sticking point.

Chava: Well, we still have one point of contention: the salary. I understand that you need to keep your costs down.

On the other hand, I deserve to be compensated fairly. What are we going to do?

Scrooge: Okay. Let's get this done. $35,000. That is absolutely it.

Chava: All right, on one condition: I get a bonus of 1 percent of gross sales for sales above my quota. That way, I'm only rewarded for bringing you more than you expected.

Scrooge: Half of 1 percent.

Chava: Okay.

Chava challenged Scrooge and did fine.

Relax. Most negotiations won't be this tough. This chapter, though, shows you everything you need to hold your own, even against Scrooge.

What Would Convince You to Give a New Employee a Fat Salary?

Imagine you're the boss. Which of these would convince you to give an employee as much as you can?

- You see a list of comparable salaries at similar organizations that justifies a higher salary.
- You're afraid of losing the candidate to another employer.
- You like the person.
- The employee can take on more responsibility than was originally envisioned.
- The employee is likely to build the bottom line more than anticipated.
- The quality of the employee's work is likely to be better than peers'.

Right. All of the above can increase your chances of an upped salary offer. Now, we show you how to make each of those happen, and how to respond if the boss is a tough negotiator.

Before the Negotiation Session

If you follow the advice in the how-to-interview chapter (see Chapter 16), you can raise your salary before the actual negotiation, and without having to be even slightly adversarial.

Negotiate with the Power Person

Remember the higher authority ploy: An employer feigns having to get permission to approve a salary offer so she can blame the "no" on someone else. To reduce the chances of the higher authority trick being used on you, ask to negotiate with the person with final decision-making power. This won't always work. The negotiator may say, "Mr. Power asks me to handle negotiations and to consult him if there's a problem." But there's no harm in asking.

Doing your homework

Negotiations are often won and lost before you even begin talking. Here's how to win.

Upgrading the position

If you haven't upgraded the position during your interviews, here's another chance. Think back on what you learned about the organization's needs from your interviews and preparation for interviews. If necessary, do a bit more research on the organization. Ask the secretary to send you some information on the organization, or talk with its employees or competitors. What higher-level tasks can you propose to do that management may perceive as worth a higher salary? For example: Is the organization thinking of expanding into the Midwest? How might you help? Are they worried about a competitor's new product? How could you assist?

Finding out what's fair

A fair way to counter a low offer is to show that other employees in similar positions are better paid. How do you get this information? Start with employees in your target organization, and perhaps a competitor. Possible sources include:

- **The Human Resources department**. Some organizations make salary information public.
- **The boss.** Say, "To get a better sense of what seems fair, might I ask what my peers in the company earn?"
- **Other company employees.** It's appropriate that you talk with company employees to help you decide if you want the position. Don't worry; you shouldn't get in trouble for doing that. In such a conversation, you might ask, "This is a bit awkward, but I'm at that moment of truth. I've just been offered at job at the company and am meeting with the boss tomorrow to discuss salary. I'm not sure how much to ask for. Any advice?" You might also ask, "Any advice about how to handle a negotiation with *(insert the boss's name)*?"
- **Your local unemployment office.** Most such offices post all your state's civil service job listings, including salaries. Pay may be similar in the private sector. The unemployment office may also have local salary survey data.

- **A local headhunter specializing in your field.** To find one, call the human resources department of a large local company in this field and ask, "When you hire a headhunter to fill a position as *(insert your job title),* who do you usually use?"

The results of national and regional salary surveys are often less applicable but more accessible:

- JobSmart (`jobsmart.org`) contains over 150 salary surveys, covering most major professions. This should be your first stop. You probably will find everything you need right here.
- The Bureau of Labor Statistics' Web site (`stats.bls.gov.comhome.htm`) offers national average wage data for 764 occupations. The BLS plans to make local data available soon.
- Dan Lauber's *Professional Job Finder* or *Non-Profits and Education Job Finder* lists salary surveys for hundreds of fields. (Costs less than $20, call 800-462-6420.)
- Many professions' magazines publish salary surveys. Contact your professional association. Don't know its name? Find it in the *Encyclopedia of Associations,* available in many libraries.

There's an understandable temptation to show the boss only those positions with the highest salaries. We recommend against that. Presenting information that doesn't help you is not only honest, but it will impress your boss with your integrity. Who knows, maybe that in itself will incline the boss to raise the offer. (We can't seem to shake that youthful idealism.)

A dress rehearsal

Your boss is probably a more experienced negotiator than you are. A bit of rehearsing can help level the playing field. After reading the next section, which describes the do's and don'ts of negotiation, role-play the negotiation. Have a friend play the boss. Then switch roles, and you play the boss. That can help you understand the employer's perspective, which is very helpful.

The Negotiation Session

Here's how to make all your preparation pay—literally.

Building chemistry

We know you're anxious to get down to business, but it's worth taking a few minutes for small talk. Even if the boss knows it's a ploy, it usually softens his and your desire to pinch every penny. Besides, this is your first project with your boss. Start out on a human basis.

A common mistake is to be friendly and pleasant during the small talk and then, as soon as the actual negotiation starts, to get too serious. Throughout, your tone should be informal, the conversation sprinkled with humor and little breaks for a light comment or anecdote.

Getting ammunition

During the initial small talk, you often can get key information that can help you immensely. You want to find out how badly the employer wants you and what she likes best about you. You can find these out by asking this series of innocent-sounding questions:

- **"I'm curious. How long was the job open?"** If it was open for a while, it means that the employer had a hard time finding someone. Your negotiating position is stronger.
- **"Was I clearly the person you wanted?"** If there wasn't a close runner-up, your negotiating position is stronger.
- **"What, in the end, made you choose me?"** If she says, for example, "Your ability to train people on databases," you can stress that in making your case for a higher salary.

Yes, there's a slight risk that asking these questions will make you sound insecure, but if you ask them in a confident tone, they'll probably just seem like questions you were curious about.

Getting the boss excited about you

Before starting the actual negotiation, also spend a few minutes discussing the job. The goal is to get the employer excited about what you can do. It also gives you an opportunity to try to upgrade the job. You'll probably suggest the upgrade(s) you prepared in advance.

Popping the question

At the moment when the boss seems maximally enthusiastic about the prospect of your working for him, pop *the* question: "What's the highest salary you think is reasonable of me to expect?"

If the response is lower than some of those on your list of comparable salaries, say something like, "I'm not looking to make a killing. I just want pay that's similar to that of others who do my work." Then show your boss your list of comparable salaries and wait.

To keep the wait from feeling so agonizing, count to ten in your head. A better offer may be forthcoming.

If no better offer comes, calmly ask for 10 to 20 percent more than was offered: "Joe, I want $XX,000."

Dear reader, we know that's scary, and that there is a tiny chance that the boss will say, "That's way over our budget. If you want that much, you'll be an unhappy employee if you took less. Thanks for your time." The vast majority of the time, though, your request will yield a better offer, or at least make the employer feel he'd be getting a bargain if you came on board for the salary he originally offered you.

If you think the employer's offer is just barely acceptable, don't rush to close the agreement. It makes you seem desperate. At impasse, consider a statement like, "Why don't we put salary aside for a moment and talk about the benefits." Or if benefits are not at issue, say, "I think I need to take some time to think about this." (The "I think" gives the boss room to make another offer.)

Benefits

Benefits are particularly desirable because they're tax-free. With some employers, benefits such as vacation, health and other insurance, retirement plans, and profit sharing are negotiable. More often, you can negotiate moving expenses, the opportunity to work at home at least one day a week, and reimbursement for education (that training course in Hawaii, for example). Other possibilities are association or club memberships, use of a company car, a desirable office, your title, and the timing of your next salary review, which is especially important if you're not happy with the agreed-on salary.

Don't overestimate the value of stock options. Yeah, the few hundred people who got in on the ground floor of Yahoo! made zillions. But for every Yahoo!, there are employees of countless companies who feel like yahoos, holding stock options that are worth zippo, nada, zilch. Most new companies never end up going public. Even among public companies, stocks can certainly go down as well as up. Under some circumstances, options can even cost you money.

At the end of the negotiation, offer to write a note summarizing the offer as it currently stands. She who writes the agreement gets the gray areas.

Even if you agree on all terms, ask for a few days to make up your mind. "Now that we've discussed all the terms, I'd like a few days to consider it all. Might I see where I'd be working and talk with a few of my coworkers, and perhaps customers?"

Ten things every negotiator must know . . . and most don't

In our view, a major reason that women earn less than men is that, on average, they don't negotiate as well. Some women may have been conditioned to believe that negotiating isn't ladylike. Others may simply feel that negotiating is a more competitive/testosterone-driven activity than they feel comfortable with. But, women, if you don't like the idea that women earn 80 cents for every dollar men earn, one step you can take is to burnish these ten principles in your brain. Oh, and you guys out there, you can peek too.

1. **Know if the boss is more fact-driven or emotion-driven, and make your appeals accordingly.** It's usually easy to tell. If, in describing the workplace, he talks mainly about facts, statistics, and the bottom line, he's fact-driven. If he mainly talks about the people and their feelings, he's emotion-driven.

   If the boss is mainly fact-driven, justify your salary requests with facts — for example, "I see three ways that I am likely to build the bottom line: *(Give them.)*" If your boss is emotion-driven, use feeling-based appeals such as, "Having met a number of the people I'd be working with, it feels like I'll fit in. I've really enjoyed talking with you all."

2. **Know if the boss is fast-paced or slow-paced.** Do you sense that the boss wants you to get to the point or prefers a more leisurely approach? Act accordingly.

3. **How to respond to "How much are you looking to make?"** Answer: "I just want to be paid fairly. What is the range you've budgeted for the position?"

   If you have to give a number, make it high but flexible. So if your research suggests that the position is worth around $60,000, say, "I'm looking to get a common salary for this sort of position: in the 60s."

4. **When negotiating with an employment agency, aim for 70–75 percent of the *bill rate*.** The bill rate is the amount that the employer is willing to pay for an employee, including the employment agency's fee. The agency may try to get you to work for 50–60 percent of the bill rate, pocketing the difference, but you often can do better — if you know what the bill rate is. Ask, and if the agency won't tell you, try the employer's human resource department.

5. **How to respond to "What's your current salary?"**

   If your current salary is below what you're hoping to get, chuckle and say, "Not enough! I was willing to accept that job as an investment in my future. What's the salary range that's budgeted for the position?"

   But what if your previous job *wasn't* an investment in your future? Let's say you were slinging hash for seven bucks an hour because you were still "finding yourself." While being completely honest, you can explain away even that: "I took an interim job to give me time to figure out what I really want to do. Now I've found it. What's the salary range budgeted for the position?"

   If your current salary is at market rate, say, "It's $XX,000, but to make a move, I expect more than that."

   If your current salary is above market rate, just tell the boss your salary. If the employer blanches, calmly explain, "I was paid that because *(insert two to three reasons why you're worth big money).*"

6. **The power of being heard.** Especially when the boss says something you don't like, start by restating her position. That lets the boss know you understand her stance. This is a valuable tool for all discussions, especially when fighting with a family member.

   For example, the boss says, "We're under real pressure to cut costs, so we can't pay anywhere near that much." Your response: "I understand. I know you have to keep your boss happy, yet you want me to come aboard and feel okay about it. What do you think is the most that the company can pay?"

7. **Avoid making counteroffers.** If your boss makes an offer, say something like, "I can't accept that." Sometimes, that will generate a better offer — without your having to reveal what you'd be willing to accept.

8. **Make a concession only if you get something in return.** To appear like a nice person, it may be tempting to give something away: "Okay, I'll give up *(insert concession).*" But that makes you seem desperate and can inspire the boss to get you to make other concessions without giving anything in return.

8a. **Corollary: Don't offer to split the difference between your offer and the boss's**. If you are somehow forced to make an offer, don't offer to split the difference between what your boss offered and the figure you named. That's a concession with nothing received in exchange. Let the boss offer that.

9. **Don't seem too pleased with a concession the boss makes.** Don't say, "Gee, that was great of you." Save the thank-yous for the end, at which point you might say something moderate such as, "Well, that seems fair. I look forward to working with you." If you're too gushy, it makes the boss feel that she was too generous.

10. **Don't get caught up in the game.** The goal is a fair agreement, one that leaves both people feeling that they won something. If you manage to extract every last dime, you may cause resentment, which can hurt you more than the extra dough helps.

For each negotiating item, ask yourself, "Would King Solomon think it's reasonable of you to ask for this?" If yes, that builds your confidence in making the request. If no, maybe this isn't the right time.

If you're self-employed

Employees negotiate salary, and the self-employed negotiate fees. Not surprisingly, similar rules apply.

- **Do your homework.** Ask what your customer has budgeted. Ask about any past experience your customer has had with a similar product or service. Find out what your competitors charge. Check out if there's a public record of what they've paid for similar services in the past — common among government contractors.
- **Be at ease in talking about money.** Practice if necessary. Don't be too eager. Customers are more willing to pay a fair fee to people who are in demand.
- **Get a concession for a concession.** If you must lower your price, reduce, in some way, what you're doing.
- **If your customer doesn't have a form contract, be the one to write up the agreement.** If there is a form, don't hesitate to negotiate unfavorable terms. Get a written agreement, even if it's just a brief note or a purchase order.

After the Negotiation

Puhleeze, before accepting the position, talk with people to find out about what it's really like to work there. Otherwise, you may find yourself miserable and looking for another job.

Learning about your new job

How to check out an organization? Talk with peers, prospective boss, and supervisees. Ask questions, such as

- Why did my predecessor leave?
- What does it take to be successful here?
- What sort of person is happiest here?
- What sort of hours are we expected to work?
- Is it expected that I'll ask for a fair amount of support, or am I expected to work pretty much on my own?
- Is the firm in growth mode, downsizing mode, or steady-state?

Seven signs of a job that's right for you

You angle for an extra thousand. You trade a nice office for the chance to work a day per week at home. Amid all the machinations, it's easy to lose sight of what's really important in deciding whether to accept the job offer. These questions can help bring things back into perspective:

- Will you find the work interesting?
- Does it use your skills?
- Is it an important job?
- Will you receive useful training?
- Will you enjoy working with the co-workers, especially your boss?
- Is this a good organization to work for?
- Are the salary and benefits fair?

If your answer to most of these questions is yes, congratulations! You've found a fine job.

Part IV
Customizing Your Career

"We don't care where you see yourself in five years, as long as you can see where our clients will be."

In this part . . .

You buy a suit. Off the rack, it will probably look just okay. To really look terrific, you need to tailor it and accessorize it. Same with your career. In this part, we show you how to customize an off-the-shelf career so that you're maximally likely to be happy and successful. For example, we show how to get your assigned tasks changed so that they match your strengths.

Another way to customize your career is to be your own boss. In this part, we also show you how to become successfully self-employed, even if you're not a born entrepreneur.

Chapter 18
Making Any Job Better

In This Chapter

- Molding the job to fit your strengths
- Creating a happy work environment
- Becoming a star without becoming a workaholic
- Staying fresh
- Moving up, moving out

The career you select is a fine piece of marble, but the key to making it wonderful is knowing how to sculpt it. Fortunately, you don't need to be a Michelangelo. Everything you need to know is right here in this chapter.

How Chava Turned an Okay Job into a Cool Career

In previous episodes, Chava triumphed over the interview from hell (see Chapter 16) and the salary negotiation with Scrooge (see Chapter 17). Now, she tries to sculpt her chosen career — online sales — into a masterpiece.

Getting the lowdown

Before taking a chisel to her career, Chava needed to know what she was working with. She started by asking her supervisor at Scrooge Online, Kelly Redmond, for things she could read about the company that they wouldn't have given her before she was hired; for example, its strategic plan or a consultant's report.

Next, she talked with co-workers. "Anything special I should know about how to succeed here? Anything about Kelly Redmond or my co-workers that would be helpful to know? Who are the computer whizzes? The veterans who really know the politics?" She asked customers, "Truthfully, how do we compare with our competitors?"

Starting the sculpture

Finally, Chava came back to Kelly. She asked the same sorts of questions, but added other things.

Chava: I want to get off on the right foot, so could you give me an idea of what you expect from me in these first few weeks?

Kelly *(a little embarrassed):* To tell you the truth, with all the other stuff I'm doing, I haven't had a chance to think much about it. *(A common supervisor condition.)*

Chava: Well, in talking with Judy and Ping *(two of the other salespeople),* and in thinking about what I do best, I wonder if I might make a proposal. Apparently, most of the salespeople focus on outside sales, but I'm best on the phone. On a trial basis, can I start half outside and half inside to see which works better?

Kelly: I'm worried that the other salespeople might resent that you get to stay inside while they had to traipse all over the city.

Chava: I trotted the idea by Ping and Judy, and they didn't object.

Kelly *(feeling magnanimous as bosses tend to feel during a new employee's honeymoon):* Well, I'm not crazy about it, but go ahead and try it.

Chava: Here's something you might like better. I read the division plan you gave me and noticed that retailers are one of your target markets. As you know, I worked at Macy's before coming here. So could I get some retail accounts?

Kelly: That's no problem.

That was as much as Chava could ask for in one sitting, but she wasn't finished sculpting her job. Fast forward a week.

Chava: I'm a little nervous you won't be thrilled with my next proposal, but I really want to ask you about it.

Kelly: Okay, I'm bracing myself.

Chava: Kelly, I'm a single parent with two kids. I'd love to be home when they come home from school. Can I do my by-phone sales work at home?

Kelly: Chava, I don't think so. If I let you do it, all the other parents will want to work at home too.

Chava: Maybe they should be allowed to, but at least with regard to the other salespeople, it's not an issue. They do *outside* sales, so they can't work at home.

Kelly: There's another reason I want to say no. I can't imagine you getting the same amount of work done with two kids pulling at you.

Chava: I can understand why you'd worry about that, but I know my kids and I know me. Can we try it for a few weeks? If my sales numbers are good, fine. If not, the experiment stops. That would make me very happy.

Kelly *(nervous about whether he's hired a problem, but feeling slightly stuck):* Well, we'll try it for one week, but I want an ongoing log of how you spend your time.

Chava: Deal. Thank you. The bottom line won't suffer, I promise, and my kids and I will love you!

Kelly: Well, is that all? Next you'll want the penthouse office.

Chava *(grinning):* That's next week. For today, the last thing is something I think you won't find objectionable. I'd like to do some extra work.

Kelly: Now you're talking my language.

Chava: Could I assemble a booklet of all the tips and tricks that the salespeople have used successfully? That will teach me a lot, it will help me get to know the other salespeople, and maybe I'll create something that will help everyone.

Chava also picked that project because it's something she can point to at promotion time, and something she'll find fun: Chava likes talking with people, getting their ideas, and putting them all together.

We can hear you protesting, "Doesn't that force Chava to do extra work for no pay? She was hired to be a full-time salesperson, and now in addition, she's taking on this big project." Chava was too savvy to fall into that trap. She looked for places to cut corners. She did the minimum paperwork, got a college intern to handle much of that, and avoided being roped into low-payoff activities such as chairing the Christmas party committee. Chava knew where to focus her efforts: on the things that are both important and fun. As you'll see, she also recruited an all-star support team that made her life easier.

Kelly: Sounds okay. Write me a one-pager outlining what you plan to do.

Chava: Fine. I better quit while I'm ahead.

Kelly: I'm not sure you're ahead yet.

Chava: I'm working on it. Can we meet for a few minutes each week until we're both comfortable that I'm on track?

Kelly: Okay, as long as you don't decide that next, you want a spa in the employee cafeteria.

Chava: Only a Jacuzzi. Oh, and between meetings, if you have any feedback for me, please let me know.

Kelly: Okay, Chava. Good-bye.

Chava may have used up a few chits with Kelly, but it was worth it. She took that piece of marble called an off-the-shelf job and already has done a lot to sculpt it in her own image.

Recruiting her all-star team

Chava's next order of business was to cultivate relationships with people she could call on for assistance: knowledge gurus to help with technostuff; wise old souls to help her craft strategies for getting her ideas implemented and making sure she gets credit for them; plus fun folks — she recognized that all work and no play makes for a dull Chava. So early on, she asked key players out for lunch, stopped by to say hello, and heaven forbid, even flirted a little.

Staying fresh

Sales can feel as repetitious as emptying a full swimming pool with a bucket. So Chava knew she needed to add variety to her job. Of course, there was her salespeople's tips and tricks booklet, but a key to staying fresh is to keep learning. Chava was too busy for college-based courses, so she did her learning the efficient way. In the car, when she didn't feel like vegging out, she listened to Tom Hopkins's tapes on how to sell. She passed on her employer's after-work "UNIX and You" seminar but wouldn't have missed "New Ways to Look Your Best" for the world. A social animal, she joined an association of Internet ad salespeople. That gave her entry into the association's local chapter get-togethers. There, she could trade war stories and find out what's working and what's not. Her membership also got her monthly newsletters, which, alas, soon started to pile up. Well, you can't do everything.

Moving up

Chava didn't want to turn into Willy Loman, selling until she dropped. So she did what was needed to get promoted. Her mantra: **Even if you're a clerk, think like a CEO.** That means keeping your antennae out for big ideas: a new profit center, a way to streamline a process, or make workers' lives easier. So Chava continued to ask questions of co-workers, customers, and suppliers on an ongoing basis to find out what was working and what wasn't. And she worked to come up with solutions.

Some bosses try to steal workers' ideas, but not from Chava. When she came up with an important idea, she'd first run it by a trusted colleague to make sure it wasn't stupid. Then, she'd "ask for feedback" either at a staff meeting or by broadcasting an e-mail message. That way, everyone knew the idea was hers. If she produced a special work product, she usually did the same: She sent a draft for feedback to the immediate universe.

Moving out

Despite doing everything right, promotions sometimes just don't come. The company may be in downsizing mode, the bosses could be too firmly entrenched, the chemistry between you and management may be wrong. Chava knew that the world has changed: Patience, with regard to promotions, is no longer a virtue. After a year in sales for Scrooge Online, Chava was starting to feel stale, and despite doing everything right, when she asked about a promotion to sales manager, all she heard were hollow-sounding noises: "You're doing really well, Chava. Give it another year and I could see you getting promoted." She looked around and saw that almost no one was moving up. The company's sales figures were stagnant. The bottom line was that she was not at the right place at the right time.

Chava's response was to get on the phone with her friends at the Internet ad salesperson's association. Also, she whipped out e-mailed queries to senior management at competitors' companies. It was easy to impress them because, thanks to those special projects she always cooked up, Chava could prove that she was no run-of-the-mill salesperson. Within two weeks, she got a sales manager job offer. Good bye, Scrooge Online.

Chava took her off-the-shelf career and sculpted it into quite a piece of work.

Seven More Ways to Make Any Job Better

In addition to the things Chava did, there are other ways to make your job better.

Training your boss

Yes, in the first week or two, you may need to work longer hours to get up to speed. But as soon as possible, try to get down to a workweek you're willing to sustain. If, to impress your boss, you work 60-hour weeks for a while and then start to slow down, your boss may think you've lost interest in the job. Occasionally, we all have to give up an evening or weekend, but if you want or need to work moderate hours, start conditioning your boss to accept that early on. Compensate by keeping her aware of all your accomplishments.

Getting what you want from your boss

Learn your boss's personality type — whether he's fact-driven or emotion-driven, fast- or slow-paced — and respond accordingly. If you have a slow-paced, emotion-driven boss, you'd be foolish to barge into his office saying, "Hi, Allan. If we do A, B, and C, I think we can generate big bucks. Whaddya think?" This is a sure turnoff for a slow-paced, emotion-driven boss. Yet the same approach might work well with a fact-driven, fast-paced boss.

Making your workspace feel good

If an attractive workspace makes you happier, act early. Even all cubicles are not alike. Want one near the window with the view? Far from the elevator? Near the chatterboxes? Away from them? The time to ask is now. Even if your cube is run-of-the-mill, take the time to decorate it so that you'll feel good. We recall one cubicle with an oriental rug on the floor and oil paintings on the walls, enhanced by soft classical music.

Telecommuting

For many people, telecommuting, for at least part of the week, brings a bit of heaven to their work life. All three of us work at home. We enjoy ourselves more and are much more efficient. When I used to work in an office building, there were nonstop interruptions such as, "Let me tell you about my son's bar mitzvah." Now, when I want to work, I work. And when I want to socialize, I pick up the phone or invite someone out to lunch. I get to play the piano or with my cat in between clients. I write in my underwear. Try that in an office! Perhaps best of all, we have ten-second commutes. Of course, many people find work at home too distracting, or they miss the collegiality, or they simply don't live in a place conducive to working.

Three things are key to keeping your boss and yourself happy.

- **Reassure your boss.** Many bosses are control freaks. They're afraid that if you're out of sight, your work will be out of mind. They have visions of you sleeping 'til noon, watching soap operas 'til 3, and squeezing in a little work before your kids come home at 3:30. Offer to send progress reports, documentation of how you used your time — whatever will stop him from losing sleep over that sybaritic lifestyle he thinks you're living on the company dime.
- **Set limits.** Your boss may at least be partly right. Work at home and there are endless temptations: morning tennis, housecleaning, a call to your old girlfriend, and, yes, the refrigerator — telecommuting can be a diet killer. Perhaps the biggest impediment to a successful telecommuting day: kids. If you have young children, it may be worth getting child care so that you can work in peace on days when you're working at home.
- **Try to get compensation for telecommuting.** If you're working at home, your employer saves office space, utilities, phone, computer costs, and so on. Why should you have to pay for that?

Recruiting your very own team of (free!) experts

Every successful employee has a stable of experts on call. These experts generally fall into four types. Chava utilized the first three.

- **Knowledge gurus.** Most organizations have experts at various things — for example, the computer wizard, or the nut who can recite all your company's product specifications in his sleep. If your organization doesn't have the knowledge guru you need, find an outsider: Ask people in your professional association, search Internet resume sites, or post a query at an appropriate Internet discussion group.
- **Wise old souls.** Being politically savvy is overrated, but it helps to have someone who knows the ropes, especially when trying to figure out how to get your idea implemented or get yourself out of trouble. Often, these folks, who usually are no longer interested in climbing the ladder, enjoy playing an avuncular role, passing on words of wisdom to the next generation.
- **Fun people.** In our ever-more-pressured workplaces, without a fun person to break things up, we can gyrate ourselves into whirling work dervishes. The funmeister offers badly needed perspective: some silliness she pulled off the Internet, gossip about who's sleeping with whom, or a recipe for Last-Request Chocolate Cake.
- **Bosses.** It's rare that your first boss is the one you want. Your dream boss is a mentor, confidante, and rising star — he succeeds, and you may ride on his coattails. How do you get hitched to the boss's star? Start with coffee machine chitchat or by asking for newcomer advice. After a few good interactions, ask if you might work on one of his projects. If you're still getting along famously, pop the question: Is there any way I can come to work for you?

Your team of experts requires care and feeding. Because they're so good, it means they're in demand. If you expect them to return your phone call within the decade, go out of your way to help them when you can. And when they help you, a thank-you note or little present doesn't hurt. We guarantee that if you give someone Lindt chocolate truffles — the world's most delicious morsel — they'll return your calls.

Learning the fast way

Staying current keeps you competent, confident, and increases your employability. But with the information explosion, staying current isn't easy. These can help:

- Don't take a class when you need to learn a piece of software. Hire someone who's available by phone to help you get unstuck. Or try a savvy co-worker in your office. Start with a couple of in-person sessions to get you rolling. Then use the program at work, and when you're stuck, ask your tutor. That's just-in-time learning. In a class, it's the opposite. The instructor teaches you the software's features on the semester's timetable. By the time you need a feature at work, you'll probably forget what to do.

- Skim books, read articles. If you're a member of your field's professional association, you'll probably get a useful magazine. Want more? Jump onto your favorite Internet search engine (ours are `www.metacrawler.com` and `www.hotbot.com`), search on terms you're interested in, and you'll instantly have plenty of articles to browse. Talk about an easy approach: Now you can recruit electronic slaves (often called *gobots*) to search the entire Internet 24/7 for material that includes the key words you select and deliver the articles right into your e-mail automatically. MegaCool! Find top gobots at `www.botspot.com`.
- Of the hundreds of thousands of electronic discussion groups, there is, almost assuredly, at least one related to your career. Use `www.liszt.com`, `www.dejanews.com`, or `www.forumone.com` to find the best fits.

Considering self-employment

Self-employment is often a fine later step in growing a cool career. Despite all the downsizing, many people still think of corporate or government work as the most secure, but the fact is that self-employment done right (we explain how in Chapter 19) may offer the most secure job: No one can fire you. And, of course, it feels great to be in control of all the decisions surrounding your work life. Besides, you get to keep all the profits.

We've stressed the importance of staying vigilant to the needs of co-workers, customers, and vendors. Not only can that help you as an *INtrapreneur* (someone who creates innovations within an organization) but also as an entrepreneur. For example, in talking with her fellow sales managers, Chava discovered that they would gladly pay for better-qualified leads. After a few years as a sales manager, she longed for more control over her life. And there it was: a little-known, yet lucrative self-employment niche that most people wouldn't have thought of — selling qualified leads for online ad sales.

Will You Get Ahead?

Up isn't the only way, but for many of us, getting ahead is a way to make a career better. How likely are *you* to get ahead? After you've been in your new career for a few months, hopefully having followed some of the above principles, try this self-test. Many of its items are from a *Fortune* magazine inventory that appeared at Time-Warner's `www.pathfinder.com`.

____ 1. Compare your work with that of your peers. If you think that you've added more value, give yourself 1–3 points. If you've been less productive, take away 1–3 points.

Can't figure out how valuable you are? One way is to think about your suppliers or your customers: How much do they value what you do?

____ 2. Do you have long-term career goals and specific strategies to achieve them? If so, give yourself 3 points.

____ 3. If you've already received a promotion, give yourself 3 points.

____ 4. Are you pampered? For example, if you still need a secretary to do your word processing, you look like a dinosaur and a high-maintenance one at that. Subtract 2 points.

____ 5. Are you actively upgrading your skills? If so, give yourself 1–3 points.

____ 6. Do you build your reputation by writing articles, speaking at industry events, or being active in your professional association?

____ 7. If your organization or department is ripe for restructuring, subtract 1–3 points.

How do you know? Here are some clues:

- Your department's product stacks up poorly against others in the organization or among your competitors.
- Your organization uses too many administrators. Do high-performing competitors work with half the staff you do?
- Morale is low and office politics high.
- Your department isn't central to the long-term success of the employer. For example, you're involved in cutting costs rather than building market share or creating new products.
- Your department gets to spend very little money. If you're constantly being asked to cut costs, your department is unimportant to the employer's long-range plans.

____ 8. If at least one of your suggestions for improving the organization's bottom line or simplifying procedures has been adopted and you've gotten credit, give yourself 1–2 points.

____ 9. Do co-workers and bosses frequently seek your counsel? Give yourself 2 points.

____ 10. Are you getting to do a lot of work, especially important work? Give yourself 1–2 points.

____ 11. If your co-workers and bosses were polled, would at least three-quarters of them say they like you? Give yourself 3 points.

____ 12. Have you cultivated important allies in the organization by volunteering for projects and getting to know staff and managers outside your department? If so, give yourself 1–3 points.

____ 13. Do you regularly ask friends and colleagues for feedback on how you're doing? If so, give yourself 1 point. If you really work on changing yourself as a result, give yourself 2 more points.

TIP

Be sure to ask your boss for frequent evaluations, formal or informal. Pry out negative feedback. You don't want it coming back to bite you later.

____ 14. If you lost your job today, could you tap a network of pros for advice and job leads? If so, give yourself 3 points.

____ 15. Do you have portable skills such as technical or management know-how? If so, give yourself 3 points.

____ 16. Watch your boss during a performance review. If she talks to you about your role in the organization's big picture, give yourself 2 points.

____ 17. Is your boss's star rising or in a death spiral? Give yourself between +2 and –2 points.

____ 18. If you were the boss, would you hire you? If yes, give yourself 3 points. If no, subtract 3 points.

____ 19. If you were the boss, would you promote you? If yes, give yourself 4 points.

A highly unscientific scoring system:

10 or less: You may be downsizing material. Is this a wake-up call to start working on some of the above items? Would you be more motivated to do so in a different job? In a different career?

11-20: A solid performance.

21-30: Star potential.

30+: Send us your resume.

Chapter 19

The Four Musts of Successful Self-Employment

In This Chapter

- The Self-Employment Test: Is independence for you?
- Getting off the fence
- Keeping the cash flowing
- Acting like the CEO you are
- Dealing with the details
- Getting business to come to you

What if you know what your perfect cool career is, but no one's hiring? Or what if you'd love your job if only you could do it your way, on your time schedule, in the locale of your choice, with the kind of people you like working with?

Many of the coolest careers are those we create for ourselves. So if you can't find a job pursuing the cool career of your dreams, consider creating your own.

Who's going to give you a salary to be a ghost hunter, peacock farmer, prairie preservationist, collector of antique furniture, celebrity escort, musical instrument maker, horror aficionado, nature poet, Mediterranean culinary historian, backcountry adventurer, boot maker, video biographer, surfing photographer, or Web cop? These are just a few of the thousands of cool careers people have created for themselves by becoming their own bosses.

We're not talking about building an elaborate business, as a classic entrepreneur might. If you were one of those, you probably wouldn't be reading this book. We're simply talking about creating a job for yourself in which you find customers willing to pay you to pursue your cool career. You don't need to have employees unless you want them and can afford them. You probably won't need to get bank loans or venture capital. You may not even need to shell out the big bucks for an outside office. Many self-employed people do just fine, thank you, working from home.

But What about the Downsides?

People contemplating self-employment often get teased: "So you're considering trading job security for the freedom to work 60 hours a week with no benefits?" Or "Being self-employed is being on a perpetual job search." Or "When you're on your own, you only have to work half-time — whichever twelve hours a day you want." With a little luck, and if you follow the advice in this chapter, you have a good chance of enjoying the freedom and control of self-employment, while providing yourself with the perks of a job: good benefits and reasonable vacations, plus at least as much job security as you can get in a so-called real job.

Job insecurity

Many people equate being your own boss with job insecurity. Fact is, self-employment, *well-done,* offers a good shot at a lifelong paycheck. No one can fire you on a whim. You'll never be merged, purged, right-sized, or downsized.

Insane hours

Conventional wisdom says that the self-employed work harder and longer than anyone else. Yet corporate managers routinely work more than 50 hours a week. And that doesn't even count the ever-lengthening commute time. For people working in offices of 100 or more, 73 percent must work on weekends, and to make ends meet, many people are forced to request overtime or to take a second job. The savvy self-employed often needn't work longer.

You're on a perpetual job search

And if being on your own feels like a perpetual job search, again it probably means you're not doing it right. At first, yes, you will be busy lining up your clientele, but stay with it for a while, and if you're good, and you listen to your customers, business will start coming to you.

So you may be wondering: "If all this is true, how come everyone's not self-employed?" The answer is that a lot of people aren't suited to, or interested in being their own boss. However, many people would do just fine in self-employment if they only knew how. That's what this chapter is about. We give you a chance to discover if creating your own job is a good decision for you, and we show you what it takes to do it right so that you won't flop and can enjoy a self-employed cool career.

The Self-Employment Test: Is Independence for You?

No need to study for this test. Just look inward and try to be honest about yourself.

1. Do you like being in charge?

Do you love running the show and hate having someone tell you what you can and can't do? When you're your own boss, you make all the decisions — from which brand of paper clip to buy to whether to take on a large risky project or a small but sure one. To stay motivated when on your own, it helps if you crave one of the main benefits of being self-employed: control.

2. Are you flexible?

Planning is invaluable when you're on your own, but often, you have to throw out your plan and reinvent. If you're looking for a relatively fixed job description, you'll do better in a salaried job. But if you like the idea of continually reshaping what you do, self-employment will feel good.

3. Can you get things done?

Are you unusually productive? Ideas and dreams are a dime a dozen. The key to turning them into reality is implementation. As they say, success is 5 percent inspiration and 95 percent perspiration. If you're easily distracted from work, you'll have problems.

4. Are you good at solving real-world problems quickly?

Think of the stumbling blocks you recently faced at work and at home. Did you overcome most of them reasonably quickly or did you stay bogged down? When you're your own boss, there's always a thorny issue to address. The successfully self-employed solve their problems quickly, by themselves or with inexpensive help.

5. Are you persistent?

Even the successfully self-employed face many setbacks, but they don't sulk. They quickly move to develop a new strategy. (Of course, that doesn't preclude an occasional private rant or cry.)

6. Do you have good communication and computer skills?

As the front person, you need to be able to make a good first impression, verbally and in writing. Also, in most fields, you need to be able to do word processing, use database and financial management software, send e-mail, and access the Internet.

7. Are you willing and able to market and sell?

No matter how much you enjoy doing your work, you won't get the chance to do it as your own boss unless you can find a way to let others know what you can do for them.

You don't have to make cold-calls to get customers. In this chapter and in Chapter 23, we show you many other ways to get business to come to you.

Scoring

If you couldn't honestly answer yes to all seven questions but are still eager to be self-employed, consider working as an assistant to a successfully self-employed person. You'll either acquire the skills and mind-set you need to be successfully self-employed, or realize that you'll be happier employed by someone else.

The single most important determinant of your success in creating your own career is how motivated you are to do it. If, on a 10-point scale, your desire to create your own career is less than an 8, don't do it.

Don't be tempted by advertised get-rich-quick schemes. You probably won't get rich, and it certainly won't be quick. Whatever they're selling will take time, energy, and money, just like whatever it is you really want to do. So don't fall into the trap of thinking, "Well, I'll just do this until I make plenty of money and then I'll do what I really want to do." Instead, save time and figure out how you can make money doing what you really want to do in the first place.

Four Musts for Hiring Yourself

Entire books have been written about how to become successfully self-employed. Indeed we (Paul and Sarah) have written eight. Yet, when we really think about it, the keys to success reduce to just four things.

Getting off the fence

Unless you are one of those rare birds who wants to work a 70-hour week, to achieve your goal of career happiness you probably must choose: salaried or self-employed. Too many have tried to do both at once and failed, handing out business cards during the day and sending out resumes at night.

Once you make a commitment one way or the other, doors will likely start opening for you. As long as you're sitting on the fence, most people won't take you seriously. Employers will pass over you for fear you'll leave to go out on your own. Customers will shy away because they'd rather deal with a full-timer. (Wouldn't you prefer a physician who practiced full-time?)

The thing that will best help you decide whether to be self-employed is to do a simple business plan. Don't get intimidated. All that means is making sure there's a market for your product or service, describing what you'll do to reach that market, creating a rough budget for the first year, and having an idea of where you'll get the money. Here's the key to developing a valid business plan: Interview lots of potential customers. Ask them what would make them buy from you, and how much they would be willing to pay if you delivered it. Want more guidance in doing your business plan? Try some inexpensive, simple software to walk you through the steps; for example, Bob Adams' *Small Business Startup*.

After developing your business plan, just look at it. If you were an investor, would you invest in this business? Your answer will usually make it clear whether you should open up shop or look for a salaried job.

If you decide to go out on your own, don't compromise your cool career by making either of these two waffling mistakes:

- **Jack and Jill of All Trades.** Connie wanted a cool career creating gourmet wedding cakes. She had always loved cooking, and all the wedding cakes she'd made for family and friends received rave reviews. So she left her job and, working out of a rented kitchen, began marketing her wedding creations. Business was slow coming in though, so when a friend asked Connie to join her as a partner in her desktop publishing business, she agreed. But there wasn't enough business yet to keep them both busy, so when a cousin urged Connie to get involved in her multilevel marketing skin care business, Connie bought in. Now she had three businesses, three business cards, three business names, but of course, not enough time or money to make the most of any one of them. What should Connie have done? **Answer:** Stuck to building her wedding cake business.

- **All Things to All People.** George had a lot of management experience but had been downsized three times in ten years. He decided he could make more money and have greater security as a management consultant. Being his own boss was a real boost to his morale and confidence, but he worried about whether he could line up enough business to support his family. So he decided he wouldn't be picky. He told prospective clients that he'd work with any business on any sort of problem. To his dismay, he's finding few takers. What should he do? **Answer:** Find a niche, a specialty that makes him stand out from the crowd of other management consultants. He might specialize as a franchising consultant or an optometry practice consultant, for example.

Have an entry plan that keeps the cash flowing

You shouldn't need a lot of money to launch your independent career. The myth that you need a bank loan, venture capital, or rich friends and family keeps far too many people from becoming their own boss. Creating a job for yourself is not like starting a traditional business. The average person starting a business spends under $5,000 according to the Small Business Administration. Today, most of that money goes for a computer and office equipment — the costs of which keep going down. Most of the self-employment opportunities listed in the Cool Careers Catalog require only a small investment. Before spending big, think hard about ways to launch your business less expensively. If you can't, before getting into hock, consider another business.

Keys to controlling costs

There's an old axiom, "It takes money to make money." That may be true in big business, but we've found that in creating your own little business, it actually helps if you're a cheapskate.

- **Start your business at home.** You can save literally thousands of dollars a month in rent and other business costs. If you need to meet with clients and your place is a pig sty, offer them the convenience of meeting at their place, at a quiet restaurant, or at a rent-by-the-hour office in an executive center.
- **Provide a service rather than a product.** Products must be produced or bought, and usually require you to maintain thousands of dollars of inventory.

- **Avoid the temptation to buy expensive stuff.** Office furniture, slick brochures, and pricey ads all cost money. You need that cash for more important things like your training, business phones, marketing, a computer (and, no, you don't need the latest and greatest model). Often, you spend the most on your living expenses during those first months when you have few customers.
- **Avoid hiring help.** If you need help, see if you can hire other self-employed people on an as-needed basis. Not only does that avoid the ongoing overhead of employees but also saves you from paying hefty payroll taxes.
- **Consider government-subsidized small business incubators.** These are sets of adjacent offices that allow you to share equipment and secretarial services, and provide a professional environment. Also, the presence of other budding entrepreneurs seems to inject a pioneering spirit among everyone.

Transition plans

Here are common ways to transition into self-employment:

- **The Leave Plan.** Start your independent career while on sabbatical or leave.
- **The Moonlighting Plan.** Keep your full-time job and develop your business as a sideline. When it takes off, you can go whole-hog. Be sure to work at least eight hours a week on a sideline business, and don't save all eight hours for Saturday.
- **The Part-Time Plan.** While you're building up the business, work a part-time job to provide a base income. When your business equals the base, drop the part-time job.
- **The Spin-Off Plan.** Turn your previous employer into your first major customer or, when ethically possible, take a major client with you from your previous job.
- **The Cushion Plan.** Of course, there are obvious cushions like savings, divorce settlements, or severance packages, but think about less obvious assets. Benjamin funded his new business by selling his grand piano, saying, "I wasn't playing it anyway. It was just a very expensive piece of furniture." Your cushion should be large enough to cover your expenses for the cash-poor start-up phase, typically 6 to 12 months.
- **The Piggyback Plan.** If you have a working spouse or partner, cut back your expenses so that you can live on one salary until your business gets going.
- **The Key Client Plan.** If you have sufficient stature in your field, line up one or more retainer contracts with clients for the first year to provide you with assured revenue in exchange for a discount rate.

Smart pricing

Of course, when you're first starting out, it's unfair of you to charge top dollar, but consider charging at least mid-range if only because many prospective clients will be turned off if you charge too little. They believe you get what you pay for.

Many new businesses charge too little, either because they're desperate for customers or because they fail to take into account all the costs of doing business. In setting your pricing, start by figuring out what will yield you a reasonable salary. On top of that you must factor in all your costs, for example: setting up your office, your Internet site, training time, equipment, materials, travel to clients, phones, accounting fees, utilities, marketing costs, business license fees, and your benefits.

We are a bit weary of hearing self-employed individuals lament that they don't get benefits. The self-employed have whatever benefits they provide themselves. Would you work for someone who didn't pay you any benefits? Well, don't expect anything less of yourself than you'd expect from any other employer. Build the cost of sick leave, vacation time, retirement, and health insurance benefits into what you charge.

Don't base your fees on the assumption that you will be able to bill out a 40-hour week. It is the rare person who can. How many billable hours you can expect to generate each week depends not only on how much business you can line up, but on the nature of the work. A medical transcriptionist might bill 40 hours a week, but a corporate trainer may average no more than two billable days a week. Talk to others about the norm in your field, but soon, your own experience will be your best guide.

Finding money

Okay, we've done what we can to keep you out of debt, but sometimes it's unavoidable.

If you really need to borrow money to get underway, here's the straight scoop on the most often considered sources of start-up funds:

- **Banks.** Banks are eager to give loans to small businesses and self-employed individuals for expansion. The problem is, they're looking for a two- to three-year track record.

  To find out what bank loans you might qualify for, visit Quicken's Business Cash Finder at `www.cashfinder.com`. It's free.

- **Equity loan.** Here's where a bank can help — if you have equity in your home.

- **Venture capital.** Generally forget about it. Venture capitalists want to invest at least hundreds of thousands of dollars for a piece of some action that promises millions. They're not interested in helping someone create a great career.

- **Friends, relatives, and other personal contacts.** Often a good bet, but before hitting up ol' Uncle Albert, consider what would happen to your relationship with him if, somehow, you aren't able to repay.
- **Credit cards.** Often the easiest and cheapest approach. Get at least two cards while you still have a job: one for personal use and one for your business. Find cards with low interest rates. They are available as low as 5 or 6 percent for the first six months or year. After that, you can switch cards for a new introductory rate.
- **Small Business Administration loans**. An SBA loan is a possibility, especially if you're a minority or a woman. To find out more, check your White Pages for your local office.

Acting like the CEO you are

When you're self-employed, you suddenly go from subordinate to CEO. To succeed, you have to act like the chief executive. Here are common no-no's:

- **Never use a resume.** Prepare a bio, brochure, portfolio, and/or company mission statement. Have professional-looking letterhead, business cards, and stationary.
- **Never refer to yourself as a free-lancer.** If you want to command good fees, don't ever represent yourself as less than the head of your own company. Free-lancers routinely get paid less and are paid last. Also, never put the word "just" in front of what you do — for example, "It's just a home business" or "I'm just a one-man shop." Be proud of your one-person operation. After all, your clients never have to work with an underling. They get the personal attention of the CEO.
- **Never ask for an interview.** Interviews are for jobs. You are getting business, lining up customers, serving clients. Therefore you arrange for a meeting, offer to make a presentation, make a bid, or submit a proposal.

- **Never ask what someone pays.** Tell people what you charge. However, don't announce your fees first thing, even if that's the first thing they ask for. Find out the details of what they need so that you can provide a price that both meets their needs and covers your costs and profit. Build value for what you do before announcing the price, so customers will be relieved to hear that your fee isn't higher.
- **Never work without an agreement.** Before you begin working with a new client or customer, get an agreement in writing as to what you will be doing, the price, payment arrangements, and so on. Depending on the nature of your work, your agreement can be a simple order form, a purchase order, or a letter of agreement (a less intimidating word for a contract).

You will often be the one to provide the agreement, but large organizations usually have their own standard forms. Beware when you get one of those babies — their attorney probably wrote it to benefit his or her client. If you're nervous, it may be worth hiring your own legal eagle to review it. And remember that even though those corporate contracts look official, they are not set in stone. Don't hesitate to negotiate.

When extending credit, remember that it's always a privilege, no matter how big, well-known, or established the customer. Take the time to check credit references.

- **Never complain.** Your customers have enough problems of their own. That's probably part of why they want to work with you. So don't add to their problems. If you're having difficulties in your business or personally, commiserate with family and friends if need be, but don't moan and groan to clients. Ever hear a CEO complain to a customer?

Getting business to come to you

It's every new businessperson's biggest question: How do I get customers? Eventually, if you're good, repeat business and word of mouth may largely sustain you, but for now, you've got to get the word out. People have to know, not only what you do, but how you're different from others who do similar work.

The good news is that there are plenty of ways to market, and you need to choose only those few methods that you feel most comfortable with. If cold-calling makes you sweat, no problem. Pick something else. Chances are, you won't do a marketing activity you hate. Here are several of the quickest, most effective marketing activities. They're also low cost.

Please, as long as you need more customers, market during every minute of your workday that you're not doing paying work. This is the most important sentence in this chapter.

- **Schmoozing.** Otherwise known as networking, schmoozing is the most popular way for self-employed individuals to get business. You can schmooze at professional and trade association meetings, in business organizations, Chambers of Commerce forums, and through formal networking groups like Business Network International, which has chapters all over the United States. For the chapter in your area, check out its Web page at `www.bni.com` or call 800-825-8286. In California call 909-305-1818.

If business gatherings aren't for you, schmooze by phone with colleagues, friends, and associates. Or browse Web sites and user groups, leaving helpful information along the way. Add a tag line to your online signature so that people know what you do and can reach you by e-mail.

- **Cross Referrals.** If you carve out a specialized niche, colleagues and even your competition can become valued referral sources for you. You can send them business in their areas of expertise, and they can send you business in yours.
- **Gatekeepers.** Gatekeepers are people whose business puts them in contact with lots of people who need what you offer. Make a list of everyone your potential customers do business with. These are your gatekeepers. For example, if you have a cleaning service, commercial real estate agents can be gatekeepers for you because their clients need property cleaned before sales. Let all relevant gatekeepers know about you and what you offer. Sometimes referrals from one or two good gatekeepers can keep you busy full-time.
- **Sampling.** Your work can be your own best sales force. Let people see what you do. Give them a taste, a sample. Whet their appetite for more. You can provide samples of your work through photos, portfolios, brochures, business cards, demonstrations, tapes, free consultations, speeches and seminars, or passing out actual samples.

Need more marketing ideas? See Chapter 23. Paul and Sarah offer some gems in the form of special reports that did not fit into the newest edition of their book, *Getting Business to Come to You,* at their Web site: `www.paulandsarah.com`.

But What If I Fail?

Fortunately, we were too young to ask this question of ourselves when we were learning to walk. Otherwise, many of us would be crawling our way through life. If you fall on your face, corny as it may sound, force yourself to congratulate yourself for having the courage to try, regroup, and put together another plan for achieving your cool career. Winston Churchill once said that success is moving from failure to failure with grace, composure, and confidence. Being more optimistic than that, we would add: . . . until you get the hang of it.

If you're willing to learn from your experiences, you probably will get the hang of it; you will find a way to make your cool career work. If you have trouble finding the winning combination of what people will pay for, Paul and Sarah provide hundreds of examples of unique businesses people have created for themselves in their book *Finding Your Perfect Work* (Tarcher/Putnam, `www.perfectwork.com`).

And of course, it's perfectly okay to decide at any point that being your own boss is not for you. As you can see in the Cool Careers Catalog, there are plenty of great salaried careers.

You're Not Alone

It can feel scary to go off on your own. Remember, just because you're on your own, doesn't mean you *are* alone. There are limitless support resources. Three Web sites alone — `www.edgeonline.com`, `www.business.gov`, and `www.workingsolo.com` — connect you to more support, written and human, than anyone could possibly use. And that's not counting another incredible resource: the literally millions of other people who are living their dreams in an independent cool career, many of whom would love to talk with you.

Part V
The Part of Tens

"I'm sure there will be a good job market when I graduate. I created a virus that will go off that year."

In this part . . .

Many good ideas don't require a long explanation. So we plunk every good idea that's self-explanatory into this part. Over 500 good careers not enough? We show you ten ways to find thousands more. Does a job interview make you sweat? We cut to the chase: Ten interview questions that make job seekers squirm — and honest ways to survive them. Suffering from the heartbreak of procrastinitis? Stall no more. We give you ten (all right, 29) extra-strength cures. We also offer ten cool ways to heat up your small business. Don't miss this part!

Chapter 20

Ten More Sources of Cool Careers

In This Chapter

- How an index can be your best friend
- Internet hot spots
- Potent places in periodicals
- Finding your career while watching TV
- Capitalizing on who you know
- Creating your own cool career

You scoured the Cool Careers Catalog. Nothing sounds good. You've wracked your brain. Nothing. If you hear advice from one more person, you'll explode. Yet you still can't find a career that turns you on. Here's hope: easy ways to find literally thousands of additional cool careers.

A Special Note

When you've reviewed a zillion careers and still nothing jumps out at you, your problem may not be that you need a new career. Might your discontent follow you to your new occupation?

Examples:

- Maureen realized she wanted to be loved by her boss. She didn't need a change of careers; she needed a lover.
- Maybe your problem is that you're not as good at your job as you need to be, and should bone up — or scale back your career goal.
- Is your problem not that you make too little money but that you spend too much?
- Could it be that your career is fine but that you need different co-workers?

- Are you asking too much of a job? Some people refuse to accept that work *is* work. No job — not even movie star, not professional athlete, not TV anchor — will be as fun as play.

Many, maybe even most, people who come to career counselors end up realizing that what they need is to tweak their current careers, not dump them. So before going on to the rest of this chapter and digging up more careers, ask yourself whether you need to look more closely at what you're currently doing or considering. If so, first read Chapter 18.

That said, some people do need to be exposed to even more careers than the 500 in the Cool Careers Catalog. This chapter shows you how to find them.

Lists of Careers

Had Eric not skimmed the Yellow Pages index, never in a million years would he have thought of becoming an acid dealer (industrial acid, not LSD, you Deadhead!). Had Patricia not browsed the index of the *Occupational Outlook Handbook,* she never would have considered being a zookeeper. After scanning the College Board's *Index of Majors and Graduate Degrees,* Justin knew he wanted to be something he had never heard of before: a textile scientist, someone who develops new fabrics. Your library has these and many other directories that list careers. Just a couple of hours of scanning can expose you to thousands of options.

Variation on the theme: Hundreds of career books contain descriptions of many careers. A few titles to whet your appetite follow.

Tom Stienstra's *Sunshine Jobs: Career Opportunities Working Outdoors* (Live Oak Publications).

*O*Net Dictionary of Occupational Titles.* Just the facts on 1,122 occupations, covering 95 percent of the United States workforce. ($40: 800-648-JIST.)

VGM Career Horizons publishes such titles as

- *Careers for Courageous People*
- *Careers for Animal Lovers*
- *Careers for Good Samaritans*
- *Careers for Nature Lovers*
- *Careers for Self Starters*
- *Careers for Cybersurfers*
- *Careers for High-Energy People*

- *Careers for Born Leaders*
- *Careers for Sports Nuts*
- *Careers for Bookworms*
- *Careers for Culture Lovers and Other Artsy Types*

Two of us (Paul and Sarah) have written three books you might want to look at. *Best Home Businesses for the 90s* and *Making Money with Your Computer at Home* (Putnam) profile many outstanding home businesses. *Finding Your Perfect Work* profiles hundreds of novel careers people have crafted for themselves plus a step-by-step method for creating your own.

College catalogs also contain lists of careers; look in the section describing each major. One of our favorite sources is colleges' *extension* catalogs. They often describe programs in new and locally in-demand careers.

The biggest career list of all is the want ads, especially the online listings. CareerPath (www.careerpath.com) lists every want ad from 60 major U.S. newspapers. To keep you from getting overwhelmed, the ads are categorized and keyword searchable. Hundreds of thousands of want ads, also categorized and keyword searchable, are on such sites as America's Job Bank (www.ajb.dni.us), The Job Factory (www.jobfactory.com), and The Monster Board (www.monster.com).

The Media

You hear a radio interview with a range scientist, a person who manages grazing pastures. Sound like a cool career to you?

You watch a TV segment on some new gizmo. Want to sell it?

At a career Web site, you read a profile of a flower importer. Wanna smell the roses on a full-time basis?

You spot a newspaper article in which a company was found guilty of maintaining a hostile work environment because it didn't have a written harassment prevention plan. That will scare companies fast. Want to develop those plans for a living?

Keep your antennae out. There's an ongoing, easily accessible gold mine of ideas coming at you from the media 24/7. Especially fertile media outlets are

- **The Discovery Channel.**

- **A newspaper's business, career, and science sections.** Sometimes, an article's career implications are obvious, but often it requires a little thought. You read an Election Day article on a school construction bond that just passed. That should mean a boom for construction companies that specialize in schools. A magazine article reports on the trend to interracial relationships. Want to be a counselor specializing in multicultural couples? The general principle is that when you see a feature on something new, ask yourself, "What kinds of problems will this cause? Do I want a career that would solve them?"
- **Trade and professional magazines.** These are treasure troves of cool careers and trends, written by leading insiders.

The next three career sources are for people who suspect, deep down, that they're not going to find a career they're passionate about. They just want a career that pays reasonably, that they can succeed at, and that doesn't require breathing toxic fumes or listening to clanging equipment.

Personal Connections

Personal connections are particularly helpful if you don't have extensive formal credentials. Make a list of everyone who likes you who might hire you or know someone who could. Then phone each person and describe what you're looking for. You may need to say no more than, "I've just graduated from college and don't really know what I want to do. I just want to find a decent place to start my career." You never know what might turn up. You may never have thought about working for a food brokerage. Heck, you never even knew that food got brokered. But if your cousin told you that you could get an entry-level management job in food brokerage, especially if you didn't have extensive credentials or a burning passion, mightn't you go for the interview? Asking your personal connections for career leads can turn you on to careers you never would have thought of.

Isaac was a schizophrenic whose medication finally got him under control. He was ready for a job, any job. I asked him to list everyone who cared about him. Outside of his parents, he could list only one person: his therapist. (Schizophrenics don't have lots of friends, let alone friends in a position to hire them.) I told Isaac to ask his therapist for career advice. She referred him to the manager of a mental health advocacy group, and Isaac got an internship there. His goal now is to become a spokesperson for schizophrenics. Not a career he would have otherwise have thought of.

Often, your connections will at least help you get a short-term or part-time job. That's okay. That can turn into a reference for another job or even the first step toward going into business for yourself.

The Dream Industry

The same sort of people who, despite all efforts, can't really narrow down their career goals, are sometimes clearer that they'd like to work in a particular industry. Shane knew he wanted to work in baseball even if he had to pick weeds in the outfield. And that's exactly what he did. Even though he had a college degree, he took a job as a minor league assistant groundskeeper — translation: he mowed the grass and picked weeds — and he was happy, but that's not the end of the story. One game, when staring at the scoreboard, he realized that someone had to be running all the fancy video equipment that creates the replay screen and the between-innings entertainment. Shane had worked in his college's TV studio, which gave him the background for that job, and volunteered to assist in the scoreboard room. Before long, Shane had a cool career as scoreboard operator, a career he never would have known existed.

The Dream Organization

Some people care more about which employer they work for than what they do there. Kathy felt that way about Estee Lauder. She loved their products, was intrigued that it remained a family-run business despite being so big, and simply wanted to work there. Short of sweeping the floors, she would do anything. It took her two years. Kathy kept contacting their human resources department month after month, visiting its Web site, writing letters to the president, the whole deal. Finally, a sales manager was impressed with her persistence and offered her a position as a manufacturer's rep. For Kathy, a cool career, and one she wouldn't have thought of.

Internet Searches

Go to `www.metacrawler.com` or `www.yahoo.com` and try these search terms. They can uncover career ideas you wouldn't have thought of

- Careers + (something you're interested in). For example, careers + roses.
- Trends + (something you're interested in). For example, trends + publishing.
- New career(s)
- New job(s)
- New profession(s)
- New occupation(s)

- Best new career(s)
- Best new job(s)
- Best job(s)
- Best career(s)
- Hot job(s)
- Hot career(s)

Internet Discussion Groups

Internet discussion groups exist for thousands of careers. Participants are probably on the cutting edge, so you'll likely read about careers you haven't heard of. You can post a query asking for career ideas. For a master list of career-related Internet discussion groups, visit www.careers.org.

Imitate a Successful Business

Many aspiring business owners think they need an original concept. If they see a similar business, they're discouraged. The smart reaction is to be pleased. If a similar business has been around awhile, it means it's reasonably successful. If you'd like to run that sort of business, go for it. Check out a number of businesses of that type, incorporate the best features of each, and open your business in a prime location. Sometimes prime doesn't mean downtown. Jon was fond of training corporate employees in team building and communication skills but found the market saturated. He went to Poland, where, following the fall of Communism, corporations are now just ramping up. Jon is now a wealthy man.

A franchise offers the opportunity to copy a business with the steps laid out for you. But don't think it's pure cookie cutter; inevitably there are local problems to solve. Pick a franchise that's been around for at least five years and has at least 50 franchisees so that there's a track record. You don't want the franchisor to use you as a guinea pig. Before buying, ask at least 10 franchisees chosen at random if they're happy with the franchise. Hundreds of franchises are described at the International Franchise Association Web site: www.franchise.org. For a printed list, call the IFA at 202-628-8000.

Trade Show and Business Expos

Trade shows and expos are the equivalent of career shopping malls. Hundreds of booths offer different career opportunities. Go to a garden industry show and you may find yourself in love with the idea of working for a greenhouse company, something you never would have thought of. Go to a business expo and you may hear about a terrific-sounding business fixing basement leaks. Again, something you wouldn't have thought of. No kid grows up thinking, "Gee, when I grow up, I want to go into the leak-fixing business." A plus for these events is that instead of just reading about it, you can talk with a person who's doing it. But do us a favor, leave your checkbook home. Although it's usually not legal to sell businesses on an expo floor, some vendors do. You should take months, not minutes, to decide to buy a business.

If you find an appealing business or franchise opportunity, go home, think it over, read the fine print, check references, and survey the competition. If everything checks out, great.

Creating Your Own Cool Career

Here's a cool career factory complete with tools for designing your own custom career:

Ten ways to find your perfect work

1. Do what you love.
2. Provide a service to others who do what you love.
3. Teach others to do what you love.
4. Write about what you love.
5. Speak about what you love.
6. Create a product related to what you love.
7. Sell or broker what you love.
8. Promote what you love.
9. Organize what you love.
10. Set up, repair, restore, fix, or maintain what you love.

One sentence to a career that is uniquely you

Find a market need so uniquely tailored to your skills and personal experiences that no generic name has been given to the career.

Peter is an engineer who spends his free time hiking, rock climbing, and taking wilderness photos. As he explored how he could combine these, his thoughts returned repeatedly to memories of the many evenings his family enjoyed reviewing the photo albums from their wilderness trips. That gave him the idea. His target customers are wilderness adventure companies who want to enhance their customers' experience by providing a video or still record of their trip. He created Peter's Wilderness Adventure Video Memories.

Seven career fantasies

These are provided by Arlene Hirsch, author of *Love Your Work and Success Will Follow.* Perhaps they might trigger a custom career idea for you.

1. **Hitting the open road.** Be like the Illinois scientist who gladly gave up his life of the mind to drive a big rig.
2. **Risking it all.** For example, take on a physical challenge.
3. **Letting your creative juices flow.** Become an artist or performer.
4. **Embracing a tropic paradise.** Let yourself be motivated by place and by a calmer, less stressful existence.
5. **Benefiting society.** Help others while shunning the profit motive of big business.
6. **Returning to your roots.** Embrace life's basic ingredients, such as growing your own food or living in a small town.
7. **Staying close to family.**

Find a micro-niche

In light of all the military sex scandals, Sheila, an army lifer, decided to become a gender-equity auditor for the military.

Trends are particularly fertile sources of neat niches. Trend 1: Attention Deficit Disorder is the disease du jour. Trend 2: We're ever more aware of the importance of good parenting. A business idea that capitalizes on both trends: becoming a parenting coach to children with attention deficit disorder.

The contrarian approach

No one graduates college saying, "I want to be in the scrap metal business." So the competition is much less rigorous than in popular fields. Yet your happiness is often more dependent on whether you are successful and feel you're doing good work than on working in a sexy-sounding industry. If you buy this concept, consider industries that turn off most people, such as food processing, funeral homes, or even commercial bathroom supply.

Find a need and fill it

In the mid-1980s, Erika, a graphic designer, was watching cable TV, then in its infancy. She was struck by the crudeness of its graphics, so she developed some samples, sent them to all the cable stations, and that launched a successful career.

New laws and regulations create opportunities. For example, Jane is an attorney whose best skill is translating legal mumbo jumbo into plain English. At a meeting of the Society of Technical Communication, she found out that the Securities and Exchange Commission just started requiring all mutual fund prospectuses to be converted from legalese into plain English. Right up Jane's alley.

Listen to people's complaints. They may be willing to pay for solutions. The tattoo craze has faded, but not the tattoos. Many young adults are regretting the pythons branded into their arms, the hearts inscribed in less visible places. Their problem is your business opportunity. Open a tattoo-removal clinic. Even if you're not a doctor, you can open the storefront, market it, and hire a doctor to do the laser surgery.

The meeting

Nicholas Lore, author of *The Pathfinder,* says that we are not a single personality. We may have a practical part, a hedonistic part, an intense part, a laid back part, and so on. Lore recommends this technique, developed at the Esalen Institute, to help create a career goal that satisfies all of our parts.

Start by listing up to six parts of youself. Only refer to the possibilities in the following list if you're stuck.

Ms. Responsible	The Kid	The Rebel
The Saboteur	The Saint	The Rogue
The Star	The Beast	The Know-It-All
The Guru	The Mother	The Problem Solver
The Cynic	The Lover	The Creative One
The Philosopher	The Fool	The Hedonist
The Comedian	The Radical	The Conservative
The Good Neighbor	The Basket Case	The Friend

Invite all your parts to a meeting by putting cards with each part's name on them around a table. (Of course, you're the only person at the "meeting.") As the meeting's facilitator, start by describing the problem — for example, the reasons you're having trouble deciding on a career. Then go around the table and have each part of yourself give its take on the situation. After that go-round, your parts can speak as you see fit. The meeting ends when you, the facilitator, can state a plan or goal that meets most or even all of your parts' agendas. Of course, you can decide to reconvene if the problem doesn't get solved in one meeting, or if you want to discuss another issue such as your romantic life or whether to buy those new golf clubs.

Randomness

The message behind this and most how-to books is that planning is good. Yet, sometimes — probably more often than we like to acknowledge — things just happen. Marilyn Maze, career software designer for ACT, tells about her cousin, Grace (name changed) who was a biology major in college. After graduating, Grace took an entry-level position in a bank. She had never even considered a banking career but saw it as a temporary solution when the job market for biologists was depressed. Now she's vice president of a bank and very happy. Marilyn said, "Yes, people should make some effort to decide if they have a true vocation, but many people don't, so they should take advantage of opportunities that present themselves."

Chapter 21

Ten (Okay, 29) Extra-Strength Procrastination Cures

In This Chapter

- When it's okay to procrastinate
- Overcoming excuse-making
- Conquering the fear of appearing stupid
- Managing your perfectionism
- Overcoming overwhelm
- Getting rolling again
- When you don't know what to do next

Procrastination is like a credit card: Fun when you use it, painful when the bill comes in.

Let's come back to this chapter later. (Just kidding.)

Does Your Procrastination Really Need Curing?

Sometimes procrastination, like pain, is a warning that something is wrong. Just as the ouch you get when you touch a hot stove tells you to stay away, procrastination can be your brain telling you to stay away from a task. When is your brain right? Here is a test to find out. Write down your answers to these questions:

- What are the benefits of *not* doing the activity you're procrastinating about?
- What would happen if you did the activity?
- What's the worst thing that could happen?

- How likely is that worst case?
- Could you survive if the worst occurred?
- What would you do?

Now look at what you've written and make a commitment that by a time you select, you'll either do the thing you've been procrastinating about or drop it forever.

So You Want to Stop Procrastinating

Yes, sometimes procrastination is good for us, but more often it's career cancer. The rest of this chapter is about curing the bad kind of procrastination.

It's no surprise that procrastination can cause you to fail in your career and in the rest of your life. So we pull no punches. This chapter may make you confront demons you'd rather not confront. If so, it will be tempting to put the book aside — in other words, to procrastinate. See if you can make it through the entire chapter. It's only eight pages long. You can do it, and it will be worth it. We have spent considerable time studying procrastination and helping clients overcome it, and we crammed in as much help as possible into these eight pages.

This chapter contains many cures for procrastination. That sounds good on first blush, but having many choices can be overwhelming, especially to a procrastinator. So, as you read, we suggest you keep a pencil with you and star just the few cures that you think are most likely to work for you.

Cures for Excuse-Making

Some procrastinators can be cured if they understand why their excuse for procrastinating is bogus.

The Hedonist's Excuse: "Searching for a job is yucky, no fun at all. I always find something I'd rather do."

The cure: Remember that you'll have more fun if you don't procrastinate. When you procrastinate, you suffer in many ways. You suffer ongoing guilt: Even when you're watching your favorite TV show, a little voice whispers in your ear, "You should be working on getting hired." You also suffer from staying in that same miserable situation that made you want to find a cool career in the first place: the low pay, the lousy work, your lack of success. Plus, you must endure your family's searing questions: "When *are* you going to find yourself, Melvin?" If you truly like pleasure more than pain, the key is to get your work done as efficiently as possible so that maximum time is left for pleasure, without guilt or negative consequences to spoil the fun.

The Fear-of-Failure excuse: "I don't want to risk failing."

The cure: Recognize that not trying usually means greater failure. If you don't try, you're a guaranteed failure. If you give it a shot, there is at least some chance you'll succeed, and at minimum, you will learn from your failure. You'll also gain self-respect and the esteem of others. People who try and fail are respected more than people who don't try at all.

Ask yourself, "What's the worst that can happen?" What if you call a prospective employer and she laughs, "I wouldn't hire you for all the tea in China." That's no biggie, especially if you have Plan B — someone else to call.

The Perfectionist's Excuse #1: "It takes me a long time, but I want to get it right."

The cure: Know when okay is good enough, and when you need to be perfect. It usually takes a long time to get from good to perfect, so you only want to spend that time when it's worth it — for example, in crafting a good answer to "Why have you been unemployed for the last nine years?" In nearly every other task in a career search, shooting for perfection is time that can be more valuably spent.

We've seen many clients waste weeks agonizing over the fine points of their resumes, the design of their business cards, or their cold-call script. Their job prospects would be much better if they simply started contacting employers. One reason people are perfectionists about such things as their resumes is that it's more comfortable to fiddle with things than to risk embarrassing yourself. Be aware of that tendency. Spend your time on tasks that make a difference.

The Perfectionist Excuse #2: "I'd rather not do it than do it poorly."

The cure: Sure, brain surgeons, poets, and master craftspeople must be perfect, but career searchers needn't be. That high-minded talk coming from a career searcher is usually fear talking. Such career searchers are afraid that if they make a mistake, others will think they're stupid. The fact is, most successful people don't let fear of making a mistake stop them. They dive in, make mistakes (sometimes appearing stupid), and simply learn from their mistakes. Unsuccessful people are much more likely to plan, plan, plan in hopes of getting it perfect, and give up before it ever gets done. Or if it *has* to get done, they find themselves at the eleventh hour, forced to crank out something far worse than what they would have produced had they not procrastinated. Sometimes a procrastinator's motive is to protect his ego: "I could have done it well if I had taken the time." For that cold comfort, they pay a huge price.

Another difference between winners and losers lies in how they react to failing. Winners don't waste much time on self-pity. They focus on learning from their failure, so they're more likely to succeed the next time. Mr. Honda, of car fame, was asked, "What is the secret to your success?" His answer, "I am not a success. I am a failure. I have failed 50 times for each time I have succeeded. But I continue to try. That is the secret to my success."

If you try, you may fail, but your failure will teach you something and you will be eager to try again to make it better. If you don't try, you build up more fears, and decrease your desire to achieve. Being scared and feeling like a fraud is part of the change process, so, as author Susan Jeffers says, feel the fear and do it anyway. To get you moving forward, we can tell you nothing more important than what Nike does: Just do it.

The Fear-of-Imposing Excuse: "I don't want to contact them because I don't want to impose."

The cures:

- Recognize that you may not be imposing. Many people enjoy giving advice. Plus, if you're calling for a job, and the employer happens to need an employee like you, you'll be doing him a favor. If not, you will have wasted ten seconds of his time. Big deal.
- The karma concept: Even if you *are* imposing, recognize that it's okay to ask for help as long as you remember to be kind to a job seeker who asks you for help.
- Think of your contact as you would a how-to book. If your contact turns out not to be helpful, simply go on to the next one.

The Fear-of-Success Excuse: "I'm not sure I want to succeed. If I do, I won't have time for the things and people that are important to me."

The cure: Remember that you can set limits. There's no need to accept more pressure than you want. For example, many successful executives have decided that the stressful 60-hour weeks aren't worth it no matter how high the salary, and quit to do something low-key like teach college. Others who are strongly committed to family, with some persistence, usually find jobs that allow them to preserve most of their evenings and weekends.

The Resent-Authority Excuse: "You're not going to make me do that."

The cure: You're right. Neither family nor societal pressure can make you do anything, but recognize that if you make the choice not to succeed, you, not the authority, will suffer.

The Gotta-Do-This-First Excuse: "I really can't get started on my career search until I clean my desk" (or get my divorce finalized, quit my job, or whatever).

The cure: Realize that these are delaying tactics. Yes, they are also legitimate problems, but millions of people with piled-high desks, doing full-time jobs, and yes, in the throes of divorce, have found new careers. Often, the search for a better career actually provides rays of hope and distraction from the stresses of a breakup. If you wait until all the stars are aligned, you'll never get started.

All-Purpose Procrastination Cures

No matter what your excuse for procrastinating, here's a medicine chest full of cures. They work — if you don't procrastinate using them.

Keep reminding yourself of the benefits of not procrastinating. Examples: When you find a job, you can support your family, feel useful, afford that mountain cabin you've fantasized about, and rid yourself of the guilt that you are letting life pass you by. How do you keep a benefit burnished in your brain? Write a word or draw a picture that symbolizes it. John put the letters "G-WOMB" on the cover of his appointment book. It stands for "Get Wife Off My Back."

Tomorrow, how will you feel about having procrastinated?

The less you accomplish, the less you want to accomplish. The more you accomplish, the more you want to accomplish.

Think back to times you've procrastinated. What were the consequences? Has it hurt your career? Your relationships? Your self-esteem? Sometimes, looking at the price you've paid for procrastinating can motivate you to not let it happen ever again.

Think back to a time you *didn't* procrastinate on an unpleasant task. What kept you from procrastinating then? A rigorous schedule? Someone nagging you? Does that give you a clue as to how to beat your current procrastination?

What would you say to get your twin to quit procrastinating?

Figure out where you are least likely to procrastinate. If at home you play too much with your dog or take too many tea breaks, consider working somewhere else.

Figure out *when* you are least likely to procrastinate. Block out that time as career-search time. Write it in your date book just as you would an appointment with a friend. You wouldn't fink out on your friend. Maybe you won't fink out on yourself.

Just do it. Do it now, even if you don't feel like it. If you only work on your career when you feel like it, you won't feel like it often enough. Don't expect it to be fun. That's okay. As those obnoxious but correct people say, "No pain, no gain." Fight through the discomfort and just do it. Think how good it will feel to have put in a good hour. Think of the benefits you'll derive. Realize that if you keep procrastinating, you're a loser — yes a loser. Then force yourself to start working.

Don't think about how much work you have ahead of you. That can overwhelm you into procrastination. Instead, think like a mountain climber. Just put one foot in front of the other, and when you get to the top and look down, you'll be amazed at how far you've gotten.

Before we began to write this book, we knew there were 400 pages ahead of us but we never let ourselves think about that. It would feel overwhelming. As soon as those sorts of thoughts entered our minds, we immediately replaced them with, "One step at a time. What's my next little task?"

Be aware of the moment of truth. When feeling the temptation to procrastinate, there is a moment of truth when you're still not over the edge, like when you're starting to lose your temper. At that moment, you can consciously suppress the desire to procrastinate. When you feel that temptation arise, ask yourself "What's my next one-second task?" You might also remind yourself of the benefits you'll get by staying with the task.

Use a one-second task to get you rolling. Before you start or when you reach a hard part, it's tempting to grab some coffee, call your friend, or trim your nails. That's when you have to force yourself to get working (on the task, not your nails). Ask yourself, "What is my next one-second task?" For example, "I have to open my address book to see whom I should call."

When you're stuck, don't stew, get help. Sometimes, clients sheepishly admit they didn't get much done on their job search. When asked why, they frequently say that they hit a problem they couldn't solve. When asked whether they tried to get help, they usually say no. If you don't know what to do, think about it for literally one minute. If that doesn't yield at least some progress, the odds are small that you'll be able to solve your problem in a reasonable amount of time. That, of course, will frustrate you and make you more likely to procrastinate on the whole project. So if you're still stuck after a minute, put the problem aside, go on, and come back to it later. Sometimes, fresh eyes can help. Or get help from someone in your office, by phone, or online.

The Scarlet P. (This tactic is a bit draconian, but what the heck.) Write the letter "P" (for procrastinator) on the outside of your hand so that everyone can see it. Unlike in Hester Prynne's case, no one's forcing you to do it. That P, which follows you everywhere you go, is an ongoing reminder that curing your procrastination is Job One. The P is also embarrassing, so it may motivate you to overcome the problem so that you can honorably remove it. To be honest, I've only tried this with one client so far, but he said it helped.

Create a to-do list that you check throughout the day.

Make a deal with yourself. For example, "If I work for two hours, I'll watch *Days of Our Lives*."

Do more and think less. As a child, I would lie awake worrying about dying. As a young adult, I interpreted every twinge as a sign of an impending heart attack. Doctors tried to reassure me that nothing was wrong, therapists tried to find the cause of my hypochondria, but nothing worked. I was a worrywart.

But at age 30, I suddenly stopped worrying. Who cured me? My wife. "Martin," she ordered, "The more you think about your health, the more in knots you are. From now on, every time you get a hypochondriacal thought, just force yourself to think of something else." Within two weeks, I was cured. That was 17 years ago. Of course, now I worry about little green men from Mars coming to destroy the earth. Just kidding.

Why am I telling you this? Because too often, we procrastinate taking action by thinking a problem to death — analysis paralysis. This, of course, usually leads to a worse result than if we had tried something, even if it ended up not succeeding. If you stay at the bottom of the mountain until you figure out the precise route to the top, you'll never get up there.

Avoiding analysis paralysis is particularly important for career searchers. Rarely can you make progress just sitting there and thinking. Write something, phone someone, talk out loud. Don't just sit there. What is your next one-second task?

I have found analysis paralysis to be a particular problem with clients who have been in therapy that focuses on the childhood roots of their problems. Some seem more paralyzed as a result. They seem in knots, stuck in the past. They seem more interested in doing yet more exploration of the childhood-based reasons they're stuck than in doing something to get unstuck.

Create an artificial deadline. Do you wait until the last minute because you need time pressure to motivate you? Create an artificial deadline. For example, hand a friend $100. If you don't finish the work by the agreed-on time, he keeps your hundred bucks.

A lower-stakes way to create an artificial deadline is to give yourself an insanely short amount of time to get a task done: "I want to have lunch at 12. Let's see if I can write a draft of my resume by then."

Draw a thermometer and tape it to your desk. Instead of numbers on the side, write the little steps you need to do to get the task done. Every time you complete a step, color in that part of the thermometer. This technique helps churches raise lots of money.

Find someone to check in with.

Some career seekers can go it alone, but many, especially procrastinators, find that it helps to have someone to check in with. Regular check-in is a key to the success of Weight Watchers and 12-step programs.

Some people prefer one-on-one support. Find a friend you can phone every day. I sometimes allow procrastinating clients to call my answering machine each evening to report their progress. Dave said, "Knowing I'll have to check in with you each night makes me feel like Marty Nemko is at my side all day urging me on."

Richard Bolles, author of *What Color is Your Parachute?,* suggests finding a "loving taskmaster," someone who will meet weekly with you to give you a gently-dispensed hard time if you've been a slacker during the week.

Would you prefer group support? Ongoing groups are available in most large cities. My favorite is the 5 O' Clock Club (about $40 a session). It has branches in New York City; Summit and Princeton, NJ; Philadelphia; Washington, DC; Stamford, CT; Boston; Chicago; Hamilton, Ontario; San Francisco; and soon in Los Angeles. Also good is the Forty Plus group. Call 212-233-6086 to find the nearest chapter. To find other local job-search support groups, check with your chamber of commerce, college alumni association, church, or unemployment office.

You can start your own support group. Here's an approach adapted from Barbara Sher's *Wishcraft*. Recruit members by asking friends, relatives, or colleagues, or by putting an ad in a local newspaper. Just write, "Forming a career-search support group. For information, call *(insert phone number)*."

Your group should have four to six members. Meet weekly, or at least monthly. At each session, each person gets ten minutes in the "hot seat." One member starts by telling the group her career/job-finding goal(s). Then group members offer advice on objectives for the next week. Before moving out of the hot seat, each person ends by saying what she commits to accomplishing by the next meeting.

If you're starting your own business, you can find support from a home-based business organization. One national association with many local chapters is the American Association of Home-based Businesses. Call 800-447-9710 for the nearest chapter. In addition, many communities have home-based forums as part of the local Chamber of Commerce. If yours doesn't, join the Chamber and start one.

Members of job support groups generally do well. Partly, it's because they get ideas and encouragement from the group leader and other members, and partly because it's exciting to see people who came in unhappy come out with new and better jobs and careers. It can be truly inspirational.

Chapter 22

Ten Questions That Make Job Interviewees Squirm (And Honest Ways to Survive Them)

In This Chapter

- Honesty really is the best policy
- When you've been fired
- When you're been unemployed
- When you've job hopped
- When you haven't gotten promotions
- When you're overqualified
- When you've been self-employed
- When you're asked about willingness to do overtime
- When asked about your commitment to the company

It's what you're really scared about. The team of interviewers is waiting for you to answer the question — and you're blank. After an agonizing silence, you start mumbling some gibberish that doesn't really answer the question. One interviewer sighs, another crosses his arms, the third actually scowls at you, and all three start scribbling on their score sheets.

This chapter can help prevent such embarrassment. We can't make your interview squirm-proof because interviewers are endlessly creative in coming up with ways to stump you, but interviewers seem to have a top-ten list of killer questions. Even if they never ask any, being ready to answer them can calm you enough so that your interview can reveal your best self.

Something else we hope calms you. Remember that your goal in an interview is *not* to convince them to hire you. Your goal is for both of you to assess if you're well-suited to each other. If too many of their questions are too tough, it's probably not the right job for you. This chapter's true purpose is to help you stay calm enough that you can show what you're really like.

Honesty in Interviews, an Oxymoron?

It can be very tempting to lie when an honest answer to a job interview question would make you look bad. Let's take a truly tough situation to be honest about: You committed an armed robbery. After you got out of prison, you managed to land a job but were unable to do the job well, partly because of your drug problem, which the employer found out about during a random drug test, at which point you were fired. When asked why you left, it's awfully tempting to say something like, "I was tired of the long commute."

But we truly believe that it is wiser to tell the truth, first for a pragmatic reason: The new employer may check your references. You could go through multiple interviews, get your hopes up, and then, because of your falsehood, lose the job. Better to briefly fess up, explain why it's unlikely to happen again, and prove to the employer that you're likely to be a great employee, maybe even a better one because of your previous problems. Another pragmatic benefit is that if you tell the truth about a checkered past, only a good soul will hire you. That's the sort of person most likely to help you to be more successful.

Yes, telling the truth often means it will take you longer to land a job, but we suspect that your odds of succeeding will ultimately be greater if you tell the truth. Apart from pragmatics, as you go through your time on this earth, you may feel better about yourself and your role here if, even in the face of frequent dishonesty, you insist on remaining honorable. We recognize that it's easier for us to recommend this than to do it.

Ten Killer Questions

These are questions that can make your your heart pound, your palms sweat, and your voice crack, questions that could raise the blood pressure of a corpse. And these are answers that can calm you right down — yet they're honest enough that, after the interview, you won't have to go to confession.

Note: Statements marked with an asterisk (*) actually appeared on resumes and cover letters, and are compliments of career specialist Robert Half. The other "Wouldn't you love to see . . ." answers are my twisted fantasies.

Why did you leave your previous job?

First, see if you can get off easy. Are any of these employer-pleasing answers true?

- You decided to go back to school.
- Geographic reasons:
  - To get a better school for your child.
  - You were tired of the long commute.
  - Your significant other got a job requiring a move.
  - You simply wanted to live somewhere else (like sunny California).
- You wanted to make more money.
- The job ended (through a downsizing, for example).
- You wanted more challenge.
- Your skills, personality, and goals are more suited to the new job.
- You had an ethical concern: For example, a boss asked you to do dishonest things, or you didn't believe in the company's products.
- You were expected to work 60 hours a week and felt that was unacceptable. (Some employers will be turned off if you give that reason for leaving a job, but if you want a moderate workweek, you don't want to work for those employers anyway. Better to find an employer who will be happy with 40 high-quality hours.)

Benchmark answer

"I left my job because I wanted to do more. After two years as assistant marketing manager at AmeriCare, I learned a lot about direct-mail marketing, but my boss wasn't going anywhere, so my role would always be as an assistant. I feel I'm ready to run the show, so I'm looking for a company who needs someone who can take charge of a direct-mail operation. That's why, when you answered my e-mail saying you were looking for someone to do just that, I was excited."

What makes that a benchmark answer?

- The informal, energetic tone. This sounds like a motivated employee.
- It makes a case for why she's ready to be promoted.
- It provides enough detail to convince the employer it's an honest response.
- It explains how her strengths match the company's need.

We can hear you saying, "But what if you don't have a nice, pretty reason for leaving your job? What if you left because the work was too hard? Or because you despised your co-workers? Or because your boss hated your guts and fired your butt?"

As we explain in the introduction to this chapter, you're still better off being honest. Give a brief answer, explain why you're likely to be a better employee as a result, and move on to showing how you'd be great in the new job.

Benchmark answer

"Would you like me to lie?" (Interviewer, of course, says no.) "I have to be honest, this is the question I've been dreading, but I decided I am going to be straightforward and let the chips fall as they may. This is what happened: My job required skills I simply don't have. It mainly consisted of writing reports, and I am a poor writer. They somehow tolerated that, but then I did a very stupid thing: When I was on a business trip, I took my wife and charged her expenses to the company. Of course, they fired me. John, that experience is something I will *never* repeat. I learned a lot from that experience and am committed to being a completely ethical employee. And as to the skills, I applied for this job because it requires what I'm good at: selling and computer programming. I can understand why you wouldn't hire me, but I'm willing to hold out for an employer who will hire me knowing the truth. Might you give me a chance?"

What makes that a benchmark answer?

- The humorous beginning is not only disarming, but subtly makes the interviewer more likely to not hold the truth against him.
- There was absolutely no posturing, so he was quite credible.
- After briefly making the revelation, he immediately moved on to making the case for why he'd be successful in the new job.
- He ended by asking for the job. That tends to encourage a maybe, which given what he just revealed, is a heck of a lot.

Wouldn't you love to see the interviewer's face if you said . . .

When asked why you left your previous job, wouldn't you love to see the interviewer's face if your response was, "The company made me a scapegoat. Just like my previous six employers"?*

Why have you been unemployed so long?

Employers buy some reasons: wanting to stay at home to raise your child, take care of an ailing parent, taking a year after graduating college to figure out what you want to do. But in our benchmark answer, the situation isn't so reassuring to employers. This 40-year-old got burned out on work, quit, and basically goofed off.

Benchmark answer

"I won't pull any punches. I had been working for 20 years and didn't want to spend the next 20 thinking, 'Geez, I wish I had taken some time off.' So I figured that while I was still young enough to enjoy it, I would spend a year on pure pleasure: helping my brother rebuild a sailboat, traveling for three months in Europe, playing a lot of golf. I even cleaned out my basement! And lest you think I was a total slug, I attended a landscape architecture conference, and during my drive through California, I visited a half-dozen award-winning landscape architecture projects. Now, I'm more than ready to go back to work!"

What makes that a benchmark answer?

- She makes it easy to understand why one would want to spend a year not working. I can imagine interviewers thinking, "Hmm, I wish I had the guts to do that."
- She mentions her career-related activities.
- Her last sentence makes it clear that she is rarin' to go back to work. The implication was that she is rejuvenated and therefore likely to be a better employee than someone who had been cranking away nonstop.

Wouldn't you love to see the interviewer's face if you said . . .

When asked why you've been unemployed for so long, wouldn't you love to see the interviewer's face if you said, "Work makes me nervous"?*

Why have you job-hopped so much?

If you worked for 17 employers in the last year, it often means you're disgruntled or your employers were disgruntled with you. In either case, employer #18 has every reason to wonder whether you'll be out the door before you've made it to your first office Christmas party.

Benchmark answer

"It looks worse than it is. On my first job, my company was acquired a few months after I was hired, and the new firm fired all redundant staff. At my next firm, within six months, it was clear that I had learned all I could and there was no room for promotion, so when I heard about the job at Dennison, I jumped. Maybe if I had stayed, my resume would look better but you would have gotten a weaker employee. Why am I looking again? I wasn't looking, but I heard about your job, and it sounded terrific, so I decided to apply. I've been interested in geothermal energy ever since college. I'm also excited about the position because you're looking for someone with a hydrogeology background."

What makes that a benchmark answer?

- His opening statement doesn't dispute the accusatory question, "Why have you job hopped?" but quickly moves to make the case for why the new employer shouldn't be concerned.
- He takes the time to explain his reason for leaving each job, but keeps it brief.
- He ends with a reasonable argument for why he's likely to stick around at this new job.

Wouldn't you love to see the interviewer's face if you said . . .

When asked about your job hopping, wouldn't you love to see the interviewer's face if you said, "Please don't misconstrue my 14 jobs as job-hopping. I have never quit a job"?*

Why aren't you making more money or getting promoted?

Of course, this is something you should be thinking about, long before the question is asked. If you don't have a good answer, it may be time for some soul searching, but you may have a valid explanation, for example:

Benchmark answer

"I like to think it's because I have my priorities in order. In every case, I've chosen to take the jobs I felt were the most interesting, and in which I could do the most good, and I haven't let the money or status of a title get in the way. Also, I probably haven't been the toughest salary negotiator in the world, although I suppose I could change that when you and I talk money."

What makes that a benchmark answer?

- She give credible reasons, not defensively stated.
- She ends with a humorous punch line.

Benchmark answer

"I've put family first. Most people who get promoted are willing to work evenings and weekends. I just can't do that."

What makes that a benchmark answer?

- Its honesty ensures that the person who hires her won't force her to choose between work and family. Of course, in today's world, in which many employers expect evening and weekend work, it may take her longer to land a job.

- Its brevity. You want to keep answers to tough questions short. That way, a larger percent of the interview focuses on your strengths.

Wouldn't you love to see the interviewer's face if you said . . .

When asked about your never having been promoted, wouldn't you love to see the interviewer's face if you said, "Because in the cosmic scheme of things, what difference does it make?"

What's your greatest weakness?

Don't follow the standard recommendation to finesse the question by providing some non-weakness like, "I sometimes work too hard." Even if it's true, it sounds like B.S.

Benchmark answer

"I've had a tendency to focus too much on the details. It's something I'm now aware of. That's actually my resolution for this job: On every project, I'll be asking myself what parts of this task should I prioritize? Where's the big picture here?"

What makes that a benchmark answer?

- It acknowledges a legitimate weakness.
- He describes it in the past tense.
- He keeps his description of the weakness brief.
- He makes no excuses.
- He sounds committed to improvement.

Wouldn't you love to see the interviewer's face if you said . . .

When asked about your greatest weakness, wouldn't you love to see the interviewer's face if you said, "Bosses insist that all employees take no more than an hour for lunch. I just can't work under those conditions"?*

Why us?

If you've done your homework, that question should be easy. If you haven't, you deserve to squirm.

Benchmark answer

"Because I'm in love with you guys! I've been reading about your efforts to limit cars into Yosemite Park. That's something I really believe in, and my background in transportation planning and my degree in environmental science made me think I'd fit right in."

What makes that a benchmark answer?

- She isn't afraid to be exuberant.
- She makes it clear that she shares the organization's values.
- She asserts that her skills and background are a fit.

Wouldn't you love to see the interviewer's face if you said . . .

If you were asked, "Why this company?" wouldn't you love to see the interviewer's face if you said, "I sent out 500 resumes, and you were the only one that would interview me"?

Don't you think you're overqualified for this job?

Employers don't like to hire overqualified people: They get bored quickly and leave, or become frustrated workers, bored by the lack of challenge.

Benchmark answer

"In some ways, I am overqualified. My experience is obviously more than you need on this job, but in most ways, I'm a perfect fit. I really enjoy supervising nurses and I know a lot about informatics, which sounds like it's high priority for you. That's why I applied for this job. We never use all our skills. What I'm looking for is a job that uses enough of my skills to keep me interested, and from what I've heard so far, this sounds great."

What makes that a benchmark answer?

- Acknowledges the concern without defensiveness.
- The use of the term "perfect fit" is persuasive.
- He provides a good, easy-going rationale for why he's unlikely to quit soon because he's overqualified.

Wouldn't you love to see the interviewer's face if you said . . .

When asked if you were overqualified, wouldn't you love to see the interviewer's face if you said, "I'm not as qualified as I look"?

You're going to have a lot of routine work. How do you feel about that?

Licking envelopes, alphabetizing files, cleaning test tubes. Studies have shown that repetitive work is a major cause of stress-related illness. So what are you gonna say when the boss asks, "Well Tiger, how do you feel about doing a lot of routine work?"

Benchmark answer

"I can't expect to start my career at the top, and it seems reasonable that you ask me to learn the field from the ground up. Of course, nobody wants to spend an entire career at the copy machine, but I expect that as I start learning things, I'll get more work that uses that knowledge." (Adapted from an answer given at the AboutWork site: `www.aboutwork.com`.)

What makes that a benchmark answer?

- It strikes a good balance between willingness to pay dues and desire for more responsibility.
- It makes clear that the additional responsibility will come not because of dues paid but because of expertise acquired.

Wouldn't you love to see the interviewer's face if you said . . .

When asked if you minded lots of routine work, wouldn't you love to see the interviewer's face if you said, "Hire a robot"?

Would you object to working overtime and weekends?

Oh yeah, you're thrilled at thought of evenings at work instead of hanging out at home. Yeah, you're in ecstasy at the prospect of missing ballgames. Yeah, you love the idea that you'll be cranking out some more work at the office instead of going out with your friends. Yet how can you, without blowing the interview, honestly answer Cujo's question: "Would you object to working overtime and weekends?"

Benchmark answer

"It depends. It depends on how often, the importance of the projects, whether others were doing their part, and on the compensation. Can you fill me in on some of that?"

What makes that a benchmark answer?

- He strikes a balance between rigidly rejecting the idea and unqualifiedly accepting it. (Unquestioning acceptance of overtime during an interview may make you appear desperate for a job.)
- Instead of attempting an answer based on incomplete information, he asks a reasonable question.

Wouldn't you love to see the interviewer's face if you said . . .

When asked whether you're open to overtime, wouldn't you love to see the interviewer's face if you said, "As long as you're there with me and not on the golf course"?

What's your commitment to this job?

It's remarkable that employers have the chutzpah to ask a question like that in an era in which employers have about as much commitment to employees as Casanovas have to their lovers. Yet this question is a favorite among interviewers. What's an honest yet knock-their-socks-off answer?

Benchmark answer

"It would be easiest for me to say, 'Oh, yes I'm highly committed,' but I think the most honest statement I can make is that as in all relationships, as we get to know each other, if we're right for each other, our commitment to each other will grow."

What makes that a benchmark answer?

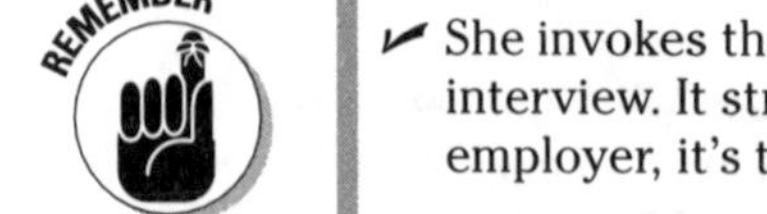

- She avoids the obvious, trite, potentially not credible answer, "Oh yes. I'm committed to the job."
- She invokes that dating metaphor, which is a good mind-set for a job interview. It stresses mutuality of commitment. If that turns off an employer, it's the wrong employer for you.
- She sounds interested, not desperate.

Wouldn't you love to see the interviewer's face if you said . . .

When asked about your commitment to a job, wouldn't you love to see the interviewer's face if you said, "About as committed as you are to me. You'd downsize me in a nanosecond if you could make an extra nickel"?

Chapter 23

Ten Keys to Success When You're Your Own Boss

In This Chapter

- Finding a niche
- Making yourself irresistible
- Getting visible
- Being unforgettable
- Staying on technology's *trailing* edge
- Keeping current
- Being ready to transform your business
- Staying positive

Many people think that self-employment requires 70-hour workweeks. Not if you work smart, and that's what this chapter is all about: smart ways to build your business.

Be One in a Million

There are a million self-help gurus, a million cookbook authors, a million photographers, and so on. The world probably doesn't need more. The world, however, can always use a true specialist: a self-help guru for people over 60; a cookbook author who concocts "Diabetic Delights;" a photographer who focuses on pictures of newborns and parents in the hospital.

Within your chosen occupation, figure out a specialty that feels quintessentially you. Talk with potential customers to find out if they'd be willing to pay you for that specialty — if so, voilà, you're one in a million, and an employable one.

If your potential customers give you the thumbs up, be sure to take the time to become expert in your niche. In the end, being an expert will build your business more than anything else. Don't be scared by the word "expert." Because you're focusing on a narrow specialization, your task is manageable. A term paper's worth of research and a mentor or two can often give you enough expertise to start your business.

Be Irresistible

No one likes to part with their money . . . unless what they will get for it is worth every penny and then some. Then just watch how fast the cash, credit cards, and checks fly out of their hands. A mistake of the newly self-employed is trying to compete on price. They keep lowering their prices, hoping to attract more business. In actuality, bargain-basement pricing is a great way to run your business into the ground.

Instead of cutting your prices to the bone, build value. Make what you offer so appealing that it's irresistible.

Michelle Weil is a psychologist. There are a lot of shrinks around, and most people think they charge too much. Weil's clients feel differently. She specializes in helping people who are suffering from *technosis* — a fear of technology. Her clients are companies whose employees must start using new technology. Michelle shows companies that by using her service, she can save them big money in lost productivity, and absenteeism. For an employer facing the challenge of getting employees comfortable with new technology, Weil's evidence is irresistible.

Here is how an artist who creates glass wind chimes makes his offer irresistible. His chimes are beautiful and melodic. They attract lots of people at art fairs, but many people are afraid that the chimes will break in the wind. Their concerns dissolve, however, as the artist begins talking about how he creates his chimes. He explains how the delicate glass is tempered by his unique process that ensures they won't break, even in the strongest gale. As he describes his process, he creates enough value that when people hear the price, they're not, pardon the expression, blown away.

So build your evidence. Make your offer irresistible.

Get Visible to Your Target Market

No matter how irresistible your offer, if no one knows about it, you obviously can't succeed. So you must make yourself visible to your target customers.

We recommend trying a few different kinds of marketing activities simultaneously. Especially in the beginning, you rarely can count on any one source to build a good-enough reputation. We discussed many marketing approaches in Chapter 19 — for example, free seminars, media appearances, articles for local newspapers, flyers, networking meetings, ads, speeches at conferences attended by potential customers or referral sources, cold-calling, direct-mail, newsletters, alliances such as cross-referrals with other businesses, or talking up your business with friends and relatives.

Be sure to keep track of where your customers come from. After say six months, you can see which marketing vehicles have worked best, and reallocate your efforts accordingly.

Another way to reduce the number of marketing approaches you need to try is to make the most of each one. For example, let's say you took the time to create a newsletter. Most people would feel pretty good if they simply mailed it out to a carefully-targeted mailing list, That's okay, but you can get much more from your newsletter without much more effort. Include a coupon in the newsletter for a free consultation, needs assessment, or demonstration. Take copies with you to professional meetings. Send it to potential referral sources as a means of introduction and call them the following week. Give copies to your customers to read and share with their friends and associates. Use them as a handout at a speech to potential clients. Take out an ad that people can clip for a free copy of your newsletter.

And one more absolute key to making the most of your marketing effort: targeting. In a small business, mass marketing amasses no one. Getting business is like sightseeing: If you're looking for elephants, you better visit places where elephants live.

Be Unforgettable and Easy to Contact

If you're going to go to the trouble of spreading the word about what you do, you'd better make a memorable impression while you're at it. As a consumer, how often have you heard about some business you might want to hire — for example, a housepainter, but when you got around to it, you couldn't find the contact information. If you're like us, you usually don't search very hard. It's easier to just call someone else, for example, someone recommended by your neighbor.

If people can't remember who you are or can't easily reach you when they decide they need you, you've wasted all your marketing efforts. In fact, you've helped make a sale for the person they hired instead of you.

One easy way to ensure that you get remembered is to pick a memorable name for your business. Don't pick a name that has special meaning to you but means nothing to anyone else: for example, names based on your granddaughter's initials. Which name do you think will generate more business: BNG Painting or Flying Colors? Joe's Dance Club or Rock Hard?

Another easy way to jog potential customers' memories is to choose a memorable phone number. Quick, when you think of ordering flowers by phone, what do you think of? 1-800-FLOWERS, of course. Just think what a bonanza that company got just by calling itself that and by getting that phone number.

After you've picked your memorable name, phone number, and perhaps Web site name, make the most of them. Don't just plaster them in big letters on all your marketing materials. Publicize the heck out of them — direct mail, ads, flyers, whatever — until they're so implanted in your customers' brains that the easiest thing for them to do when they need a product or service like yours is, of course, to call you. Sometimes, it's all in a name.

Be Top-of-Mind

You've heard the saying: out of sight, out of mind. It's never more true than when it comes to getting and keeping a steady flow of business. To keep yourself and your business top-of-mind with your customers and referral sources, develop a contact list using software like ACT!, Goldmine, or Maximizer that includes all your past, present, and potential customers and key referral sources. Then make contact by phone, fax, e-mail, or regular mail once a month or at least once a quarter.

Power Your Business

Today's small office/home office equipment is equivalent to having a small workforce. The right equipment can often save you money and hours. So be on the lookout for cost-saving technology. Often, you can power your business by powering up your office.

Several years ago, we (Paul and Sarah) wanted to add a color printer to our home office. At that time they were expensive, so it wasn't something we would buy just for the heck of it. We kept our eye on the prices and kept looking for profit-making ways that we could use that printer. As soon as the cost came down enough that we could see it paying for itself within a few months, we sprung. Stay alert for the cost-effective moment.

Sometimes the savings you get from technology are not directly in money, but in quality of life. My most recent techno-purchase? A spread spectrum cordless phone, which sounds virtually as good as a corded phone, even hundreds of feet away from the base. The freedom to have sessions with my phone clients in my rose garden instead of being chained to my desk came at a cost of $90.

Just because we encourage you to consider technological solutions doesn't mean you necessarily need the latest and greatest. Often the leading edge turns out to be the bleeding edge, not to mention the most expensive edge. Small businesses often are wiser to be on the trailing edge. Last year's model of computer, printer, or software will probably give you 95+ percent of the productivity at 50 – 75 percent of the cost. Also, you're likely to have fewer problems with a year-old model. The first-delivered products of a new model often have bugs, which by the end of the model year have usually been worked out. There's no reason to be a guinea pig and pay extra for the privilege.

Technophobic? Find a computer consultant who works with small businesses. That person can set up your technology, teach you to use it, walk you through problems, and come out to fix the inevitable glitches. To ease your techno-frayed nerves, read *TechnoStress* by Dr. Michelle Weil and Dr. Larry Rosen (Wiley, 1997).

Team Up

Just because you're working on your own doesn't mean you have to be alone. Teaming up with others is a hot trend among the self-employed. Sixty-one percent of the successfully self-employed individuals we interviewed tell us they are teaming up more often than five years ago and 70 percent say they would like to do even more in the future.

The reasons for teaming up are clear. You can serve more clients and avoid downtime between jobs; you can bid on larger projects and elicit greater respect by affiliating with other experts. This all can mean increased income and greater success, sooner.

To enjoy these benefits, people are teaming up in ways other than partnering: everything from joint promotions and mutual referrals to time-limited joint ventures.

Explore more possibilities for teaming up at `www.teamingup.com`.

Stay Current

Keeping up with what's new in your field is not only helpful, it's fun. It makes you feel more competent and confident, and it's exciting to see the rapid advancements occurring in most fields.

Here are some ways to stay current:

- Subscribe to (and read) your quarterly trade or professional journal.
- Read the trade or professional journal of your best clients and customers.
- Read a major national newspaper like *The Wall Street Journal* or *The New York Times*.
- Read your local daily newspaper.
- Subscribe to an online service like Pointcast (`www.pointcast.com`) that creates a customized newspaper for you from leading news sources and delivers it to your e-mailbox.
- Subscribe to your local business periodical.
- Browse Web sites of pertinent trade and professional organizations. Participate in their online bulletin boards and chats.
- Attend the exhibits, trade shows, and annual conference for your profession.

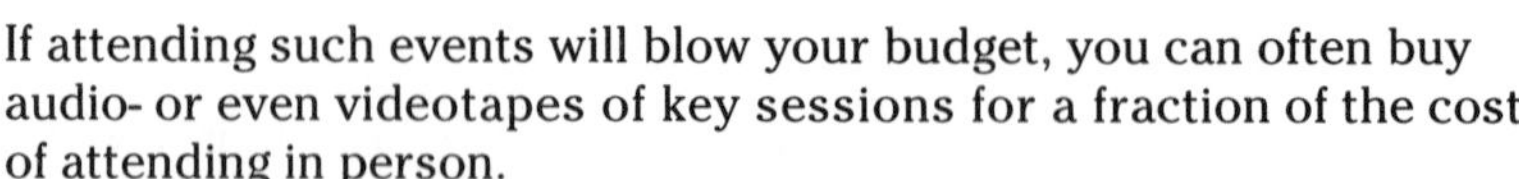

If attending such events will blow your budget, you can often buy audio- or even videotapes of key sessions for a fraction of the cost of attending in person.

- Subscribe to a trend report or magazine like *Futurist* magazine, *The Roper Report,* or *American Demographics*.
- Keep your eye on industry leaders. What are they doing? What are they saying?
- Listen to your client's complaints about the changes they're facing. They will give you clues as to what's in the offing.
- Keep your eye on the horizon.

Be Ready to Change

A key benefit of staying current is that you become aware of new ways to improve your business. If your business is to survive long-term, you'll probably need to make improvements regularly, and even be open to radically transforming your operation.

When we poll people who have been self-employed more than five years, more than 75 percent tell us that their current business is substantially different from the one they originally started.

When career counselor Jim Gonyea saw the growth in the online world, he decided to capitalize. He approached America Online and started an online career counseling center. He now has four counselors working for him and over 30 online career forums.

The good news is that as a small company, flexibility is one of your greatest assets. There's no huge hierarchy you must convince. There's no massive infrastructure that must be revamped. If advances in your field or feedback from your customers suggest that your business needs to change, you can turn on a dime to meet the need. After all, you're the CEO and emperor.

Look on the Bright Side

It's easy to fall into the habit of moaning about the challenges of being self-employed: Taxes are too high; there's too much or too little business; the computer refuses to behave itself; a frantic client wants major changes at the last minute.

It's been said that the secret to a good life is having interesting problems. Well, when you're self-employed, you do have interesting problems. They're the problems of being responsible, the problems of choices, the problems of opportunity, the problems of creating something you believe in. As problems go, they're not bad ones.

Afterword

Our Best Thoughts on How to Have a Happy Work Life

Here, we though we would take the liberty of speaking as individuals.

Marty Nemko's Thoughts

I believe six somewhat unconventional things about work.

Work is work

Many career searchers want to hold out for work that would be fun. They fantasize about jumping out of bed each morning rarin' to start their work day, but the fact is, few people — even those with carefully chosen careers — jump regularly.

Despite what many career guide authors and motivational speakers tell you, work is generally work. Even an ostensibly glamorous job such as writing a book for a fine publisher or hosting a radio show, for the most part, is work.

To wit, this story from *Satire* magazine. "A writer dies and due to a bureaucratic snafu in the afterworld, is allowed to choose her own fate: heaven or hell. Being a very shrewd dead person, she asks St. Peter for a tour of both. The first stop is hell where she sees rows and rows of writers sitting chained to desks in a room as hot as a thousand suns. Fire licks the writers' fingers as they try to work, demons whip their backs with chains. Your general hell scene. 'Wow, this sucks,' quoth the writer, 'let's see some heaven.' In a moment, they were whisked to heaven and the writer saw rows and rows of writers chained to desks in a room as hot as a thousand suns. Fire licks the writers' fingers as they try to work, demons whip their backs with chains. It looks and smells even worse than hell. 'What gives, Pete?' the writer asked. 'This is worse than hell!' 'Yes,' St. Peter replied, 'but here your work gets published.'"

A key to a contented work life is to not expect work to be play; that's why they call it work. Appreciate being able to work: that you can use your mind and perhaps your body to do something useful, and get paid for it to boot. I try to embrace work, and concentrate, really concentrate, on trying to make the most of each working *moment*. I find that when I do that, the work actually feels more pleasant.

Want to succeed? Consider lowering your self-esteem

Many people would be more successful if they *lowered* their self-esteem. American students score near the bottom among industrialized nations, but have the highest self-esteem. Asian students have the lowest self-esteem but score at the top. Within the United States, African-American achievement is below average, but they have above-average self-esteem. These are not coincidences. If you have more than moderate self-esteem, you believe you're wonderful, which takes the edge off feeling that you need to work hard. In contrast, if your self-esteem is only moderate, you are at least a little scared that your work won't turn out well. Your only chance, you believe, is to work hard. Most successful people I know, when beginning a project, are usually fearful it won't come out well. That worry motivates them to work hard. Of course, you can't be so afraid of failing that you don't even start a task, but you have to be a little worried. I was anxious before beginning each chapter of this book, and although I've been hosting a radio show for years, I'm still nervous before every show. If I went into preparing for a radio show thinking, "I'm great, I can do this, no problem," the work would come out poorly, guaranteed. I simply wouldn't work as hard. Instead, I worry. It's ironic that self-esteem, so often promulgated as the cure for low achievement, can cause it.

Think twice about following long-shot dreams

Many career guides tell you to do what you love and the money will follow. They're filled with stories of starving artists who no longer starve, aspiring novelists who no longer have to aspire.

Those books don't tell you that for every person who achieves his long-shot dream, there are many who don't: talented artists who still starve, terrific actors and novelists who still wait tables.

Here is more realistic advice: If you believe that your life will feel empty unless you pursue a long-shot career full-time, then do it, but give it no more than a fixed amount of time — say, one year. If, after a year, you don't have a clear sign that you're going to "make it," the odds are great that you never will.

If you can see yourself having a good life even without that long-shot career, please take that long-odds dream and make it an after-work activity. The key to achieving your long-shot dream is to not insist that you get paid. That allows you to keep doing what you love while ensuring that you don't spend your entire life unemployed.

Fact is, there are plenty of miserable artists, writers, and actors, and plenty of happy plumbers, salespeople, and managers. For most people, career happiness, in the end, comes from doing something they're good at and feel is worthwhile, having co-workers who appreciate them, and making a reasonable living.

In praise of the anonymous achievers

Who gets the attention? The performers, athletes, and politicians. My hero is the anonymous achiever: the smart, hard-working people who make the world run and get few rewards for it. These days, we're not allowed to say that one person is better than another, but I believe those are our better people: the smart geologist who labors in anonymity trying to find oil reserves; the restaurant owner who is out buying fresh produce at four in the morning and working into the night to provide fresh meals at fair prices; the Social Security eligibility worker who simultaneously ensures that people get the help they need while protecting the taxpayers' dollars. It saddens me that these bulwarks of our society, thanks to a 40–60 percent state/federal marginal tax rate, sometimes even with a second income, cannot afford to buy even a modest home in a safe neighborhood. We spend a lot of time admiring entertainers and athletes — people who make millions for doing something non-essential. I would love to see the media pay attention to the real contributors, the anonymous achievers without whom our quality of life would be decimated.

Balance is overrated

I believe that many people would be wise to work long hours rather than embrace the vaunted work/play balance. How can I assert such heresy? After all, since the days of Aristotle, the golden mean has been revered. Today's women's movement deifies work/play balance. We ridicule people who work 60 hours per week as "workaholics" — people whose lives are out of balance. Yet I believe that balance is overrated. I believe that if you choose a meaningful career, you may be more satisfied with your life and do more good if you work long hours.

I'm not saying that everyone should work 60 hours per week. My goal here is simply to encourage you to consciously decide how much you want to work rather than be swept along by the popular consensus.

Because I do work that I believe makes a difference and uses my best skills, I choose to work long hours as long as it doesn't shortchange my family. I believe more good is done by writing an extra article, seeing another client, doing another radio show, or talking to another reporter, than by watching TV or playing golf — even if I have already worked 50 hours that week. In addition to being more productive, it simply feels good to use my strengths while doing good. To boot, those long hours also earn me a few extra bucks.

Please remember that I'm not advocating that everyone work 60-hour workweeks. I'm simply saying that there are some people who prefer working long hours, and they shouldn't be guilt-tripped into playing golf by calling them workaholic. Rather, these people should be revered as our unrecognized heroes, the people who toil long hours in anonymity to improve the quality of our lives.

Up is not the only way

Climb the ladder — it's the American way. Earn more so that you can buy more stuff that you don't really need.

If high income is important to you, fine, but it's easy to shoot for a high-income job without really thinking about the trade-offs. This section merely asks you to make that decision consciously.

With a 40–60 percent marginal tax rate for many American middle income earners, it's usually difficult to raise your standard of living significantly without plenty of extra hours at work and time away from the people and things you love. You may well have to spend a lot of effort on something you don't really believe in. You may have to do a lot of apple polishing, maybe some ethical compromising.

And what are the likely benefits? Material. Is it really worth those compromises so that you can drive a nice car rather than a functional one, live in an upscale place instead of an adequate one, fly to a faraway vacation spot rather than drive to a nearby one?

Imagine what would happen if you agreed to trade away some income for work that required fewer, or at least different, compromises.

Thirteen years ago, I said goodbye to the university, where I was essentially forced to pass prospective teachers I wouldn't allow to teach my own child, where I was forced to teach theoretical constructs that my students didn't need to know, where I was forced to write journal articles that would do nothing for the world.

Now I spend my time telling my truth and helping others find their truth. I feel alive.

Here are some decidedly low-paying but potentially rewarding careers that you might consider, at least for part of your employment:

- Lead wilderness tours. Over the campfire, talk about life.
- Write grant proposals for important things.
- Train baby-sitters.
- Teach people how to use the Internet.
- Tutor children — or grown-ups.
- Help people manage their money. Be amazingly honest with them.
- Give massages.
- Become a parenting coach.
- Paint murals on ugly concrete walls in the community. If you don't know how to paint, find children who do.
- Work in a hospice.

I ask you to consciously consider whether the upsides of climbing the ladder are likely to be worth the price — for you and the others you affect.

Paul & Sarah's Thoughts

Having traded in livelihoods that sapped our energies and literally made us ill, for careers that feed our bodies, minds, and souls, we hold strong beliefs about making a living.

If play is child's work, why cannot work be adult's play? It's possible. On our weekly radio show, we interview three people each week, each in a different business. From these exchanges, and the hundreds of interviews we've conducted in writing our books, we know that many people would continue to do the work they do even if they won the lottery. Sure, they'd delegate out the parts they dislike, but they would continue doing the work they enjoy.

For some, work means even more. It means making a difference, leaving the world a bit better. We believe that these values, along with loving and being loved, are what matter most in life. And we firmly believe that it's realistic to find a career that provides plenty of this kind of sustenance. It's a choice we can make.

Sometimes, the key is choosing to tackle something big, maybe even something so big that it feels scary: to go beyond your comfort zone, stretch yourself, and strive to surpass what you and others expect of you. Consider approaching your career in the spirit expressed by President John Kennedy in the early '60s when he said that we choose to go to the moon in this decade, not because it is easy, but because it is hard.

Especially if you are self-employed, but even if you are not, you can be the artist of your life. You hold the brush in your hands. The events that life presents are your watercolors, your dreams are your guide, and your canvas is the 24 hours that lie ahead. If you don't like the color, the texture, and form of your life, you can usually change it until you get something more to your liking.

There is no need to compare your canvas to that of others. The good life means different things to different people. Only you know what it is for you. Courage is being willing to take a stand for what *you* want and to get busy creating it from the realities at hand. For us, that's what livelihood is all about.

Appendix

The Cool Career Finder

Here are 16 special lists of careers, all of which are discussed in the Cool Careers Catalog (see Chapter 2). We present the careers most likely to impress your family, those that are too much fun to be work, those offering the surest routes to big bucks, and those likely to make the biggest difference to society, plus 12 more lists that can make it easier to home in on the right career for you.

Each career is accompanied by the page number where you can find its scoop in the Cool Careers Catalog.

Make a big difference

Too much fun to be work

Impress your friends and family

Express yourself

Could lead to big bucks

I have no degree, but I want a good job and I want it fast!

For the brainy

Employers are begging

Little-known but great

Maximum security

Hands-on

Weird careers

The leading edge

Kick-back careers

Our favorite shoestring businesses

Supercool careers (the best of the best)

These careers scored highest overall on our criteria: little-known, make a difference, ease of entry, good pay, enjoyable to many people, and good job prospects.

Index

Numbers & Symbols

• A •

• B •

• C •

• D •

• G •

• H •

• J •

• L •

• O •

• P •

• T •

• U •

Discover Dummies Online!

The Dummies Web Site is your fun and friendly online resource for the latest information about *...For Dummies*® books and your favorite topics. The Web site is the place to communicate with us, exchange ideas with other *...For Dummies* readers, chat with authors, and have fun!

Ten Fun and Useful Things You Can Do at www.dummies.com

1. Win free *...For Dummies* books and more!
2. Register your book and be entered in a prize drawing.
3. Meet your favorite authors through the IDG Books Author Chat Series.
4. Exchange helpful information with other *...For Dummies* readers.
5. Discover other great *...For Dummies* books you must have!
6. Purchase Dummieswear™ exclusively from our Web site.
7. Buy *...For Dummies* books online.
8. Talk to us. Make comments, ask questions, get answers!
9. Download free software.
10. Find additional useful resources from authors.

Link directly to these ten fun and useful things at **http://www.dummies.com/10useful**

For other technology titles from IDG Books Worldwide, go to **www.idgbooks.com**

Not on the Web yet? It's easy to get started with *Dummies 101*®: *The Internet For Windows*® *95* or *The Internet For Dummies*®, 5th Edition, at local retailers everywhere.

Find other *...For Dummies* books on these topics:
Business • Career • Databases • Food & Beverage • Games • Gardening • Graphics • Hardware
Health & Fitness • Internet and the World Wide Web • Networking • Office Suites
Operating Systems • Personal Finance • Pets • Programming • Recreation • Sports
Spreadsheets • Teacher Resources • Test Prep • Word Processing

IDG BOOKS WORLDWIDE BOOK REGISTRATION

We want to hear from you!

Visit **http://my2cents.dummies.com** to register this book and tell us how you liked it!

- Get entered in our monthly prize giveaway.
- Give us feedback about this book — tell us what you like best, what you like least, or maybe what you'd like to ask the author and us to change!
- Let us know any other *...For Dummies®* topics that interest you.

Your feedback helps us determine what books to publish, tells us what coverage to add as we revise our books, and lets us know whether we're meeting your needs as a *...For Dummies* reader. You're our most valuable resource, and what you have to say is important to us!

Not on the Web yet? It's easy to get started with *Dummies 101®: The Internet For Windows® 95* or *The Internet For Dummies®*, 5th Edition, at local retailers everywhere.

Or let us know what you think by sending us a letter at the following address:

...For Dummies Book Registration
Dummies Press
7260 Shadeland Station, Suite 100
Indianapolis, IN 46256-3945
Fax 317-596-5498